CRISIS AND CONSOLIDATION IN THE FORMATIVE PERIOD OF SHI'ITE ISLAM

CRISIS AND CONSOLIDATION IN THE FORMATIVE PERIOD OF SHIʿITE ISLAM

Abū Jaʿfar ibn Qiba al-Rāzī and His Contribution to Imāmite Shīʿite Thought

Hossein Modarressi

THE DARWIN PRESS, INC.
PRINCETON, NEW JERSEY

Library of Congress Cataloging in Publication Data

Modarressi, Hossein, date
Crisis and consolidation in the formative period of Shīʿite Islam : Abū Jaʿfar ibn Qiba al-Rāzī and his contribution to imāmite Shīʿite thought / Hossein Modarressi.
p. cm.
Includes bibliographical references (p.) and index.
ISBN 0–87850–095–2 (alk. paper): $35.00
1. Shīʿah—Doctrines—History. 2. Ibn Qibah, Abū Jaʿfar Muḥammad ibn ʿAbd al-Raḥmān, 9th/10th cent.—Contributions in Shiite doctrine. 3. Shīʿah—Doctrines—Early works to 1800. I. Title.
BP194.M63 1993
297′.2042—dc20 92–41266
CIP

The paper in this book is acid-free neutral pH stock and meets the guidelines for permanence and durability of the Committee on Production Guidelines for Book Longevity of the Council on Library Resources.

Printed in the United States of America

CONTENTS

Preface

THE YEARS 260-329/874-941, known among the Shī'ites as the period of Minor Occultation, comprised undoubtedly the most difficult and critical period in the history of Imāmite Shī'ism. It began with the death of the eleventh Imām, Ḥasan al-'Askari, of no apparent successor, thus creating a total doctrinal chaos in the Imāmite Shī'ite community, particularly in Mesopotamia. That resulted in turn in internal conflicts, many desertions and conversions, and the emergence of numerous splinter groups and subsects within the Imāmite community. The situation encouraged other groups such as the Mu'tazilites and Zaydites to criticize and attack more aggressively the traditional Imāmite doctrines, which were now more vulnerable than ever before. Continuation of the old internal disagreements and schisms in the Imāmite community itself over some of the main theoretical issues, such as the validity of reason, the nature of the Imām, and the scope of his authority, only further complicated the situation. Beyond these elements, political suppression of the Shī'ite community, which reached its peak during the reign of the Abbasid Mutawakkil (232-247/847-861) and continued throughout most parts of the period of Minor Occultation, added to the tension. The need for reconstruction of some of the fundamental principles of the doctrine, such as the question of why humanity should always need an Imām, was real and pressing.

The Imāmite theologians of that period thus had the difficult task of defending the doctrine against attack while trying to offer new interpretations of fundamental principles to accommodate new realities and developments. Gradually, in this period, which continued for most of one century, Imāmite Shī'ism developed into what later came to be known as Twelver Shī'ism with its special theological analyses and points of view. Abū Ja'far b. Qiba al-Rāzī, one of the most prominent and active Imāmite theologians of this period, had a major role in all of these reconstructions and developments.

The present work attempts to shed light on some aspects of the Imāmite doctrine during the period of Minor Occultation and on the contributions of Abū Ja'far b. Qiba to the formation of the developed Imāmite doctrine. The second part of this volume contains the texts of three short works of this scholar together with their English translation.

The author would like to express his gratitude to Professors Wilferd Madelung and Michael Cook, who read the work and made valuable suggestions, and to Mr. John Cooper, who produced the typescript of the Arabic texts and helped with their translation.

PART ONE

Imāmite Shī‘ism in the Late Third/Ninth Century

I

From Responsibilities to Rights

AFFECTION FOR THE household of the Prophet is an old phenomenon in Islam that dates back to the time of the Prophet himself. Among his companions some were especially devoted to his family. Historical accounts suggest that after the death of the Prophet, when succession to his position was contested, those companions upheld the priority of the House of the Prophet, represented at the time by 'Alī b. Abī Ṭālib, first cousin of the Prophet and husband of his beloved daughter, Fāṭima, and supported him as the most eligible candidate. This opinion failed, however, to get enough support as did the suggestion that the leadership of the Muslim community be divided between the Emigrants (*Muhājirūn*) and the Medineans (*Anṣār*). Instead, the Quraysh, the powerful tribe of the Prophet, managed to appoint one of their seniors from another clan to the position. 'Alī did eventually assume the caliphate twenty-five years later but for less than five years; he was assassinated in 40/661. With the failure of the brief rule of his son, Ḥasan al-Mujtabā, political leadership passed from the Prophet's family to the Umayyad clan, which had been among the most bitter enemies of the Prophet until the last years of his life. The circle of followers that gathered around 'Alī, especially from the time of 'Uthmān, the third caliph, expanded immensely during the short period of 'Alī's caliphate, which was marked by fervent religiosity. During the reign of Mu'āwiya (41-60/661-680), the followers of 'Alī comprised a distinct group within the larger Muslim community and were severely persecuted by the government. In the course of their involvement in subsequent issues, such as the rise and fall of Ḥusayn in 61/680, the revolt of the *Tawwābūn* (the Penitents) in 64-65/683-684, and the rise of Mukhtār al-Thaqafī in Kūfa in 66-67/686-687, they emerged as an active anti-Umayyad group that supported the 'Alīds as the legitimate rulers of the Muslim state.[1]

1. See the letter of the caliph Hishām b. 'Abd al-Malik to his governor in Kūfa in Ṭabarī, 7:169; also Ḥasan b. Muḥammad b. al-Ḥanafiyya: 24.

The Shī'ite movement would eventually become one of the two main divisions of Islam. Until the end of the first century of the *Hijra*, however, it did not distinguish itself from the main body of the Muslim community except by the mentioned political tendency. As Islamic legal schools began to form early in the second/eighth century, Shī'ism gradually became a distinct legal school, most of whose members followed the teachings and legal opinions of the most learned member of the House of the Prophet at the time, Muḥammad b. 'Alī al-Bāqir (d. 114/733).[2] Soon, during the explosion of theological debates in Islamic society and the emergence of different schools of *kalām*, the Shī'ite movement gradually began to take specific positions on various theological topics, mainly following the positions of Imām Muḥammad al-Bāqir and his son, Imām Ja'far al-Ṣādiq (d. 148/765). By the time of the Abbasid revolution in 132/749, the Shī'ite movement had thus grown into a complete and independent political, legal, and theological school.

After the death of 'Alī b. Abī Ṭālib, his two sons by Fāṭima, Ḥasan and Ḥusayn, became the focus of devotion for those who supported the claim of the House of the Prophet to leadership of the Muslim community. After the death of these two, the son of Ḥusayn, 'Alī Zayn al-'Ābidīn, came to be recognized by most of the community as the head of the Prophet's House. One radical splinter sect, the Shī'ites of Kūfa who supported Mukhtār al-Thaqafī in his revolt against the Umayyads, however, chose a third son of 'Alī b. Abī Ṭālib, Muḥammad b. al-Ḥanafiyya, as their spiritual

2. See Kashshī: 425 quoting Imām Ja'far al-Ṣādiq as saying: "Before Abū Ja'far [Muḥammad al-Bāqir] the Shī'ites did not know what they needed from among the lawful and unlawful except for what they had learned from the people [the overwhelmingly Sunnite community], until Abū Ja'far came along. He opened [the way] for them, explained [religion] to them, and taught them." See also 'Ayyāshī, 1:252–3, where a similar report says: "Before Abū Ja'far, the Shī'ites did not know the [right way to perform] the ceremonies for the pilgrimage to Mecca (*ḥajj*) nor what was lawful and unlawful until he emerged and performed the pilgrimage for them, explaining to them how to do it as well as to the lawful and unlawful until they no longer needed the people [the Sunnites] [for these things]. And whereas they had previously learned from the people, the people now learned from them."

leader. This group, which came to be known as the Kaysānites,[3] did not survive beyond the second/eighth century. After 'Alī Zayn al-'Ābidīn, his son, Muḥammad al-Bāqir,[4] and then Muḥammad's son, Ja'far al-Ṣādiq, each enjoyed in turn wide public recognition as the head of the House of the Prophet.[5] In the time of Ja'far al-Ṣādiq, however, a further split divided the Shī'ite community into two camps, Zaydites and Ja'farites. The Ja'farites later came to be known as the Imāmites.

After Ja'far al-Ṣādiq, the majority of his followers continued to recognize, as a general rule, the most distinguished (usually the eldest) son of the previous Imām of his descendant as the next Imām. The common belief was that each Imām designated his successor from among his male descendants through testament (*waṣiyya*), sometimes also called explicit designation (*naṣṣ*). The list of the Imāms came, therefore, to be a chain of fathers and sons (except for the second and third Imāms, Ḥasan and Ḥusayn, who were brothers) as follows:

1. 'Alī b. Abī Ṭālib (d. 40/661)
2. Ḥasan b. 'Alī al-Mujtabā (d. 49/669)
3. Ḥusayn b. 'Alī al-Shahīd (d. 61/680)
4. 'Alī b. al-Ḥusayn Zayn al-'Ābidīn (d. 95/713)
5. Muḥammad b. 'Alī al-Bāqir (d. 114/733)
6. Ja'far b. Muḥammad al-Ṣādiq (d. 148/765)
7. Mūsā b. Ja'far al-Kāẓim (d. 183/799)
8. 'Alī b. Mūsā al-Riḍā (d. 203/818)
9. Muḥammad b. 'Alī al-Jawād (d. 220/835)

3. See the article "Kaysāniyya" in *EI*², 4:836–8 (by W. Madelung).
4. This, of course, did not mean that all Shī'ites who gathered around Muḥammad al-Bāqir and followed him considered him to be an Imām in the same sense that the title later implied (see below, chapter 3).
5. These facts are well attested by the letter that the second Abbasid caliph, Manṣūr (r. 136–158/754–775) wrote to Muḥammad b. 'Abd Allāh b. al-Ḥasan al-Nafs al-Zakiyya (d. 145/762) in which he said: "No one born from among you [the 'Alīds] after the death of the Prophet was more virtuous than 'Alī b. al-Ḥusayn. . . . After him, no one among you was like his son, Muḥammad b. 'Alī . . . , nor like his [Muḥammad b. 'Alī's] son, Ja'far" (Ibn 'Abd Rabbih, 5:82–3; Mubarrad, *Kāmil*, 4:119; Ṭabarī, 7:569–70).

10. 'Alī b. Muḥammad al-Hādī (d. 254/868)
11. Ḥasan b. 'Alī al-'Askarī (d. 260/874)
12. Muḥammad b. al-Ḥasan al-Mahdī al-Muntaẓar

* * * * *

Islamic legal and theological works describe the office of imāmate as the supreme leadership over the affairs of religion (*dīn*) and mundane life (*dunyā*). The *imām* was, thus, the head of the Muslim community, the successor to the Prophet, and the guardian of all Muslim religious and social affairs. The right to that position was publicly claimed for 'Alī against the incumbent caliph by his supporters during the reign of the third caliph, 'Uthmān. In subsequent ages, many Muslims, including many orthodox Sunnites,[6] maintained that the 'Alīd Imāms possessed a legitimacy that the reigning caliphs lacked. The Shī'ites believed that when the time came, the true Imām would take up arms, expel the usurpers, and regain his proper place.[7] Many Shī'ites hoped that when this occurred, they would be the reigning party and would finally be free from the persecution they had so long endured.[8] On the other hand, it seems that by the late first/early eighth century, the belief was already well established in the Muslim community that at some future time, a revolutionary leader from the House of the Prophet would rise up, overthrow the unjust government, and establish the rule of justice and truth. This millenarian figure was called by the Shī'ites the *qā'im*, "the one who rises up."

In the early second century of the *Hijra*, as popular discontent with the Umayyads grew ever more pervasive, many hoped that

6. See, for instance, Dhahabī, *Siyar a'lām al-nubalā'*, 13:120, where he says that Ḥasan, Ḥusayn, 'Alī b. al-Ḥusayn and Muḥammad al-Bāqir were all well qualified for the position of caliph; Ja'far al-Ṣādiq had a greater right to the caliphate than his contemporary caliph, Manṣūr; and Mūsā al-Kāẓim had a greater right to it than Hārūn al-Rashīd who was the caliph in his time.
7. See Ḥasan b. Muḥammad b. al-Ḥanafiyya: 24.
8. See especially Nu'mānī: 287, 288, 295 (see also 266); also 'Ayyāshī, 2:218; Kulaynī, 1:369, 5:19, 8:81; Ibn Qūlawayh: 336.

Imām Muḥammad al-Bāqir, would lead an insurrection.[9] He did not do so. This stance surprised Shī'ites whose conceptions of the Imām of the House of the Prophet required him to take action when conditions were propitious. When asked why despite his many followers in Iraq he had not led the awaited rising, he excused himself by saying that he was not the awaited *qā'im* and that the *qā'im* would appear in the future when the time was right for such a step.[10] Two decades later, however, his son, Ja'far al-Ṣādiq, also failed to act at a time that many considered ideal for the Imām, if he had sincerely wished to do so. He did not act, and the disillusionment engendered led the Shī'ites to reexamine long-established beliefs.

Imām Ja'far al-Ṣādiq was the most respected member of the House of the Prophet[11] during the time of upheaval that saw the overthrow of the century-old Umayyad rule. Ja'far was an obvious candidate to succeed the Umayyads as leader of the Islamic state, and many expected him to step forward into the role.[12] Iraq was full of his followers. A passionate follower told him that "half of the world" supported his claim.[13] The people of Kūfa waited only for his order to seize the city from its garrison.[14] Even the Abbasids, who eventually took the reins of power, reportedly looked to him in the early days of their insurrection as their first choice for the spiritual leadership of their movement.[15] His failure to take advantage of the situation led to various reactions: some of his followers even held that it was unlawful for him not to rise up;[16] others simply showed disappointment that despite the new developments the promised golden age of the Shī'ites was no closer to its realization.[17]

9. Kulaynī, 8:80, 341; Khuṣaybī: 242–3
10. Kulaynī, 1:342, 536 (see also 1:368); Nu'mānī: 167–8, 169, 215, 216, 237; *Kamāl*: 325. See also Sa'd b. 'Abd Allāh: 75; Mufīd, *al-Risāla al-khāmisa fī 'l-ghayba*: 400.
11. See Kulaynī, 8:160; Dhahabī, *'Ibar*, 1:209.
12. Kulaynī, 1:307, 8:331; Kashshī: 158, 398; *Tahdhīb*, 7:2; *Manāqib*, 3:362.
13. Kulaynī, 2:242. See also *Manāqib*, 3:362.
14. Kulaynī, 8:331; Kashshī: 353–4.
15. *Manāqib*, 3:355–6 (quoting from earlier sources); Shahrastānī, 1:179. See also Kulaynī, 8:274.
16. Kulaynī, 2:242.
17. Ibid., 1:368; Nu'mānī: 198, 288, 294, 330; *Ghayba*: 262, 263, 265.

The Imām, however, remained quiet and did not enter any political activity.[18] He also forbade his followers to engage in any political activity[19] or to join any armed group,[20] make Shī'ite propaganda,[21] or recruit new members into the Shī'ite community.[22] Possibly along the same line, he at times did not even like to be called the Imām.[23] He explicitly told his people that he was not the *qā'im*, and that there would be no change in the political status of the Shī'ite community during his generation.[24] Some Shī'ites thereupon turned to the more active and politically ambitious Ḥasanid branch of the House of the Prophet and joined the revolt of Muḥammad b. 'Abd Allāh al-Nafs al-Zakiyya[25] who was widely believed to be the long awaited savior. The belief that the *qā'im* would imminently appear was by now so strongly held that people continued to look for him even after al-Nafs al-Zakiyya had been defeated and killed (145/762); according to some, the *qā'im* was to appear as soon as fifteen days after the killing of al-Nafs al-Zakiyya.[26] It did not come to pass.

Other groups of Shī'ites did not consider the principal role of the Imām to be political. They instead viewed him as the most learned man from among the descendants of the Prophet who was to teach people what was lawful and what was not and to exhort them to turn toward God.[27] He was the one to distinguish truth

18. See Ṭabarī, 7:603; Abu 'l-Faraj: 273; Kashshī: 362, 365. This, however, did not suffice to convince the caliph that he was not conspiring against him. See Ibn 'Abd Rabbih, 3:224.
19. See Ibn Bābawayh, *'Uyūn*, 1:310; Ṭūsī, *Amālī*, 2:280.
20. See Kashshī: 336, 383–4; Najāshī: 144–5.
21. Kulaynī, 2:221–6, 369–72. For an example of the Shī'ite propaganda in that time see Ṣaffār:244.
22. Barqī, 1:200, 201, 203; Kulaynī, 1:165–7.
23. See, for instance, Barqī, 1:288–9; 'Ayyāshī, 1:327; Kulaynī, 1:181, 189; Kashshī: 281, 349, 419, 421, 422–3, 427. A similar reaction is quoted from his son, Mūsā al-Kāẓim. See Kashshī: 283.
24. *Ghayba*: 263.
25. On him see the article "Muḥammad b. 'Abd Allāh al-Nafs al-Zakiyya" in *EI*[1], 3:665–6 (by Fr. Buhl).
26. *Kamāl*: 649; Sulamī: 116, 119. See also Ibn Abī Shayba, 8:679; Haytamī: 55; and Kulaynī, 1:534 (quoting a Shī'ite of the time who vowed to keep fasting until the *qā'im* appears), 8:310.
27. Kulaynī, 1:178, *Kamāl*: 223, 224, 229.

from falsity,[28] to protect the religion from being distorted and corrupted by the ignorant and misguided,[29] and to reestablish whatever truth suffered distortion or corruption at their hands.[30] He guarded the integrity of the religion: if the people added anything to it he would reject it, and if they omitted anything he would restore it.[31] Society needed an Imām to whom they could refer problems they encountered in religious practice, an Imām who would act as the ultimate authority in explicating the law of God and the true meaning of the Qur'ān and the Prophetic tradition so that differences of opinion among the believers could be removed by following his instructions in every question.[32]

Even for those who emphasized the political role of the Imām, Ja'far al-Ṣādiq's failure to assume an active political role resulted in a major reconsideration of the institution of Imāmate. The Imām was no longer the long-awaited savior; at least, this was no longer considered to be his major role. Now, for them like the others, the Imām was the head of religion. In this manner, the community changed the emphasis of the institution of Imāmate from political to religious authority. Hishām b. al-Ḥakam's theory of the Imām's divine protection against sin and error (*'iṣma*)[33] was a major contribution to further accommodate the shift. In their times, Muḥammad al-Bāqir and Ja'far al-Ṣādiq were each venerated by the entire Muslim community as profoundly learned men and indisputable authorities on the *sharī'a*. In the view of the followers of the Imāms, however, their knowledge was qualitatively different from that of other learned men for it was the knowledge of the House of the Prophet, which derived ultimately from the Prophet himself. It was, therefore, unquestionable truth and indisputable authority, representing in effect a part of the revelation that the Prophet had received from God.

While these changes were taking place, new opinions and ideas were put forward by a new extremist wing of the Imāmite tradition, which had links to the now-vanished Kaysānite movement

28. Kulaynī, 1:178.
29. *Kamāl*: 221, 281.
30. *Kamāl*: 221.
31. Ṣaffār: 331–2; Kulaynī, 1:178; *Kamāl*: 203, 205, 221, 223, 228.
32. Kulaynī, 1:170, 172.
33. See the article "iṣma" in *EI*², 4:182–4 (by W. Madelung).

of the late first/seventh century. The extremists[34] emphasized the supernatural qualities of the Imām, maintaining that he was the centerpiece of the universe: "If the earth were left without an Imām for even one minute, its entire structure would collapse."[35] The result, nevertheless, was the same—a downgrading of the political aspect of the institution of Imāmate.

The old expectations were, however, renewed during the time of Ja'far al-Ṣādiq's successor, Mūsā al-Kāẓim. The circulation of a *ḥadīth* among the Shī'a of his time that suggested that the seventh Imām would be the *qā'im*[36] created widespread expectations within the Shī'ite community that it was Mūsā who would establish the rule of truth. The establishment of the institution of representation, which he initiated and which, as will be seen below, provided him with a chain of representatives across the Muslim world who systematically collected religious funds and donations on his behalf and sent them to him in Medina, made those expectations look more realistic than at any time before. He personally was a brave person, outspoken against the government[37] and daring to challenge the caliph in his presence.[38] Many people, later even some Sunnites,[39] considered him to be the legitimate caliph,[40] which was tantamount to declaring the Caliph of Baghdad illegitimate. The situation provoked the suspicion of his contemporary caliph, Hārūn al-Rashīd (r. 170-193/786-809). Mūsā was arrested in Medina and brought to Iraq, where he was imprisoned for several years before he was put to death in 183/799. Some of his partisans were also arrested and ruthlessly tortured.[41] The announcement of his death in jail was a strong blow to the Shī'ites' hopes and expectations. For many

34. See Murtaḍā, *Shāfī*, 1:42.
35. Ṣaffār: 488–9; Kulaynī, 1:179; Ibn Bābawayh, *'Uyūn*, 1:272; *Kamāl*: 201–4.
36. Muḥammad B. al-Muthannā al-Haḍramī: 91; 'Alī b. Bābawayh: 147; Nawbakhtī: 92; Sa'd b. 'Abd Allāh: 91; Abu 'l-Qāsim al-Balkhī: 180:; Kashshī: 373, 475; Mufīd, *Irshād*, 302; Shahrastānī, 1:197, 198. See also Abū Ḥātim al-Rāzī: 290; 'Ayyāshī, 2:250–1.
37. Kashshī: 441.
38. Ibn Qūlawayh: 18; 'Ayyāshī, 2:229–30; Abū Manṣūr al-Ṭabrisī, 2:167.
39. Nawbakhtī: 95; Sa'd b. 'Abd Allāh: 94.
40. Kulaynī, 1:486.
41. See, for instance, Kashshī: 591–2; Najāshī: 326, 424.

years thereafter,[42] most refused to believe he had really died, hoping that someday he would reappear to inaugurate the rule of truth. The belief that he was the *qā'im*, based on a *ḥadīth* that was widely known in his time, could not so quickly disappear.

The political component of the Imāmate was once more renewed in 201/817 when the Abbasid Ma'mūn (r. 198–218/813–833) designated Imām 'Alī al-Riḍā as his heir apparent, but the Shī'ites' hopes were dashed once again by the death of 'Alī al-Riḍā in 203/818. The ninth and tenth Imāms succeeded their fathers when they were very young, which led to controversy in the Shī'ite community after the death of 'Alī al-Riḍā as to whether a child of seven years was legally qualified or knowledgeable enough to become an Imām. The solution that was offered[43] and that was widely and well received by the Imāmite community strengthened the extremists' ideas about the nature of the Imāmate and further downgraded the political aspect of the office. This solution involved the suggestion that the Imām became the Imām through divine grace and that knowledge or political status were mere contingent effects of the possession of the divine light and not essential elements of the Imāmate.

By this time, however, the Shī'ite community was already well established both socially and doctrinally. A vast body of theological and legal literature existed—quotations from the Imāms Muḥammad al-Bāqir and Ja'far al-Ṣādiq and, to a lesser extent, from Mūsā al-Kāẓim compiled in books and collections by Shī'ite scholars—that made the Shī'ite community self-sufficient except in odd cases where a new question arose or reports conflicted or opinions regarding interpretation differed. The office of Imāmate now also regularly received the gifts, alms, and charitable donations and endowments that faithful Shī'ites regularly sent to the Holy Threshold[44] (*al-nāḥiya al-muqaddasa*), the house of the Imām. For the last few decades of the period of the "presence" of the Imāms and then to the end of the period of Minor Occultation this situation remained unchanged. The faithful Shī'ites in this period changed the balance of demand

42. In the beginning there was an idea that he would return within eight months (Kashshī: 406). The time limit was later modified.

43. See below, chapter 2.

44. For this term see Ṭabrisī, *I'lām*: 418. See also Kashshī: 532, 534; Najāshī: 344; *Ghayba*: 172.

and expectation to the benefit of the Imām. They no longer asked the Imām to rise against the political system. With the caliphs in firm control this would have been an unthinkable task. They faithfully fulfilled their duties toward the Imām and did not neglect his rights. The list of the payments made by the faithful to the Imām now included the *khums*, a tax of 20 percent levied on the incomes of all Shīʿites. The Imāms Muḥammad al-Bāqir[45] and Jaʿfar al-Ṣadiq[46] had previously not collected this tax from their followers. The belief was widespread that this levy would be instituted by the *qāʾim* when he came to establish his rule of justice.[47] The systematic collection[48] of the levy as a mandatory tax seems to have started in 220/835 when Imām Muḥammad al-Jawād ordered his financial representatives to collect the *khums* on certain kinds of income.[49] In the same document, he emphasized that he was collecting the *khums* in that one year, which happened to be the last year of his life, because of a certain reason he did not want to specify (perhaps the financial need of some members of the House of the Prophet at the time). As attested by historical reports, however, the collection of this tax by local representatives of the Imām became a quite well-established practice during the latter part of the incumbency of the next Imām, ʿAlī al-Hādī.[50]

The Imāms reportedly had received funds from their followers from the time of Jaʿfar al-Ṣādiq.[51] In the beginning, these consisted mainly of the obligatory alms (*zakāt*) that many Shīʿites chose to

45. Kulaynī, 1:544.
46. Ibid., 1:408; Ṭūsī, *Tahdhīb*, 4:138, 143, 144.
47. See Kulaynī, 1:408; Ṭūsī, *Tahdhīb*, 4:144. See also Nuʿmānī: 237; Sulamī: 40.
48. Some reports suggest that Mūsā al-Kāẓim received *khums* from one of his followers (Ibn Bābawayh, *ʿUyūn*, 1:70) and that ʿAlī al-Riḍā instructed his followers to pay this tax (Kulaynī, 1:547–8). The referred to document from Muḥammad al-Jawād, however, attests to the fact that the tax was not systematically collected before the date mentioned.
49. Ṭūsī, *Tahdhīb*, 4:141. See also *Manāqib*, 4:389.
50. See Ḥurr al-ʿĀmilī, 6: 348–9.
51. For Muḥammad al-Bāqir's refusal to accept religious funds see Nuʿmānī: 237 (and Sulamī: 40). For Jaʿfar al-Ṣādiq's occasional acceptance of the same see Ṣaffār: 99; Kulaynī, 2:512; Ḥusayn b. ʿAbd al-Wahhāb: 87; Rāwandī, 2:777.

give to the Imām,[52] voluntary donations and endowments (*nadhr, waqf,* etc.), and gifts.[53] Shī'ites originally gave their donations to Ja'far al-Ṣādiq in person. In 147/765, the Abbasid caliph Manṣūr ordered Ja'far to come to court where he took him to task on a number of points, among them that the people of Iraq had chosen Ja'far as their Imām and paid their obligatory alms to him.[54] According to another report, the caliph also accused Ja'far of receiving *kharāj*, administrative taxes, from his followers.[55]

Ja'far al-Ṣādiq does not, however, appear to have appointed representatives to collect taxes for him.[56] The system by which agents (*wukalā'*, sing. *wakīl*) of the Imāms collected religious funds—which had already grown into an elaborate and well-organized institution by the middle of the third/nineth century—was established by Ja'far's son, Mūsā al-Kāẓim. Mūsā's representatives served in all the major Shī'ite communities in Egypt,[57] Kūfa,[58]

52. See Ṭūsī, *Tahdhīb*, 4:60, 91.
53. See Kulaynī, 1:537–8; Kashshī: 434; Ṭūsī, *Tahdhīb*, 4:91. For later periods see Kulaynī, 1:524, 548, 4:310, 7:38, 59; Khuṣaybī: 342; Ibn Bābawayh, *Faqīh*, 2:442, 4:232, 237; *Kamāl*, 498, 501, 522; Ḥasan al-Qummī: 279; Ṭūsī, *Tahdhīb*, 9:189, 195–6, 198, 210, 242; idem, *Istibṣār*, 4:123, 124, 126, 129, 133; *Ghayba*: 75, 91, 225; Pseudo Mas'ūdī: 247; Majlisī, 50:185, 51:29.
54. Ibn Ṭalḥa: 82. See also Kulaynī, 6:446.
55. See Majlisī, 47:187. The same charge was made against his son, Mūsā al-Kāẓim, during his Imāmate. See Kashshī: 265; Ibn Bābawayh, *'Uyūn*, 1:81.
56. *Ghayba*: 210, reports that Nasr b. Qābūs al-Lakhmī and 'Abd al-Raḥmān b. al-Ḥajjāj acted as financial representatives of Ja'far al-Ṣādiq, but there is no evidence in the early Shī'ite literature to support this claim. 'Abd al-Raḥmān b. al-Ḥajjāj was later an agent of Mūsā al-Kāẓim (Ḥimyarī: 191; Kashshī: 431. See also ibid.: 265, 269, where the Imām is said to have sent a message to another disciple of his through 'Abd al-Raḥmān b. al-Ḥajjāj). According to another report (Kulaynī, 6:446; Ibn Ṭāwūs, *Muhaj al-da'awāt*: 198), Ja'far's servant, Mu'allā b. Khunays, also collected donations on the Imām's behalf. This obviously does not mean that he was a financial representative (*wakīl*) in the sense understood in the later history of the Imāmate administration.
57. Kashshī: 597–8; *Ghayba*: 43.
58. Kashshī: 459; Najāshī: 249.

Baghdad,[59] Medina[60] and elsewhere. At the time of his death, Mūsā's agents had large sums for him in their possession,[61] from ten[62] to thirty[63] and even seventy[64] thousand *dīnār*s. These funds came from a variety of levies, including the *zakāt*.[65] Imām 'Alī al-Riḍā continued his father's initiatives, appointing his own representatives in various places.[66] The new financial institution continued to grow under later Imāms. It seems that Muḥammad al-Jawād periodically sent special envoys to the Shī'ite communities to collect the levies and donations,[67] including funds that had been gathered during the year by his numerous local representatives.[68]

The Imāmate's financial administration was further developed into a very well-organized institution in the time of Imām 'Alī al-Hādī as attested by references in early sources about how the institution worked.[69] The Imām regularly sent letters to local Shī'ite communities and urged the faithful to fulfill their financial obligations toward the Imām by regular payment of his rights to his representatives.[70] This payment was "an obedience to God that guaranteed lawfulness and cleanliness for their wealth and the protection of God for their lives."[71] The revenues of the office of the Imāmate had increased dramatically with the addition of the *khums* tax, which the Imām's agents systematically collected from the faithful as his right.[72] Because it was a new imposition, there were

59. Kashshī: 886–7.
60. Ibid.: 446.
61. Ibid.: 405, 459, 467, 468, 493, 598.
62. *Ghayba*: 44.
63. Kashshī: 405, 459, 493.
64. Ibid.: 467, 493.
65. Ibid.: 459.
66. Ibid.: 506; Najāshī: 197, 447; *Ghayba*: 210–11.
67. See Kashshī: 596 where Zakariyyā b. Ādam al-Ash'arī is quoted as reporting to the Imām a disagreement that came up between his two emissaries to Qum, Maymūn and Musāfir.
68. See, for instance, Kashshī: 549; Najāshī: 197.
69. See, for instance, Najāshī: 344.
70. Kashshī: 513–14.
71. Ibid: 514.
72. See Kulaynī, 1:545, 548; Kashshī: 514, 577, 579, 580–81; Ṭūsī, *Tahdhīb*, 4:123, 138, 143.

questions about the scope of the "right." Three main representatives of 'Alī al-Hādī[73] reported to him that they had faced questions from the Shī'ite community about the right of the Imām that the representatives did not know how to answer.[74]

In 233/848 Imām 'Alī al-Hādī was brought to the capital Sāmarrā' on orders of Caliph Mutawakkil and put under constant observation. His activities were severely restricted there, and for the rest of his life the Imām's financial representatives were the main channel through which he kept contact with his followers in other parts of the Shī'ite world.[75] The Shī'ite community experienced

73. They were Abū 'Alī b. Rāshid, who was appointed as the Imām's chief representative in Iraq in 232/846–847 (Kashshī: 513–14; see also Kulaynī, 7:59; Ṭūsī, *Tahdhīb*, 9:234) to replace 'Alī b. al-Ḥusayn b. 'Abd Rabbih, who had died three years before (Kashshī:510); 'Alī b. Mahziyār, who followed 'Abd Allāh b. Jundub as chief representative in Ahwāz (ibid.:549); and Ibrāhīm b. Muḥammad al-Hamadānī, the sole representative in Hamadān (ibid.: 608, 611–12; Najāshī: 344). The Imām, of course, had many other financial agents in other parts of the Shī'ite world (see, for instance, Kashshī: 512–14). It is worth noting that almost all Imāmite notables that were described by the last Imāms as trustworthy or reliable were financial representatives and agents (see, for instance, Kashshī: 557 where *al-Ghā'ib al-'alīl* ['Alī b. Ja'far al-Humānī, 'Alī al-Hādī's principal agent; see Kashshī: 523, 527, 606–8; *Ghayba*: 212], Ayyūb b. Nūḥ b. Darrāj al-Nakha'ī [the Imām's financial representative in Kūfa; see Kashshī: 514, 525, 572, 612; Najāshī: 102; Ṭūsī, *Tahdhīb*, 9:195–96; idem, *Istibṣār*, 4:123; *Ghayba*: 212], Ibrāhīm b. Muḥammad al-Hamadānī [mentioned above, the Imām's representative in Hamadān] and Aḥmad b. Isḥāq al-Ash'arī al-Qummī [the agent in charge of the endowments made for the Imāms in Qum; see Ḥasan al-Qummī: 211; *Ghayba*: 212] are described as *thiqa* [trustworthy]). Many of the Imām's agents were not scholars, a point certainly true with 'Uthmān b. Sa'īd al-'Amrī and his son, Muḥammad (see below), who were described by 'Alī al-Hādī and Ḥasan al-'Askarī as reliable and trustworthy (*Ghayba*: 146–7, 215–20). The word *thiqa* in these cases means financial trustworthiness, *al-thiqa al-ma'mūn 'alā māli 'llāh* (ibid.: 216). The description was meant to direct the faithful to these agents for the payment of their donations and religious dues and not for doctrinal and legal questions and as sources of religious knowledge, as many Shī'ite scholars of the past (see, for instance, Ḥurr al-'Āmilī, 18:100) and modern scholars of the field (such as Kohlberg, "Imām and Community": 38–9) have thought.

74. Kulaynī, 1:547; Ṭūsī, *Tahdhīb*, 4:123.

75. See Kashshī: 509, 580–1.

severe persecution during Mutawakkil's reign. He purged Shī'ites from all administrative positions and ostracized them socially.[76] The shrine of Ḥusayn in Karbalā', a major center for Shī'ite gathering and pilgrimage, was razed to the ground.[77] Many Shī'ite notables, including some of the Imām's representatives, were imprisoned[78] or put to death.[79]

The Zaydite branch of Shī'ism was by now a well-established school of thought and a major rival of Imāmite Shī'ism. In a treatise from that period entitled *al-Radd 'ala 'l-rawāfiḍ,* the Zaydite author who was a contemporary of Imām 'Alī al-Hādī criticized him for levying the *khums* on the general income of all Shī'ites, for appointing financial representatives in all towns to collect funds, and for, he claimed, "using the money for himself rather than distributing it to the needy."[80] Similar criticism was launched a few decades later by Abū Zayd al-'Alawī in his *Kitāb al-Ishhād*,[81] among others, which was answered by the Imāmite authors.[82]

The emphasis on the financial right of the Imām in the Shī'ite community continued through the incumbency of the next Imām, Ḥasan al-'Askarī, and into the period of the Minor Occultation. Some of the letters that Ḥasan al-'Askarī wrote to his local representatives are preserved as well.[83] In these letters, the Imām attaches major significance to the regular collection of religious funds, obviously because of the pressing needs of the office to meet the needs of Shī'ite society, which was passing through a very difficult time. In an untraditionally long letter that the Imām wrote to one of the notables in the Shī'ite community of Nīshāpūr,[84] he complained that the community there was not paying its dues to the Imām as properly as they had during the time of his father. He equated any negligence in payment of the Imām's rights to unbelief. In the same

76. See Mas'ūdī, *Murūj*, 5:50– 51.
77. Ṭabarī, 9:185; *Murūj*, 5:51.
78. Kashshī: 607–8.
79. Ibid.: 603 (cf. Ṭabarī, 9:200–201).
80. Pseudo Qāsim b. Ibrāhīm, *al-Radd 'ala 'l-rawāfiḍ*: 106b, 108a.
81. Abū Zayd al-'Alawī: para. 39.
82. See Ibn Qiba, *Naqḍ kitāb al-ishhād*: paras. 41–2.
83. See Kashshī: 577–81.
84. Ibid.: 575–80.

letter he noted that his correspondence with the Shīʿite community of Nīshāpūr in demand of his rights had been going on for a long time and that if it was not for the fact that he did not want them to become subject to God's punishment, he would not insist or contact them again. At the end of the letter he named several of his agents in different towns whom he praised for their good service and reliability. As might be expected, some of these local agents later misappropriated funds, and others who had not received authorization from the Imām claimed to be his representatives and fraudulently collected money from the people. Numerous associates of the Imām were excommunicated in this period for such transgressions, including one of those named and praised in the letter just mentioned.[85]

ʿUthmān b. Saʿīd al-ʿAmrī served as a financial agent first to Imām ʿAlī al-Hādī (apparently from the time of the Imām's removal to Sāmarrā')[86] and then as the principal financial aide to Imām Ḥasan al-ʿAskarī[87] during whose time ʿUthmān was in full control of the office.[88] ʿUthmān outlived both of his masters and remained head of the Imāmate administration after the death of Ḥasan al-ʿAskarī,

85. That was ʿUrwa b. Yaḥyā al-Dihqān, the Imām's chief representative in Baghdad (Kashshī: 543, 579), who was later excommunicated by the Imām because he had embezzled the funds (ibid.: 536–7, 573–4). Another one of those named in the letter (Abū Ṭahīr Muḥammed b. ʿAlī b. Bilāl, known as Bilālī) was excommunicated later by the second agent of the Twelfth Imām (*Ghayba*: 245).

86. ʿUthmān b. Saʿīd started working in Imām ʿAlī al-Hādī's house when he was 11 years old (Ṭūsī, *Rijāl*: 420); later he became one of the chief aides to the Imām (see, for instance, Kulaynī, 1:330; Kashshī: 526).

87. See Kulaynī, 1:330; *Ghayba*: 215. In a rescript that was sent from the Holy Threshold to the Imām's representative in Nīshāpūr, who was at the time in Sāmarrā', the representative was ordered not to leave the town until "you meet ʿAmrī, God may be satisfied with him as a result of my satisfaction with him, and say hello to him and make yourself known to him, because he is the pure, the trustworthy, the chaste, and the [one] close to us and to our hearts. Whatever is brought to us from various regions eventually ends with him so that he passes it to us" (Kashshī: 580).

88. Mufīd, *al-Fuṣūl al-ʿashara*: 355. See also Kashshī: 544 where the phrase implies that it was not even quite clear if he always acted under the instruction of the Imām.

continuing to receive religious funds on behalf of his son who had passed into occultation beyond the reach of ordinary Shī'ites. Upon 'Uthmān's death, his position was assumed by his son, Muḥammad b. 'Uthmān, and then by two others. This period of the Minor Occultation ended with the death of the last deputy, who had not named a successor, and thus began the Major Occultation when the Shī'ites lost all contact with the Imām.

II

Moderation or Shortcoming?

IT HAS BEEN insisted throughout the Qur'ān that God is the only one who creates all beings and provides them with their living[1] without anyone's help or support,[2] the only one who never dies whereas every other being dies,[3] the only one who has knowledge of the unseen,[4] and the only lawmaker in the universe.[5] In numerous verses as well, the Qur'ān insists that the prophets were ordinary people who lived and died like everyone else.[6] It especially speaks of Muḥammad as an ordinary person whose only difference from other people was that he received revelation from God in order to deliver it to mankind.[7] Muḥammad was asked by God especially to emphasize this point to those who asked him to perform miracles and to prove that he was someone special.[8]

In spite of these cautions, the idea that the Prophet was a supernatural being started immediately after his death. It is reported that as soon as the news of his death spread, a certain Companion asserted that he did not die but disappeared from his people and would return and "cut off the hands and feet of those who alleged that he was dead,"[9] an assertion that other Muslims rejected on the basis of a Qur'ānic verse that spoke of the Prophet's death in the future.[10] A similar claim was heard after the assassination of 'Alī when some people maintained that he was still alive and that he would not die until he conquered the whole world and drove the

1. Qur'ān, e.g. 6:102, 27:64, 30:40, 35:3.
2. Ibid., e.g. 17:111, 34:22.
3. Ibid., 28:88.
4. Ibid., e.g. 27:65.
5. Ibid., e.g. 6:57, 12:40, 67, 39:3.
6. Ibid., e.g. 5:75, 14:38, 25:20.
7. Ibid., 18:110.
8. Ibid., 17:90–94.
9. Ibn Hishām, 4:305–6; Ṭabarī, 3:200–201.
10. Qur'ān, 3:144.

Arabs with his stick.[11] It was again heard after the death of his son, Muḥammad b. al-Ḥanafiyya in 81/700 when many of his followers claimed that he did not die but only concealed himself from the people and will reappear before the end of time "to fill the earth with justice as it was filled with injustice and despotism."[12] This idea was labeled by the mainstream of the Muslim community as *ghuluww*[13] (exaggerations, conventionally translated as "extremism") and the people who supported it as *ghulāt* (exaggerators, conventionally "extremists").[14]

From the beginnings of the second century of the *Hijra,* numerous heretic persons and groups emerged who proclaimed one or another prominent figure of the House of the Prophet as God. This idea reportedly was begun in the previous century by a group that, sometime after ʿAlī's death, claimed that he was God and that he concealed himself from the people as a sign of anger.[15] Later sources even claim that this idea started in ʿAlī's lifetime when during his caliphate some people, for unspecified reasons, maintained that he was their God, and he subsequently ordered them to be burned after they refused to repent and give up that idea.[16] During the second/eighth century, however, the idea that one or the other Imām was God was normally the first half of a two-part claim; the second half was that the claimant himself was that god's messenger. This was the case with Ḥamza b. ʿUmāra al-Barbarī[17] who separated from his fellow Kaysānites by claiming that Muḥammad b. al-Ḥanafiyya was God and Ḥamza was his messenger.[18] It was also the case with

11. Jāḥiẓ, *al-Bayān wa 'l-tabyīn*,3:81; Nawbakhtī: 40–44; Saʿd b. ʿAbd Allāh: 19–20.
12. See Wadād al-Qāḍī, *Kaysāniyya*: 168ff.
13. See, for instance, *Kamāl*: 33 where the poet Al-Sayyid al-Ḥimyarī (d. ca. 173/789) is quoted as describing his own state of belief before his alleged conversion to Imāmite Shīʿism as the time when he "adhered to *ghuluww* and believed in the occultation of Muḥammad b. al-Ḥanafiyya." See also Nawbakhtī: 52.
14. See Wadād al-Qāḍī, "The Development of the Term *Ghulāt* in Muslim Literature": 295–300.
15. Saʿd b. ʿAbd Allāh: 21.
16. For sources and an evaluation of the authenticity of these reports see Wadād al-Qāḍī, "The Development . . .": 307.
17. On him see Wadād al-Qāḍī, *Kaysāniyya*, 206–8.
18. Nawbakhtī: 45; Saʿd b. ʿAbd Allāh: 32.

the numerous groups that believed Ja'far al-Ṣādiq[19] and the Imāms among his descendants[20] were God. All of these groups had their own special allegoristic and esoteric interpretations of the religious symbols; they subsequently abrogated the *sharī'a,* legalized unlawful acts, and, consequently, split from the Muslim community. The Imāms and their followers, however, consistently condemned and publicly disassociated themselves from these groups. This might have been partly in order to protect the Shī'ite community from possible discredit by the blasphemies of those groups whose leaders started as Shī'ites and claimed association with the Imāms, and the wild ideas of those groups could, therefore, be harmful to the image of Shī'ism.

Some time in the first decades of the second century of the *Hijra* during the time of Imām Ja'far al-Ṣādiq, another category of extremists emerged within the Imāmite community. This group inherited and adopted[21] many of the points of view of the extremists in the defunct school of Kaysānite Shī'ism on the divine nature of the Imāms,[22] namely, that the Imāms were supernatural beings who possessed limitless knowledge, including that of the unseen,[23] and had power of disposal over the universe. This new group of Shī'ite extremists did not proclaim the Prophet and the Imāms as God but believed that God had empowered them to create and provide for all beings and had vested in them the authority to legislate and abrogate the *sharī'a* as they decided. The Prophet and the Imāms were, thus, fulfilling nearly all the functions that God was supposed to do; the only difference was that His power was original and theirs subordinate. This idea soon came to be known in the Shī'ite tradition by the term *tafwīḍ* (delegation), after which the group came to be more specifically known among the Shī'a as the *Mufawwiḍa*, just

19. See Nawbakhtī: 57–9; Sa'd b. 'Abd Allāh: 51–55; Qāḍī Nu'mān, 1:62.
20. See Kashshī: 480, 518–21, 555.
21. The extremists in question themselves regarded the Kaysānites as their predecessors as this statement that they ascribed to Ja'far al-Ṣādiq attests: "Our secret was undisclosed until it went into the hands of the descendants [*sic*] of Kaysān who disclosed it in the streets and amongst communities" (Kulaynī, 1:223).
22. See Wadād al-Qāḍī, *Kaysāniyya*: 238–61.
23. Nawbakhtī: 49, 51, 65; Sa'd b. 'Abd Allāh: 39, 41; Shahrastānī, 1:170.

as the splinter heretic groups who deified the Imāms were sometimes more specifically called *Ghulāt Ṭayyāra,* or simply *Ṭayyāra*[24] (overflyers).[25] In early Shī'ite biographical dictionaries the latter, who split from the community and established their own heretical sects on the basis of their esoteric interpretations, are sometimes distinguished by the term *fāsid al-madhhab* or *fāsid al-i'tiqād* (of corrupt doctrine)[26] or by stating that the scholarship of the person concerned

24. See Kashshī: 324, 363, 401, 407, 507; Maqdisī, 5:129; Ṭūsī, *Rijāl*: 515.

25. See for this translation Kashshī: 507–8 (para. 978, 981) where Ṣafwān b. Yaḥyā al-Bajalī (d. 210/825–826), a prominent figure in the Shī'ite community of his time, is quoted as having said that Muḥammad b. Sinān, a well-known figure among the Mufawwiḍa, "was from the *Ṭayyāra* (or, according to another report, "repeatedly tried to fly") but we clipped [his wings] until he settled with us." The word was possibly related to the word *irtifā',* which was used for the Mufawwiḍa—the latter had gone up a distance away from the truth, the radical extremists had flown far beyond it (see also Nu'mānī: 19). Cf. Maqdisī, 5:129 where it is said that the followers of 'Abd Allāh b. Saba' (see below, chapter 7) are called *Ṭayyāra* because they maintain that they do not die, rather their souls fly into the dark.

26. The list of the transmitters of *ḥadīth* who were described by those definitions includes the following:

—Aḥmad b. Muḥammad b. Sayyār, a transmitter of *ghuluww* and *takhlīṭ* (Najāshī: 80; Ṭūsī, *Fihrist*: 23), who believed in metempsychosis (Ibn al-Ghaḍā'irī, 1: 150)

—'Alī b. 'Abd Allāh al-Khadījī, author of a book that is described as *kitāb mal'ūn fī takhlīṭ 'aẓīm* (Najāshī: 267);

—'Alī b. 'Abd Allāh al-Maymūnī (Najāshī: 268);

—'Alī b. Aḥmad al-Kūfī (Najāshī: 265), who later in his life became a member of the *bāṭinī* sect of the Mukhammisa (Ṭūsī, *Rijāl*: 485; idem, *Fihrist*: 211; 'Umarī: 108);

—'Alī b. Ḥassan al-Hāshimī (Najāshī: 251), author of a book called *Tafsīr al-bāṭin,* which is described by Ibn al-Ghaḍā'irī, 4: 176, as heretical;

—Dāwūd b. Kathīr al-Raqqī (Ibn al-Ghaḍā'irī, 2: 190), whom the Ghulāt counted among their leaders (Kashshī: 408);

—Fāris b. Ḥātim b. Māhawayh al-Qazwīnī, who had *takhlīṭ* in his works and beliefs (Ibn al-Ghaḍā'irī, 5: 11);

—Ḥasan b. Asad al-Ṭufāwī (Ibn al-Ghaḍā'irī, 2: 98);

—Ḥusayn b. Ḥamdān al-Khuṣaybī, the Nuṣayrite (Najāshī: 67; Ibn al-Ghaḍā'irī, 2: 172), whose works suffered from *takhlīṭ* (Najāshī: 67);

—Isḥāq b. Muḥammad b. Aḥmad b. Abān al-Aḥmar (Ibn al-Ghaḍā'irī, 1: 197), the source of *takhlīṭ* and author of works of *takhlīṭ* (Najāshī: 73);

—Ja'far b. Muḥammad b. Mālik al-Fazārī (Najāshī: 122);

suffers from *takhlīṭ* (confusion with esoteric, *bāṭinī*[27] teachings).[28] The Mufawwiḍa, on the other hand, are frequently distinguished by descriptions such as *ahl al-irtifāʿ*,[29] *fī madhhabihi*[30] (or *fī ḥadīthihi*)

—Mufaḍḍal b. ʿUmar al-Juʿfī, the Khaṭṭābite (Najāshī: 416);

—Muḥammad b. ʿAbd Allāh b. Mihrān, the Khaṭṭābite (Najāshī: 350);

—Abū Sumayna Muḥammad b. ʿAlī al-Ṣayrafī, *fāsid al-iʿtiqād* (Najāshī: 332), whom Kashshī: 546 put in the same rank as Abu 'l-Khaṭṭāb;

—Muḥammad b. al-Ḥasan b. Shammūn, a Wāqifite extremist with *takhlīṭ* (Najāshī: 335);

—Muḥammad b. Jumhūr al-ʿAmmī (Najāshī: 337);

—Sahl b. Ziyād al-Ādamī (Ibn al-Ghaḍā'irī, 3: 179);

—Ṭāhir b. Ḥātim b. Māhawayh al-Qazwīnī (Ibn al-Ghaḍā'irī, 3: 228), whose beliefs and works suffered from *takhlīṭ* (Najāshī: 208).

27. See the article "Bāṭiniyya" in *EI*², 1:1098–1100 (by M. G. S. Hodgson).

28. See, for instance, Najāshī: 67, 73, 80, 164, 208, 221, 226, 251, 270, 284, 332, 336, 350, 373, 396, 448; Ṭūsī, *Rijāl*: 211, 486; idem, *Fihrist*: 23, 91–92, 143, 145, 146. The expression *mukhalliṭ*, thus, can describe either a person who does not have a sound doctrinal base and who takes all sorts of odd ideas from anywhere and puts them together and holds to them (see, for instance, Abū Manṣūr al-Ṭabrisī, 2:74; also ʿAbd al-Jabbār, *Mughnī*, 20[2]: 175) or the work of the person concerned in the same sense as the expressions *fāsid al-ḥadīth* or *fāsid al-riwāya*, of corrupt transmission (Najāshī: 368, 421; Ibn al-Ghaḍā'irī, 5:184; Ṭūsī, *Fihrist*: 284). ʿAlī b. Aḥmad al-ʿAqīqī is, for instance, called *mukhalliṭ* (Ṭūsī, *Rijāl*: 486) because his *ḥadīth* contained *manākīr*, bizarre ideas (idem, *Fihrist*: 97). Kashshī: 476 states that Abū Baṣīr Yaḥyā b. Abi 'l-Qāsim al-Asadī was not a *ghālī* himself but was *mukhalliṭ*, that is, he transmitted *ghuluww* traditions. Compare with cases where a person is said to be *fāsid al-madhhab wa 'l-riwāya* (e.g., Najāshī: 122; Ibn al-Ghaḍā'irī, 3:179). This is, of course, the more specific sense of this term as used in the Imāmite *ḥadīth* literature. The term *mukhalliṭ* is also used in the works on *ḥadīth* in the sense of careless transmitter who quotes and mixes all sorts of *ḥadīth*, whether sound or "weak."

29. See Kashshī: 326 (describing three transmitters, one of whom, Isḥāq b. Muḥammad al-Baṣrī, had [according to ibid.: 531] a special interest in transmitting Mufaḍḍal b. ʿUmar's reports on the themes of *tafwīḍ*). See also Khuṣaybī: 431 where the word *murtafiʿa* is used in the same sense.

30. See Najāshī: 24 (Ibrāhīm b. Yazīd al-Makfūf), 155 (Khaybarī b. ʿAlī al-Ṭaḥḥān), 228 (ʿAbd Allāh b. Khidāsh al-Mahrī), 384 (Muḥammad b. Baḥr al-Ruhnī, who was accused, according to Ṭūsī, *Rijāl*: 510 of supporting the idea of *tafwīḍ*); Ibn al-Ghaḍā'irī, 1:37 (Ibrāhīm b. Isḥāq al-Aḥmarī), 126 (Aḥmad b. ʿAlī al-Rāzī), 237 (Umayya b. ʿAlī al-Qaysī), 2:42 (Jaʿfar

irtifāʿ, *murtafiʿ al-qawl*[31] or *fīhi ghuluww wa taraffuʿ*,[32] all describing the doctrine of or the nature of the *ḥadīth* transmitted by the concerned person to be "elevated"[33] and exaggerated as they elevated the Imāms from human beings to supernatural beings by ascribing miracles and superhuman characters to them. Nevertheless, in general usage, the term *ghulāt* was also liberally and systematically used for both categories in Shīʿite circles as well as in the traditions and sources.[34] However, if the two terms *ghulāt* and *mufawwiḍa* are

---

b. Muḥammad b. Mālik al-Fazārī), 45 (Jaʿfar b. Maʿrūf al-Samarqandī), 124 (Ḥasan b. ʿAlī b. Abī ʿUthmān Sajjāda), 5:45 (Qāsim b. al-Ḥasan b. ʿAlī b. Yaqṭīn), 127 (Muḥammad b. Aḥmad al-Jāmūrānī), 162 (Muḥammad b. Baḥr al-Ruhnī), 219 (Muḥammad b. Sulaymān al-Daylamī, *murtafiʿ fī madhhabih*), 264 (Muḥammad b. ʿAlī al-Ṣayrafī).

31. Kashshī: 571 (Abū Hāshim al-Jaʿfarī whose narration betrays *irtifāʿ fi 'l-qawl*); Najāshī: 406 (Mūsā b. Jaʿfar al-Kumaydhānī); Ibn al-Ghaḍāʾirī, 3:266 (ʿAbd Allāh b. Baḥr al-Kūfī), 268 (ʿAbd Allāh b. Bakr al-Arrijānī), 278 (ʿAbd Allāh b. al-Ḥakam al-Armanī), 284 (ʿAbd Allāh b. Sālim al-Ṣayrafī), 4:25 (ʿAbd Allāh b. ʿAbd al-Raḥmān al-Aṣamm), 74 (ʿAbd al-Raḥmān b. Aḥmad b. Nahīk al-Kūfī), 6:131 (Mufaḍḍal b. ʿUmar al-Juʿfī), 279 (Yūsuf b. al-Sukht al-Baṣrī), 289 (Yūsuf b. Yaʿqūb al-Juʿfī).

32. Najāshī: 97 (Aḥmad b. ʿAlī al-Rāzī).

33. The expression was possibly taken from a then well-known statement attributed to the Prophet: "Do not exalt me above my actual rank [*la tarfaʿūnī fawqa ḥaddī*]; God picked me up as a slave [of His] before He picked me up as a prophet" (Ḥimyarī: 181; Ibn Bābawayh, *ʿUyūn*, 2:201).

34. Ibn Dāwūd: 538–42 gives a list of 65 persons described in the Shīʿite biographies of the transmitters of *ḥadīth* as *ghulāt*, and Wadād al-Qāḍī, "Development . . .": 317–18, gives a list of 56 based on the information available in the biographical dictionaries of Kashshī, Najāshī, Ṭūsī and Ibn Shahrāshūb. She, however, missed these names: Ismāʿīl b. Mihrān (Kashshī: 589), Muḥammad b. al-Furāt (ibid.: 554), Muḥammad b. Nuṣayr al-Numayrī (ibid.: 520–21), Muhammad b. Mūsā al-Shurayqī (ibid., 521: Ṭūsī, *Rijāl*: 436), Munakhkhal b. Jamīl al-Kūfī (Kashshī: 368; also Ibn al-Ghaḍāʾirī, 6:139), Muḥammad b. Ṣadaqa al-Baṣrī (Ṭūsī, *Rijāl*: 391), Muḥammad b. ʿĪsā b. ʿUbayd al-Yaqṭīnī (idem, *Fihrist*: 311), Ḥasan b. Khurzādh (Najāshī: 44), and Ḥusayn b. Yazīd b. ʿAbd al-Malik al-Nawfalī (ibid.: 38). Other names can be found in Ibn al-Ghaḍāʾirī, 2:24 (Jaʿfar b. Ismāʿīl al-Minqarī), 272 (Khalaf b. Muḥammad al-Māwardī), 275 (Ḥasan b. ʿAlī al-Ṭaḥḥān), 3:205 (Ṣāliḥ b. Sahl al-Hamadānī), 206 (Ṣāliḥ b. ʿUqba b. Qays b. Samʿān), 4:204 (ʿAlī b. ʿAbd Allāh al-Maymūnī), 5:45 (Qāsim b. al-Rabīʿ al-Ṣaḥḥāf), 6:112 (Muʿallā b. Rāshid al-ʿAmmī), 156 (Mūsā b. Saʿdān al-Ḥannāṭ), 164 (Mayyāḥ al-Madāʾinī), 290 (Yūnus b. Bahman).

mentioned together, *ghulāt* definitely refers to those who deified the Imāms or, alternatively, considered them prophets or angels.[35]

The doctrines of the Mufawwiḍa were more developed versions of those of the earlier extremists. The trend, it seems, was helped by the introduction of two ideas into the extremist doctrine some time around the beginning of the second/eighth century by the Kaysānite extremists.[36] First came the idea of incarnation of the divine spirit or light in the bodies of the Prophet and the Imāms. Earlier extremists had believed that the Prophet and the Imāms represented divinity itself.[37] According to this new idea, they possessed a part of the spirit of God or a spark of the divine light (but not necessarily the totality of God) which they had inherited from

---

Many of these *ghulāt* belonged to sectarian extremist groups, whereas others were from the Mufawwiḍa. Ṭūsī, for instance, describes Muḥammad b. Baḥr al-Ruhnī as a *ghālī* in his *Fihrist*: 132 but as a *mufawwiḍ* in his *Rijāl*: 510, and Furāt b. al-Aḥnaf al-ʿAbdī as being attributed to *ghuluww* and *tafwīḍ* in his *Rijāl*: 99 (as quoted by Ibn Dāwūd: 492 who possessed the autograph of that work, although in the printed copy it appears as *ghuluww* and *tafrīṭ*, two concepts with opposite meanings). Sometimes, however, only the adherence to *tafwīḍ* is mentioned as in the case of Ādam b. Muḥammad al-Qalānisī al-Balkhī in Ṭūsī, *Rijāl*: 438.

35. See, for instance, Ibn Bābawayh, *ʿUyūn*, 2:203 where a quotation from Imām ʿAlī al-Riḍā states that the "Ghulāt are infidels and the Mufawwiḍa are polytheists" (naturally because the more radical extremists, referred to here as the Ghulāt, believed in a god other than Allāh, whereas the latter, the Mufawwiḍa, virtually added other acting gods to Him); ibid, 1:215 (and idem, *Khiṣāl*: 529; idem, *Iʿtiqādāt*: 100; *Ghayba*: 18) where it is said that the Ghulat and Mufawwiḍa denied that the Imāms were actually killed or actually had died (Ṭūsī, in *Talkhīṣ al-shāfī*, 4:198, says that the Mufawwiḍa doubted that Ḥusayn was actually killed, in the same way that the Ghulāt hesitated about ʿAlī's death); idem, *Faqīh*, 1:359 where he says that "the Ghulāt and the Mufawwiḍa, may God curse them, deny the inadvertence of the Prophet"; Mufīd, *Awāʾil*: 38 where he states that the idea that the Imāms did not possess knowledge of the unseen is held by the entire Shīʿite community "except those who split away from them of the Mufawwida or those who allege to belong to them [the Shīʿites] of the Ghulāt" (compare with other cases in that work, such as the beginning of the same page, where he speaks of "the Mufawwiḍa and others among the Ghulāt." See also Kashshī: 479).
36. See Wadād al-Qāḍī, *Kaysāniyya*: 246, 248, 250–53.
37. See ʿAbd al-Jabbār, 20(1):13.

Adam through a line of prophets. The second was an interpretation that seems to have been offered first by the Kaysānite Bayān b. Sam'ān al-Nahdī (d. 119/737)[38] of a Qur'ānic verse that speaks of the God in Heaven and the God on earth.[39] He commented that this verse indicated that the one who is the god in heaven was different from the one who is the god on earth, although the one in heaven is greater and the one on earth lesser and obedient to him.[40] The two ideas were combined in the fourth decade of the second/eighth century by Abu 'l-Khaṭṭāb Muḥammad b. Abī Zaynab al-Asadī (d. ca. 138/755-756),[41] head of the Khaṭṭābite extremists,[42] who maintained that the spirit of God descended to the earth, manifested in Ja'far al-Ṣādiq,[43] and that now he was the god on earth.[44] The doctrine of the Mufawwiḍa, who appeared about the same time and was championed by Mufaḍḍal b. 'Umar al-Ju'fī, the money changer[45] (d. before 179/795), a former disciple of Abu 'l-Khaṭṭāb,[46] was clearly a further modification of that same idea.[47]

38. On him see Wadād al-Qāḍī, *Kaysāniyya*: 239–47; the article "Bayān b. Sam'ān al-Tamīmī" in *EI*², 1:1116–17 (by M.G.S. Hodgson); William Tucker, "Bayān b. Sam'ān and the Bayāniyya," in the *Muslim World*, 65, (1975): 241–53.
39. Qur'ān, 43:84: "and it is He who is God in heaven and God on earth."
40. Kashshī: 304 (see also Nawbakhtī: 59).
41. On him see the article "Abu 'l-Khaṭṭāb" in *EI*², 1:134 (by B. Lewis); Halm, *Die Islamisch Gnosis*, 199–206.
42. On them see the article "Khaṭṭābiyya" in *EI*², 4:1132–3 (by W. Madelung); Halm, *Die Islamische Gnosis*: 199–217.
43. Shahrastānī, 1:210–11.
44. Kashshī: 300. See also Nawbakhtī: 59 and Sa'd b. 'Abd Allāh: 53 where some followers of Abu 'l-Khaṭṭāb are quoted as describing his successor as "the god on earth who was obedient to the god of heaven and acknowledged his superiority and rank."
45. On him see Halm, "Das Buch der Schatten," in *Der Islam*, 55 (1978): 219–60.
46. Kashshī: 321, 324.
47. See ibid., 324–5. Abu 'l-Ḥasan al-Ash'arī, 1:79, thus, classifies the Mufawwiḍa as a subsect of the Khaṭṭābiyya whose only difference with the mainstream Khaṭṭābites was that they disassociated themselves from Abu 'l-Khaṭṭāb after Ja'far al-Ṣādiq anathematized him, but they remained faithful to Abu 'l-Khaṭṭāb's teachings.

The Mufawwiḍa maintained that the Prophet and the Imāms were the first and only beings to be directly created by God[48] from a substance different from that of the rest of humanity.[49] God then gave them authority and responsibility for all affairs of the world, whatever movement and action takes place in the universe.[50] They, as noted above, actually perform whatever functions are normally and conventionally ascribed to God, such as creation, providence, death, and so forth.[51] They make the *sharī'a* and abrogate it, make things lawful or unlawful.[52] They have knowledge of everything, seen or unseen.[53] (At least some upheld that the Imāms received

48. Sa'd b. 'Abd Allāh: 60–61; Mufīd, *Taṣḥīḥ*: 112. To be more precise, the first and only direct creature was a single entity, a single perfect being. This perfect being was then manifested in the world in various shapes, first as the Prophet and then as 'Alī, Fāṭima, and the Imāms from their descendants (Sa'd b. 'Abd Allāh: 60–61). Bursī: 258 names a certain Jālūt (?) al-Qummī who held that the Imām was "the perfect man" and as such the manifestation of God. The idea was that the first creature had all qualities of God save His exclusive quality of being self-existing. The first creature was, thus, the manifestation of all names and attributes of God except for His name *qayyūm* (self-subsisting) because God is the only being whose existence does not depend on anyone or anything else. Thus, in the hierarchy of existence, the Prophets, his daughter Fāṭima and the Imāms (or, as the Mufawwiḍa called them, *silsilat al-muḥammadiyyīn*) occupy the highest rank save that of God. Some described their rank to be the rank of *mashiyya* (God's will), which is God's first manifestation and action. They thus represent the will of God, that is, whatever they do is the manifestation of what God wants (see, *inter alia*, 'Abd al-Jabbār, 20(1):13; Bursī, 32–8, 45–7).
49. 'Ayyāshī, 1:374; Ṣaffār: 14–20; Kulaynī, 1:387; Khuṣaybī: 354; Ibn Bābawayh, *Khiṣāl*: 428; Ṭūsī, *Amālī*, 1:315. See further Kohlberg, "Imām and Community": 31.
50. See Ṣaffār: 152; Sa'd b. 'Abd Allāh: 61; 'Abd al-Jabbār, 20(1): 13.
51. Ṣaffār: 61–6; Sa'd b. 'Abd Allāh: 61; Abu 'l-Ḥasan al-Ash'arī, 1:86, 2:239; Kashshī: 332; Khuṣaybī: 431; Ibn Bābawayh, *'Uyūn*, 1:124; 2:202–3; idem, *I'tiqādāt*: 100–101; 'Abd al-Jabbār, 20(2):175; *Ghayba*: 178; Abū Manṣūr al-Ṭabrisī, 2:288–9; Ibn al-Jawzī, *Talbīs*: 107; Bursī: 257–8.
52. Ṣaffār: 378–87; Abu 'l-Ḥasan al-Ash'arī, 1:88; Kulaynī, 1:265–6, 441. See also Namāzī, 8:319–26 for other references.
53. Ṣaffār: 122–30; Kulaynī, 1:260–62; Kashshī: 540; Ḥasan b. Sulaymān: 2; Majlisī, 26:18–200. See further Kohlberg, "Imām and Community": 26–30.

direct revelation.)[54] They knew not only all the languages of mankind but also those of the birds and animals.[55] They were omnipotent, omniscient, omniefficient, and omnipresent.[56]

The first spokesman for this tendency, in fact the first person who is known for supporting these views[57] in the Imāmite community,[58] was, as noted above Mufaḍḍal al-Ju'fī, who was then followed by[59] Abū Ja'far Muḥammad b. Sinān al-Zāhirī (d. 220/835)[60] and found significant support in the Imāmite Shī'ite community of that time. A few decades later in the middle of the third/ninth century, Muḥammad b. Nuṣayr al-Numayrī,[61] a prominent scholar from Basra[62] and a follower of Mufaḍḍal and Muḥammad b. Sinān, developed their doctrine by adding much *bāṭinī* material to their teachings. This brought the tendency back to the original fully extremist Khaṭṭābite theories of metempsychosis and incarnation. He enjoyed the support of Muḥammad b. Mūsā b. al-Ḥasan b.

54. Kashshī: 540; Abu 'l-Ḥasan al-Ash'arī, 1:88.
55. Ṣaffār: 335–54; Kashshī: 540.
56. See on these points Ṣaffār, passim; Kulaynī, 1:168–439. Many of the Mufawwiḍa further denied that the Imāms were actually killed or died and held that, as in the case of Jesus as mentioned in the Qur'ān 4:157, they simply ascended to God. See Ibn Bābawayh, *I'tiqādāt*: 100; idem, *Khiṣāl*: 529; idem, *'Uyūn*, 1:215; Ṭūsī, *Ghayba*: 18; idem, *Talkhīṣ al-shāfī*, 4:198.
57. See Kashshī: 323, 326, 380, 531. See also Ṣaffār: 24; Kulaynī, 8:232.
58. See Pseudo Mufaḍḍal, *Kitāb al-Haft*: 31 where Mufaḍḍal is described as *aṣl kull riwāya bāṭina* (see also Kashshī: 531). Cf. Ibn Bābawayh, *I'tiqādāt*: 101 where Zurāra b. A'yan is quoted as reporting to Imām Ja'far al-Ṣādiq that "a man from the descendants [*sic*] of 'Abd Allāh b. Saba'" upheld the idea of *tafwīḍ*. The Imām asked what the term meant. Zurara explained that the man maintained that God created Muḥammad and 'Alī and then delegated the authority to them, so they created, provided, and gave life and death.
59. See Kashshī: 508–9.
60. On him see Halm, *Die Islamische Gnosis*: 242–3.
61. On him see Nawbakhtī: 102–3; Sa'd b. 'Abd Allāh: 100–101; Kashshī: 520–21; Ibn Abi 'l-Thalj: 149; Khuṣaybī: 323, 338, 367, 395.
62. Ibn al-Ghaḍā'irī, 6:62–3 where it is said that Muḥammad b. Nuṣayr was *min afḍal ahl al-baṣra 'ilman*.

al-Furāt,[63] a member of the influential Shī'ite family of high-ranking government officials of Banu 'l-Furāt,[64] and managed to establish his own splinter group, the Nuṣayriyya.[65] The movement was further consolidated by the works of one of its next heads,[66] Ḥusayn b. Ḥamdān al-Khuṣaybī (d. 346/958 or 358/969)[67] and lived henceforth within the Islamic community as a heretic sect that now has several million followers in Syria, Lebanon, and Turkey.[68] The bulk of the Mufawwiḍa, however, remained in the mainstream of the Imāmite community until the end of the time of the Imāms.

From the time that extremist ideas started to gain some following in the Imāmite community many Imāmites opposed the idea of any supernaturality of the Imāms and insisted that they were simply virtuous learned men (*'ulamā' abrār*). The followers of this tendency, however, firmly believed that absolute obedience to the Imāms was required, as the Prophet, according to the Shī'ite analysis and conclusion, instructed the people to follow them as the true interpreters of the Book of God and heirs to the Prophetic knowledge. This doctrine of the necessity of absolute obedience to the Imām distinguished the supporters of this Shī'ite trend from the many Sunnites of the time who also favored those Imāms whose authority was widely accepted, such as Muḥammad al-Bāqir and Ja'far al-Ṣādiq. Those Sunnites attended the circles of the Imāms, studied with them, cared about their opinions on various legal questions

63. Nawbakhtī: 103; Sa'd b. 'Abd Allāh: 100; Kashshī: 521. See also Khuṣaybī: 338 where Aḥmad b. Muḥammad b. al-Furāt al-Kātib is mentioned among the associates of Muḥammad b. Nuṣayr. On the family's connection to the Ghulāt see further Kashshī: 303, 554; Khuṣaybī: 323; ibn Abi 'l-Thalj: 148; Pseudo Mufaḍḍal, *Kitāb al-Haft*: 20–21; Bursī: 258.
64. On them see the article "Ibn al-Furāt" in *EI*[2], 3:767–8 (by D. Sourdel). Muḥammad b. Mūsā was father of Abu 'l-Ḥasan 'Alī b. al-Furāt (d. 312/924), the vizier of the Abbasid Muqtadir (r. 295–320/908–932).
65. See Ibn Abi 'l-Thalj: 149; Ibn al-Ghaḍā'irī, 6:63; *Manāqib*, 1:265; Ibn Abi 'l-Ḥadīd, 8:122; Bursī: 257. See also Abu 'l-Ḥasan al-Ash'arī, 1:86 where they are called Numayriyya instead (possibly, however, a misspelling of Nuṣayriyya).
66. See the table in Halm, *Die Islamische Gnosis*: 296.
67. On him see especially Ziriklī, 2:255; Sezgin, 1:584 and the sources mentioned in these two works.
68. On them see the article "Nuṣayriyya" in *EI*[1], 3:963–7 (by L. Massignon).

and transmitted *ḥadīth* from them but only as some of the many religious authorities of the time, or even as some of the most, or the most, learned among them. Unlike the Shī'ites, those Sunnites, however, did not consider following the Imāms to be religiously binding by Prophetic designation. The followers of that Shī'ite trend denied and rejected any idea or report that would attribute any supernaturality to the Imāms, including claims about their knowledge of the unseen.

In the first decades of the second/eighth century, the most distinguished figure in this latter tendency was a profound Shī'ite scholar of Kūfa,[69] Abū Muḥammad 'Abd Allāh b. Abī Ya'fūr al-'Abdī (d. 131/748-749)[70] who was a very close associate of Imām Ja'far al-Ṣādiq.[71] He was an especially devoted and faithful follower of the Imām[72] and was praised by him as the only[73] or one of only two[74] disciples of his who were the most obedient to him and with whom he was totally satisfied. In numerous statements from the Imām, 'Abd Allāh is praised with unusual and unprecedented complimentary phrases where he is said, for instance, to be living in Paradise in a house between the houses of the Prophet and 'Alī.[75] He maintained, however, that the Imāms were merely righteous and pious learned men (*'ulamā' abrār atqiyā'*).[76] He once had a debate

69. See Kashshī: 162, 427; Najāshī: 213.
70. According to Kashshī: 246, he died in the year of the plague during the time of Imām Ja'far al-Ṣādiq. That was the year 131/748–749 (Ibn Sa'd, 5:355, 7[2]: 21, 60 [see also 7(2):11, 13, 17]; Khalīfa b. Khayyāṭ, 2:603; Mubarrad, *Ta'āzī*: 212; Ibn Qutayba, *Ma'ārif*: 470 [also 471, 601]; Ibn al-Jawzī, *Muntaẓam*, 7: 287–8; Dhahabī, *Ta'rīkh al-islām*, 5:199; Ibn Taghrībirdī, 1:313. Cf. Ṭabarī, 7:401; Ibn al-Athīr, 5:393 who dated the plague to 130/747–748).
71. Kashshī: 10. See also Kulaynī, 6:464.
72. Kashshī: 249 (para. 462). See also Durust b. Abī Manṣūr: 162; 'Ayyāshī, 1:327; Pseudo Mufīd, *Ikhtiṣāṣ*: 190.
73. Kashshī: 246, 249, 250 (paras. 453, 463, 464).
74. Ibid.: 180.
75. Ibid.: 249.
76. Ibid.: 247. See also Abān b. Taghlib's definition of the Shī'a (quoted in Najāshī: 12) as "those who follow the opinion of 'Alī when quotations from the Prophet are contradictory, and the opinion of Ja'far b. Muḥammad [al-Ṣādiq] when quotations from 'Alī are contradictory."

on this issue with Mu'allā b. Khunays,[77] a servant of Imām Ja'far al-Ṣādiq, who ranked the Imāms as prophets. The Imām reportedly confirmed Ibn Abī Ya'fūr and strongly denounced Mu'allā's idea.[78] Ibn Abī Ya'fūr's ideas clearly had wide support in that period. At the time of his death a huge crowd of those who supported his anti-extremist ideas attended his funeral.[79] Some Muslim heresiographers, the first of them Ibn al-Muq'ad[80] in the time of the Abbasid Mahdī (r. 158-169/775-785), mentioned a Shī'ite sect as Ya'fūriyya, clearly denoting the followers of Ibn Abī Ya'fūr, who maintained moderate positions on various theological and sectarian questions. They, for instance, did not allow wrangling in religious matters and, unlike the extremists,[81] did not consider the acknowledgment of the Imām to be an essential component of Islam.[82]

The extremists were working actively against Ibn Abī Ya'fūr and his supporters during his lifetime and after.[83] In his lifetime, they tried to discredit him even in the presence of the Imām who always supported him and condemned his opponents.[84] They labeled the big crowd that attended his funeral as the *murji'at al-shī'a*,[85] the Shī'ite Murji'ites, obviously trying to accuse his supporters of Sunnite inclinations in their doctrinal views as they considered the Imāms human beings, not acting gods. The situation created considerable tension and exchanges of verbal attacks between the two factions during the period of Ja'far al-Ṣādiq[86] but reportedly became

77. On him see Kashshī: 376–82; Najāshī: 417; Ibn al-Ghaḍā'irī, 6:110.
78. Kashshī: 247 (para. 456); *Manāqib*, 3:354.
79. Ibid.: 247 (para. 458).
80. Ibid.: 265–6.
81. See, for instance, Nawbakhtī: 65; Sa'd b. 'Abd Allāh: 69.
82. Abu 'l-Ḥasan al-Ash'arī, 1:122. The sect was, thus, obviously different from an extremist subsect with the same name that allegedly followed a certain Muḥammad b. Ya'fūr (Khwārazmī: 50). On Ibn Abī Ya'fūr and his ideas, see further Kulaynī, 1:277, 3:133; Kashshī: 305, 307; Majlisī, 23:53.
83. In general, the extremists detested the prominent and learned disciples of the Imāms who were regarded by the community as most authentically representing the views of the Imāms. See Kashshī: 138, 148.
84. Kashshī: 246.
85. Ibid.: 247.
86. See Kulaynī, 8:78, 223, 285.

much worse and more bitter after him.[87] Even the learned mainstream disciples of Imām Mūsā al-Kāẓim were divided on the issues concerning the position of the Imāmate, and the difference of opinion on those issues caused heated debates, and, in some cases, permanent breakdowns of friendship[88] between them.

The turning point for the Mufawwiḍa came with the death of Imām 'Alī al-Riḍā, who left a seven-year-old son as his only descendant. This led, as noted above, to controversy in the Imāmite community as to whether a child of seven years was legally qualified or knowledgeable enough to become an Imām. The mainstream of the Imāmite community eventually accepted him as the Imām but disagreed in their interpretations and the solution offered. One group held that the meaning of his being an Imām was that he was the Imām to be, that is, that the Imāmate was his right. When he reached his age of maturity and obtained the knowledge necessary for the holder of the position, he would then be the Imām. This knowledge he would obtain not through revelation, as the Prophet was the last to receive it and there would be no revelation after him, nor through any supernatural means, but through reading the books of his forefathers and acquainting himself properly with the principles of religious law. This solution could not, of course, solve the problems entirely because the Imām later had inevitably to decide what the law was in many instances which might not be specifically mentioned in the books of his forefathers. Therefore, some of the supporters of that opinion suggested that he might arrive at his legal conclusions about those cases through rational reasoning.[89] This mode of reasoning was not recognized by most early authorities of the Imāmite doctrine to be valid in law because one could not guarantee the absence of errors in one's argument that could eventually lead to wrong conclusions and to ascribing things to religion that were not parts of it. This rationale, however,

87. *Manāqib*, 4:250.
88. See Kulaynī, 1:410.
89. The word used here in the sources is *qiyās*, which in the Shī'ite terminology of the time implied any sort of rational argument, not only analogical reasoning which the word more specifically implied in the Sunnite tradition. See my *An Introduction to Shī'ī Law*: 29–30; also al-Muḥaqqiq al-Ḥillī, *Ma'ārij*: 187.

would not be true in the case of the Imām, who was protected by God against error in religion. Thus his rational argument would always lead him to truth.[90] Others held that one could be given the perfect knowledge of the *sharīʿa* and be appointed by God as the Imām even as a child in much the same way that Christ and John the Baptist were, according to the Qur'ān,[91] prophets from their childhood.[92] This second interpretation and idea eventually received the most support in the community and contributed greatly to the popularization of extremist ideas about the cosmic position of the Imāms, the belief that they were superhuman beings possessed of a divine light, and that it was this divine light, not any mere knowledge or specific political right, that was the true essence of the Imāmate. The Imām became the Imām through divine grace; knowledge or political status were mere contingent effects of the Imāmate.

From this point on,[93] the Mufawwiḍa intensified their efforts to spread their literature, a vast body of material quoted by Mufaḍḍal al-Juʿfī and his colleagues on the authority of Imām Jaʿfar al-Ṣādiq,

90. Nawbakhtī: 98–99; Saʿd b. ʿAbd Allāh: 96–98. See also Ṣaffār: 387–90. According to Saʿd b. ʿAbd Allāh: 96, this view was supported by the prominent Imāmite scholar and theologian of the time Yūnus b. ʿAbd al-Raḥmān al-Qummī (on him see below, chapter 4).

91. Qur'ān, 19:12, 29–30.

92. Ṣaffār: 238; Nawbakhtī: 99; Saʿd b. ʿAbd Allāh: 95–96, 99; Kulaynī, 1:321, 322, 383–4; Abu 'l-Ḥasan al-Ashʿarī, 1:105; Abu 'l-Qāsim al-Balkhī: 181–2; Mufīd, *Irshād*: 317, 319; idem, *Majālis*, 2:96; Majlisī, 50:20, 21, 24, 34, 35 (quoting other sources). Nāshi': 25 quotes a similar controversy among earlier Shīʿites on the Imāmate of ʿAlī Zayn al-ʿĀbidīn who, according to some reports, had not yet reached the age of puberty when his father was killed. According to Nāshi', a group of the Shīʿites offered the same analysis cited above to support the truth of the Imāmate of ʿAlī Zayn al-ʿĀbidīn, arguing that Christ and John the Baptist became prophets when they were still children. The group was headed by Abū Khālid al-Kābulī, an early Shīʿite that the extremists greatly admired and considered as one of their pioneers (see Pseudo Mufaḍḍal, *Kitāb al-Haft*: 20–21; also Ibn Abi 'l-Thalj: 148). For similar ideas among the Shīʿites in the beginning of the second/eighth century, see Nawbakhtī: 68–9; Saʿd b. ʿAbd Allāh: 72; Nāshi': 43.

93. On the split in the Imāmite community in the early third/ninth century on the nature of the Imāms, see Kulaynī, 1:441.

in addition to that already produced by radical extremists such as Abu 'l-Khaṭṭāb and others.[94] The Mufawwiḍa also added extensively to that literature.[95] In line with a statement attributed to the Imāms that permitted the attribution of whatever supernatural quality or miracle one wanted to the Imāms as long as one did not identify them with God,[96] the Mufawwiḍa offered much material quoted on the authority of the Imāms on the divine aspect of their nature, as well as many stories of miracles performed by any one of the Imāms and narratives that traced their signs and effects to the antediluvian world. The whole of the third/ninth century was, thus, a period in which the extremists' literature in general and the Mufawwiḍa's in particular greatly flourished. Much of the material in those genres that is preserved in the later works was contributed by the Mufawwiḍa of this period. To further consolidate their own position, they also quoted many complimentary remarks and praises of Mufaḍḍal and their other notables on the authority of the Imāms.[97] By the middle of the third/ninth century they had properly established themselves as a group within the mainstream Imāmite community, and they were struggling to overwhelm the moderates.

The Imāmite scholars and transmitters of *ḥadīth* in Qum, which was by now the main Imāmite center of learning, reacted very harshly to the Mufawwiḍa's expansionism. They tried to contain the flow of extremist literature that was spreading fast. The scholars of Qum began to declare anyone who attributed any sign of superhumanity to the Prophet or the Imāms an extremist[98] and to expel such people from their town. Many of the transmitters of *ḥadīth* were banished from Qum for transmitting reports that contained that genre of material during the first half of the third/ninth cen-

94. See Kashshī: 224–5.

95. See, for instance, Ibn al-Ghaḍā'irī, 6:131 where he commented about Mufaḍḍal that "much additional material has been added to him and the extremists have loaded a big load in his reports."

96. Ḥimyarī, *Dalā'il* (quoted in Irbilī, 2:409); Ṣaffār: 241; Muḥammad b. al-Qāsim al-Astarābādī: 44; Khuṣaybī: 432; Ibn Bābawayh, *Khiṣāl*: 614; Abū Manṣūr al-Ṭabrisī, 2:233; Ḥasan b. Sulaymān: 59.

97. See, for examples, Ṣaffār: 237; Kashshī: 321, 322–3, 365, 402, 508–9.

98. See Majlisī, 52:89.

tury.[99] This was, of course, the punishment for merely transmitting reports of that genre. The actual belief in the supernaturality of the Imāms was another matter; it was a grave heresy that could be punished by death. There is, in fact, a report that the people of Qum once tried to kill a scholar of their town who was accused of holding such opinions because they thought he was an unbeliever, but they stopped when they found him praying.[100] This response indicates that the Imāmite community of Qum did not differentiate between the two concepts of *ghuluww* and *tafwīḍ*[101] and regarded

99. Kashshī: 512 (see also Najāshī: 38, 77). They included famous Imāmite transmitters of *ḥadīth* such as Sahl b. Ziyād al-Ādamī al-Rāzī (Ibn al-Ghaḍā'irī, 3:179; Najāshī: 185), Abū Sumayna Muḥammad b. 'Alī al-Qurashī (Ibn al-Ghaḍā'irī, 5:264; Najāshī: 332), Ḥusayn b. 'Ubayd Allāh al-Muḥarrir (Kashshī: 512), as well as Aḥmad b. Muḥammad b. Khālid al-Barqī, author of *Kitāb al-Maḥāsin*, who was expelled from the town because he was not careful and quoted inauthentic material (Ibn al-Ghaḍā'irī, 2:138).

100. Najāshī: 329; Ibn al-Ghaḍā'irī, 5:160. The man was Abū Ja'far Muḥammad b. Ūrama al-Qummī, a *ḥadīth* transmitter of the mid-third/ninth century. Among his numerous works mentioned in Najāshī: 329–30 was a book against the Ghulāt. There was, however, some *bāṭinī* material in a book attributed to him, which generated suspicions about him. He was, therefore, at most one of the Mufawwiḍa and not of the radical extremist splinter groups.

101. The sectarian Ghulāt, as said before, normally abrogated the *sharī'a* and did not consider themselves bound by religious obligations, including prayer. They regarded such obligations as duties imposed on those like the Muqaṣṣira (see below), whose minds, unlike those of the Ghulat, were not developed enough and blessed enough to know the secrets of the Universe and the true rank of the Imāms (Sa'd b. 'Abd Allāh: 61), and they maintained that the recognition of the true status of the Imām would make them unneedful of prayer and other religious obligations (ibid.: 39; Kashshī: 325). This is why in the early centuries people thought that they could ascertain whether someone was from the Ghulāt by watching him in the time of prayer, because if he was an extremist he would not pray (Kashshī: 530). In a statement reported from Mufaḍḍal he also downgraded the value of prayer in contrast to serving the Imām (ibid.: 327). Another report suggests that in a pilgrimage to Karbalā' he personally failed to say his prayers (ibid.: 325), a report that presumably attempts to prove that he was actually a full-force extremist. An opposite example is a statement quoted from a mid-third/ninth century transmitter of *ḥadīth* who denied

anyone who attributed supernaturality to the Imāms to be a heretic, virtually a nonbeliever, whether he deified them or not. The Mufawwiḍa counterattacked by calling the scholars of Qum and other moderates *muqaṣṣira,* the shortcomers, suggesting that the moderates fell short of recognizing the true nature of the Imām.[102] At times they even accused them of having Sunnite inclinations.[103] The term *taqṣīr* subsequently assumed a new sense in the post second/eighth century Imāmite usage[104] as the opposite of *tafwīḍ,*[105]

---

that Muḥammad b. Sinān was a *ghālī* on the basis that he was the one who taught that transmitter how to perform ritual purity (Ibn Ṭāwūs, *Falāḥ al-sā'il*: 11). This explains why the people of Qum who wanted to kill Muḥammad b. Ūrama stopped when they found him praying, because, in their minds, if he were a *ghālī*, he would not pray and, therefore, in their judgment his praying proved that he was innocent of that accusation, not knowing that the Mufawwiḍa branch of the Ghulāt did not differ from the mainstream of the Muslims in respect to the *sharī'a* and that they fulfilled the Islamic religious obligations.

102. In a statement attributed in an anonymous work of the Mufawwiḍa to the Prophet, the Muqaṣṣira are defined as "those who fell short in the recognition of the Imāms . . . to know that God delegated His authority to those whom He blessed with His grace: to create by His permission and to resurrect by His permission and to know what is in the mind of the people and the past and the future until the day of resurrection" (Majlisī, 26:14–15; see also Khuṣaybī: 431; Mufīd, *Awā'il*: 45).

103. See the quotation from the above-mentioned anonymous work of the Mufawwiḍa in Majlisī, 26:9 where a reference is made to *al-nāṣiba al-malā'īn wa 'l-qadariyya al-muqaṣṣirīn*, and 26:6 where it is said that whoever hesitated about the divine nature of the Imām—that he is the "face of God, the eye of God and the tongue of God"—is a *muqaṣṣir* and a *nāṣibī* (anti-'Alīd).

104. The most common sense of the term *taqṣīr* was, of course, negligence of one's religious duties. It was, however, freely used in the general Islamic usage to refer to shortcomings in recognition of religious facts and truths (e.g., Kulaynī, 2:19, 8:394; Kashshī: 424; Mufīd, *Awā'il*: 48).

105. The contrast already existed between the two terms of *taqṣīr* and *ghuluww* in the Shī'ite (see, for instance, Ṣaffār: 529; Kulaynī, 1:198, 8:128; Khuṣaybī: 419, 431, 432; Ibn Bābawayh, *Khiṣāl*: 627; Majlisī, 26:1, 5, 6, 9, 14, 16) as well as in the general Islamic usage (see, for instance, Rāghib al-Iṣfahānī, *Muqaddama fi 'l-tafsīr*: 120, where he quotes some earlier scholars as describing the opinions of those who restricted the right of the interpretation of the Qur'ān to the Prophet and those who allowed it for anyone who had good command of Arabic as falling into the two

each referring to one extreme within the mainstream of the Imāmite community.[106]

---

extremes of *ghuluww* and *taqṣīr*; Jishumī, *Risālat iblīs*: 96). A well-circulated anecdote suggested that both *ghuluww* and *taqṣīr* in religion were disapproved (Majd al-Dīn b. al-Athīr, *Nihāya*, 5:119; see also Nāṣir Khusruw: 410, 436). In the usage of the early pro-'Alid groups it referred to the disrespectful statement and accusations that the pro-Umayyad and anti-'Alid elements used to make against 'Alī (see, for instance, Ibn al-Iskāfī: 31 where it is said: "*afraṭa fīhi* [i.e. 'Alī] *qawmun fa-'abadūhu wa qaṣṣara fīhi qawmun fa-shatamūhu wa qadhafūh*; see also 32, 33). In the more general Shī'ite usage, however, it referred to the shortcoming of the non-Shī'ites who did not acknowledge the right of the 'Alīd Imāms in the succession to the Prophet in the leadership of the Muslim community. A statement quoted on the authority of Imām 'Alī Zayn al-'Ābidīn, therefore, speaks of those who denied the right of the House of the Prophet as those "who came short in our matter" (Irbilī, 2:311 quoting Ibn al-Akhḍar; also Sunnite sources mentioned in Ibn 'Ayyāsh, introduction to the edition: 17). Another statement attributed to Imām Ja'far al-Ṣādiq asserted that "the *ghālī* comes back to us but we do not accept him, but the *muqaṣṣir* joins us and we accept him . . . [because] the *ghālī* develops a habit [of neglecting his religious obligations], it would be impossible for him to give up the habit and obey God, whereas the *muqaṣṣir* will fulfill [his obligations] and obey [God] if he comes to know [the true path]" (Ṭūsī, *Amālī*: 2:264; an abridged version of this statement is ascribed to Imām Muḥammad al-Bāqir in 'Ayyāshī, 1:63). The reference is clearly to an outsider; a *muqaṣṣir* is someone who currently does not follow the Imām and is not a member of the Shī'ite community. The term clearly retained this meaning until the time of Imām 'Alī al-Riḍā (see Ibn Bābawayh, *'Uyūn*, 1:304), although the trend to label the non-extremist Imāmites as the *muqaṣṣira* had already reportedly started in the second/eighth century when some early Ghulāt are quoted as calling the mainstream Imāmites who opposed them *muqaṣṣira* (Sa'd b. 'Abd Allāh: 55).

106. Shahrastānī is obviously using the term in its general sense of shortcoming when he states that "the Shī'a fell into *ghuluww* in connection with the Imāms as they made them similar to God and into *taqṣīr* through making God similar to man" (*Milal*, 1:105) and that some of the Ghulāt brought God down to the level of man and others elevated man to the status of God, so they are at the two ends of *ghuluww* and *taqṣīr* (ibid., 1:203). Fakhr al-Dīn al-Rāzī clearly did the same when he interpreted a statement from an early 'Alīd who said "the extravagant in love for us is like the extravagant in spite of us" as referring to the point that, in affection for the House of the Prophet, both *ghuluww* and *taqṣīr* are disapproved (*al-Shajara al-mubāraka*: 121). This is not, however, true with the editor's footnote

The rank and file Imāmites and many of their transmitters of *ḥadīth,* however, stood somewhere between the two extremes. They seem to have maintained that the Imāms possessed a divine blessing that had been bestowed on the family of the Prophet, and, thus, they believed in some sort of supernaturality for the Imāms, although not to the extent upheld by the Mufawwiḍa. The Imāms up to the middle of the third/ninth century are reported in the Imāmite *ḥadīth* as condemning the extremists and denouncing the attribution of supernaturality to themselves. "The Ghulāt are infidels and the Mufawwiḍa are polytheists"; whoever maintains any sort of contact or friendship with them is cutting his ties with God, the Prophet and his House, said Imām 'Alī al-Riḍā.[107] A similar statement from Imām Ja'far al-Ṣādiq warned the Shī'ites to be extra careful and not to let their youth be misled by the extremists. The extremists, he said, are the most wicked among the creatures of God, worse than any other category of infidels, because they try to desecrate God.[108] Many other similarly harsh statements are quoted from the Imāms in condemnation of the extremists.[109] Nevertheless, as noted above, the situation of the office of Imāmate in the third/ninth century helped the extremist ideas to gain more ground within the Shī'ite community, although not necessarily among the circle of the close associates of the Imāms and certainly not in the principal Imāmite center of learning at Qum.

By the time of Imām Ḥasan al-'Askarī the heated debates on the nature of the Imāms had already split the Imāmite community in some places into two hostile camps.[110] In Nīshāpūr, for instance, the community was divided, and each group was excommunicating the other. One group supported the Mufawwiḍa's opinion on the supernatural knowledge of the Imāms, and so they believed that the Imāms knew the languages of all humans and birds and animals as well as whatever was happening in the world. They believed that the divine revelation did not stop with the death of the Prophet but continued, and the Imāms still received it when they needed

---

in *Kamāl*: 470 where the term *muqaṣṣira* is misinterpreted as those who cut their hair in the pilgrimage to Mecca (a required act in the pilgrimage that marks the end of the ceremonies, which is mentioned in the Qur'ān, 48: 27).

107. Ibn Bābawayh, *'Uyūn*, 2:203; idem, *Tawḥīd* :364.

108. Ṭūsī, *Amālī*, 2:264.

109. See, for instance, Ḥimyarī: 31, 61; Kashshī: 297–302, 306–8; Ibn Bābawayh, *I'tiqādāt*: 100–101; idem, *Khiṣāl*: 1:63; idem, *'Uyūn*, 11:143, 2:202–3; Majlisī, 25:261–350.

110. See Kulaynī, 1:441.

it. Another group headed by the prominent Shī'ite scholar of that century, Faḍl b. Shādhān al-Naysābūrī (d. 260/873), denied all of these claims and maintained that the Imām was a man who had a thorough knowledge of the *sharī'a* and of the correct interpretation of the Qur'ān.[111] A few months before Faḍl b. Shādhān's death,[112] however, the emissary of the Imām's office to Nīshāpūr for the collection of the community's donations chose to stay with the first group. That caused great difficulty. The moderates discredited the emissary and abstained from paying their dues to him. The matter was reported to the Imām, who sent a letter to the community in which he condemned the beliefs of the Mufawwiḍa[113] but at the same time complained about Faḍl b. Shādhān, who had prevented the people from paying their religious dues to the Imām's agent.[114] Kashshī, who has quoted this letter, suggests that the letter perhaps had been sent by 'Uthmān b. Sa'īd al-'Amrī,[115] the Imām's chief agent, who by that time controlled the financial affairs of the office. The whole episode, however, signifies a noticeable change in the practical position of the office to satisfy the entire community. (The change had obviously become necessary by the difficult political and social conditions of the Shī'ite community in those years.) In another instance, two disputing groups, the Mufawwiḍa and the Muqaṣṣira, of an unspecified region (possibly of Sāmarrā' itself) are said to have

111. Kashshī: 539–41. See also his own *Kitāb al-Īḍāḥ*: 461; Ibn Bābawayh, *'Uyūn*, 2:20; Najāshī: 325, 328.
112. As Kashshī quoted, the Imām's letter concerning the event in question was sent, or at least received, two months after Faḍl b. Shādhān's death in the *Hijrī* year 260. Because the Imām himself died early in the third month of that year, the event should have happened mostly in the year before, and Ibn Shādhān's death must have occurred quite early in 260. The fact that Ibn Shādhān died very early in the year is also verified by another quotation in Kashshī: 538 that reports that a Shi'ite from Khurāsān met the Imām on his way back from the annual pilgrimage to Mecca and later came to know that Ibn Shādhān had died around the same time that he met the Imām. If one considers the distance between Mecca and Sāmarrā' and the time of annual pilgrimage, the meeting must have taken place sometime in Muḥarram, the first month of the *Hijrī* year, by any account.
113. Ibid., 540.
114. Ibid.: 542–3.
115. Ibid.: 544.

sent a representative to the Imām to ask for his instructions. According to the report, the Imām denounced the Mufawwiḍa by name and called them liars.[116]

The internal disputes and splits in the Imāmite community continued to the period of Minor Occultation.[117] The case was referred several times to the agents of the vanished Imām to ask for the Imām's judgment. In a rescript received from the Holy Threshold,[118] the Imām complained about the "ignorants and idiots" among the Shī'a who attributed the knowledge of the unseen or any supernatural power to them or exalted them above their actual rank.[119] In another rescript sent by the second agent, Muḥammad b. 'Uthmān al-'Amrī, the Mufawwiḍa standpoints that attributed the creation of and providing for all beings to the Imāms were rejected, although the special grace that God had bestowed on the Imāms was confirmed.[120] This seems to be an attempt to bring the official position closer to the prevailing view among the rank and file who, as noted above, stood somewhere between the two extremes. An old and well-circulated anecdote that condemned both *ghuluww* and *taqṣīr* (in their general Islamic senses) in religion[121] would be now taken by many as confirming this middle position against those two concepts in their new and more specific Shī'ite senses. Because the extremists had been condemned by the Imāms and the Shī'ite community for a very long time, this and similar quotations would actually be used to discredit the moderates and to suggest that they, too, had gone

116. Khuṣaybī: 359, who mentioned the Mufawwiḍa as the *mu'minūn* (the faithful); *Ghayba*: 148–9.
117. See *Ghayba*: 178, 238.
118. Abū Manṣūr al-Ṭabrisī, 2:288–9 (quoted also in Majlisī, 25: 266–8). The rescript was issued to Muḥammad b. 'Alī b. Hilāl al-Karkhī who was ordered at the end of rescript to show it to others until all the Shī'ites come to know its content and learn about it.
119. Abū Manṣūr al-Ṭabrisī, 2:289.
120. *Ghayba*: 178.
121. See above, n. 105. Clearly referring to the same general meanings of the two terms, a statement from Imām Ḥasan al-'Askarī also maintained that the right path is always the middle path, that stands between the two scales, lower than *ghuluww* but higher than *taqṣīr* (Muḥammad b. al-Qāsim al-Astarābādī: 44; Ibn Bābawayh, *Ma'ānī al-akhbār*: 33).

too far in denying the divine qualifications of the Imāms.[122] The position of scholars such as Muḥammad b. Ibrāhīm al-Nuʿmānī of the first half of the fourth/tenth century, who complained that groups of the Shīʿites went beyond the line of truth by either exaggeration or shortcoming,[123] is in the same line of thought.[124]

The moderate tendency, however, remained strong throughout these periods to the last decades of the fourth/tenth century. In a report, clearly authored by a pro-Mufawwiḍa transmitter, he suggests that of thirty Shīʿite pilgrims who were present at the grand mosque of Mecca on the sixth day of Dhu 'l-Ḥijja, 293/23 September 906, only one was "purely faithful" (*mukhliṣ*) and the rest were *muqaṣṣira*.[125] In another report from the post-Occultation period, an imaginary dialogue between Jābir b. Yazīd al-Juʿfī (d. 128/745-746) and Imām Muḥammad al-Bāqir, it is said that the majority of the Shīʿites are *muqaṣṣira*[126] who fell short of recognizing the true nature of the Imām: that he is the one who creates and provides with the authority given to him by God and that by this grace he is omniscient and omnipotent.[127] The scholars of Qum, who were the highest authority of religious knowledge in this

122. See, for instance, Bursī: 240 where the attempt is made to present the Mufawwiḍa as those who followed the middle path; also Goldziher: 229 where it is quoted that the Nuṣayriyya identify the common Shīʿites as *muqaṣṣira*.

123. Nuʿmānī: 19. See also Mufīd, *Awāʾil*: 45.

124. Some of the Imāmite scholars of the third and fourth/ninth and tenth centuries wrote books against the Ghulāt and Mufawwiḍa. One such work was written by Ibn Bābawayh; another by Ḥusayn b. ʿUbayd Allāh al-Ghaḍāʾirī (d. 411/1020) as mentioned by Najāshī: 69. The work by Ibn Bābawayh was entitled *Kitāb Ibṭāl al-ghuluww wa 'l-tafwīḍ* as mentioned by the author himself in his other work, *ʿUyūn akhbār al-riḍā*, 2: 204. The title, however, appears in Najāshī: 392 as *Kitāb Ibṭāl al-ghuluww wa 'l-taqṣīr*, possibly a mistake caused by an oversight which, in turn, may have been caused by the change of emphasis in the mentality of the Imāmite community of Iraq from condemnation of *tafwīḍ* to that of *taqṣīr*.

125. *Kamāl*: 470, 473. See also al-Ṭabarī al-Shīʿī: 298–300; *Ghayba*; 156, in both the reference to the Muqaṣṣira is omitted but the sentence that states that only one of thirty was a "pure faithful" stands.

126. Majlisī, 26:15.

127. Ibid., 26:14–15.

period,[128] remained firmly anti-Mufawwiḍa until the end of the fourth/tenth century, opposing and rejecting any idea that attributed any supernatural quality to the Prophet and the Imāms. They held that whoever believed that the Prophet or the Imāms were immune to inadvertence (*sahw*) was an extremist.[129] They continued to discredit the transmitters who related reports that attributed any supernaturality to the Imāms[130] and considered the transmission of that genre of material to be unlawful. A group of the scholars of Qum even held that the Imāms did not know many laws of the *sharī'a* and had to rely on personal judgment and *ijtihād* to derive the appropriate laws.[131] The Mufawwiḍa consistently endeavored to discredit the scholars of Qum, derogatorily calling them *muqaṣṣira*. This denigration angered Ibn Bābawayh, the most prominent representative of the school of Qum in the middle and second half of the fourth/tenth century.[132] In his work on the Shī'ite creed, after reemphasizing that to the Shī'ites the Ghulāt and Mufawwiḍa are infidels, more wicked than all other infidels and wrong thinkers, he asserted that "the sign to know the Mufawwiḍa and Ghulāt and their like is that they accuse the masters and scholars of Qum of shortcoming."[133]

The period of the Minor Occultation was especially marked by the tireless efforts of the Mufawwiḍa to establish themselves as the true representatives of Shī'ism and their doctrine as the middle path between extremism and shortcoming. To this end, they missed no opportunity and failed no chance. They continued assiduously to spread countless quotations on the authority of the Imāms, some of which, despite all efforts of the masters and scholars of Qum,

128. This fact is well verified by the fact that Ḥusayn b. Rūḥ al-Nawbakhtī (d. 326/938), the third chief agent of the vanished Imām, sent a book of doubtful authority to the scholars of Qum and asked them to look at it and see if anything in it contradicted their views (*Ghayba*: 240).
129. Ibn Bābawayh, *Faqīh*, 1:359–60. See also my *An Introduction to Shī'ī Law*: 40.
130. See, for instance, Majlisī, 25:347.
131. Mufīd, *Taṣḥīḥ*: 66.
132. See Ṭūsī, *Fihrist*: 157.
133. Ibn Bābawayh, *I'tiqādāt*: 101 (read *mashāyikh qum* [as in Mufīd, *Taṣḥīḥ al-i'tiqād*: 65 and manuscripts of the work itself] for *mashāyikhihim*).

penetrated the Shī'ite *ḥadīth*. Tampering with the material in books written by reliable authors and inserting new material into them had been done successfully by heretics in the periods of the two Imāms, Muḥammad al-Bāqir and Ja'far al-Ṣādiq,[134] and the option was still available to all conflicting groups. The transmission system of *ḥadīth* could not always prevent these forgeries. Like their predecessors in the time of Imām Ja'far al-Ṣādiq, the Mufawwiḍa continued their effort to discredit their opponents by accusing them of weak faith,[135] of debasing the glorious position of the Imāmate, of opposing the authority of the Imāms and knowingly denying their qualifications, and of being influenced by the Sunnite doctrines.

To counter a widely reported statement from the Imāms that gave a much more favorable status to the Muqaṣṣira than to the extremists,[136] the extremists came forward with their own interpretation of that statement by construing the term *muqaṣṣira* to refer to other groups of the Shī'a and not the moderates.[137] Then the extremists ascribed to the Imāms their own similarily phrased statements, which favored the extremists against the Muqaṣṣira.[138] One of the Mufawwiḍa's contributions[139] in this period which later became a popular Shī'ite practice,[140] in spite of the opposition of

134. See Kashshī: 224–5. These activities brought the condition of the Shī'ite *ḥadīth* to a situation that Zurāra b. A'yan, the most prominent Shī'ite scholar of the first half of the second/eighth century, wished he could "make a fire and burn all of it" (Majlisī, 25:282).

135. See, for instance, Khuṣaybī: 385 where he accuses the "Muqaṣṣira and weak faithful among the Shī'a" of growing doubt about Imām 'Alī al-Hādī after his elder son Muḥammad, who was reportedly his successor designate, died during 'Alī al-Hādī's lifetime.

136. 'Ayyāshī, 1:63; Ṭūsī, *Amālī*, 2:264.

137. Khuṣaybī: 431.

138. Ibid.: 432.

139. See Ibn Bābawayh, *Faqīh*, 1:290–91, who after quoting the traditional formula of *adhān* said: "This is the correct *adhān*, nothing should be added to or omitted from it. The Mufawwiḍa, may God curse them, have fabricated reports and added in *adhān* . . . 'I witness that 'Alī is the friend of God' . . . I mentioned this in order that those suspected of being among the Mufawwiḍa but who have mixed themselves with us be distinguished [from us]."

140. This was not a common practice among the Shī'a until 907/1501–1502 when the Safavid Ismā'īl I (r. 906–930/1501–1524) issued a decree that

generations of Shīʿite jurists who regarded it a legally unwarranted innovation,[141] was the addition of testimony to the spiritual authority (*wilāya*) of ʿAlī in the call to prayer (*adhān*). Some of their ideas also gained the acceptance of Imāmite theologians of that and later periods. The Nawbakhtīs, for instance, adopted their theory of the Imām's perfect knowledge of all languages and arts,[142] as well as the theory that his Imāmate is a necessary conclusion of his inborn merits.[143] However, they opposed the Mufawwiḍa on other questions such as the Imām's power to perform miracles,[144] his receiving of divine revelation,[145] his ability to hear the voices of the angels,[146]

---

the formula *ashhadu anna ʿaliyyan waliyyu ʾllāh* be added to the *adhān*. At that time, it was suggested that it was a Shīʿite practice that had been abandoned for more than five centuries (Rūmlū, 12: 61). By early next century (eleventh/seventeenth) it had already become such a popular practice in most Shīʿite towns that if someone did not say it in the *adhān* he was accused of having become a Sunnite. Therefore, although the jurists regarded it as an unauthorized addition, they could not publicly denounce it, so they considered it to be a case wherein they had to practice precautionary secrecy (Majlisī I, *Lawāmiʿ*, 1: 82). However, in the middle of the following century (twelfth/eighteenth) many Shīʿites still refrained from adding that formula to the *adhān* (Muḥammad Muʾmin al-Ḥusaynī: 43–4; Muḥammad Naṣīr b. Muḥammad Maʿṣūm: 2–3). The Prominent Imāmite jurist, Jaʿfar b. Khiḍr al-Najafī, Kāshif al-Ghiṭāʾ (d. 1228/1813) sent a petition to the Qājār king of his time, Fatḥ ʿAlī Shāh (r. 1212–1250/1797–1834) and asked him to ban this unwarranted innovation (Akhbārī, *Risāla dar shahādat bar wilāyat*: 181–3). Later in that century the Shīʿite *ʿulamāʾ* in India, too, tried to encourage the community to abandon the practice but failed (Muḥsin al-Amīn, 2:205; Mudarris Tabrīzī, 4: 229). It is now an almost universal Imāmite practice (see, for instance, Muḥsin al-Ḥakīm, 5: 545).

141. See, for instance, Ṭūsī, *Nihāya*: 69; ʿAbd al-Jalīl al-Qazwīnī: 97; al-Muḥaqqiq al-Ḥillī, *Muʿtabar*, 2:141; Ibn al-Muṭahhar, *Tadhkira*, 1:105; al-Shahīd al-Awwal, *Dhikrā*: 170; idem, *Lumʿa*: 12; al-Shahīd al-Thānī, *Rawḍ*: 242; idem, *Rawḍa*, 1:240; Ardabīlī, *Majmaʿ*, 2:181; Majlisī I, *Lawāmiʿ*, 1:182; Sabzawārī, *Dhakhīra*: 254; Fayḍ, *Mafātīḥ*, 1:118; Kāshif al-Ghiṭāʾ: 227–28.
142. Mufīd, *Awāʾil*: 37–8.
143. Ibid.: 32–5.
144. Ibid.: 40.
145. Ibid.: 39–40.
146. Ibid.: 41.

and, after his death, the voices of visitors to his shrine[147] and to know their conditions, and his knowledge of the unseen.[148] Other Imāmite theologians such as Mufīd disagreed with the Nawbakhtīs on their two pro-Mufawwiḍa ideas.[149] Mufīd, however, agreed with the Mufawwiḍa on the basis of what he thought to be "sound reports"[150] that the Imām could perform miracles and hear the voices of the angels and the pilgrims to his shrine. These are the reports that the transmitters of Qum[151] and many other early Imāmite authorities[152] rejected as unauthentic and apocryphal accounts fabricated by the extremists, including the Mufawwiḍa. As will be seen below, Abū Ja'far b. Qiba also maintained the possibility that God "may manifest miracles by the hand of the Imām"[153] although he,

147. Ibid.: 45.
148. Ibid.: 38.
149. Ibid.: 33, 35, 38.
150. Ibid.: 40, 41, 45. Abu 'l-Ḥasan al-Ash'arī 2:125 noted the division in the Imāmite community of his time over the possibility of miracles from the Imām, where "groups" of the Rāfiḍites (in his words) supported this possibility.
151. See, for instance, Najāshī: 329 (also Ṭūsī, *Fihrist*: 143), also 348 where a long list is given of the transmitters whose reports were rejected by Abū Ja'far Muḥammad b. al-Ḥasan b. al-Walīd (d. 343/954–955), head of the school of Qum in his time (ibid.: 383).
152. Faḍl b. Shādhān al-Naysābūrī, for instance, considered it unlawful to quote the reports ascribed by Muḥammad b. Sinān to the Imāms (Kashshī: 507). 'Alī b. al-Ḥasan b. Faḍḍāl, a prominent Imāmite scholar of the early third/ninth century, had the same opinion about whatever was reported by Ḥasan b. 'Alī b. Abī Ḥamza al-Baṭā'inī, who was an extremist and a liar (ibid.: 443), in spite of the fact that he had formerly studied with Baṭā'inī and heard many *ḥadīth*s from him and copied his entire commentary on the Qur'ān from beginning to end (ibid.: 404, 552). Ḥasan b. 'Alī b. Ziyād al-Washshā', another prominent Imāmite *ḥadīth* transmitter in the beginning of the third/ninth century, refused to transmit to his students a pro-Mufawwiḍa *ḥadīth* that was in a book that he was reading with his student ('Ayyāshī, 1:374). The expression *lā yuktabu ḥadīthuhu* (or *lā yajūzu an yuktaba ḥadīthuhu*) repeatedly occurs in the early Imāmite biographical works in reference to the *ḥadīth* transmitters of the Mufawwiḍa (see, for instance, Ibn al-Ghaḍā'irī, 5:184 [on Muḥammad b. al-Ḥasan b. Jumhūr al-'Ammī], 6:131 [on Mufaḍḍal b. 'Umar al-Ju'fī]; see further Najāshī: 122).
153. See his *Mas'ala fi 'l-imāma*, paras. 5–7.

too, categorically rejected other ideas of the Mufawwiḍa such as the Imām's knowledge of the unseen[154] or the Imām as anything more than a pious scholar.[155]

154. See his *Naqḍ kitāb al-ishhād*, paras. 34, 55. The idea that the Imām had such knowledge was, as noted, originally put forward by the Kaysānite extremists and then followed by other heretic groups (see, for instance, Abu 'l-Ḥasan al-Ash'arī, 1:77; Kashshī: 291, 292, 298–9, Abu 'l-Faraj, *Aghānī*, 23:243; Ibn Abi 'l-Ḥadīd, 5:119) and the Mufawwiḍa. The pro-Mufawwiḍa elements among the Twelver Imāmites have since continued to support this idea, whereas the anti-Mufawwiḍa have always strongly rejected it; in fact some (such as Ibn Qiba in his *Naqḍ kitāb al-ishhād*, para. 55) considered the attribution of such knowledge to anybody other than God to be tantamount to infidelity (see *inter alia* and apart from those mentioned above, Kashshī: 541 [see also 326, 443]; Ibn Bābawayh, *Khiṣāl:* 428; idem, *Ma'ānī:* 102; Mufīd, *Majālis,* 1:73; idem, *Awā'il:* 38; idem, *al-Masā'il al-'ukbariyya* [quoted in Majlisī, 42:257–8]; Murtaḍā, *Dhakhīra:* 436; idem, *Intiṣār*: 243; Ṭūsī, *Tibyān*, 4: 152; idem, *Talkhīṣ al-shāfī*, 1:252, 4:182–8; idem, *Tamhīd*: 365–6; Ṭabrisī, *Majma'*, 6:230–31, 7: 230–1, 12: 238– 9; Abu 'l-Futūḥ al-Rāzī, 5:347; Ibn Shahrāshūb, *Mutashābih al-qur'ān*, 1:211; 'Abd al-Jalīl al-Qazwīnī: 286; Ibn Maytham, 3:209; Fatḥ Allāh al-Kāshānī, 1:418; Nūr Allāh al-Tustarī, *al-As'ila al-yūsufiyya*: passim; Muḥammad Ḥasan al-Najafī, 1:182 and many other sources mentioned in Najafābādī: 464–5 and Qalmdārān: 166–185). Abu 'l-Ḥasan al-Ash'arī, 1:117, noted the division between the Imāmite community of his time on this issue. Abu 'l-Qāsim al-Balkhī: 176 attributed to the Imāmites the opinion that the Imām knew everything related to the religious law. Other opponents of the Imāmites, however, accused all of them of believing in the Imām's knowledge of the unseen (Pseudo Qāsim b. Ibrāhīm: 104b; 'Abd al-Jabbār, *Fawā'id al-qur'ān*, quoted in Ibn Ṭāwūs, *Sa'd al-su'ūd*: 184). Among the Imāmites themselves Mufīd (*Awā'il*: 38) and Ṭabrisī (*Majma'*, 6:230–1, 7:230–1, 12: 238–9) categorically denied that any of the Imāmites in their time held such an opinion (the first asserted that only the Ghulāt and Mufawwiḍa held it), whereas 'Abd al-Jalīl al-Qazwīnī: 286 referred to a small group of the Imāmite *ḥashwiyya* (traditionists) who still quietly existed within the Imāmite community of his time (see my *An Introduction to Shī'ī Law*: 34; also Muntajab al-Dīn: 161 where the title of a work written by the head of the Imāmite community of Qazwīn in the early or mid-sixth/twelfth century, Muḥammad b. Ḥamdān b. Muḥammad al-Ḥamdānī, *al-Fuṣūl fī dhamm a'dā' al-uṣūl,* may be taken as a further testimony to the existence of some of the Imāmite *ḥashwiyya* in those days) and who advocated the idea of the Imām's knowledge of the unseen. Ibn Ṭāwūs, *Sa'd al-su'ūd*: 185, also acknowledged the division among the Imāmites on the issue.

155. See his *Naqḍ kitāb al-ishhād*, para. 34. See also al-Shahīd al-Thānī, *Ḥaqā'iq*

As can be gathered from the above, parts of the Mufawwiḍa's literature had begun to gain some sort of recognition in Imāmite scholarship by the later decades of the fourth/tenth century. They had already found their way into the collections of Imāmite *ḥadīth,* such as Kulaynī's *Kitāb al-Kāfī,* a work that reportedly contains 9,485 reports of doubtful and inauthentic origin,[156] two-thirds of its total contents of 16,199 reports.[157] Further material from works of the Mufawwiḍa, and even from the writings of heretical authors such as Ḥusayn b. Ḥamdān al-Khuṣaybī, were later introduced into the Imāmite literature by populist authors who tended to put together and offer whatever report in their judgment could strengthen the faith of the people in the Imāms although the authors themselves could never guarantee the authenticity of many reports or many of the sources they quoted.[158] A cultural situation existed in which

---

al-īmān: 150–51, who attributes this opinion to "many" of the early Imāmite authorities. He also asserts that many of the early Imāmites did not believe in the Imāms' *'iṣma*, that is, that they were divinely protected against sin and error (see also Baḥr al-'Ulūm, 3:220, where the opinion is attributed to the majority of the early Imāmites; also Abū 'Alī: 45, 346). In the time of Mufīd, however, only a minority of the Imāmites denied the Imāms' *'iṣma* (*Awā'il*: 35).

There were, of course, other points on which the two divisions of the Imāmite community, the pro-Mufawwiḍa and the anti-Mufawwiḍa, disagreed. Many Imāmites, for instance, denied the concept of *raj'a*, that the Imāms and some others would physically return to the world before the Day of Judgment (see Ṭabrisī, *Majma'*, 20:252). Numerous monographs are exchanged between the supporters and rejecters of this concept, many of them published. They differed also on the question of whether the non-Imāmite Muslims, including the Sunnites, will be saved and live in Paradise in the hereafter as suggested by numerous reports from the Imāms (see, for instance, Barqī: 287; Kulaynī, 2:19; Ibn Bābawayh, *Khiṣāl*: 408; *Manāqib* [quoted by Majlisī, 8:139]. See also Ṭabāṭabā'ī's footnote in Majlisī, 3:8).

156. See Yūsuf al-Baḥrānī: 395; Khwānsārī, 6:116; Āghā Buzurg, 17:245.

157. On the number of the *ḥadīth*s of the *Kāfī* see the introduction to its most recent edition: 28 and the sources cited therein.

158. These include books such as al-Ṭabarī al-Shī'ī's *Dalā'il al-imāma* and *Musnad fāṭima*, Ḥusayn b. 'Abd al-Wahhāh's *'Uyūn al-mu'jizāt*, Furāt b. Ibrāhīm al-Kūfī's *Tafsīr*, Muḥammad b. Aḥmad b. Shādhān's *al-Rawḍa fi 'l-faḍā'il* or *Mi'at manqaba*, 'Imād al-Dīn al-Ṭūsī's *Thāqib al-manāqib*, Quṭb al-Dīn al-Rāwandī's *al-Kharā'ij wa 'l-jarā'iḥ*, and numerous other works.

collecting and preserving as many *ḥadīth*s as possible was a feature of quality and pride for the collector, a mentality that prevailed in the entire community of Muslim traditionists from all schools during the early and middle Islamic ages. Much of the material contained in different versions of the earlier books[159] as well as in works attributed to early authors (at times famous ones), even though there was no evidence to verify these attributions,[160] was quoted in later works by non-Mufawwiḍa authors who themselves did not believe in the content and could not guarantee the authenticity of their sources. In more recent centuries the preoccupation of some Shī'ite authors with preserving whatever early Shī'ite material has survived has spread the material from the works of heretic authors. Some authors even tried to rehabilitate those heretics and criticized the early Shī'ite authorities who "accused" them of heresy and corruption of faith. The result of this centuries-long process is manifest in the monumental collection of *Biḥār al-anwār* of Muḥammad Bāqir al-Majlisī (d. 1110/1699),[161] which includes most of the remains of the scholarship of the extremists of the early centuries that found their way into Imāmite works through the channels mentioned.[162]

The history of these two trends of Imāmite thought, the conflict of which comprised a major chapter in the history of the Imāmite community in the periods following the period of Minor Occultation, is outside the topic of the present work. In brief, although the Mufawwiḍa came to be regarded in theory as a heretical splinter group[163] and their ideas were rejected unanimously[164] by the Imāmite

159. These differences sometimes made two books of a single book as was the case with Ṣaffār's *Baṣā'ir al-darajāt* (see its editor's introduction: 4–5).

160. These include books such as the present version of *Kitāb sulaym b. qays al-hilālī*, Pseudo Mas'ūdī's *Ithbāt al-waṣiyya*, Pseudo Mufīd's *al-Ikhtiṣāṣ* and other similar works (see further Najāshī: 129, 258; Ibn al-Ghaḍā'irī, 5:160).

161. This work is available in two editions, the old lithograph in 25 large volumes and the new edition in 110 volumes.

162. See especially volumes 23–27 of its new edition and the section on the miracles under each Imām's biography in volumes 35–53.

163. See, for instance, *Ghayba*: 254 where a former Shī'ite is said to have been converted to the doctrine of the Mufawwiḍa and that "the Shī'a did not know him except for a short time."

164. Shubbar, *Maṣābīḥ al-anwār*, 1:369. See also Majlisī, 2:175, footnote.

community, many of their teachings (although not their fundamental ideas on cosmological matters) that were put in the form of *ḥadīth,* especially on the scope of knowledge of the Imām, found supporters among later Imāmites. Heretical persons and sects appeared in the Imāmite community who even supported the cosmological theories of the Mufawwiḍa, including authors such as Rajab al-Bursī (d. after 813/1410)[165] and the splinter group of the Shaykhiyya (founded in the thirteenth/nineteenth century), all of whom were anathematized by the Imāmite mainstream as extremists. Many Shī'ite Sufis, too, supported those opinions, and, thus, the accession of the Sufi Safavids to power in Iran in the beginning of the tenth/sixteenth century contributed greatly to the spread and popularization of those ideas.

The introduction of Sufi ideas and interpretations into Islamic philosophy in the Safavid period brought about a new Shī'ite school of Islamic philosophy in the eleventh/seventeenth century and helped the Sufi cosmological theories of Ibn al-'Arabī to become established in Shī'ite philosophical thought. Some of the adherents of this philosophical school put forward a theory of the Imām's "existential authority" (*al-wilāya al-takwīniyya*) that was virtually the same as the Mufawwiḍa's cosmological theory on the authority of the "first creature" or the "perfect man" in the creation and supervision of the world. Although many of the followers of that Sufi philosophical school have not supported that concept of the Imām's existential authority to its full logical conclusion, others have done so. Those that have must be regarded as the true heirs to the Mufawwiḍa (even though they strongly deny it, at least verbally) because their doctrines are identical. Although always a very small minority, some of their ideas, which were in line with the pro-Mufawwiḍa reports in the collections of *ḥadīth,* as well as their terminology, have gained some degree of support in the community.

165. On him see especially 'Abd al-Ḥusayn al-Amīnī, 7:33–68. He was identified during his life (see his *Mashāriq anwār al-yaqīn*: 14–16, 219, 272) and after (see, for instance, Majlisī, 1:10; Ḥurr al-'Āmilī, *Amal*, 2:117; Afandī, p. 37; 2:307; Muḥsin al-Amīn, 6:466; 'Abd al-Ḥusayn al-Amīnī, 7: 34) as an extremist and certainly adhered to the school of the Mufawwiḍa as is well attested by his above-mentioned work.

For the past few centuries, therefore, the Shī'ite scholastic community has been once again divided between supporters and rejecters of the supernaturality of the Imāms. The absolute majority of the rank and file and many of the scholars stand somewhere between the two trends, as was the case during the time of the Imāms. The relation between the two trends has remained as it was during the early centuries: calm and quiet at times, bitter and problematic at others, depending on whether something or someone provoked hostilities between them. The last outbreak of violent conflict between the two trends which started in Iran and soon spread to other Shī'ite communities, followed the publication of a book late in 1970 by a member of the Shī'ite seminary of Qum on one of the most popular Shī'ite themes, the rise and fall of Ḥusayn. The analysis offered in this book was very much in line with that of the early Shī'ite scholars such as Mufīd and the Sharīf al-Murtaḍā, namely that the Imām did not know that his rising was not going to succeed and that he later tried all possible honorable ways to prevent bloodshed. The book received the written or verbal endorsement and support of other scholars of that seminary as well as of other members of the Shī'ite religious establishment in different towns.[166] The unmistakable implication that the whole episode was a failed personal initiative, however, provoked extremely hostile reactions from those who believed in the perfect knowledge of the Imām and in the authenticity of some related reports recorded in the collections of *ḥadīth* that the author ignored. Some twenty books were published against that book. Using the same familiar and thirteen-century-old tactics, the supporters of the perfect knowledge and limitless power of the Imāms, who now called themselves *wilāyatī* (the supporters of the absolute authority of the Imāms) accused their opponents of lack of faith in the Shī'ite doctrine and in the Imāms and of having Sunnite inclinations, and labeled them *wahhābī*, or *nāṣibī* (anti-'Alīd). The popular preachers, most of whom were in the *wilāyatī* camp, managed to provoke many of the common people against the so-called *wahhābī*s and to prevail against them. The so-called *wahhābī* group included almost all of those

166. See further Enayat: 190–91.

who later led the Islamic Revolution, save the leader, and came to power in Iran. The *wilāyatīs* continued their thoroughgoing and harsh attacks on their opponents for several years and did not let the case rest. The situation got out of hand, very ugly and violent in some towns in Iran. In Iṣfahān in central Iran, it led to unfortunate bloodshed; an old religious scholar, who was among the opponents of the book, was murdered. Actually, if it had not been for the Revolution, which brought the suppressed group to power and prevailed over all other social questions, many more lives would have been lost.

Many works have been exchanged between the two lines of thought during almost thirteen centuries. Many more are written by the supporters of each trend to elaborate their own lines of thought.[167] The standpoints of each group on the nature of the Imāmate inevitably affected their views on every other subject, particularly toward the rest of the Muslim community and on sectarian topics. Outsiders who face different interpretations and opposite views on those sorts of questions from Shī'ite authors become puzzled and have some difficulty deciding which one represents the true Shī'ite position. At times the moderate views of some Shī'ite writers on sectarian issues have led outsiders to suspect or presume that they are insincere, that they have exercised precautionary secrecy, or that they have attempted to offer a more moderate and presentable (or else reconciliatory) version of the Shī'ite doctrine because completely different judgments on the same subjects are given by otherwise similarly authoritative Shī'ite writers. What these outsiders fail to note is that each of the two groups is sincere in expressing its own mind but that each represents a totally different trend with different visions of some important dogmatic questions, although all agree on the basic and fundamental question on which the whole Shī'ite doctrine is built—that the Imāms of the House of the Prophet are the ultimate source and authority of religious knowledge, of the true interpretation of the Qur'ān, and of the sound tradition of the Prophet.

167. One of the most recent examples is a book called *Umarā'-i hastī* (in Persian), on the comprehensive authority of the Prophet and Imāms over the universe, written by a certain Abu 'l-Faḍl Nabawī (Tehran, 1345 sh/1966–1967). It was refuted by a book entitled *Rāh-i nijāt az sharr-i ghulāt* by Ḥaydar 'Alī Qalamdārān (Qum, [1974]).

III

The Crisis of Succession

IN THE FIRST half of the second/eighth century, the overwhelming majority of the Shī'ites, as noted, followed Imām Ja'far al-Ṣādiq, who was widely recognized as the head of the House of the Prophet in his time. During his time, however, the radical wing of the Shī'ite community first joined the revolt of Zayd b. 'Alī in 122/740 and then turned to the Ḥasanid branch of the 'Alīds.[1] At this time the Ḥasanids were represented by 'Abd Allāh b. al-Ḥasan, known as 'Abd Allāh al-Maḥḍ (d. 145/762), who was the most senior in age among the living members of the House of the Prophet[2] and considered himself to be the head of the House.[3] The radical elements eventually followed 'Abd Allāh's son, Muḥammad al-Nafs al-Zakiyya, in his open revolt in 145/762. They controlled Medina for a short time before their defeat, and during this period gave Ja'far al-Ṣādiq a difficult time for failing to support their insurrection.[4] The disputes between the Ḥasanid and Ḥusaynid branches of the 'Alids incited some members of the Shī'ite community to say that although the right to leadership of the Muslim community lay with the House of the Prophet, it was not known who the actual Imām was because there was disagreement on this issue within the House itself. The Imām, they maintained, would be the individual

1. See Ṣaffār: 66; Kulaynī, 1:349, 7:376; Kashshī: 427; *Manāqib,* 3:349. See also Nawbakhtī: 68; Sa'd b. 'Abd Allāh: 73.
2. 'Umarī: 37; Ibn 'Inaba, *'Umda*: 101; idem, *Fuṣūl*: 101. See also Kulaynī, 1:358.
3. See his debates with Ja'far al-Ṣādiq on this matter in Kulaynī, 1:358, 8:363–4 (see also 2:155, 3:507, 7:21, 376; Ṣaffār: 156, 160; 'Ayyāshī, 1:368, 2:208–9; Irbilī, 2:384).
4. Kulaynī, 1:363.

who was accepted by the consensus of all members of the House of the Prophet.[5] Nevertheless, all Imāmites[6] accepted the authority of Ja'far al-Ṣādiq[7] and from that time on came to be known as Ja'fariyya.[8]

The first major crisis of leadership in the Imāmite community occurred after the death of Ja'far al-Ṣādiq when his followers divided on the question of succession. One group, which included some of his distinguished disciples,[9] did not recognize anyone after him as Imām. This group apparently consisted of those who followed Ja'far al-Ṣādiq as *primus inter pares,* the most distinguished scholar of the

5. Nu'mānī: 133–5.
6. They were those Shī'ites who maintained the father-to-son succession of the Imāmate, the believers in the *niẓām al-imāma* as termed by Mufīd, *Majālis,* 2:88, 93, or *aṣḥāb al-nasaq* as called by Nāshi': 23, 26 (or *al-qā'ilūn bi-nasaq al-imāma,* ibid.: 24, 25, 46, 48) and Mas'ūdī, *Tanbīh*: 232. The derogatory term of *rāfiḍa* or *rawāfiḍ* (sing. *rāfiḍī* = rejector) in Sunnite usage refers to the same group. According to the Sunnite authors, this term was first used by Zayd b. 'Alī for those of his followers who deserted him after he allegedly refused to condemn Abū Bakr and 'Umar as illegitimate rulers (see Friedlaender, "The Heterodoxies of the Shīites in the Presentation of Ibn Ḥazm": 137–59; Kohlberg, "The Term *Rāfiḍa* in Imāmī Shī'ī Usage": 677–9). The Shī'ites themselves in the third/ninth century thought that the heresiarch Mughīra b. Sa'īd al-Bajalī (d. ca. 119/737) who started as a Shī'ite and then separated and established his own special group (see the article *al-Mughīriyya* in *EI*[2], 7:347–8 [by W. Madelung]) invented this term against them (see Nawbakhtī: 75; Sa'd b. 'Abd Allāh: 77; Ṭabarī, 7:181; Abu 'l-Qāsim al-Balkhī: 179; Qāḍī Nu'mān, 1:62).
7. Kashshī: 473. It seems, however, that some of the senior disciples of his father, Muḥammad al-Bāqir, did not completely submit to him. He is quoted as having said: "O God, give Your mercy to the disciples of my father, for I know that some of them consider me inferior in rank" (Ḥimyarī: 101).
8. See Kulaynī, 2:77; Kashshī: 255; Abu 'l-Qāsim al-Balkhī: 179, 180, 181 (see also Ḥimyarī: 276). The term *taja'fur,* in the sense of following Ja'far al-Ṣādiq, apparently came into existence in this period also. It appears in a poem attributed to the Sayyid, Ismā'il b. Muḥammad al-Ḥimyarī, the well-known poet of that period (see his *Dīwān*: 202), and in later sources as well (e.g., Jishumī, *Jalā' al-abṣār*: 128. See also Qāḍī, *Kaysāniyya*: 331–37).
9. They included Abān b. 'Uthmān al-Aḥmar (Kashshī: 352), who was one of the six most learned among the younger generation of Ja'far's disciples (ibid.: 375), Sa'd b. Ṭarīf al-Iskāf (ibid.: 215) and 'Anbasa b. Muṣ'ab

sharī'a or the most learned and distinguished among the members of the House of the Prophet, but not as an Imām in the Imāmite Shī'ite sense.[10] In their judgment, therefore, it was not necessary for an Imām always to be succeeded by another, let alone that the successor should be from among the descendants of the deceased Imām. They probably simply did not consider any of those who claimed his successorship to be knowledgeable enough to be recognized as a teacher and a religious authority.[11] The Muslim heresiog-

---

(ibid.: 365). There is some doubt about whether Abān belonged to this group because the phrase *kān min al-nāwūsiyya* in Kashshī: 352 is said to appear in some manuscripts of that work as *kān min al-qādisiyya,* and it is argued that this may be the right version because the man is said by Najāshī: 13 and Ṭūsī, *Fihrist*: 18 to be from Kūfa to which Qādisiyya belonged (Muḥammad Taqī al-Tustarī, *Qāmūs al-rijāl,* 1:114, 116). Kashshī, however, asserts that Abān was from Baṣra although he was living in Kūfa, so the expression *wa kān min al-qādisiyya* would not fit in his sentence because it is against what the author has said previously in the same line. There is no other evidence to suggest that the man was from Qādisiyya, whereas there is a point to support that he actually "stopped" with Ja'far al-Ṣādiq. Contrary to what Najāshī: 13 and Ṭūsī, *Fihrist*: 7 asserted, he seems to have never quoted from Ja'far's successor, Mūsā (Muḥammad Taqī al-Tustarī, 1:115), in spite of the fact that he lived during the latter's period of Imāmate. (The date of Abān's death is not known. However, that he lived until well into the second half of the second/eighth century is well verified by the fact that many of the transmitters of *ḥadīth* who started their careers in the last decades of that century studied with him. See a list of them in Khu'ī, 1:164. See also Ibn Ḥajar, *Lisān*, 1:24.)

10. A prolific Imāmite scholar of the fourth/tenth century, Abū Ṭālib 'Ubayd Allāh b. Aḥmad al-Anbārī (d. 356/966–967), is also reported to have been among the Nāwūsiyya (Ṭūsī, *Fihrist*: 103; compare with Ibn al-Nadīm: 247 where he is said to have been from the "Bābūshiyya." However, the point that this scholar had Wāqifite tendencies in "stopping" with a certain Imām is also attested to by Najāshī: 232).

11. See, for instance, 'Alī b. Bābawayh: 198 where the Prophet is quoted as predicting that upon the passing away of his two grandsons, Muḥammad al-Bāqir and Ja'far al-Ṣādiq, the chapter of knowledge will categorically close.

raphers,[12] however, made a special sect out of this group, saying that its members held that Ja'far al-Ṣādiq had not actually died but was alive and would come back someday to the world as the *qā'im.*[13] The heresiographers named the group the Nāwūsiyya, allegedly because the head of the group was a man of Baṣra called Nāwūs.[14] Two completely different accounts are given of the reason why these people "stopped" with Ja'far and thought that he must be alive.[15]

12. Nawbakhtī: 78; Sa'd b. 'Abd Allāh: 79; Nāshi': 46; Abū Ḥātim al-Rāzī: 286; Abu 'l-Ḥasan al-Ash'arī, 1:100; Abu 'l-Qāsim al-Balkhī: 179 (misspelled as *bārūsiyya* in this edition); Mufīd, *Majālis*, 2:88; 'Abd al-Qāhir al-Baghdādī, *Uṣūl al-dīn*: 273 (misspelled as *ya'ūsiyya* in this edition); idem, *Farq*: 61; Isfarā'īnī: 37; Ibn Ḥazm, 5:36; Shahrastānī, 1:195; Nashwān: 162; Fakhr al-Dīn al-Rāzī, *Muḥaṣṣal*: 354; idem, *I'tiqādāt*: 64 (appears in the edition as *nāmūsiyya*); Maqrīzī, 2:351; Sam'ānī, 13:19 (who erroneously ascribed to them that they doubted that Muḥammad al-Bāqir had actually died and awaited the return of Ja'far al-Ṣādiq, too!). See also Ibn Qiba, *Naqḍ kitāb al-ishhād*: paras. 14, 23; *Kamāl*: 37; Mufīd, *al-Fuṣūl al-'ashara*: 373; *Ghayba*: 18, 119.
13. A variant version of this account quotes them as saying that Ja'far did die, but there would be no Imām after him and he would return to the world in a future time. See Fakhr al-Dīn al-Rāzī, *Muḥaṣṣal*: 354.
14. Nawbakhtī: 78 who calls him *fulān* b. *fulān* al-Nāwūs from Baṣra; Sa'd b. 'Abd Allāh: 80 (*fulān* b. al-Nāwūs); Kashshī: 365 (*fulān* b. *fulān* al-Nāwūs); Abū Ḥātim al-Rāzī: 286 (Ibn al-Nāwūs); Abu 'l-Qāsim al-Balkhī: 180 (*fulān* b. Nāwūs [printed yāwūs]); Abu 'l-Ḥasan al-Ash'arī, 1:100 ('Ijlān [obviously a misreading of *fulān*] b. Nāwūs); Khwārazmī :50 ('Abd Allāh b. Nāwūs); Mufīd, *Majālis*, 2:88 ('Abd Allāh b. al-Nāwūs); Ṭabrisī, *I'lām al-warā*: 295 ('Abd Allāh b. al-Nāwūs); Ibn Ḥazm, 5:36 (Ibn Nāwūs al-Baṣrī [in the edition: al-Miṣrī]); Nashwān: 162 (Ibn Nāwūs, a notable among the people of Baṣra). Consider also these variations: the leader of the group was a man called Māwūs or Ibn Nāwūs (above-mentioned sources) or was from a village called Nāwūsā (Shahrastānī, 1:195) or Nāwūsī (Nashwān: 162) [Yāqūt, 5:254 mentions a Nāwūsā near Baghdad and a Nāwūs al-Ẓabya near Hamadān], or was attributed to a *nāwūs* (Christian cemetery) in Baṣra (*Farq*: 61; Isfarā'īnī: 37).
15. Compare Nawbakhtī: 78; Sa'd b. 'Abd Allāh: 79–80; Mufīd, *Majālis,* 2:88; Shahrastānī, 1:195 with Kashshī: 414. One of the two quotations given as the basis for this opinion in the first account is also mentioned as one of the main arguments of those who later denied that Mūsā al-Kāẓim died. Compare Abū Ḥātim al-Rāzī: 286; Shahrastānī, 1:195; Fakhr al-Dīn al-Rāzī, *Muḥaṣṣal*: 354 with Abū Ḥātim: 290; Nawbakhtī: 90; Sa'd b. 'Abd Allāh: 89–90.

It is very difficult, however, to imagine that anyone could have maintained such a belief in someone like Ja'far who had consistently and openly insisted that he was not the *qā'im.*[16] Unlike his son Mūsā, he was a totally apolitical person. There were no political expectations in him to continue after his death, and he did not die in prison. People could not have questioned his actually passing away. Furthermore, unlike the case of Mūsā, in whose case the people for many years[17] argued with his son, asking him to prove that his father had actually died, there is no report that anyone ever challenged the authority of Ja'far's successors or even raised a doubt based on the possibility that Ja'far might still be alive. It is, therefore, very possible that all accounts on the existence of an idea about the occultation of Ja'far that are based on the narrations of Shī'ite authorities represent an understanding of the Imāmite Shī'ite mentality that an Imām from the House of the Prophet must always exist and that followers of Ja'far should have shared this doctrine. To that mentality, "stopping" with Ja'far, or, in other words, believing in no further Imām after him would mean belief in his occultation.[18]

16. See above, chapter 1. According to a report recorded by Kulaynī, 1:307 and Khuṣaybī: 243, even 'Anbasa b. Muṣ'ab, one of the future so-called *Nāwūsīs*, himself quoted that he once asked Ja'far al-Ṣādiq whether he was the *qā'im*, to which question the Imām replied that he was *qā'im* in the sense that he was the one to rise to the position of Imāmate after his father.
17. See especially Kashshī: 426, 450, 458, 463, 473–4, 475 (dated 193/905, which was ten years after Mūsā's death), 477, 614.
18. Among the Muslim authors Mufīd was the only one who doubted if any group ever existed that denied the death of Ja'far al-Ṣādiq and maintained that he was the *qā'im* (*Majālis,* 2:90). Abū Ḥātim al-Rāzī: 285 also emphasized that there was no one in his time who held such an opinion. It should also be noted that some Sunnite sources describe the Nāwūsiyya as a sect of the Ghulāt who, according to different accounts, either awaited the return of 'Alī with no reference at all to Ja'far (Shahrastānī, 1:195 [quoting Abū Ḥāmid al-Zawzanī]; Ibn al-Jawzī, *Talbīs iblīs*: 22) or were later joined and influenced by a group of Saba'iyya and held exaggerated opinions about Ja'far (*Farq*: 61; Isfarā'īnī: 37. See also Sam'ānī, 13:19), whereas the Shī'ite sources only attribute to them the opinion that Ja'far al-Ṣādiq did not die and that he would return to the world as the *qā'im*. It can be suggested with some confidence that the Sunnite sources mixed the Shī'ite material on the Nāwūsiyya with material about another sect whose name was spelled somehow similarly in Arabic script and ascribed

A second group comprised the disciples of Ismā'īl, a son of Ja'far al-Ṣādiq who had predeceased his father by one or two years. Ismā'īl had been the eldest son and his father's favorite, and it had been widely believed that he would be the next Imām.[19] There were even rumors within the Shī'ite community that Ismā'īl's father had explicitly designated him as his successor.[20] Ismā'īl's unexpected death thus created a doctrinal problem for those among the Imāmites who believed that the order of the Imāms was prefixed and that each Imām appointed his successor according to that order as revealed to him by God or delegated by the Prophet or the previous Imāms. It also created a problem for those who thought that the Imāms possessed knowledge of the future. This quandary led to the introduction of the early Kaysānite concept of *badā'* into Imāmite thought, a concept originally understood as a change in the divine decision but later reinterpreted by Imāmite theologians as referring to an unexpected divine decision, that is, that people came to realize that the divine decision had been different from what they had thought it was.[21] Others among the disciples of Ismā'īl maintained either that Ismā'īl had not really died and had succeeded his father as a living but vanished Imām or that his right to the succession had been transferred to his son, Muḥammad, who was to be followed as the Imām after the death of his grandfather, Ja'far al-Ṣādiq. The latter was the position of the followers of Abu 'l-Khaṭṭāb who

---

the beliefs of the second group to the first. It is, therefore, plausible to think that the name *bābūshiyya* mentioned by Ibn al-Nadīm: 247 as the name of a Shī'ite sect to which 'Ubayd Allāh b. Aḥmad al-Anbārī belonged is not a misspelling of the name Nāwūsiyya; rather, it is the name of a later little-known splinter group of the Ghulāt with certain ideas that the Sunnite sources attributed to the Nāwūsiyya, because they thought they were the same. If this was the case, the Shī'ite scholar Ṭūsī should have fallen victim to that same confusion when he described that scholar as a *Nāwūsī,* when he actually belonged to a fourth/tenth century sect of the Ghulāt, the Bābūshiyya.

19. See 'Alī b. Bābawayh: 210; Nawbakhtī: 79; Sa'd b. 'Abd Allāh: 80; Kashshī: 473–4; Mufīd, *Irshād*: 284; Irbilī, 2:392.
20. Nawbakhtī: 79; Sa'd b. 'Abd Allāh: 78, 80; *Kamāl*: 69. See also Kulaynī, 2:92; Ibn Qūlawayh: 302.
21. See especially the article "badā'" in *Encyclopaedia Iranica*, 3:354–5 (by W. Madelung).

accepted Muḥammad b. Ismā'īl as the true Imām after the execution of Abu 'l-Khaṭṭāb left them without a leader.[22] The Ismā'īliyya branch of Shī'ism thus came into existence; it has survived into the present.

The overwhelming majority of the Imāmites,[23] however, accepted 'Abd Allāh, the eldest of the remaining sons of Ja'far al-Ṣādiq, as the true successor to his father. He lived only seventy days[24] after his father and died without a son. Most of his followers then transferred their allegiance to Mūsā, the next eldest son of Ja'far, who had already built his own circle of followers among close associates of his father[25] but had not openly challenged his brother while 'Abd Allāh still lived.[26] 'Abd Allāh's followers divided after his death with some deciding that they had been wrong to believe he was the true Imām. The main arguments against his truth were his inadequate knowledge of the *sharī'a* and his reported earlier Sunnite inclinations although many also argued that if he had been the true

22. Nāshi': 47; Nawbakhtī: 82; Sa'd b. 'Abd Allāh: 81, 83–4; Abū Ḥātim al-Rāzī: 289; Abu 'l-Qāsim al-Balkhī: 180; Kashshī: 321; Mufīd, *Irshād:* 285. They were also reputedly joined later by a branch of the Faṭḥites (see below), who were also bereft of guidance when their leader died with no son and without appointing a successor. See Abū Zayd al-'Alawī, para. 15; Ibn Ḥazm, *Jamhara*: 53. See also Madelung, "Bemerkungen zur imāmitischen Firaq-Literatur": 39.
23. Nawbakhtī: 88; Sa'd b. 'Abd Allāh: 87; Abū Ḥātim al-Rāzī: 287; Abu 'l-Qāsim al-Balkhī: 181; Kashshī: 154, 254, 282; *Kamāl*: 74.
24. As cited by most sources. 'Alī b. Bābāwayh: 179, however, states that 'Abd Allāh outlived his father by one month only.
25. According to Ṣaffār: 250–51 and Kashshī: 282–4, this group was headed by two well-known Imāmite *mutakallim*s, Hishām b. Sālim al-Jaqwālīqī and Abū Ja'far al-Aḥwal Ṣāḥib al-Ṭāq, who reportedly tested 'Abd Allāh by putting some legal questions to him and concluded that he was not knowledgeable in the matters of the *sharī'a* and so was unqualified for the Imāmate (see also Nawbakhtī: 89; Sa'd b. 'Abd Allāh: 88; 'Alī b. Bābawayh: 209–10; Kulaynī, 1:351). Others such as Abu 'l-Ḥasan al-Ash'arī, 1:103; Ibn Ḥazm, *Jamhara*, 53; Shahrastānī, 1:218 attributed this testing to Zurāra b. A'yan, which is incorrect (see Kashshī: 154–6). Ibn Ḥazm's account here is particularly confused as he first identifies 'Abd Allāh al-Abṭaḥ (*sic*), head of the Abṭaḥiyya (*sic*, possibly a later misspelling in both cases), as son of Muḥammad al-Bāqir and then as son of Ja'far al-Ṣādiq.
26. Sa'd b. 'Abd Allāh: 88; Kashshī: 255; *Manāqib,* 3:351.

Imām he would not have died without issue. Mūsā was, thus, the true successor to Ja'far al-Ṣadiq. This group later formed the mainstream of the Imāmite community. Another group was of the opinion that 'Abd Allāh had been a true Imām and was the legitimate successor to Ja'far al-Ṣādiq, and Mūsā was the successor to 'Abd Allāh. This group remained within Imāmite Shī'ism until the late third/ninth century and produced some of the most distinguished Imāmite scholars.[27] Agreeing with the mainstream Imāmites on the chain of succession from Mūsā al-Kāẓim on, they differed only on the addition of the name of 'Abd Allāh.[28] This group was known as the Faṭḥites after 'Abd Allāh, who bore the epithet *afṭaḥ* (the flatfooted). Their belief that succession to the Imāmate need not necessarily be from father to son later contributed, as will be seen below, to another split in the Imāmite community after the death of the eleventh Imām.

The death of Mūsā al-Kāẓim in 183/799 led to another major succession crisis. A number of the most distinguished among his close associates and regional representatives maintained that Mūsā had actually not died but had gone into hiding until he would return to the world as the *qā'im.* Many of the Imāmites, probably the majority of them in the beginning when there was a rumor that the Imām would reappear in eight months,[29] supported this claim. This group came to be known as the Wāqifites, later called the Mamṭūra by their opponents,[30] and, like the Faṭḥites, included and

27. See Kashshī: 345, 385, 530, 562, 563, 565, 570, 612. For a list of the Faṭḥite scholars mentioned in the early Imāmite sources see Ibn Dāwūd: 532–33.
28. See Kashshī: 530, 565.
29. Ibid.: 406.
30. The word can mean either "wet by rain" or "the recipients of rain." There are two completely different accounts about why these Shī'ites were called the Mamṭūra. According to one account, they once in a year of drought went out of the town and prayed for rain. That was after everybody else had gone and prayed with no result. It rained when they prayed and so they became known as the Mamṭūra, those for whom the rain came ('Abd al-Jabbār, *Mughnī*, 20 [2]:182. See also Pseudo Mas'ūdī, *Ithbāt al-waṣiyya*: 187). According to the other, the reason they were called Mamṭūra was that once one of their opponents argued with them and said to them: "you

produced many distinguished scholars.[31] Unlike what some Shī'ite scholars of the fifth/eleventh century thought that the supporters of this sect had disappeared,[32] the sect seems to have survived for quite a long time, at least until the mid-sixth/twelfth century.[33]

---

are wet dogs" or "In my eyes you are inferior to wet dogs." (The dog is considered unclean in Islamic law. It is worse when it is wet because it contaminates other things it contacts.) The opponent who made this statement is variously identified as 'Alī b. Ismā'īl al-Maythamī (Nawbakhtī: 92; Abū Ḥātim al-Rāzī: 290; Shahrastānī, 1:198), Yūnus b. 'Abd al-Raḥmān (Sa'd b. 'Abd Allāh: 92; Abu 'l-Ḥasan al-Ash'arī, 1:103; *Farq*: 64) or Zurāra b. A'yan (Isfarā'īnī: 39; in actual terms, Zurāra had already died more than thirty years before Mūsā al-Kāẓim died and this sect came into existence) or an unidentified "group" (Fakhr al-Dīn al-Rāzī, *I'tiqādāt*: 66). The first account, however, does not seem accurate because the name Mamṭūra was considered a derogatory title that their opponents used to call them (see Abu 'l-Qāsim al-Balkhī: 181. See also Kashshī: 460–61; Najāshī: 393 for examples of the derogatory use of that title), whereas it had to be a compliment if the basis for this naming was that story.

31. See a list of them in Ibn Dāwūd: 528–32 and Riyāḍ Muḥammad Ḥabīb al-Nāṣirī's monograph on this sect, 1:211–19, 261 ff.
32. See, for instance, Murtaḍā, *Dhakhīra*: 503; idem, *Risālā fī ghaybat al-ḥujja*: 295 (in his *Shāfī*, 3:148, however, he was more accurate as he confirmed that a few of the supporters of this opinion still existed); Ṭūsī, *Ghayba*: 42.
33. See Madelung, "Some Notes on Non-Ismā'īlī Shī'ism in the Maghrib": 87–97. According to Madelung, "Ibn Ḥawqal, writing ca. 378/988, mentions that the people of the extreme Sūs in the western Maghrib were partly Mālikī Sunnīs and partly Mūsawī Shī'īs who cut the line of Imāms after Mūsā (al-Kāẓim) b. Ja'far and belonged to the followers of 'Alī b. Warsand (Ibn Ḥawqal, *K. Ṣūrat al-arḍ*, ed. K. H. Kramers, pp. 91f.) . . . al-Idrīsī, writing ca. 548/1154, mentions that the people of the capital of Sūs, Tārūdānt, were Mālikīs while the people of the second major town, Tiyūywīn, located a day's trip from Tārūdānt, adhered to the *madhhab* of Mūsā b. Ja'far (al-Idrīsī, *Description de 'l-Afrique septentrionale et saharienne*, ed. H. Pérès, Algiers, 1957, p. 39)." The sect was known in Maghrib as Bajaliyya after its head, 'Alī b. al-Ḥusayn b. Warsand al-Bajalī, the Shī'ite author of the early third/ninth century. For this scholar and the sect of Bajaliyya see the same article of Madelung and his article on Ibn Warsand in *EI*[2], supplement: 402. See also al-Sharīf al-Raḍī, *Khaṣā'iṣ al-A'imma*, p. 37.

Imāmite sources have tried to find an economic basis for this split in the Shī'ite community. They suggest that at the time of Mūsā al-Kāẓim's death, large sums of money had accumulated with his representatives in different towns, which they had not forwarded to the Imām because he was in prison for several years. To keep the funds for themselves and not send them to his successor, they denied Mūsā's death and claimed that he would return to the scene.[34] This actually may have been one of the factors that contributed to the emergence of that doctrine; in fact there are numerous reports concerning distinguished members of the group who held assets that they did not want to surrender to a new Imām.[35] It does not, however, tell the whole story. As noted in chapter 1, even during his lifetime, people had expected Mūsā to lead a rising as the *qā'im*, and it was, thus, quite natural that many could not accept that he was actually dead, specially because he had died in prison and none of his followers had witnessed his death.

In due course, however, most of the Imāmites accepted 'Alī al-Rīḍā as the true Imām. They came to be known as the Qaṭ'iyya (people of certitude),[36] allegedly because they were convinced that Mūsā al-Kāẓim was categorically dead.[37] Theoretical problems arose, as noted, when 'Alī al-Riḍā died leaving a son, Muḥammad al-Jawād, who was in his seventh year. During the lifetime of 'Alī

34. See 'Alī b. Bābawayh: 213–14; Kashshī: 405, 459–60, 467; Ibn Bābawayh, *'Ilal,* 1: 225; idem, *'Uyūn*, 1:22, 113–14; *Ghayba*: 42–4; Ṭabrisī, *I'lām*: 314.
35. Kashshī: 405, 459, 467, 468, 598, 599; Najāshī: 300.
36. See, for instance, Pseudo Qāsim b. Ibrāhīm: 104a; Abū Zayd al-'Alawī, para. 24; Nāshi': 47; Nawbakhtī: 90; Sa'd b. 'Abd Allāh: 89; Abū Ḥātim al-Rāzī: 287, 291, 293; Abu 'l-Ḥasan al-Ash'arī, 1:90, 103, 104; Abu 'l-Qāsim al-Balkhī: 176, 180, 182; Mas'ūdī, *Murūj,* 4:28; idem, *Tanbīh*: 231, 232; *Kamāl*: 84; Khwārazmī :50,51; Mufīd, *Majālis*, 2:98; Ibn Ḥazm, 5:38; *Farq*: 64, 70, 71; Shahrastānī, 1:198–9; Nashwān: 166; Isfarā'īnī: 39; Fakhr al-Dīn al-Rāzī, *Muḥaṣṣal*: 355. See also Ṭūsī, *Tahdhīb*, 4:150.
37. There are statements which confirm that allegation. See, for instance, Sa'd b. 'Abd Allāh: 101; Kashshī: 612; *Ghayba*: 41; Ṭabrisī, *I'lām*: 364. Malaṭī: 38 (hence Maqrīzī, 2:351) erroneously identified the Qaṭ'iyya as those who "stopped" with 'Alī al-Riḍā and did not believe in the Imāmate of his descendants, so they were called *Qaṭ'iyya* because they cut the order of Imāmate after him (see also 'Umarī: 157). Fakhr al-Dīn al-Rāzī, *I'tiqādāt*:

al-Riḍā, rumors circulated to the effect that Muḥammad was his adopted, not his natural, son.[38] That uncertainty was compounded by questions about his youth and the state of his knowledge when he succeeded his father as Imām. Despite this, the fact that no other clear alternative existed made the transition relatively painless. Hardly anybody could challenge the succession of the only[39] son of a venerated head of the House of the Prophet who had died at the peak of his popularity. Adequate solutions were also found to the questions about the qualifications of a child Imām. Therefore, after

---

66 identified them as those who believed wholeheartedly and most faithfully (from *qaṭaʿa,* believed with certainty) in the Imāmate of Mūsā al-Kāẓim. Both of these latter assertions are obviously wrong. There is, however, a quotation in Kashshī: 374 in which the expression *qaṭaʿū ʿalayh* is used by the transmitter of the report in the sense that he categorically determined, after ʿAlī al-Riḍā explained to him that his father was not the *qāʾim*, that ʿAlī al-Riḍā was the true Imām. See also Nawbakhtī: 95 and Saʿd b. ʿAbd Allāh: 94, who spoke of a group of the Wāqifites who later followed ʿAlī al-Riḍā and *qaṭaʿū ʿalā imāmatih* but after his death returned to their former doctrine.

38. Kulaynī, 1:322–3; al-Ṭabarī al-Shīʿī: 201; Khuṣaybī: 295–6; *Manāqib,* 4:387. The reason for the doubt is said to be the fact that Muḥammad al-Jawād was extremely dark skinned (Kulaynī, 1:322; Khuṣaybī: 290; *Manāqib*, 4:387), which encouraged many people, including the close relatives of the Imām, to suspect that Muḥammad might have been a son of Sayf or Lu'lu', the two black slaves of ʿAlī al-Riḍā (Khuṣaybī: 295) and that the Imām might have adopted him. The assertion of ʿUmarī :128 that ʿAlī al-Riḍā himself was *aswad al-lawn* (very dark skinned) seems thus to be unfounded. Both ʿAlī al-Riḍā and Muḥammad al-Jawād were reportedly born of Nubian mothers. The tenth (Kulaynī, 7:463–4) and the eleventh (Kashshī: 574) Imāms were also very dark skinned.

39. Ḥimyarī, *Dalāʾil* (quoted in Irbilī, 3:92); Kashshī: 596; al-Ṭabarī al-Shīʿī: 184; Ibn Bābawayh, *ʿUyūn*, 2:250; Mufīd, *Irshād*: 316; Ḥusayn b. ʿAbd al-Wahhāb: 118; Ṭabrisī, *Iʿlām*: 344; idem, *Tāj*: 51; *Manāqib*, 4:367; ʿAlī b. Yūsuf b. al-Muṭahhar: 294 (quoting *Kitāb al-Durr*). Others name a second son for ʿAlī al-Riḍā as ʿAlī (Ibn Ḥazm, *Jamhara*: 55) or Mūsā (Ibn Abi 'l-Thalj: 109; Ḥasan al-Qummī: 200; ʿUmarī: 128 [quoting Naṣr b. ʿAlī al-Jahḍamī in his *Mawālīd al-aʾimma*]; Ibn Ṭāwūs, *Muhaj al-Daʿawāt*: 378; ʿAlī b. Yūsuf b. al-Muṭahhar: 294). Others added yet three more sons (Ibn al-Khashshāb: 193–4; Ibn Ṭalḥa: 87; Irbilī, 3:57 [quoting ʿAbd al-ʿAzīz b. al-Akhḍar], 74; Sibṭ Ibn al-Jawzī: 202). Both of these latter assertions are clearly wrong.

a short period of uncertainty that the community experienced,[40] the Imāmate of Muḥammad al-Jawād was accepted by almost[41] the entire mainstream of the Imāmite community.

With this precedent, the transfer of authority went even more smoothly when it passed in turn from Muḥammad al-Jawād to his son, 'Alī al-Hādī (who, like Muḥammad, was a child of only seven years when he succeeded to the Imāmate). According to a report, a servant of Muḥammad al-Jawād, Khayrān al-Khādim, testified that Muḥammad had named 'Alī al-Hādī as his successor, and the leaders of the Shī'ite community, who gathered on the day of Muḥammad al-Jawād's death to decide the issue of the succession, eventually accepted his word. One notable who had been present at the Imām's deathbed, the influential chief of the Shī'ite town of Qum, Abū Ja'far Aḥmad b. Muḥammad b. 'Īsā al-Ash'arī, did contest Khayrān al-Khādim's story, but the situation was quickly brought under control by other close associates of the late Imām.[42] This episode, if it can be substantiated, however, clearly indicates that even in this late phase of the history of the Imāmate, mere descent or seniority among the descendants of the deceased Imām was not considered sufficient for succession. The Shī'ite community had to be convinced that the new Imām had actually been appointed by his predecessor.[43]

40. Abu 'l-Ḥasan al-Ash'arī, 1:105; al-Ṭabarī al-Shī'ī: 204; Ḥusayn b. 'Abd al-Wahhāb: 119–20.
41. According to Nawbakhtī: 95, 97; Sa'd b. 'Abd Allāh: 93, 95; Abu 'l-Qāsim al-Balkhī: 181; and Mufīd, *Majālis*, 2:95, a group of the followers of 'Alī al-Riḍā followed, after his death, his brother Aḥmad, who had earlier, too, been followed by some Imāmites as the legitimate successor to his father Mūsā al-Kāẓim (Kashshī: 472; Abu 'l-Qāsim al-Balkhī: 181), and another group held that 'Alī al-Riḍā's death without leaving a qualified successor indicated that he was not a true Imām; they thus joined the Wāqifites and held that the Imām was Mūsā al-Kāẓim who was still alive in occultation and was to reappear in the future as the *qā'im*. According to another report (Ṭūsī, *Tahdhīb*, 3:28) a third group "stopped" with 'Alī al-Riḍā and did not believe in any Imām after him. These groups must have been very small. None of the Imāmite notables or transmitters of *ḥadīth* are reported to have been among these groups.
42. Kulaynī, 1:324.
43. See also Sa'd b. 'Abd Allāh: 106.

Special problems appeared again toward the end of the incumbency of ʻAlī al-Hādī with the death of his eldest son, Abū Jaʻfar Muḥammad. A well-mannered young man,[44] Muḥammad had been adored by his father and by the Shīʻite community as a whole. He was the obvious choice to succeed his father, and this was the widespread expectation. Some reports even suggest that his father had explicitly singled out Muḥammad from among his sons to succeed to the Imāmate.[45] Nevertheless, Muḥammad died three years before his father,[46] and ʻAlī al-Hādī named as his successor his next son, Abū Muḥammad al-Ḥasan, later known as Ḥasan al-ʻAskarī. The Imāmite community thus experienced once more the "unexpected divine decision" encountered first at the death of Ismāʻīl, the eldest son of Imām Jaʻfar al-Ṣādiq.[47] The overwhelming majority[48] of the Imāmites accepted Ḥasan al-ʻAskarī as the Imām after the death of ʻAlī al-Hādī in 255/869 although the circumstances seem to have led many to question his authority, which led in turn to an unprecedented lack of faith in and lack of deference toward the new Imām.[49] In one report, Ḥasan al-ʻAskarī is quoted as complaining that none of his forefathers had been as much doubted by the Imāmites as he was.[50] On another occasion he asked a visitor from the town of Qum about the state of the Imāmite community there "when the people [presumably referring to the Imāmites of Iraq] were in doubt and suspicion."[51] Numerous references in the early sources cite the widespread disagreement among the Imāmite community of the time about his Imāmate.[52] The lack of faith among the community was so great that for the first time ever in the history of the Imāmate one hears that some Shīʻites doubted

44. See Nawbakhtī: 111; Saʻd b. ʻAbd Allāh: 109; ʻUmarī: 131.
45. Khuṣaybī: 385; *Ghayba*: 55–6, 120–21.
46. Mufīd, *Irshād*: 337.
47. Ibid.: 336–7; *Ghayba*: 55, 120–21, 122.
48. Khuṣaybī: 384–5.
49. Ibid.: 385.
50. *Kamāl*: 222.
51. Ibid.
52. See, for instance, Ḥimyarī, *Dalāʼil* (quoted in Irbilī, 3: 206–7); Ibn Shuʻba: 361; Rāwandī, 1: 440, 448–50; Pseudo Masʻūdī: 239, 243.

the chastity of the Imām and accused him of wrongdoing in secret.[53] Some of the Imāmites of the time claimed that they had tested the Imām and concluded that his knowledge of the *sharī'a* was not up to the perfect standard required for an Imām.[54]

Throughout the period of his Imāmate, in fact from the very first day of his tenure, Ḥasan al-'Askarī faced the criticism of his followers, who complained occasionally about what they called his untraditional and unprecedented actions. In the funeral procession for his father, for example, he rent his collar. This was a well-known and familiar expression of grief in the Arab tradition, but no previous Imām had ever done it, and so he was criticized for the action. He responded to his detractors by reminding them of how "Moses rent his collar in grief for the death of his brother, Aaron."[55] Later, he was criticized for dressing in what some considered to be a sumptuous fashion.[56] In a letter sent to the people of Nīshāpūr, he complained that the prominent Imāmite scholar of that town, Faḍl b. Shādhān, "draws away our followers from us . . . and whenever we write a letter to them he criticizes us for that."[57] Some Shī'ites even argued that the Imām was making grammatical mistakes in his letters.[58] There were also complaints about the excessive spending of one of the Imām's financial agents, 'Alī b. Ja'far al-Humānī,[59] on a pilgrimage to Mecca; complaints that the Imām rejected as infringements on his authority. It had been his own decision, the Imām stated,

53. See Abū Ḥātim al-Rāzī: 292; Shahrastānī, 1:201. See also Nawbakhtī: 110–11; Sa'd b. 'Abd Allāh: 109.
54. Abū Ḥātim: 291; Shahrastānī, 1: 200.
55. Kashshī: 572 (see also 574); Pseudo Mas'ūdī: 234. Cf. Khuṣaybī, 249–50 where Jacob and Joseph are mentioned instead (note that Ḥasan is quoted as having rent his collar on the death of his brother Muḥammad, too. See Kulaynī, 1:327).
56. *Ghayba*: 148.
57. Kashshī: 541. Ibn Shādhān's criticisms of the Imām and the Imām's unhappiness with him seem to have been well known in the Shī'ite community of Khurāsān at that time. See Kashshī: 538.
58. Pseudo Mas'ūdī: 244.
59. On him, see Kashshī: 606–8 (also 523, 527, 557); Najāshī: 280; *Ghayba*: 212.

to grant his financial aide 100,000 *dīnār*s and then to double that for him later.[60] Naturally, the common people could not understand the divine interest behind the Imām's decisions.[61] There were also doubts about how much he was in actual control of the office of Imāmate. The financial affairs of the office, as noted above, were entirely administered by his close associate, 'Uthmān b. Sa'īd al-'Amrī, who was reportedly also writing and sending rescripts out in the name of the Imām.[62] The community was not, therefore, sure about the authority of the orders and statements they received in the name of the Imām.[63] This was apparently the reason that the

60. *Ghayba*: 130, 212; *Manāqib*, 4:424–5.

61. See Ṣaffār: 386 where a report ascribed to Ja'far al-Ṣādiq says: if you see the *qā'im* gives one hundred thousand to a man but only one *dirham* to another do not feel uncomfortable because he is given the full authority to do what he decides (*fa-inna 'l-amra mufawwaḍun ilayh*).

62. Kashshī: 544.

63. The Imāmite community of Baghdad, therefore, doubted the authenticity of a rescript they received in his name about a well-known and prominent Imāmite scholar of that town, Aḥmad b. Hilāl al-'Abartā'ī (on him see Kashshī: 535; *Kamāl*: 76; Najāshī: 83; Ṭūsī, *Fihrist*: 36) whom the rescript anathematized on the basis that he embezzled the Imām's property without his permission. The community asked the Imām again, and a new rescript was issued confirming the former one (Kashshī: 535–7). According to both Kashshī and Najāshī: 83, his anathematization was in the period of Ḥasan al-'Askarī (although this does not seem to be the case with *Kamāl*: 489; *Ghayba*: 214). A contemporary Shī'ite author (Muḥammad Taqī al-Tustarī, 1:675) has cast doubt on this on the basis of a reference in the first rescript to Ibn Hilāl's death, while his date of death is given by Najāshī: 83 and Ṭūsī, *Fihrist*: 36 as 267/880– 881. He also argues that Ṭūsī (in his *Ghayba*: 245) mentioned that the man contested the authority of the second agent of the vanished Imām, Muḥammad b. 'Uthmān, and that consequently (according to *Ghayba*: 245, 254) he was anathematized by a rescript of the Imām by the hand of his third agent, Ḥusayn b. Rūḥ al-Nawbakhtī. The second argument is certainly wrong. The one who contested the authority of the second agent was another disciple of Ḥasan al-'Askarī, Aḥmad b. Hilāl al-Karkhī, whose anathematization was because of this challenge, not the embezzlement of the Imām's property, which was the case with 'Abartā'ī. This is explicitly mentioned in the rescript (Kashshī: 536). This author, like many others (such as Māmaqānī, 1:100; Khu'ī, 2:357), has failed to notice that Ṭūsī mentioned the two Ibn Hilāls in two different parts of his work, the 'Abartā'ī in the section on the "rebuked agents" of

Imām's representative in Qum, Aḥmad b. Isḥāq al-Ash'arī, asked the Imām to write a line for him so that he could always recognize his handwriting whenever he received a rescript in his name.[64]

There were, indeed, some new practices that set Ḥasan al-'Askarī's period of Imāmate apart from former periods. For obvious political reasons, he, unlike his forefathers, regularly attended the court, usually every Monday and Thursday during the caliph's public audience,[65] as one of the dignitaries of rank.[66] He also occasionally visited other court dignitaries during their public audiences.[67] He had vicious and rude enemies among the common people who shouted disrespectful words at him whenever he came out to go to the court[68] despite the great respect and reverence that the community and the government held for him.[69] Owing to the ever-increasing financial needs of the members of the House of the Prophet,

---

the former Imāms until the time of Ḥasan al-'Askarī, and the Karkhī in the section on the rebuked agents of the Twelfth Imām. These authors also failed to note that Ṭūsī said that the Karkhī was anathematized in a rescript to Ḥusayn b. Rūḥ "together with others," a point which is true in his case (see the rescript in *Ghayba*: 254; see also 228), not the 'Abartā'ī who was anathematized with two *ad hoc* rescripts (Kashshī: 535–7) addressed to 'Uthmān b. Sa'īd al-'Amrī (*Ghayba*: 214). The first argument of that contemporary author, however, has some truth in it. If one assumes that the date given for the 'Abartā'ī's death is authentic, there will actually be a conflict between Kashshī and Najāshī's accounts on the one hand and the related rescript on the other. The document, however, seems to be much more authoritative than the date, which may well be inaccurate, possibly by ten years. The man, thus, must have actually died before the death of Ḥasan al-'Askarī in 260/874.

64. Kulaynī, 1:513; *Manāqib*, 4:434.
65. Kulaynī, 1:511; *Ghayba*: 123, 129. See also Khuṣaybī: 337; Rāwandī, 1:426, 439, 445, 446, 447; *Manāqib*, 4:431; Irbilī, 3:302, 305; Pseudo Mas'ūdī: 243. For the days of the caliphs' public audiences see, *inter alia, Manāqib,* 4:368.
66. See *Ghayba*: 129.
67. Kulaynī, 1:503–4; *Kamāl*: 40–41, both quoting his visit to the vizier 'Ubayd Allāh b. Yaḥyā b. Khāqān (d. 263/877).
68. *Ghayba*: 123; *Manāqib*, 4:430.
69. See Kulaynī, 1:503–5; *Kamāl*: 40–43.

for whom the generosity of the Imām was always available,[70] he reportedly had to use his discretionary authority at times and deviate from the practices of his forefathers. It was a common phenomenon in the Shī'ite community of the third/ninth century that many of its members willed all their belongings to the Imām. According to Shī'ite law, however, a man could will only one-third of his belongings, and the remainder would go as inheritance to his heirs. The previous Imāms used to return to the heirs two thirds of any inheritance that was willed completely to them.[71] There is, however, a report that Ḥasan al-'Askari ordered the executor of the will of a deceased Shī'ite who had willed his entire property for the Imām, to sell it and send the entire value to him in spite of the fact that the executor explained in his letter to the Imām that the deceased man had left two nieces.[72] The language that the Imām used against his criticizers was unusually tough. In response to a Shī'ite who criticized the Imām's rending of his collar in his father's funeral procession, the Imām called him an idiot and predicted that he would die both an infidel and mad.[73] Clearly for the purpose of preparing the community for the situation it was going to experience in the imminent future, his style in answering legal questions was also significantly different from that of previous Imāms and much

70. See, for instance, Kulaynī, 1:506–10; Mufīd, *Irshād,* 1: 341–4; Rāwandī: 426–7, 434–6; *Manāqib*, 4:431–2; Irbilī, 3:202–4. For the Imām's extraordinary moral support of the descendants of the Prophet see Ḥasan al-Qummī: 211–12.

71. See, for Muḥammad al-Jawād, Ṭūsī, *Tahdhīb*, 9:189, 198, 242; idem, *Istibṣār*, 4:124, 125–6, 129, and for 'Alī al-Hādī, Kulaynī, 7:60.

72. Ṭūsī, *Tahdhīb*, 9:195; idem, *Istibṣār*, 4:123. This author thought that there were similar cases during the time of the two previous Imāms, but in the cases that he cited the legator or the executor had satisfied and obtained the consent of the heirs to the will. One of the author's own interpretations is that the will to the Imām is an exception to the general rule and that the limitation of one-third is for wills made for other charitable purposes, not for donations to the Imāms. The Imāms have the right to take the entire property willed into their possession; if they return any part of it to the heirs, it is their special favor and generosity, not a legal obligation. After all, the law is what they do; we have to obey and submit without asking about its legal basis (*Tahdhīb*, 9:196).

73. Kashshī: 573–4. (See also 541 for another example.)

closer to the way an ordinary jurisconsult would issue a *fatwā* (legal opinion) on a given matter.[74] This fact may have been behind the very unusual request of a disciple of his who, in a letter to the Imām concerning a legal matter, asked him to "consult the jurists" around him and return an answer with the right opinion.[75] The community asked the Imām to write for them a book of religious practice that could be used as a code of conduct. The book that he gave them[76] was later found to be a copy of an earlier work called *Kitāb Yawm wa layla* or *Kitāb al-Ta'dīb*[77] by Abū Ja'far Aḥmad b. 'Abd Allāh b. Mihrān, known as Ibn Khānabih.[78] The discovery was, thus, a great tribute to the book because it had gained the Imām's complete approval. When viewed from a distance, the history of the Imāmate from the ascension of Ḥasan al-'Askarī through the Minor Occultation seems to have been a period of preparation for the future transformation, an intermediary stage in which the Imāmite community evolved procedures for solving its doctrinal and legal problems without the authority of a present Imām. It did this by using its own well-established cultural resources.

Another problem that added to the difficulties of this period, and contributed greatly to the turmoil that followed the death of Ḥasan al-'Askarī was the claim of his brother, Ja'far b. 'Alī—later

74. See Kulaynī, 4:124, 5:118, 239, 293, 307, 310, 6:35, 7:37, 45–7, 150, 402; Ibn Bābawayh, *Faqīh*, 1:114, 2:153, 444, 3:67, 173, 242–3, 296, 304, 488, 508, 4:208–9, 227, 269; Ṭūsī, *Tahdhīb*, 1:431, 4:139, 6:192, 196, 7:35, 75, 90, 138, 150–51, 277, 9:129, 132, 161, 185, 214–15, 317; idem, *Istibṣār*, 1:195, 383, 2:108, 4:100, 113, 118, 167. See also his letter to the people of Qum in *Manāqib*, 4:425, in which he argued with the statement of a former Imām (*li-qawli 'l-'ālim salāmu 'llāhi 'alayh*).

75. Ṭūsī, *Tahdhīb*, 9:161–2; idem, *Istibṣār*, 4:113.

76. This seems to be the same as the *Risālat al-Muqni'a*, a compendium of religious laws that he issued to his followers in the year 255/869. A description of its material given in *Manāqib*, 4:424, shows that it was in the form of a collection of narratives that the Imām quoted from his father, 'Alī al-Hādī (cf. Najāshī: 166 where Rajā' b. Yaḥyā b. Sāmān al-'Abartā'ī al-Kātib, a transmitter from 'Alī al-Hādī, is said to have transmitted a treatise called *Risālat al-Muqni'a fi abwāb al-sharī'a*, obviously from that Imām).

77. Najāshī: 346.

78. On him, see Kashshī: 566; Najāshī: 91; Ṭūsī, *Fihrist*: 26.

to become known among the Shīʿites as Jaʿfar the Liar—to the position of Imām. The problem stemmed ultimately from the introduction of the Imām's financial representation system; its proximate origin lay in the time of Imām ʿAlī al-Hādī in, or shortly before, 248/862[79] when one of the Imām's chief agents in Sāmarrā', Fāris b. Ḥātim b. Māhawayh al-Qazwīnī,[80] became embroiled in a dispute with another aide, the aforementioned ʿAlī b. Jaʿfar al-Humānī. This dispute led eventually to bitter quarrels and mutual vituperation,[81] which led in turn to uneasiness within the Shīʿite community[82] and the unwillingness of some to pay their financial obligations to the Imām.[83] Furthermore, local representatives of the Imām who had previously forwarded their collections to the Imām through these two aides no longer knew which one they could trust.[84] The Imām sided with ʿAlī b. Jaʿfar against Fāris and ordered his representatives to stop using the latter for their business with the Imām; at the same time, however, he asked his representatives to keep silent about his decision and to avoid provoking Fāris.[85] The Imām did this because Fāris was an influential man. He was the main intermediary between the Imām and the Shīʿites of Jibāl, the central and western parts of Iran, who normally sent their religious obligations to the Imām through him.[86] Fāris continued to receive funds from that region despite the Imām's instructions to the contrary

79. Kashshī: 527.
80. The man is said to have held some exaggerated and heretical views (Kashshī: 522), a fact attested by the title of one of his works, *Kitāb ʿAdad al-aʾimma min ḥisāb al-jumal* (Najāshī: 310). Two of his brothers also were among the disciples of ʿAlī al-Hādī, Ṭāhir, who, too, later deviated from the mainstream Imāmism (Najāshī: 208; Ibn al-Ghaḍā'irī, 3:228; Ṭūsī, *Fihrist*: 86; idem, *Rijāl*: 379, 477; see also Kulaynī 1:86) and Aḥmad (Kashshī: 4–5). On Fāris's close association with ʿAlī al-Hādī see also Khuṣaybī: 317, 318.
81. Kashshī: 523,527.
82. Ibid.: 527, 528.
83. Ibid.: 527.
84. See the letter of the representative in Hamadān to the Imām in 248/862–863 in Kashshī: 523, 527, and that of the representative in Baghdad (ibid.: 543, 579) in the same source: 528.
85. Kashshī: 522, 528.
86. Ibid.: 526.

and no longer forwarded them to his putative master.[87] At this juncture the Imām decided to make the matter public and asked his representatives to announce to the Shī'ite community that Fāris was no longer associated with him and should not be given funds meant for the Imām.[88] He then formally anathematized Fāris in two letters,[89] one dated Tuesday, 9 of Rabī' I, 250/April 20, 864.[90] Fāris thereupon began an open campaign against the Imām. The sources provide no details about his activities other than to say that he became a major troublemaker, calling people to *bid'a* and seeking to win them over to his own faction.[91] In a message sent to some of his followers who had come to Sāmarrā' from central Iran,[92] the Imām charged Fāris with having made "a wicked utterance."[93] The gravity of the situation is seen in the Imām's next move, an extraordinary, although not totally unprecedented,[94] call by the Imām for the assassination of his rogue agent. The order was carried out by one of the Imām's followers.[95]

87. Ibid.: 525.
88. Ibid.: 525, 526.
89. Ibid.: 525–6; *Ghayba*: 213–14.
90. This letter was addressed to 'Alī b. 'Umar al-Qazwīnī (*Ghayba*: 213), who seems to be the same as 'Alī b. 'Amr (*sic*) al-Qazwīnī al-'Aṭṭār mentioned by Kashshī: 526, who came to Sāmarrā' from Qazwīn carrying religious funds for the Imām and stayed with Fāris. A messenger was immediately sent by 'Uthmān b. Sa'īd al-'Amrī to inform the man that the Imām had disavowed Fāris and that the funds should be forwarded to 'Amrī. The Qazwīnī followed the instruction, and, then, the Imām pronounced a formal curse on Fāris (Kashshī : 526). This is apparently a reference to the same letter recorded in *Ghayba*: 213.
91. Kashshī: 524.
92. Ibid.: 557.
93. Ibid.: 527.
94. See Kashshī: 529 where Imām Muḥammad al-Jawād is quoted as instructing one of his followers to assassinate two deceitful fellows who pretended to be followers and propagandists of the Imām and managed to attract people to themselves and presumably made money by collecting funds that were to be paid to the Imām.
95. Ibid.: 524. The assassin continued to receive a payment from Ḥasan al-'Askarī until his death in 260/874 shortly after the death of Ḥasan (Kulaynī, 1:524).

Fāris had been very much attached to Muḥammad,[96] the son of 'Alī al-Hādī who died one year or two[97] after the assassination of Fāris, presumably on the expectation that he would serve as the chief agent of the next Imām. After the death of 'Alī al-Hādī, the followers of Fāris remained loyal to Muḥammad and maintained that he was the true Imām in spite of the fact that he died before his father.[98] This was, perhaps, partly an act of defiance directed against 'Alī al-Hādī, who had named Ḥasan as his successor, and partly against Ḥasan himself who, unlike 'Alī al-Hādī's third son, Ja'far, had supported his father's actions against Fāris. The followers of Fāris, thus, formed their own splinter group within the Imāmite community against Ḥasan's followers and held that Muḥammad had appointed his younger brother, Ja'far, as his successor and that Ja'far was the true Imām after 'Alī al-Hādī.[99] There were claims that before his death Muḥammad had received the sacred paraphernalia of the Imāmate from his father as the designated successor and had given them to his servant Nafīs who, in turn, passed them on to Ja'far.[100] It should be noted that a few others claimed that 'Alī

96. Khuṣaybī: 385. See also 'Abd al-Jabbār, 20 (2):182, quoting from Nawbakhtī.
97. According to Khuṣaybī: 385, he died four years and ten months before his father's death, which occurred on 25 Jumādā II/21 June (Khuṣaybī: 313; Ibn Abi 'l-Thalj: 86; Ibn al-Khashshāb: 197; Khaṭīb, 12:57), or 26 Jumādā II/22 June (Ṭabarī, 9:381; Kulaynī, 1:497; Mas'ūdī, *Murūj*, 5: 81–2) or 3 Rajab/28 June (Nawbakhtī: 101; Sa'd b. 'Abd Allāh: 99–100; Ṭabrisī, *Tāj al-mawālīd*: 132; *Manāqib*, 4:401 [quoting Ibn 'Ayyāsh]—Everyone, however, seems to agree that it was on a Monday) of the year 254/868. This will set Muḥammad's death at around the beginning of Ramaḍān 249/mid-September 863, which cannot be correct as it is before even the public anathematization of Fāris by 'Alī al-Hādī and naturally is before Fāris's assassination, whereas Muḥammad's death, as noted above, occurred after Fāris's assassination (see also 'Abd al-Jabbār, 20 [2]:182 quoting from Nawbakhtī). Another report in Kulaynī, 1:327 sets Ḥasan's age at the time of Muḥammad's death at around twenty or a little more. This sets the date of the latter's death at around 252/866, which agrees with the above reference.
98. Ibn Qiba, *Naqḍ kitāb al-ishhād*: para. 27.
99. Nawbakhtī: 95; Abū Ḥātim al-Rāzī: 291; Khuṣaybī: 384–5, 388; 'Abd al-Jabbār, 20 (2): 182; Shahrastānī, 1:199.
100. Nawbakhtī: 114–15; Sa'd b. 'Abd Allāh: 112–14.

al-Hādī himself had appointed Ja'far, rather than Ḥasan, as his successor.[101]

Ja'far had thus assembled a small following, mainly from among the followers of Fāris, during the incumbency of his brother Ḥasan al-'Askarī.[102] Some of Ja'far's followers were quite outspoken in their opposition to Ḥasan and his followers,[103] denying that he possessed the level of learning required of an Imām and even calling his followers the "Party of the Jackass" (*Ḥimāriyya*).[104] Some went so far as to call Ḥasan and his followers infidels.[105] The leader of these schismatics was a sister of Fāris who never accepted Ḥasan as a legitimate Imām and was a major and influential supporter of Ja'far in his campaign for the Imāmate after the death of Ḥasan.[106] In return, Ja'far praised Fāris as a pious and virtuous man,[107] openly rejecting his father's and brother's pronouncements on the case. The whole episode led to bitter animosity between Ja'far and his brother, whose associates accused Ja'far of being morally corrupt and openly committing such sins as drinking wine.[108] Later, they also accused

101. Nawbakhtī: 104–5, 108–9 (with several errors in the latter case); Sa'd b. 'Abd Allāh: 101, 110–11. See also Khuṣaybī: 320, which claims that disagreement on whether the successor to the Imāmate will be Ḥasan or Ja'far had already started during the lifetime of 'Alī al-Hādī.
102. Khuṣaybī: 388. See further Abu 'l-Ḥasan al-Ash'arī: 116; Mufīd, *Majālis*, 2:97; Shahrastānī, 1:199.
103. Nawbakhtī: 115, Sa'd b. 'Abd Allāh: 113; Abū Ḥātim al-Rāzī: 291.
104. Abū Ḥātim al-Rāzī: 291, 292; Shahrastānī, 1:200. The account of *Dustūr al-munajjimīn*: 345b that assigns this name to those Imāmites who recognized Ja'far as Ḥasan's successor seems, thus, to be inaccurate.
105. Nawbakhtī: 115; Sa'd b. 'Abd Allāh: 113.
106. Nawbakhtī: 108; Abū Ḥātim al-Rāzī: 291. See also Shahrastānī 1:199 where Fāris himself is mentioned instead.
107. Ibn Qiba, *Naqḍ ibn bashshār*, para. 10.
108. Nawbakhtī: 110–11; Sa'd b. 'Abd Allāh: 109; Abu 'l-Ḥasan al-Ash'arī, 2:114; Kulaynī, 1:504, 509; Khuṣaybī, 249, 382; *Kamāl*: 42, 475, 477; Mufīd, *Majālis*, 2:103; *Ghayba*: 7, 133, 137, 175; 'Imād al-Dīn al-Ṭūsī: 609. Some sources even mention that Ja'far was popularly nicknamed *ziqq al-khamr* (wineskin) because of his well-known love for wine (see Khuṣaybī: 248; 'Umarī: 131; Ṭabrisī, *Tāj al-mawālīd*: 56; Ibn Shadqam: 61, 65). These sources also scorn him for having ordered his servants to carry candles in front of him wherever he went in town, even during daylight ('Umarī: 131; Ibn Shadqam: 61, 65). It was noted above that the Shī'a commonly

him of having skipped his daily prayers for forty days in a row, during which time he was occupied learning the art of juggling.[109] Although it is difficult to believe that people could accept as their Imām a man so notoriously irreligious, it seems that there is some truth in these reports, especially those concerning the time when Ja'far was young. In their refutation of the charges against Ja'far, some of his supporters made a point of saying that he had "distanced himself from the characteristics of his youth, and given up improper deeds."[110]

Ja'far and Ḥasan remained at odds with each other until Ḥasan's death, and never spoke to each other again.[111] As long as Ḥasan was alive, Ja'far was a continual source of trouble for him.[112] The counteraccusations, hatred, and animosity between Ja'far and the associates of Ḥasan reached their peak, and the matter became very violent. The unfortunate Nafīs, who was claimed to have passed the sacred paraphernalia from Muḥammad to Ja'far, was found drowned in a pool.[113] Two members of the Imāmite community of Sāmarrā' who had openly supported the claim of Ja'far were chased, according to a report by the order of Ḥasan. They had to escape for their lives to Kūfa and stay there until he died.[114] Taking all these and similar facts into account, the death of Ḥasan without a son and with no brother besides Ja'far[115] would pose a terrible problem

---

know him as Ja'far the Liar. His descendants and followers, however, normally mention his name with the epithet *al-zakī*, the pure (see, for instance, 'Arashī: 51; Husameddin, 1: 20).

109. *Ghayba*: 175.

110. See 'Umarī: 136, quoting his teacher Shaykh al-Sharaf al-'Ubaydalī (d. 435–437/1043–1046), in a treatise that he wrote in support of Ja'far called *al-Raḍawiyya fi nuṣrat ja'far b. 'alī*.

111. Nawbakhtī: 107; Ibn Qiba, *Naqḍ ibn bashshār*: para. 5. See also 'Umarī: 132, which traces these unhappy relations back to earlier stages in their lives when they were still young children.

112. Nawbakhtī: 107. See also Khuṣaybī: 382.

113. Nawbakhtī: 115; Sa'd b. 'Abd Allāh: 114.

114. Khuṣaybī: 385.

115. Ya'qūbī, 2:503; Ibn Abi 'l-Thalj: 111; 'Umarī: 130. See also Ibn Qiba, *Naqḍ ibn bashshār*, paras. 4– 5. It should be noted that some sources (al-Ṭabarī al-Shī'ī: 217; Khuṣaybī: 313; Ḥasan al-Qummī: 203; Mufīd, *Irshād*: 334; Ṭabrisī, *I'lām*: 366; idem, *Tāj al-mawālīd*: 56; *Manāqib*, 4:402)

for the Imām's close associates, who were now in control of the Imāmate administration,[116] for they were absolutely unwilling to turn it over to Ja'far.[117] It would also plunge the entire Imāmite community into the most difficult doctrinal turmoil it had ever experienced.[118] Fortunately, that situation did not come up and the

---

name a fourth son for 'Alī al-Hādī (besides Ḥasan, Ja'far and Muḥammad) as Ḥusayn. Some mentioned that this son also died in his father's lifetime in Sāmarrā' (Fakhr al-Dīn al-Rāzī, *Shajara*: 78). Others mentioned that the voice of the Twelfth Imām was very much like this uncle of his. They argued with a report in Ṭūsī, *Amālī*, 1:294, in which, according to them, an Imāmite is said to have heard the Twelfth Imām, whose voice he described as resembling the voice of Ḥusayn, son of Imām 'Alī al-Hādī (see, for instance, Muḥammad Taqī al-Tustarī, *Tawarīkh al-nabī wa 'l-āl*: 66). However, the one named in that report is Ḥusayn b. 'Alī b. Ja'far, Ibn al-Riḍā, clearly a great-grandson of 'Alī al-Hādī via his son Ja'far. The Imāmite who claimed he had seen the Twelfth Imām and described his voice, Abu 'l-Ṭayyib Aḥmad b. Muḥammad b. Bū Ṭayr, was a grandson of a servant of 'Alī al-Hādī (Ṭūsī, *Amālī*, 1:305–6), clearly a contemporary of 'Alī al-Hādī's above-mentioned great-grandson and not of a son of his. The actual existence of such a son is, therefore, extremely doubtful. At any rate, at the moment of 'Alī al-Hādī's death, Ḥasan and Ja'far were his only surviving male descendants (Ibn Qiba, *Naqḍ ibn bashshār,* paras. 4–5. See also Mufīd, *Irshād*: 351).

116. See *Ghayba*: 76. They included 'Uthmān b. Sa'īd al-'Amrī, his son Muḥammad, Abū Hāshim Dāwūd b. al-Qāsim al-Ja'farī, the most senior in his time among the Ṭālibids (Mas'ūdī, *Murūj*, 5:62), and a few others. See Abu 'l-Ṣalāḥ al-Ḥalabī: 185–6.

117. That would be especially unfavorable to 'Uthmān b. Sa'īd al-'Amrī, who was instrumental in the anathematization of Fāris. See Kashshī: 526.

118. Furthermore, there was a technical problem too because lateral succession to Imāmate was disallowed (except for the second and third Imāms) according to a well-known report originating from the sectarian debates between the Faṭḥites and mainstream Imāmites in the middle of the second/eighth century (see Nawbakhtī: 80; Sa'd b. 'Abd Allāh: 102, 103; Abū Sahl al-Nawbakhtī: 92; 'Alī b. Bābawayh: 179, 188–9, 191; Kulaynī, 1: 285–6; *Kamāl*: 414–17, 426; *Ghayba*: 136, 176). Nevertheless, had the situation been different and Ja'far been qualified to be the next Imām, his could have been another case of the *badā'*. Indeed, some of his followers used that concept for this purpose (see Sa'd b. 'Abd Allāh: 110) as did Ja'far himself (Kulaynī, 1: 391; see also *Kamāl*: 488) and some other Shī'ite groups of the time (Sa'd b. 'Abd Allāh: 108) for similar purposes.

Twelfth Imām was born, although until his father's death, the news about his birth and existence was not publicized.[119]

Immediately after the abrupt death of Imām Ḥasan al-ʻAskarī in 260/874, his close associates,[120] headed by ʻUthmān b. Saʻīd al-ʻAmrī, made it public that the Imām had a son who was the legitimate successor to the Imāmate. The son, according to ʻAmrī, was in hiding because he feared he would be captured and killed by the government.[121] The mere fact that this possibility was suggested and accepted by many indicates that many feared the government had run out of patience with the Shīʻites in general and their leaders in particular.[122] There were, however, disagreements about the age of the son, for his birthdate is given differently in different sources.[123] Some Shīʻites even held that he was still *in utero* when his father died.[124]

119. Nawbakhtī: 105 (*wa lam yuʻraf lahu waladun ẓāhir*); Saʻd b. ʻAbd Allāh: 102 (*wa lam yura lahu khalaf...*).
120. Abū Sahl al-Nawbakhtī: 92–3; Abu 'l-Ṣalāḥ al-Ḥalabī: 185, who points out that the birth of the Twelfth Imām and the fact that his father appointed him as his successor were both attested to and reported by this group of his father's associates. Their *naṣṣ* (explicit designation, an Imāmite requirement for the establishment of the Imāmate of any Imām), therefore, substituted for the *naṣṣ* of his father.
121. *Ghayba*: 199.
122. See also Saʻd b. ʻAbd Allāh: 105; Kulaynī, 1:504; *Kamāl*: 44.
123. His birthdate is variously given as 1 Ramaḍān 254/24 August 868 (*Kamāl*: 473, 474), 8 Shaʻbān 255/23 July 869 (Ḥasan al-Qummī: 204; *Dustūr al-munajjimīn*: 345b), 15 Shaʻbān 255/15 July 869 (Kulaynī, 1:514; *Kamāl*: 430; see also *Ghayba*: 141 on the basis of a report from Ḥakīma, daughter of Imām Muḥammad al-Jawād, but the same report appears without that date in *Kamāl*: 424 and with a different date in Khuṣaybī: 355), 8 Shaʻbān 256/11 July 870 (*Kamāl*: 432; *Ghayba*: 241–2; see also Kulaynī, 1:329; *Kamāl*: 430; *Ghayba*: 164, 258 [the latter three mentioning the *Hijrī* year 256 without specifying the day and month]), 8 Shaʻbān 257/24 June 871 (al-Ṭabarī al-Shīʻī: 270–71, 272; Khuṣaybī: 334, 355, 387), 15 Shaʻbān 257/1 July 871 (al-Ṭabarī al-Shīʻī: 271), 19 Rabīʻ I, 258/3 February 872 (Ibn Khallikān, 4: 176 [quoting Ibn al-Azraq in his *Ta'rīkh mayyāfāriqīn*]), 23 Ramaḍān 258/3 July 872 (Ibn Ṭalḥa: 89; Irbilī, 3:227; see also Kulaynī, 1:515; *Kamāl*: 436; Ibn Abi 'l-Thalj: 88; Ḥasan al-Qummī: 204); and 259 (Ibn Abi 'l-Thalj: 88, editor's footnote quoting a manuscript of Khuṣaybī [MS 2973, Marʻashī Library, Qum]).
124. Nawbakhtī: 112, 113; Saʻd b. ʻAbd Allāh: 114, 115; Kulaynī, 1:337; Nuʻmānī: 166; Mufīd, *Majālis*, 2:98–9; Ibn Ḥazm, *Jamhara*: 55.

This latter assertion was, however, put forward by Ḥasan's mother,[125] Ḥudayth, for a different purpose. She was the one named in Ḥasan's will, with no mention of a son or anyone else.[126] She was in Medina when Ḥasan died, but she came to Sāmarrā' immediately when she heard the news[127] to try to stop Ja'far from seizing her son's inheritance. According to the Sunnite law of inheritance followed by the caliphate, if Ḥasan had died without a son, his inheritance would be divided between his mother and Ja'far. Shī'ite law, however, would give it all to her, because it did not allow siblings to inherit while a parent still lived. To prevent Ja'far from getting any part of her son's inheritance, she told the government officials that one of Ḥasan's slave girls[128] was pregnant by him. Considering this to be a total fabrication designed with no other aim in mind than to exclude him from his brother's inheritance, Ja'far denounced Ḥudayth to the government.[129] This was another

125. *Dustūr al-munajjimīn*: 345b. Other sources attribute this to one of Ḥasan's slave girls who claimed that she herself (*Kamāl*: 474, 476) or another slave girl (Kulaynī, 1:505; *Kamāl*: 43) was pregnant.

126. Mufīd, *al-Fuṣūl al-'ashara*: 348, 357; *Ghayba*: 75, 138. See also Kulaynī, 1:505; *Kamāl*: 43. She was also the one considered by many Imāmites as the caretaker of the office in the absence of her vanished grandson. See *Kamāl*: 507; Khuṣaybī: 366 where Ḥakīma (or Khadīja), the aunt of Ḥasan al-'Askarī, refers a wandering follower of his in the year 262/875–876 to the "*Jaddah* (grandmother), mother of Abū Muḥammad (al-Ḥasan)." The same report appears with the date 282/895–896 in *Kamāl*: 501, which is an obvious error.

127. *Kamāl*: 474, 476.

128. According to Khuṣaybī: 248, he had two slave girls, Narjis (same as Ṣaqīl [*Ghayba*: 241; 'Umarī: 132] mentioned in other sources as the mother of the Twelfth Imām; see, for instance, *Kamāl*: 475), and Wardās, who is described as *kitābiyya*, a non-Muslim from the People of the Scripture, undoubtedly a Christian. They are apparently the same as Nasīm and Māriya mentioned in Khuṣaybī: 357 (Nasīm is also mentioned in *Kamāl*: 441). According to a report in *Kamāl*: 419–423 Narjis was also originally a Christian-Roman slave girl, in fact a member of the Byzantine royal family who was captured by the Muslims in a war and brought to *Dār al-islām*. Having Roman slave girls was a common phenomenon in the Islamic community of those ages. Imām 'Alī al-Riḍā also reportedly had a Christian slave girl (see Ṭūsī, *Tahdhīb,* 1:399).

129. *Kamāl,* 474, 476; *Dustūr al-munajjimīn*: 345b. See also Mufīd, *al-Fuṣūl al-'ashara*: 348, 354–5, 356.

of Ja'far's departures from Shī'ite tradition, which prohibited recourse to an "unjust" judicial system, whether one's claim was true or false.[130] The slave girl was put in the house of Muḥammad b. 'Alī b. Ḥamza al-'Alawī, a respected scholar from the 'Alīd family,[131] under government surveillance until it became clear that she was not pregnant. She was then released and lived for many years in Baghdad, at least for a while in the house of a member of the influential Shī'ite family of Banū Nawbakht, Ḥasan b. Ja'far al-Kātib. Later, she was seized once again by the government and put under surveillance until she died around the turn of the century.[132] Meanwhile, after seven years of struggle, the inheritance of Ḥasan had been divided between Ḥudayth and Ja'far.[133]

'Uthmān b. Sa'īd al-'Amrī continued as caretaker of the office of Imāmate in the absence of Ḥasan's son.[134] Although some harbored deep doubts about the actual existence of such a son,[135] most of the

130. See 'Ayyāshī, 1:254; Kulaynī, 1:67, 7:411–12; Qāḍī Nu'mān, 2:530; Ibn Bābawayh, *Faqīh,* 3:2–4; Ṭūsī, *Tahdhīb,* 6:301–3.

131. Najāshī: 347–8. See also *Dustūr al-munajjimīn*: 345b where it is said that she was put under the care of an 'Alīd for four years because it was claimed that she was pregnant. Some reports suggest that she was imprisoned in the house of the caliph (*Kamāl*: 474) or put under the care of the chief judge (ibid.: 476). The detention or surveillance continued for two years (Abū Sahl al-Nawbakhtī: 90; Ibn Ḥazm: 4:158. See also *Kamāl*: 43 where the figure "two years or more" is given in a report, but the same report in Kulaynī, 1:505, does not mention that figure. This latter report does not specify her whereabouts during that period. See further Khuṣaybī: 248, 320; Mufīd, *Fuṣūl*: 348, 354–5, 356).

132. Ibn Ḥazm, 4:158.

133. Ibid. See also Nawbakhtī: 105; Sa'd b. 'Abd Allāh: 102.

134. A report even suggests that Ḥasan al-'Askarī instructed his followers to obey 'Amrī after his own death because he would be the deputy of the Imām and the affairs (of the Imāmate) would be entrusted with him (*Ghayba*: 217). The report seems to be a later contribution.

135. See Kulaynī, 1:318; *Kamāl*: 485, 487; *Ghayba*, 146, 218. See also Kulaynī, 1:329 (quoted also in *Ghayba*: 146, 218) where it is quoted that Aḥmad b. Isḥāq al-Ash'arī, Ḥasan al-'Askarī's representative in Qum (Kashshī: 557–8; al-Ṭabarī al-Shī'ī: 272; Khuṣaybī: 372, 383), urged someone to ask 'Amrī if he had personally seen the son. The name of Aḥmad b. Isḥāq himself is, however, included in the list of those who had personally seen

local representatives publicly acknowledged his existence. Those who did so were confirmed in their posts and were authorized to collect funds from the Imāmite community on behalf of the hidden Imām.[136] Most Shī'ites in various towns of Iran and especially Qum, which was the main center of Shī'ite scholarship in this age, accepted the new situation and continued to pay their taxes to the local representatives, who were now the agents of 'Amrī.[137] In Iraq, however, the situation was different. Kūfa had been a Shī'ite town for two centuries and was, by reason of its proximity to Sāmarrā', closely attuned to movements and disputes within the inner core of the Imāmate and always rife with unorthodox tendencies. The sources name many different sects that emerged after the death of Ḥasan al-'Askarī within the Imāmite community,[138] presumably basically referring to the community in Kūfa and other towns of Iraq. Many members of that community were puzzled by the situation and did not know how to react.[139] Many left the community

---

the son (*Kamāl*: 442; see also Ṭūsī, *Fihrist*: 26), apparently on the basis of a story that is included in *Kamāl*: 454–65. He had also reportedly received a letter from Ḥasan al-'Askarī when the son was born, in which the Imām gave him the news of the birth of his son (ibid.: 433–4).

136. Kulaynī, 1:518. In a somewhat similar case those Ṭālibids of Medina who maintained good relations with the Imāms and acknowledged them used to receive an allowance from the house of the Imām in Sāmarrā'. After the death of Ḥasan those who acknowledged the existence and Imāmate of the son continued to receive their payment but for those who did not the payment was discontinued (Kulaynī, 1:518–19; Khuṣaybī: 370).

137. See *Kamāl*: 478–9, 501–3, 509, 516, 518.

138. Nawbakhtī: 105–119 (14 sects); Sa'd b. 'Abd Allāh: 102–116 (15 sects); Abū Ḥātim al-Rāzī, 292 (11 sects); Mas'ūdī, *Murūj*: 5:108 (20 sects); Mufīd, *Majālis*: 2:97–9 (14 sects); Shahrastānī, 1:200–202 (11 sects); *Dustūr al-munajjimīn*: 345b (15 sects). See also Iqbāl: 160–65.

139. *Kamāl*: 408; Khazzāz: 290. For examples of the uncertainties and doubts among the Shī'ites immediately after the death of Ḥasan, see *Kamāl*: 426, 429, 487; *Ghayba*: 138, 172; also Abū Ghālib al-Zurārī: 141 who reports that in 260/874 the Shī'ite community sent an emissary to Medina to investigate the existence of the son, clearly because it was claimed that the son had been sent by his father to that town (*Kulaynī*, 1:328; see also 340).

for other Islamic sects.[140] A large number,[141] possibly even the majority,[142] recognized Ja'far as the Imām.[143] The Faṭḥites, who maintained that the succession need not necessarily pass from father to son and that two brothers could both become Imāms, did not face a doctrinal problem and followed Ja'far as Imām after Ḥasan.[144] Ḥasan b. 'Alī b. Faḍḍāl,[145] the most prominent jurisconsult in the Imāmite community of Kūfa,[146] and 'Alī al-Ṭāḥin, a Kūfan *mutakallim* and prominent member of the Faṭḥite community,[147] were among the Faṭḥites who followed Ja'far. It is obviously for this reason that Ja'far was described by some as "the Imām of the second [generation of the] Faṭḥites" (*imām al-faṭḥiyya al-thāniya*).[148] Ja'far's following was more diverse than this, however. In addition to the Faṭḥites, it included those who counted him as successor to 'Alī al-Hādī or to his other brother, Muḥammad.[149] Some of these were originally followers of Ḥasan who had lost faith in him when he died with no apparent

140. *Kamāl*: 408. For examples of that see Kulaynī, 1:520; 'Abd al-Jabbār, *Tathbīt dalā'il al-nubuwwa,* 2:390; Ḥusayn b. 'Abd al-Wahhāb: 146.
141. See the report narrated in *Kamāl*: 320, 321; *Ghayba*: 136; Irbilī, 3:246, according to which Imām 'Alī al-Hādī predicted at Ja'far's birth that he would mislead "a large number of people."
142. Abū Ṭālib: 210.
143. Nawbakhtī: 107–9, 115; Sa'd b. 'Abd Allāh: 110–14; Abu 'l-Ḥasan al-Ash'arī, 1:116; *Kamāl*: 408; Khazzāz: 290; Abū Ḥātim al-Rāzī: 291; Mufīd, *Majālis*, 2: 98–99, 103; *Ghayba*: 55, 57, 133, 135; Ibn Ḥazm, 4: 158; 'Umarī: 135; *Dustūr al-munajjimīn*: 345b; Shahrastānī, 1:199–200; Fakhr al-Dīn al-Rāzī, *I'tiqādāt*: 68; idem, *Muḥaṣṣal*: 356.
144. Nawbakhtī: 107–8, 119; Sa'd b. 'Abd Allāh: 110, 111–12; *Ghayba*: 55, 57, 135.
145. Abū Ḥātim al-Rāzī: 291; Khuṣaybī: 382, 389; Shahrastānī, 1:200.
146. Najāshī: 257.
147. Nawbakhtī: 108; Abū Ḥātim al-Rāzī: 291; Shahrastānī, 1:199. He is 'Alī b. Ṭāḥī al-Khazzāz in Nawbakhtī, but 'Alī b. *fulān* al-Ṭāḥin in the latter two works. According to Nawbakhtī, he was among the followers of Ḥasan and joined Ja'far's campaign after Ḥasan's death, but according to the other two sources, he joined Ja'far immediately after the death of 'Alī al-Hādī.
148. Ibn Bābawayh, *Ma'ānī*: 65.
149. Nawbakhtī: 108–9, 114–15; Sa'd b. 'Abd Allāh: 110–11, 112–14; Abu 'l-Ḥasan al-Ash'arī: 116; Abū Ḥātim al-Rāzī: 291; Mufīd, *Majālis*, 2:97, 98: Shahrastānī, 1:199–200.

son.[150] The majority, however, simply considered Ja'far to be another name on the list of Imāms after Ḥasan. For some he was the twelfth Imām, whereas for the Faṭḥites, who had already added to their list the name of 'Abd Allāh, son of Ja'far al-Ṣādiq, he was the thirteenth. The followers of Ja'far became known in this period as the *Ja'fariyya,*[151] a title coined in the previous century for the followers of Imām Ja'far al-Ṣādiq. Their opponents, who believed in the Imāmate of the vanished son of Ḥasan, used to call them *Ṭāḥiniyya* after the head of the movement and its main apologist in Kūfa, 'Alī al-Ṭāḥin.[152] Heated sectarian debates flared between the two groups,[153] and tracts and treatises were exchanged.[154]

These disputes raged for quite some time. The house of the Imāmate was divided. The mother of Ḥasan, Ḥudayth, and his aunt, Ḥakīma, the daughter of Imām Muḥammad al-Jawād,[155] supported the existence and Imāmate of the son,[156]whereas Ḥasan's only

150. Nawbakhtī: 108–9; Sa'd b. 'Abd Allāh: 110–11; Mufīd, *Majālis*, 2:97; Fakhr al-Dīn al-Rāzī, *Muḥaṣṣal*: 356.

151. Sa'd b. 'Abd Allāh: 101; Ibn Qiba, *Naqḍ ibn bashshār*: para. 5; Fakhr al-dīn al-Rāzī, *I'tiqādāt*: 68. See also the title of Sa'd b. 'Abd Allāh's polemic against them in Najāshī: 177 (see below, n. 154).

152. Abū Ḥātim al-Rāzī: 291.

153. For examples of that see *Kamāl*: 511. See also *Ghayba*: 175.

154. These include the tract in support of Ja'far written by Abu 'l-Ḥasan 'Alī b. Aḥmad b. Bashshār and the refutation of it by Ibn Qiba (both texts follow in the second part of the present work); also the treatise by Sa'd b. 'Abd Allāh b. Abī Khalaf al-Ash'arī al-Qummī (d. 299–301/912–914) against the followers of Ja'far entitled *Kitāb al-Ḍiyā' fi 'l-radd 'ala 'l-muḥammadiyya wa 'l-ja'fariyya* (Najāshī: 177). This latter treatise was extant at least until the late fifth/eleventh century as evidenced by a quotation from it in a work of that period, *Dustūr al-munajjimīn*: 344b.

155. See Khuṣaybī: 334, 355–7; *Kamāl*: 418, 423, 424–30; *Ghayba*: 138 (where it is Khadīja instead of Ḥakīma, also in Khuṣaybī: 366), 141–144; Ḥusayn b. 'Abd al-Wahhāb: 138–41; 'Umarī: 128, 130, 132; *Manāqib*, 4:394, Ibn Ṭāwūs, *Muhaj*: 44.

156. The account of the son's birth is quoted on the authority of this aunt of Ḥasan al-'Askarī, who was present at the birth (*Kamāl*: 424–30). In a different report, however, she is quoted as telling that she had not herself seen the son; she rather came to know it through a note that Ḥasan had sent his mother when the son was born, giving her the news of the birth (ibid.: 501, 507).

sister,[157] the only other surviving descendant of 'Alī al-Hādī[158] besides Ja'far, supported the claim of Ja'far.[159] High-ranking Shī'ite officials were also divided; some supported Ja'far and others Ḥasan's mother.[160] Ja'far did not live long.[161] His followers then turned to his son, Abu 'l-Ḥasan 'Alī,[162] although some held that he shared

157. The name of this sister is variously given as Fāṭima (Abū Ḥātim al-Rāzī: 292; Shahrastānī, 1:200), Dalāla (al-Ṭabarī al-Shī'ī: 217), 'Aliyya (Ṭabrisī, *I'lām*: 366; *Manāqib*, 4:402) and 'Ā'isha (Mufīd, *Irshād*: 334; Ṭabrisī, *Tāj*: 56; Ibn al-Muṭahhar, *Mustajād*: 225.) Some genealogists, therefore, have thought that 'Alī al-Hādī had three daughters, Fāṭima, 'Ā'isha, and Burayha. (See, for instance, Fakhr al-Dīn al-Rāzī, *Shajara*: 78.) It can confidently be suggested that the first name (Fāṭima) was the real one and one or both of the next two (Dalāla and 'Aliyya) the nicknames. The name 'Ā'isha is presumably the misspelled form of 'Aliyya.

158. See Dhahabī, *Siyar*, 12:121, quoting Ibn Ḥazm in his *Fiṣal*, that the inheritance of Ḥasan was seized by his brother Ja'far and a sister of his (read *ukhtun lahu* for *akhun lahu*). The reference does not, however, appear in the edited copy of Ibn Ḥazm's *Fiṣal*, 4:158.

159. This fact is attested to by the point maintained by many followers of Ja'far that she was one of his two successors after his death (see below, n. 163).

160. See Ibn Ḥazm, 4:158; Subkī, *Fatāwā*, 2:568; Dhahabī, *Siyar*, 13:121. See also 'Umarī: 130.

161. 'Umarī: 135 gave the date of his death as 271/884–885, but added that he was forty-five years old when he died. This sets the birth of Ja'far in 226/840–841, which clearly cannot be correct because Ja'far was younger than his brother Ḥasan (Kulaynī, 1:326, 328; Khuṣaybī: 386), and Ḥasan was born in 231/845 (Khaṭīb, 7:366; Irbilī, 3:271–3; Ḥusayn b. 'Abd al-Wahhāb: 134; Ibn Abi 'l-Thalj: 87; Ibn al-Khashshāb: 198–9; Ibn al-Jawzī, *Muntaẓam*, 12:158; Sibṭ Ibn al-Jawzī: 362) or 232/846 (Ḥimyarī, *Dalā'il* [quoted in Irbilī, 3:308]; Kulaynī, 1:503; Mufīd, *Irshād*: 335; Ibn al-Athīr, 7:274) [the year 233/847 given by Khuṣaybī: 327 (see also al-Ṭabarī al-Shī'ī: 223) is most likely wrong]. In the editor's introduction to the first volume of the Qur'ānic commentary of Ja'far's descendant, Seyyid Ahmed Husameddin, Ja'far's birth date appears as 849 (Husameddin, 1:20), that is, 235–236 *Hijrī* era, which seems to be correct. So if he was forty-five years old when he died, he must have died in 281/894–895.

162. He is described in some of the sources as the chief syndic of the Ṭālibids (*sayyid al-nuqabā'*) of Baghdad (Marwazī: 9; Fakhr al-Dīn al-Rāzī, *Shajara*: 79, 80. See also Ibn Funduq, 2:692). His descendants later were notable people in Baghdad (Fakhr al-Dīn al-Rāzī, *Shajara*: 80) and several of them served as syndics of the Ṭālibids (*naqīb*) in different towns (Najāshī: 269; 'Umarī: 135; Fakhr al-Dīn al-Rāzī, *Shajara*: 80; Kammūna, 1:143, 2:3).

the Imāmate with Fāṭima, the sister of Ja'far.[163] After 'Alī and Fāṭima, they carried the same claim to other descendants of Ja'far.[164] At the turn of the century, the Iraqi Imāmites were divided into two opposing camps; those who adhered to the son of Ḥasan and those who championed Ja'far's descendants.[165]

It is not quite clear how much longer the supporters of Ja'far and his descendants existed as a separate sect in the Shī'ite community. By 373/983-984 when Mufīd was writing the chapter on various Imāmite sects in his *Kitāb al-Majālis,* he did not know anyone who believed in Ja'far as the Imām.[166] By 410/1019-1020 when he was writing his main book on the Occultation,[167] many of the descendants of Ja'far had already converted to mainstream Twelver Shī'ism; in fact, Mufīd did not know any descendant of Ja'far who disagreed with the Twelvers on the question of the Imāmate of Ḥasan al-'Askarī's son.[168] Ṭūsī emphasized the same point in his book on the Occultation written in 447/1055-1056;[169] by then this sect had completely disappeared and none of its followers remained.[170]

A descendant of his, Yaḥyā b. Ḥamza b. 'Alī b. Ibrāhīm b. Muḥammad b. Idrīs b. 'Alī b. Ja'far ('Arashī: 51, presumably with missing names of additional intermediate persons in this genealogical table), a prolific Zaydite scholar (on him see Ḥibshī: 67–78; Ziriklī, 9:175 and the sources mentioned in these two works), emerged in 729/1328– 1329 in Yemen and called people to himself as the *imām* al-Mu'ayyad bi 'llāh. He was recognized and accepted as *imām* by many people until his death in 749/1344–1349. A descendant of this scholar, Sharaf al-Dīn b. Muḥammad b. 'Abd Allāh (d. 1307/1890), assumed the imāmate of a part of Yemen as the *imām* al-Hādi li-Dīn Allāh from 1295/1878 until his death ('Arashī: 79). The family has produced other notables and scholars up to the present (see the editor's introduction to Yaḥyā b. Ḥamza's *Tasfiyat al-qulūb:* 5).

163. Abū Ḥātim al-Rāzī: 292; Shahrastānī, 1:200.
164. Abū Zayd al-'Alawī: para. 24; 'Umarī: 135; Shahrastānī, 1:200.
165. Abū Ḥātim al-Rāzī: 293.
166. Mufīd, *Majālis*, 2:99.
167. This is his *al-Fuṣūl al-'ashara fī 'l-ghayba.* See its date of compilation in pp. 349 and 366 of the book.
168. Mufīd, *al-Fuṣūl al-'ashara*: 356.
169. *Ghayba*: 218.
170. Ibid.: 133, 137.

These accounts seem to be reliable for the area within the traditional boundaries of Shī'ite land, from Medina to Khurāsān. Many of Ja'far's descendants, however, emigrated to Egypt,[171] India,[172] and other areas which at that time were far from the Imāmite homeland. Many of those who emigrated as well as those who remained in Iraq became notables[173] in their various societies. Some became spiritual mentors of Sufi orders.[174] One of those orders, whose sequence of leadership is based on a father-to-son succession, is presently stationed in Turkey. In their publication they name

171. 'Umarī: 135. Fakhr al-Dīn al-Rāzī, *Shajara*: 80–81; Marwazī: 9; Ibn 'Inaba: 200–201.

172. The large clan of Naqawī *sayyid*s in the Indian subcontinent traces its genealogical ancestry back to Ja'far. See also Marwazī: 8, 219 (read *naqawī* for *taqawī* in both cases as also suggested in the footnote in the second case).

173. Among his many sons apart from 'Alī, his eldest son and successor, some were respected notables. One of them, 'Īsā (d. 334/965) was a respected public figure in Baghdad and a transmitter of *ḥadīth* (Ṭūsī, *Rijāl*: 480; Ibn Ḥazm *Jamhara*: 55). Another, Muḥsin (or Muḥassan) was killed during the time of the Abbasid Muqtadir (r. 295–320/908–932) on the accusation that he called a rebellion against the government (Abu 'l-Faraj, *Maqātil*: 703; *Jamhara*: 55). Another, Yaḥyā al-Ṣūfī (d. 354/965), was syndic of the Ṭālibids in Baghdad (Fakhr al-Dīn al-Rāzī, *Shajara*: 79) and moved to Qum later in his life (Ḥasan al-Qummī: 216–17; on him see also *Jamhara*: 53). Another, Mūsā, is said to have become a Sunnite, frequenting regularly the circles of the Sunnite traditionists (*Jamhara*: 55–6; possibly the same one mentioned in Ṣūlī: 98 as having died in 326/937). Among his descendants, who formed a very large clan, were many holders of official positions, such as syndics of the Ṭālibids in different towns (in addition to those mentioned above among the descendants of his son, 'Alī, see 'Umarī: 135; Marwazī: 9, 219, 39; Fakhr al-Dīn al-Rāzī, *Shajara*: 79–80; Ibn 'Inaba: 200–201; Kammūna, 1:116, 2:156–7), emissaries from the caliphs (Ṣarīfīnī: 256) and the like, scholars and transmitters of *ḥadīth* (see, for instance, 'Umarī: 135; *Jamhara,* 56 [which mentions as a great-grandson of Ja'far, a Ja'far b. Muḥammad b. Ibrāhīm b. Muḥammad b. 'Ubayd Allāh b. Ja'far, a learned *muḥaddith* who died in Mecca in 341/951–2 at the age of 100. Unless the correct date is 441/1049–50, this man, obviously, cannot be a great-grandson of Ja'far b. 'Alī]; Ibn 'Asākir, *Ta'rīkh,* the biography of 'Alī, 2:253; Ibn 'Inaba: 200; Ibn Shadqam: 61–2).

174. See, for instance, Sha'rānī, 1:181 (the biography of the Sufi *shaykh,* Ibrāhīm b. Abi 'l-Majd al-Dusūqī [d. 676/1277–8], who descends from Ja'far as a twelfth-generation descendant of his).

their spiritual leaders back to Ja'far, whom they call Ja'far al-Mahdī.[175] One of their most recent heads, Seyyid Ahmed Husameddin (d. 1343/1925), author of a partly published commentary on the Qur'ān,[176] was in the twenty-ninth generation from Ja'far.[177] In an indirect reference in the introduction to his Qur'ānic commentary, he unmistakably refers to himself as the "heir to the Prophet and the Imām of the age."[178]

For the mainstream of the Imāmites who maintained the Imāmate of the vanished son of Ḥasan al-'Askarī the puzzlement and uncertainties continued and increased in the course of time. In the first days when that idea was put forward and accepted by the community, nobody, obviously except for 'Uthmān b. Sa'īd al-'Amrī and his close associates, had ever imagined that it was going to be such an unusually long occultation. The Shī'ites clearly expected the son to become manifest in a short time and the office of the Imāmate and the order of the Imāms to continue their normal and natural courses.[179] A contemporaneous rumor suggested that he

175. A group of supporters of Ja'far in the late third/ninth century maintained that he was the *qā'im*, a concept which by then had become equivalent to the concept of *mahdī*. See Nawbakhtī: 115; Sa'd b. 'Abd Allāh: 113.

176. *Kur'an'in 20.asra gore anlami*, ed. M. Kāẓim Öztürk, vol. 1: *Fatiha ve Amme cuzu okunusu tercumesi ve aciklamasi* (Izmir, 1974), vol. 2: *Tebareke cuzu. Okunusu tercumesi ve aciklamasi* (Izmir, 1976). They are numbers 4 and 5 from a series of his works published by the same editor, who is the son of the author, under the general title of *Seyyid Ahmed Husameddin Kulliyatindan*. According to the editor's introduction to the mentioned Qur'ānic commentary, 1:25, other works by Husameddin edited in that series include *Thamarat al-ṭūbā min aghṣān āl al-'abā, Mawālīd ahl al-bayt, Maqāṣid al-sālikīn* and *Zubdat al-marātib,* which are published in a single volume, and *Wajīzat al-ḥurūf 'alā manāṭiq al-ṣuwar,* which is published together with its Turkish translation as *Esrar-i Ceberut-ül A'la.* The editor has also translated the *Mawālīd ahl al-bayt* into Turkish, which was published in Ankara in 1969 as *Islam Felsefesine Isik veren Seyyidler.*

177. See his Qur'ānic commentary, 1:20–21. According to the genealogical table that appears there, he was the ninteenth-generation from the above-mentioned Sufi *shaykh*, Ibrāhīm b. Abi 'l-Majd al-Dusūqī. However, the names in the genealogical table here vary from those in Sha'rānī, 1:181, in minor ways.

178. See ibid., 1:27–28.

179. See Nawbakhtī: 116, 118; Sa'd b. 'Abd Allāh: 102, 106. See also Ibn Qiba, *Mas'ala fi 'l-imāma,* para. 5 where it is said that when the vanished

would have to remain in hiding for either six days or six months with a maximum possibility of six years before circumstances would allow him to emerge without fear of harm.[180] It did not, however, take long before the community started to identify the case with the concept of Occultation, whose occurrence some time in the future was forecast in reports that had already been in circulation among the Shī'ites for almost one century. The reports predicted that the *qā'im* would first disappear from the public scene to emerge later and establish the rule of truth.[181] One report even predicted two periods of concealment for the *qā'im*; after the first short one he was to reappear and then go into a longer period of occultation during which most of his followers would lose their faith and leave the true doctrine.[182] A different version of this report predicted that the first period of Occultation would be longer and the second period would be shorter.[183] The Waqifites used to quote these reports in support of their idea that Mūsā al-Kāẓim was the *qā'im*,[184] identifying the two Occultations with his two periods of imprisonment.

---

son of Ḥasan al-'Askarī reappears, the truth of his claim to be the vanished son will have to be confirmed by his associates, that is, those who had previously seen him and can identify him. Clearly, the author expected the son to reappear while those witnesses were still alive.

180. 'Alī b. Bābawayh: 146; Kulaynī, 1:338; *Kamāl*: 323 (In Nu'mānī: 61, who quoted the report from Kulaynī, the phrase "six days, six months or six years" is changed to "a period of time." *Ghayba*: 204 omitted the part of the report that mentioned the duration of the Occultation altogether.)
181. See, for instance, *Ghayba*: 38, 40, 41 quoting 'Alī b. Aḥmad al-'Alawī al-Mūsawī in his book in support of the Wāqifite doctrine; Ṭabrisī, *I'lām*: 444 quoting Ḥasan b. Maḥbūb al-Sarrād (d. 224/839) in his *Kitāb al-Mashyakha*.
182. *Kamāl*: 323.
183. Nu'mānī: 170.
184. Numerous works were compiled during the late second/eighth and early third/ninth centuries by the Wāqifite scholars and their opponents as *Kitāb al-Ghayba,* obviously all discussing the concept of the alleged occultation of Mūsā al-Kāẓim as suggested by the Wāqifites (see the article *al-Mahdī* in *EI*², 5:1230– 38 [by W. Medelung]: 1236). These include works by the Wāqifites Ibrāhīm b. Ṣāliḥ al-Anmāṭī (Najāshī: 15, 24), Ḥasan b. 'Alī b. Abī Ḥamza al-Baṭā'inī (ibid.: 37); Ḥasan b. Muḥammad b. Samā'a (Ṭūsī, *Fihrist*: 52), 'Abd Allāh b. Jabala (Najāshī: 216), 'Alī b. al-Ḥasan al-Ṭaṭarī (ibid.: 255), 'Alī b. 'Umar al-A'raj (ibid.: 256), and 'Alī b. Muḥammad b. 'Alī b. 'Umar b. Rabāḥ al-Qallā' (ibid.: 260) and non-

It was also true that most of those who supported the Wāqifite idea about Mūsā al-Kāẓim later rejected it as "predicted" in those reports and recognized 'Alī al-Riḍā as the next Imām.[185]

The general idea of the occultation of a future Imām who would be the *qā'im* was, thus, a well-established concept in the Shī'ite mentality.[186] This fact is well evidenced by the views of those who denied the death of 'Alī and awaited his return and those of the Kaysānites and other early heretic movements on the living and future return of their respected leaders. After the death of Ḥasan al-'Askarī, too, some of his followers are quoted as suggesting that he actually went into his first concealment from which he would emerge in a short time as the *qā'im*.[187] By around 290/903 when the prominent Imāmite theologian Abū Sahl al-Nawbakhtī finished his *Kitāb al-Tanbīh*,[188] it was already known, apparently for many years, that the vanished son of Ḥasan was the one to emerge as the *qā'im* to establish the rule of truth.[189] Otherwise, one could hardly imagine any reason why he was so afraid for his life if he were to live calm and quiet as his forefathers had done.[190] The time period of the Occultation was not yet long enough for one to assert that it was impossible for someone to still be in hiding.[191] It was not

---

Wāqifites 'Abbās b. Hishām al-Nāshirī (ibid.: 280), and 'Alī b. al-Ḥasan b. Faḍḍāl (ibid.: 258). As noted, the latter author lived into the period of Minor Occultation but did not believe in the occultation of the son of Ḥasan al-'Askarī and was a follower of Ja'far. So his book was most likely in the same Wāqifite–non-Wāqifite line of polemics.

185. See above, chapter 1.

186. Abū Sahl al-Nawbakhtī: 94.

187. Nawbakhtī: 106–7; Sa'd b. 'Abd Allāh: 106–7; Mufīd, *Majālis,* 2:98; Shahrastānī, 1:200.

188. Abū Sahl al-Nawbakhtī: 90 (where it is said that some thirty years had already lapsed by the time the work was being written since the son went into hiding, that is, from 260/874), 93 (where in the last paragraph of the book it is said that more than one hundred and five years [read *mi'a wa khams* for *mi'a wa khamsīn*] had passed since the death of Mūsā al-Kāẓim, that is, from 183/799).

189. Ibid.: 94. See also Ibn Qiba, *Naqḍ ibn bashshār*: para. 5; also Nawbakhtī: 118; Sa'd b. 'Abd Allāh: 105.

190. On this point see also 'Abd al-Jabbār, *Mughnī,* 20(1): 196.

191. For the mentality behind this judgment see Kashshī: 458 where Imām

like the alleged occultation of Mūsā al-Kāẓim which, as Abū Sahl stated, more than one hundred and five[192] years had passed since his death (or concealment as the Wāqifites claimed) and the duration of his alleged occultation had already exceeded the maximum normal duration.[193]

A short time later, the concept of *mahdī*, "the rightly guided one," thus far essentially a non-Imāmite concept,[194] was also introduced into the case.[195] This concept was based on a statement reported from the Prophet that predicted that before the end of time a descendant of his would emerge who would restore the religion

---

'Alī al-Riḍā is quoted as saying that if God were to prolong someone's life because society needed him, He would have prolonged the life of the Prophet.

192. Read *mi'a wa khams* for *mi'a wa khamsīn*, as noted.

193. Ibid.: 93–4.

194. See the article "al-Mahdī" in *EI*², 5:1230–38 [by W. Madelung]. The Prophetic statement about the *mahdī* does not seem to have been recorded by the Imāmite authors until the post-Occultation period. The assertion of some Sunnite authors of the past and present who accused the Imāmites of fabricating the reports about the *mahdī* is, thus, totally misplaced. The statement, however, is widely quoted in the post-Occultation Imāmite literature, especially in the reports where the Prophet and previous Imāms are quoted as miraculously predicting the exact number and names of the twelve Imāms where the vanished son of Ḥasan al-'Askarī is said to be the *mahdī* who is to "fill the earth with equity and justice as it was filled with oppression and injustice" (see Kulaynī, 1:338, 525, 534; Nu'mānī: 58–60, 86, 93). There are a few cases in the supposedly pre-Occultation Imāmite literature where the concept of *mahdī* is mentioned (see, for instance, Kulaynī, 1:281, 372; Nu'mānī: 60, 189, 212–15, 231, 247, 264). Most of these, however, seem to have been subject to later rewordings. Compare, for instance, Kulaynī, 1:372, report no. 6 in which the word *mahdī* is used with 1:372–3, reports nos. 2, 4, 5, and 7 (also Nu'mānī: 200, 329, 330, 331) where the words *qā'im*, *muntaẓar* and *ṣāḥib hādha 'l-amr* are used in other versions of the same statement; also Nu'mānī: 283–4 where a statement is quoted with the word *qā'im* in one version and with *mahdī* in the other.

195. This is, of course, the chronological order of how the community came to know the fact. This certainly does not exclude that the fact was already revealed by God to the Prophet and via him to the Imāms and that they had already informed their reliable associates, as verified by many Imāmite and even non-Imāmite reports.

and "fill the earth with equity and justice as it was filled with oppression and injustice." The rank and file of the Imāmites tended to identify this savior of the earth with the *qā'im* who would establish the rule of truth.[196] The link between the two concepts had already been reportedly advocated by some splinter groups who "stopped" with certain Imāms on the assumption that they were the *qā'im* and the *mahdī*.[197] This identification presented some technical problems because, according to widespread reports, the *mahdī* was to be a namesake of the Prophet.[198] Many Imāmites, however, expected any of the Imāms to be the *qā'im*, whereas the names of most of the Imāms did not satisfy that condition.[199] This problem did not exist in the case of the Twelfth Imām, whose name was first unknown

196. See, for instance, the reports that suggest that the *qā'im* must be a namesake of the Prophet (Sa'd b. 'Abd Allāh: 43; Nu'mānī: 230) or that the *qā'im* or *ṣāḥib hādha 'l-amr* will fill the earth with justice (Kulaynī, 1:341).

197. This assertion is quoted from those who allegedly "stopped" with Ja'far al-Ṣādiq (Nāshi': 46; Nawbakhtī: 78; Sa'd b. 'Abd Allāh: 79; *Farq*: 61; Isfarā'īnī: 79; Shahrastānī, 1:195), Mūsā al-Kāẓim (Nāshi': 48; Nawbakhtī: 90, 92; Sa'd b. 'Abd Allāh: 89, 91), and Ḥasan al-'Askarī (Nawbakhtī: 106, 108; *Kamāl*: 40). Some non-Imāmite Shī'ite groups are also quoted as having considered their leaders to be *al-qā'im al-mahdī* (Nawbakhtī: 52, 74; Sa'd b. 'Abd Allāh: 43, 76). Ja'far al-Ṣādiq was asked by one of his disciples whether he was the *qā'im* and the *mahdī* or not (Kulaynī, 1:536). The combination of *al-qā'im al-mahdī* or the connection between the two appears in some other reports, too (see, for instance, Nu'mānī: 235, 237–8).

198. See, for instance, Aḥmad, 3:376, 377, 448; Tirmidhī, 9:74–75; Ṭabarānī, 2:148. See also Sulamī: 27–32; Ṣāfī: 182–4 who refers to forty-eight *ḥadīth*s to that effect, some quoted in several sources. See also al-Sayyid al-Ḥimyarī: 49, 183 for the common belief about that. According to another report, the father of the *mahdī* was also to be a namesake of the Prophet's father (see Ibn Abī Shayba, 8: 678; Abū Dāwūd, 4: 106–7; Hākim, 4: 442; Khaṭīb, 1: 370; Baghawī, 3: 492; Sulamī: 27, 29, 30). This report, which was in wide circulation in the middle of the second/eighth century, encouraged many people to consider Muḥammad b. 'Abd Allāh al-Nafs al-Zakiyya as the long awaited *mahdī* see, for instance, Nawbakhtī: 74; Sa'd b. 'Abd Allāh: 43; Nu'mānī: 230; Abu 'l-Faraj, *Maqātil*: 244; Ibn Zuhra: 20. See also Qāḍī, *Kaysāniyya*: 227).

199. There were other technical problems too. The *mahdī* was to emerge close to the end of the time, according to some reports right before the day of judgment. According to a report, he was to come after an interval during which there would be no Imām at all, just as the Prophet came in a time when the sequence of the prophets had been cut for a long period of time

even to the most prominent Imāmite persona of the time who asked his first deputy about it.[200] Furthermore, a report circulating in this period among the Shī'ite community quoted Imām Muḥammad al-Jawād telling a disciple, who was wondering whether the *mahdī* was the same as the *qā'im* or different, that both concepts referred to the same person.[201] Thus while the reference to the concept of *mahdī* in connection to the vanished son of Ḥasan al-'Askarī is absent in the Imāmite works written in the last decades of the third/ninth century, even in those that describe him as the *qā'im,* by the first decades of the following century when Kulaynī finished his *Kitāb al-Kāfī*[202] and 'Alī b. Bābawayh al-Qummī wrote his *Kitāb al-Imāma wa 'l-tabṣira min al-ḥayra*[203] the vanished Imām was already the one who was to reappear to "fill the earth with equity and justice as it was filled with oppression and injustice."[204]

(Kulaynī, 1:341). This was against the Imāmite's main principle that the earth would never remain without an Imām (Ṣaffār: 484–9; 'Alī b. Bābawayh: 157–62; Kulaynī, 1:168, 177–80). It, however, contributed to the emergence of one of the several groups that rose after the death of Ḥasan al-'Askarī as some of his followers held that there was no Imām after him, and the sequence of the Imāms was cut until God appoints the next Imām. During this period of vacuum the Shī'ites were to follow the already well-established teachings and principles of their own school (see Nawbakhtī: 113–14; Sa'd b. 'Abd Allāh: 107–8; Mufīd, *Majālis*, 2:99).

200. See Kulaynī, 1:328, 330, 331; Nu'mānī: 288; Ibn Bābawayh, *'Uyūn*, 1:67; *Kamāl*: 331, 338, 369, 370, 378, 380–81, 403, 442, 482–3; *Ghayba*: 147, 215, 219, 222.

201. See *Kamāl*: 377.

202. The compilation of this book took twenty years (Najāshī: 377). The author died in 329/940–941.

203. According to the author, the age of the vanished Imām at the time the book was compiled had already reached the maximum of the normal life of people of that time (ibid.: 149), presumably referring to age seventy. The book must, therefore, have been written in or shortly after 325/937 when, according to the most supported view on his birth date (the year 255/869) the Imām had passed his seventieth birthday. The author died in 329/940–41.

204. See Kulaynī, 1:338 (where the vanished Imām is explicitly called the *mahdī*), 341, 525, 534; 'Alī b. Bābawayh: 147. However, the vanished Imām is already Muḥammad b. al-Ḥasan in Ibn Qiba, *Mas'ala fi 'l-imāma,* para. 5, a name that was apparently determined by the introduction of the concept of *mahdī* into this case.

'Uthmān b. Sa'īd al-'Amrī moved to Baghdad and continued as the caretaker of the office of Imāmate until the end of his life. He insisted that he had direct contact with the son of Ḥasan and received the correspondence sent to the son by the community as well as the religious funds in the same way that he had during the time of Ḥasan. It is said that the entire community agreed to recognize his claim to be the deputy of the Imām.[205] Some reports, however, suggest that rather serious doubts existed about his authority to receive the religious funds.[206] As noted above, some doubted the scope of his credibility even during the time of Ḥasan and whether he was always acting at the Imām's instruction and wish.[207] Nevertheless, there was no doubt that he was the closest associate of the Imām. His position was further strengthened at the Imām's death when he was the one who performed the funeral and burial ceremonies,[208] an extremely important privilege in the Imāmite tradition, reserved, according to popular opinion, for the successor to the deceased Imām.[209]

'Amrī was succeeded by his son, Muḥammad b. 'Uthmān, also a well-known agent who had previously served in the office of Ḥasan al-'Askarī in the company of his own father and later as the chief aide to his father when he was the caretaker for the vanished Imām. Muḥammad carried on in this job for a long time despite more open challenges to his authority as the caretaker of the office raised by some prominent members of the community who had not contested his father's claim.[210] Before his death in 305/917, he appointed one

205. *Ghayba*: 216, 221.
206. See Kulaynī, 1:517.
207. See Kashshī: 544 where, after quoting the text of a letter that Ḥasan al-'Askarī's representative in Nīshāpūr received from the Imām that included harsh words against the prominent Imāmite scholar of the time, Faḍl b. Shādhān, the author expressed doubt on the credibility of the latter on the basis that "it has been mentioned that that letter as well as all other instructions that [the representative in Nīshāpūr] received were sent by 'Amrī." The hesitation in this statement about 'Amrī's credibility and authority is unmistakable.
208. *Ghayba*: 216.
209. See 'Ayyāshī, 2:281; Kulaynī, 1:384–5, 459; *Kamāl*: 71; *'Uyūn*, 1:106, 2:246, 248; Ḥasan b. Sulaymān al-Ḥillī: 13; Majlisī, 27:288.
210. They included Abū Ṭāhir Muḥammad b. 'Alī b. Bilāl (*Ghayba*: 245–6),

of his junior aides,[211] Ḥusayn b. Rūḥ al-Nawbakhtī, as his successor. The latter continued in that office, meeting the same sort of challenge and doubt from some members of the community,[212] until 326/937 when he died, leaving ʿAlī b. Muḥammad al-Samarrī, presumably an aide of his, as his successor. The latter held that position for only three years and died in 329/941 without naming anyone as his successor. The office was, thus, formally closed.

During the period between the deaths of Ḥasan al-ʿAskarī and the fourth agent, later termed the Minor Occultation, the chief agent used to receive the correspondence to the vanished Imām from the community and the religious funds and donations for the Imām. The agents occasionally issued written statements to the community and instructions to the local agents as rescripts of the vanished Imām.[213] Until the time of the second agent, Muḥammad b. ʿUthmān, they were all written in the same handwriting that the community received from the office of Imāmate during the time of Ḥasan and later during the incumbency of Muḥammad's father,[214] which suggests that all were copied by Muḥammad himself at the instruction of the Imām. The rescripts were mostly instructions to

---

a respected scholar and *ḥadīth* transmitter (Kashshī: 564, 566; *Kamāl*: 499; Ṭūsī, *Rijāl*: 435; *Ghayba*: 238), and formerly an agent of Ḥasan al-ʿAskarī who praised him in a letter as a "reliable and trustworthy man who knows his duties very well" (Kashshī: 579; see also *Kamāl*: 442; incidentally he was the one who complained to Ḥasan about the excessive spending of his agent ʿAlī b. Jaʿfar al-Humānī, quoted above); Aḥmad b. Hilāl al-Karkhī (*Ghayba*: 245), also a companion of Ḥasan al-ʿAskarī (and possibly the uncle of Muḥammad b. ʿAlī b. Hilāl al-Karkhī, a later recipient of a rescript from the vanished Imām [Abū Manṣūr al-Ṭabrisī, 2:288–9]), who had accepted ʿUthmān b. Saʿīd as the agent of the vanished Imām but disputed the authority of Muḥammad; and Muḥammad b. Nuṣayr al-Numayrī, head of the Nuṣayrites (*Ghayba*: 244).

211. See *Ghayba*: 225 (cf. ibid.: 227).
212. Ibid.: 192.
213. Cf. Ḥusayn b. ʿAbd al-Wahhāb: 143 where it is said that the Shīʿite community agreed that the rescripts of the Twelfth Imām were coming out to the community in Iraq for a while after his disappearance at the hand of ʿUthmān b. Saʿīd al-ʿAmrī. There is no mention there of any rescript by the hands of later agents.
214. *Ghayba*: 220, 221, 223.

the local agents or receipts for the donation made to the Imām and, occasionally, answers to legal questions asked by the community. For this last point, however, the community was ordered in a rescript to refer to the Imāmite jurists.[215] Sometime around 280-285/893-898 the correspondence from the Holy Threshold stopped, and no more rescripts were issued. The situation continued at least until around 290/903. This was taken by the community to mean the beginning of the second and greater occultation during which the Shī'ites were supposed to lose their contact with the Imām.[216] The correspondence seems to have resumed during the term of office of the third agent when some rescripts were issued to anathematize those who challenged the authority of the agent.[217] The legal questions were now forwarded by the agent to some Imāmite jurists to answer,[218] jurists to whom the agent also turned with his own questions.[219] The rescripts were now in the handwriting of an agent's secretary and dictated by the agent himself.[220]

215. *Kamāl*: 484.
216. See Abū Sahl al-Nawbakhtī: 93.
217. *Ghayba*: 228, 252–4. There were also quasi rescripts in the form of answers given to legal questions. Some Shī'ites used to put their questions in scrolls to the agent, which he would return with short answers on the back of the paper (*Ghayba*: 228, 229) or in the space between the questions (Najāshī: 355). See, for instance, the four examples of this kind of rescript sent by the Imāmite scholar of Qum, Muḥammad b. 'Abd Allāh b. Ja'far al-Ḥimyarī (on him see Najāshī: 354–5; Ṭūsī, *Fihrist*: 156; Ibn Shahrāshūb, *Ma'ālim*: 111; Āghā Buzurg, 1:241) in Abū Manṣūr al-Ṭabrisī, 2:301–318 (the first two also in *Ghayba*: 229–236) including one dated 307/919–920 (ibid., 2:306–9) and another dated 308/920–921 (ibid., 2:309–15).
218. See, for instance, *Ghayba*: 181, 228. Some people apparently knew this fact as may be verified by their asking the agent to "ask the jurists that he trusts" and return an answer (*Ghayba*: 230, 231, 232. It is, however, probable that the Imām himself was meant by that expression). Others were in doubt (ibid.: 228). The answers sometimes clearly demonstrated that they were given by an Imāmite jurist and not by the Imām, as they referred to the conflict of the reports and that one could choose whichever he wanted (ibid.: 232) or, alternatively, argued with consensus (Abū Manṣūr al-Ṭabrisī, 2:307) or the reports from the former Imāms (ibid.: 308, 311, 314).
219. *Ghayba*: 240.
220. Ibid.: 228, 229.

There seems to have been a widespread expectation in the Imāmite community that the vanished Imām would reappear before his fortieth birthday, which was to occur before the turn of the century. This idea originated from suggestions in a number of reports that the *qā'im* had to be an energetic young man[221] of either thirty or thirty-one years, with a maximum age of forty,[222] and that anyone who exceeded the age of forty would not be the *qā'im*.[223] When the expectation did not come true, it was first suggested that the limit mentioned was to mislead the unjust rulers who were gathering their whole power to crush such a rise of the *qā'im*[224] Later, it was decided that the reports meant that whenever the *qā'im* appears, regardless of whatever number of years that he lives and even if he lives for thousands of years, he will look like a young

221. Kulaynī, 1:536.
222. See also Sulamī: 35–6, 38; Haytamī: 43.
223. 'Alī b. Bābawayh: 146; *Ghayba*: 258; *Dustūr al-munajjimīn*: 345b; Shahrastānī, 1:202. See also Khuṣaybī: 242–3. It may have been because of these reports that some of the Imāmites in this period thought that the son of Ḥasan al-'Askarī might have died in hiding and been succeeded by his own son. They seem to have come to this conclusion by a juxtaposition of several facts, that (1) the existence of the son of Ḥasan was proved by reports, that (2) he was in occultation because he was to be the *qā'im*, otherwise there would be no reason for him to hide because the time was not more difficult than that of his forefathers, and that (3) the *qā'im* was not to have passed his fortieth birthday. Because the son of Ḥasan had not reappeared although he was no more to be the *qā'im* as he had already passed his fortieth birthday, this had to be a sign that he had passed away while in hiding. Because the next Imām had to be his descendant he must, thus, have left a son who was the current Imām. Because this one was also unseen, one had to determine that he was now the one who would rise to establish the just rule. The application of the principle of *badā'* could facilitate this transition of the task. The opinion is attributed by Ibn al-Nadīm: 225 (also quoted by Dhahabī, *Siyar,* 15:328) to Abū Sahl al-Nawbakhtī. His own statements in his *Kitāb al-Tanbīh* (quoted above), however, do not support this view though the book was written before the fortieth birthday of the vanished Imām when the above theoretical problems arose. Should he have held such an opinion, he should have started it some years after the completion of that work. The attribution is not, however, supported by any other source and seems to be unfounded (see also *Ghayba*: 240).
224. 'Alī b. Bābawayh: 146–7.

man of thirty odd years.[225] There was some background for this mode of interpretation. A clearly Wāqifite report on the authority of Ja'far al-Ṣādiq had suggested that the *qā'im* would live for 120 years but emerge as a thirty-two-year-old man.[226] Before this stage, however, in the first days of the Occultation the Zaydites used to criticize the Imāmites for the belief in the Imāmate of a child. They argued that the Imām was needed for the administration of the Islamic state and the protection of the Muslim homeland from enemies, which required the ability to fight and to lead the Muslim army, functions that could not normally be performed by a young child.[227] The Imāmites used to answer these criticisms by saying that if such a situation arose, God would immediately turn the child Imām into a well-grown man, powerful and strong enough to lead such a fight.[228] Some quoted a report that suggested that the son of Ḥasan al-'Askarī was growing as much in one month as normal babies grew during one year.[229]

Nevertheless, the failure of the old expectations and justifications created an atmosphere of severe doubt and uncertainty. At the turn of the century, the Zaydite Imāms had already established their independent rules in Yemen and the northern part of Iran. The political situation started to change dramatically in the first decades of the fourth/tenth century; the pro-Shī'ite Būyid dynasty came to power and extended their power over the caliphate of Baghdad for quite a long time. During the Būyid time, the better part of the fourth/tenth century, the situation changed everywhere to the benefit of the Shī'ite community. It was now believed that the Imām could safely become manifest should he, as was upheld by his chief agent in the first days of his occultation, have vanished because of a threat to his life and that if he managed to gather as many as 313 loyal supporters around him he would rise up.[230] This

225. Mufīd, *Majālis,* 2:98; *Ghayba*: 259.
226. Nu'mānī: 189; *Ghayba*: 259.
227. *Kamāl*: 78.
228. Ibid.: 79 describing it as the answer given by an Imāmite scholar to Abu 'l-Qāsim al-Balkhī.
229. Ibid.: 429.
230. *Kamāl*: 378. Mufīd wrote a treatise in support of this idea published as *al-Risāla al-thālitha fi 'l-ghayba*.

rationalization was, however, modified by a rescript[231] issued by the second agent; the real reason given for the Imām's hiding was that he had tried to avoid committing himself to allegiance to any of the unjust rulers of his time so that when he rose up he would not violate the term of allegiance—considered a capital sin in the Islamic tradition. If he had been manifest, he would have had to pledge allegiance to the government as all members of the Muslim community in those ages, including his forefathers,[232] had had to do and continued to do.

By the third decade of the century, therefore, when ʻAlī b. Bābawayh was writing his book on the Occultation, many of the Imāmites were in a state of severe doubt and uncertainty.[233] By the end of the fourth decade when Muḥammad b. Ibrahīm al-Nuʻmānī wrote his work on the topic,[234] the absolute majority of the Imāmites in the western parts of the Shīʻite homeland (in fact, the whole community with very few exceptions)[235] were in a similar state of fierce doubt and one way or another rejected the existence of a vanished Imām. The situation was not much better in the eastern

231. *Kamāl*: 485. Some reports attributed to the earlier Imāms also mention the same reason for the hiding of the *qā'im* in the future (Nuʻmānī: 171, 191; Ibn Bābawayh, *ʻUyūn*, 1:273; *Kamāl*: 479–80), including one with a small chronological problem in the chain of transmission because a transmitter from an earlier generation appears in it quoting from one of the later generation (see Nuʻmānī: 171, n. 1). The idea is, however, based on an ultraorthodox, pro-Umayyad and anti-Shīʻite view that regarded the unjust rulers who forcefully seized political power as legitimate and allegiance to them as binding, even if paid under duress and in fear. It is apparently for this reason that neither Mufīd in his treatise on the reason for the Occultation (published as *al-Risāla al-rābiʻa fi 'l-ghayba*) nor Ṭūsī in his *Kitāb al-Ghayba* mentioned any of these reports but insisted that the reason for the Imām's occultation was only his fear for his life (see Mufīd, *al-Risāla al-rābiʻa*: 395–8; *Ghayba*: 199–201).

232. *Kamāl*: 485.

233. ʻAlī b. Bābawayh: 142.

234. The book was written when some eighty-odd years had already passed since the birthdate of the Twelfth Imām (p. 157) and before Dhu 'l-Ḥijja, 342/April 954 when the book was read with the author by his student (p. 18, n. 2). These references put the date of compilation at around 340/951–952 (see also pp. 161, 173–4).

235. Nuʻmānī: 21, 157, 160, 165, 170, 172, 186.

region either; a decade or two later Ibn Bābawayh found most of the Shī'ites he met in Khurāsān, even respected scholars of the Imāmite community, extremely doubtful about the vanished Imām.[236] Numerous references in the reports that circulated in the Shī'ite community during these periods attest to a universal uncertainty about this question[237] and to widespread conversions from the "True Doctrine."[238] Some reports even suggest that the greater portion of the community converted during these periods of uncertainty, as they quote earlier Imāms as predicting that the majority[239] (according to some, up to two-thirds)[240] of those who followed the truth would turn to other doctrines.[241] The reports also speak of severe hostility and mistrust among the Shī'ites, some of whom called others liars, cursed each other, and spat into each other's faces,[242] as well as similar sorts of violent behavior.[243]

236. *Kamāl*: 2–3 (see also 16).

237. See, for instance, Nu'mānī: 185, 186, 190; *Kamāl*: 258, 286, 287, 302, 304, 330; Majlisī, 51:109, 118, 142, 158 where these reports are quoted from other early sources (see also Khuṣaybī: 357–8; Ibn Abi 'l-Thalj: 116; *Alqāb al-rasūl*: 287). Reference to this state of doubt, traditionally referred to as *ḥayra* (uncertainty), can also be found in the names of several books that were written on the question of Occultation in this period, including the above-mentioned work by 'Alī b. Bābawayh (*Kitāb al-Imāma wa 'l-tabṣira min al-ḥayra*), another one by Muḥammad b. Aḥmad al-Ṣafwānī (Najāshī: 393), another by Salāma b. Muḥammad al-Arzanī (ibid.: 192), and a fourth by 'Abd Allāh b. Ja'far al-Ḥimyarī (ibid.: 219). The full title of Ibn Bābawayh's *Kamāl* (which appears at the end of its first volume: 332 as well as in his *Khiṣāl*: 187 and *'Uyūn*, 1:54, 69) also refers to it: *Kamāl al-dīn wa tamām al-ni'ma fi ithbāt al-ghayba wa kashf al-ḥayra*.

238. Nu'mānī: 22, 25, 61, 154, 170, 172, 186, 190, 207–8; *Kamāl*: 16, 17, 253, 286, 287, 304, 317, 356, 360, 408; *Ghayba*: 41, 204, 206; Ibn 'Ayyāsh: 23; Mufīd, *al-Risāla al-khāmisa*: 400; Ibn Bābawayh, *Nuṣūṣ* (quoted by Hāshim al-Baḥrānī: 335).

239. Nu'mānī: 165, 172, 186; *Kamāl*: 323– 4, 378; *Ghayba*: 206.

240. *Kamāl*, 656 (read *thuluthay* for *thuluth*); *Ghayba*: 206.

241. Many of these Imāmites converted to other branches of Shī'ism, including Ismā'īlism (see, for instance, 'Abd al-Jabbār, *Tathbīt dalā'il al-nubuwwa*, 2:390). They included even some Imāmite jurists and notables (see, for instance, Kulaynī, 1:520). Others turned to other non-Shī'ite heretical sects (see, for instance, Tanūkhī, 8:70).

242. Kulaynī, 1:340; Nu'mānī: 159, 210, 260; *Kamāl*: 317, 348, 361.

243. Abū Zayd al-'Alawī, para. 24; *Kamāl*: 317, 361; Ibn 'Ayyāsh: 23. Obviously

It was thanks mainly to the tireless efforts of the Imāmite transmitters of *ḥadīth* that this situation gradually changed. The turning point apparently came around the turn of the third/ninth century[244] after the earlier hopes for the appearance of the Imām before his fortieth birthday were dashed. It was made possible by the application of a quotation from the Prophet about the number of the Imāms.

There was a well-known statement attributed to the Prophet by the Sunnite transmitters of *ḥadīth* according to which he predicted that there would be twelve caliphs[245] after him, all from his tribe, the Quraysh.[246] One version of the statement spoke of twelve caliphs during whose reign the Islamic community would be united.[247] In other versions, it was also predicted that anarchy would prevail after the reign of those twelve. It is almost certain that the statement was in circulation in the time of Walīd II (r. 125-126/743-744) when the first signs of the anti-Umayyad revolution had already emerged, and the rebel forces, joined by Yazīd b. al-Walīd and the Qadarites, were threatening the long-established Umayyad orthodoxy. It might even have started to circulate in the final years of the reign of Hishām b. ʿAbd al-Malik (r. 105-125/724-743), the ninth Umayyad ruler to whom the Muslims universally submitted as they had done to the first three *Rāshidūn,* the years that were already clouded by troubles concerning the succession. The state-

---

for the same reason Abū Ghālib al-Zurārī: 131 speaks of this period as the time of "*al-fitna allatī umtuḥinat biha 'l-shīʿa.*"

244. This dating is based on the fact that the argument with the Prophet's prediction of the exact number of the Imāms is absent from the works of Nawbakhtī, Saʿd b. ʿAbd Allāh, Ibn Qiba, and Abū Sahl al-Nawbakhtī, the last of which was compiled around the year 290/903, but is already used by ʿAlī b. Bābawayh, writing shortly after 325/937.

245. Variations of the report mention twelve *amīr*s or *qayyim*s, (guardians).

246. Ṭayālisī: 105, 180; Nuʿaym b. Ḥammād: 20b–21a, 26b; Aḥmad, 1:398, 5:86–108; Bukhārī, 4:407; Muslim, 3:1452–3; Abū Dāwūd, 4:106; Tirmidhī, 9:67; Ṭabarānī, 2:213–18, 227–9, 236, 238, 241, 248, 251, 258, 268, 277, 282–6; Abū ʿAwāna, 4:394–6, 398–9; Ḥākim, 3:617–18; Khaṭīb, 2:126, 14:353; Ibn ʿAsākir, *Taʾrīkh*, the biography of ʿUthmān: 173–4.

247. Abū Dāwūd, 4:106.

ment had thus been in circulation long before the beginning of the occultation of the Twelfth Imām in 260/874. It was already on record as early as the middle of the second/eighth century in, for instance, the *Amālī* of the Egyptian scholar Layth b. Sa'd (d. 175/792),[248] later in the *Musnad* of Abū Dāwūd al-Ṭayālisī (d. 204/819-820) and in others. No one can, therefore, claim that the statement was in any way authored by the Imāmites in the post-Occultation period. In fact, there is no evidence in any work written before the last decades of the third/ninth century that suggests that this statement had ever attracted the attention of the Shī'ite traditionists or that anyone in the Shī'ite community had ever thought that it might concern them. The Imāmite scholar Muḥammad b. al-Ḥasan al-Ṣaffār (d. 290/903), for instance, does not refer to that statement in his book, *Baṣā'ir al-darajāt*, which is a collection of *ḥadīth*s on the virtues of the Imāms.[249] Other scholars, such as the two Nawbakhtīs, Sa'd b. 'Abd Allāh al-Ash'arī and Ibn Qiba, all from the latter part of the third/ninth century, also failed to refer to that statement in any of their surviving works.[250] The only exception[251]

248. See Ibn Shahrāshūb, *Mutashābih al-qur'ān,* 2:56.
249. Kohlberg, "From Imāmiyya to Ithnā'ashariyya": 522–3.
250. That includes the surviving section of Abū Sahl al-Nawbakhtī's *al-Tanbīh fi 'l-imāma,* the related part of Ḥasan b. Mūsā al-Nawbakhtī's *Firaq al-shī'a,* the corresponding part of Sa'd b. 'Abd Allāh's *al-Maqālāt wa 'l-firaq* as well as the abridged version of his *Baṣā'ir al-darajāt,* and all three works of Ibn Qiba which are reproduced in the second part of the present work.
251. Another exception is suggested by Etan Kohlberg: "Al-Barqī [d. 274/887 or 280/893] quotes a well-known Imāmī tradition, in which al-Khiḍr meets 'Alī and his son al-Ḥasan and reveals to them the names of the Imāms [Barqī: 332f]; but in the version cited by al-Barqī, unlike other . . . versions of this tradition, al-Khiḍr mentions by name only 'Alī, al-Ḥasan and al-Ḥusayn; the tradition adds: ànd he counted every last one of them,' . . . but the names or the number of Imāms who are to follow al-Ḥusayn are not specified. In the *Tafsīr* by 'Alī b. Ibrāhīm al-Qummī (d. 307/919), the Khiḍr tradition appears already with the names of the twelve Imāms ['Alī b. Ibrāhīm al-Qummī, *Tafsīr,* 2:45]" ("From Imāmiyya to Ithnā'ashariyya": 523). It should, however, be noted that the version of this *Tafsīr* now available was compiled by 'Alī b. Ibrāhīm's pupil, Abu 'l-Faḍl 'Abbās b. Muḥammad b. al-Qāsim b. Ḥamza (Āghā Buzurg, 4:303–8), presumably sometime during the first decades of the fourth/tenth century, by which time the complete version of the Khiḍr tradition was already

was an anti-Sunnite polemic, apparently from the first decades of the second/eighth century, which was attributed to a certain Sulaym b. Qays al-Hilālī, allegedly a disciple of 'Alī. In that book,[252] the Prophet was quoted as saying to 'Alī that he, that is, 'Alī, and twelve of his descendants (thirteen all together)[253] are the leaders of truth.[254] The book seems to use widely accepted principles of the Sunnite community to support the Shī'ite points of view, a characteristic preserved in the present fourth/tenth-century version of the book, which is presumably modeled after the original one and seems to have preserved parts of its contents. The quotation, therefore, possibly reflects the understanding of the Shī'ite author of the book of that widespread statement rather than the existence of a Shī'ite version of it.[255]Nevertheless, the reference obviously never attracted the attention of the Imāmites until the late third/ninth century. As noted before, the Imāmite community in the first decades of the Occultation still expected that the order of the Imāms would continue its normal path in the descendants of Ḥasan al-'Askarī until the end of time. It was, possibly, not until after 295/908, when

in full circulation (see Kulaynī, 1:525; Nu'mānī: 58–60; Ibn Bābawayh, *'Uyūn,* 1:67; *Kamāl*: 213–15).

252. Mas'ūdī, *Tanbīh*: 231; Najāshī: 440.

253. Abū Naṣr Hibat Allāh b. Aḥmad al-Kātib, a late fourth/tenth-century Imāmite scholar who was also a maternal grandson of the second agent of the Twelfth Imām (Najāshī: 440; *Ghayba:* 216, 220, 221, 227, 238, 246, 248), wrote a book on the Imāmate for a Zaydite patron of his. Arguing with this report in *Kitāb sulaym b. qays*, he suggested that the Imāms were thirteen: the twelve plus Zayd b. 'Alī (Najāshī: 440).

254. In the printed copy of the book, which is apparently an early fourth/tenth-century contribution, the number appears as eleven (see pp. 62, 201 [also 94, 109, 125, 151, 167, 168]; see also Muḥammad Taqī al-Tustarī, *al-Akhbār al-dakhīla*: 1–10).

255. Two similar reports that quoted the Prophet as predicting twelve noble chiefs "from among his descendants," the last of them being the *qā'im* who would fill the earth with equity and justice, appeared in a collection of *ḥadīth*s ascribed to the Kūfan Zaydite transmitter of *ḥadīth*, 'Abbād b. Ya'qūb al-Rawājinī (d. ca. 250/864) (Kulaynī, 1:534). However, in the edited version of Rawājinī's work (entitled *Aṣl abī sa'īd 'abbād al-'usfurī*): 15, the number appears as eleven. Both reports were quoted from Imām Muḥammad al-Bāqir.

the community started to realize that the situation was more unusual than they had originally thought and that possibly there would not be a manifest Imām for the foreseeable future, that the question of the number of the Imāms came under serious consideration,[256] although many may have guessed and some reports may have started to circulate before that date.

The two prominent Shī'ite traditionists of the early fourth/tenth century, Muḥammad b. Ya'qūb al-Kulaynī and 'Alī b. Bābawayh al-Qummī, both of whom died in the late third decade of that century, are the first among those Imāmite authors whose works have survived to put forward the idea. In the introduction to his *al-Imāma wa 'l-tabṣira,* 'Alī b. Bābawayh mentions that because he found many Imāmites of his time in doubt about the truth of the doctrine because the Occultation had continued for such a long period, he wrote that book and collected some *ḥadīth*s that specified the exact number of the Imāms so that the community would know that it was following the right doctrine.[257] There is a chapter in Kulaynī's *Kitāb al-Kāfī* on the *ḥadīth*s which set the number of the Imāms at twelve[258] although the chapter is not in its most proper place and very much looks like a later supplement, possibly added by the author later in his life.[259] Later scholars managed to find many more *ḥadīth*s of this genre, so numerous that they formed the basis for later sizable monographs on the subject. According to these *ḥadīth*s the Prophet and the earlier Imāms had not only predicted the exact number of the Imāms but had even disclosed the full list of their names, including the vanished one that was the last on the list.

256. According to Najāshī: 310, Fāris b. Ḥātim wrote a book on the number of the Imāms on the basis of chronogrammatic calculation (*Kitāb 'Adad al-a'imma min ḥisāb al-jumal*). This work, however, clearly was not related to our discussion and most likely did not come to the same conclusion that the Imāmite community later reached on the exact number of the Imāms either.

257. 'Alī b. Bābawayh: 142, 151.

258. Kulaynī, 1:525–35.

259. Muḥammad b. Ibrāhīm al-Nu'mānī was a pupil and close associate of Kulaynī and personally copied his above-mentioned work (see Maḥfūẓ: 19). In the chapter of his *Kitāb al-Ghayba* that deals with the question of the exact number of the Imāms (pp. 57–111), Nu'mānī tried his best to collect

Many, however, questioned the originality and authenticity of these *ḥadīths*.[260] Their main argument was that if these *ḥadīths* were correct and original and the names of the Imāms were already determined and well known from the time of the Prophet, in fact, from antediluvian time,[261] then why had all of those disagreements on the question of succession occured among the Shī'ites, and why had all the many sects been formed, each following a different claimant to the Imāmate? Moreover, many of the authorities on

---

all reports he could find on that matter. After the completion of the book he found yet two more reports and he added them to the chapter (pp. 97–101) as attested by a note that the principal transmitter of the book, Abu 'l-Ḥusayn Muḥammad b. 'Alī al-Shujā'ī (Najāshī: 383), added before those two reports (p. 97). The work, as noted, was compiled some ten years after the death of Kulaynī. Nu'mānī, however, failed to quote sixteen of the total of twenty reports included in that chapter of the *Kāfī,* though he quoted some of those reports from other Shī'ite authorities of *ḥadīth.* This clearly indicates that in his copy of the *Kāfī* those sixteen reports, especially those that he quoted on other authorities, did not exist, particularly if one notes Nu'mānī's special preference for what is reported by Kulaynī. This is well attested by the fact that in one case in which he received one of those reports recorded in the *Kāfī* through a different source too, he quoted that on the authority of Kulaynī and merely referred to some additional words in a different transmission of it that was narrated by "some others" (pp. 94–95). Apart from four reports that Nu'mānī quoted from the above-mentioned chapter of the *Kāfī,* he quoted also a fifth report on the authority of Kulaynī that he quoted from 'Alī in the chapter of the Occultation of the *Kāfī,* but major differences exist between Nu'mānī's quotation from Kulaynī and what is in the present version of the *Kāfī.* In the *Kāfī,* 1:338, the duration of the Occultation is, as noted before, given as "six days, six months or six years." In Nu'mānī: 61 this phrase is recorded as "a period of time." In the *Kāfī* the *mahdī* is said to be the eleventh (or the twelfth according to another variation of the *ḥadīth*; see Nu'mānī, 61, n. 3; also Khuṣaybī: 262; Khazzāz: 316; and *Ghayba*: 204, depending on whether the phrase is *min ẓahrī, al-ḥādī'ashar min wuldī* or *min ẓahr al-ḥādī'ashar min wuldī*; in 'Umarī: 134 it is, however, *al-'āshir min wuld al-thānī*) generation from the descendants of 'Alī; the reference is missing in Nu'mānī (the Twelvers' *mahdī* is, in fact, the tenth generation from 'Alī).

260. See Khazzāz: 289.

261. See 'Alī b. Bābawayh: 145.

whose authority those *ḥadīth*s are quoted belonged to other groups.[262] Why should one follow a false doctrine when he himself had heard and, more importantly, had quoted the true doctrine from the Prophet or the Imām? The most prominent Imāmite scholar of the second/eighth century, Zurāra b. A'yan, reportedly did not know who the successor to Ja'far al-Ṣādiq was. According to numerous reports, when the news of the Imām's death reached Kūfa, Zurāra immediately sent his son to Medina to find out who the new Imām was. However, before the son returned, Zurāra became ill to the point of death. To fulfill the obligation that requires any Shī'ite to know his Imām at any given time he reportedly took a copy of the Qur'ān and said, "my Imām is the one whose Imāmate is determined in [or, variantly, 'established by'] this Book."[263] Clearly, if Zurāra had heard the name of Ja'far al-Ṣādiq's successor from him, as suggested by a report,[264] he would hardly have needed to resort to that option. Similarly, if the most learned of the disciples of Ja'far al-Ṣādiq did not know the Imām's successor, how then can one imagine that a new convert such as the poet al-Sayyid al-Ḥimyarī knew the full list of the Imāms so as to be able to include it in a poem ascribed to him?[265]

The Imāmite scholars rejected these criticisms. The fact that many of those on whose authority those reports were quoted did not admit the truth of their own words did not prove that the reports were not authentic. Those authorities may well have been driven by their worldly desires away from truth, while they actually knew what the truth was. The point made that such a prominent scholar as Zurāra did not know the new Imām was not true. He

262. That included persons such as the Companion Abū Hurayra (Ibn Bābawayh, *Nuṣūṣ* [quoted by Hāshim al-Baḥrānī: 210–12]) and 'Abd Allāh b. al-Ḥasan (Hāshim al-Baḥrānī: 125–6), none known to have had any pro-Imāmite tendency.

263. Kashshī: 154–5; *Kamāl*: 74–6. See also Abū Ghālib al-Zurārī: 114.

264. Nu'mānī: 327–8.

265. See his *Dīwān*: 357–69. According to a report quoted in *Kamāl*: 33, he had also told a friend that the *qā'im* would be the sixth generation from Ja'far al-Ṣādiq. See also Mufīd, *al-Risāla al-khāmisa fi 'l-ghayba*: 400–401; Hāshim al-Baḥrānī: 193.

knew who the successor to Ja'far al-Ṣādiq was; he did not disclose it because he was not sure whether it was permissible for him to publicize it. It was then a matter of precautionary secrecy that he did not make it public.[266] After all, in some of these *ḥadīth*s, the Imām or the first transmitter of the *ḥadīth* is quoted as advising the one who heard it from him to keep it a secret and not to disclose it to the wrong people.[267]

These *ḥadīth*s henceforth became the central point in the Imāmites' argument on the Occultation and in support of the truth of the Twelver Shī'ism doctrine. They were extremely instrumental in gradually removing the doubts and uncertainties of the Imāmite community and persuading the Imāmites of the truth of their doctrine. This entire success was made possible by the hard work and tireless efforts of the Imāmite transmitters of *ḥadīth* during the last decades of the Minor Occultation up to the middle of the fourth/tenth century. The Twelver Shī'ism doctrine and the Imāmite community owe a great deal to those faithful and courageous men.[268]

266. *Kamāl*: 75. See also 'Alī b. Bābawayh: 148.
267. Kulaynī, 1:528; Nu'mānī: 66; Ibn Bābawayh, *'Uyūn*, 1:45, 46; *Kamāl*: 311, 313.
268. A statement quoted from Imām 'Alī al-Hādī reportedly predicted this situation. It asserted that "if it were not for the learned men who exist in the community after the occultation of the *qā'im*, which learned men call [others] to him and instruct people about him, protect the doctrine with the divine proofs, and save the weak among the servants of God [the Shī'ites] from the nets of Satan and his followers and from the traps of the anti-Shī'ites, nobody would remain who had not converted from the religion of God. But they, the learned men, will take the reins of the hearts of the weak among the Shī'a in the same way that the pilot controls the rudder of the ship. Those [learned men] are the best people before God, the mighty, the exalted" (Abū Manṣūr al-Ṭabrisī, 2:260).

PART TWO

Abū Ja'far ibn Qiba al-Rāzī: His Life and Works

IV

Ibn Qiba: A Prominent Theologian

THEOLOGICAL DEBATES ON topics such as man's free will and predestination and the attributes of God started quite early in the Islamic community. This was due in part to the way that these topics were treated in different parts of the Qur'ān, which in some cases appear, at first glance, to be contradictory, and in part to the introduction of new ideas to Muslim society via converts and Muslim encounters with the followers of other religious traditions. There are reports which suggest that debates on the topic of man's free will and predestination had already started during the time of the Prophet.[1] These reports cannot possibly be substantiated, but heated debates about that question were reportedly quite common in such places as Baṣra[2] and Kūfa[3] two and one half decades after his death and were soon followed by debates on other theological questions that eventually led to the emergence of various theological schools in Islamic tradition. The second caliph, 'Umar, however, is reported to have been bitterly opposed to any debate on religious matters, including even questioning the meaning of some ambiguous words in the Qur'ān. He never engaged himself in that sort of questioning,[4] and he punished and banished those who did.[5] Following his lead, most later religious authorities in Sunnite Islam also opposed

1. See Suyūṭī, *Ṣawn al-manṭiq*: 35.
2. See Kashshī: 397.
3. See my introduction to Jishumī's *Risālat iblīs*: 3–5.
4. See Suyūṭī, *Itqān*, 2:113 (where it is quoted that 'Umar once hesitated about the meaning of a word in the Qur'ān but immediately tried to distract his attention so as not to engage his mind with something that God did not impose on him to know); idem, *al-Durr al-manthūr*, 6:317.
5. See the story of Ṣubaygh b. 'Isl al-Tamīmī (who was reported to 'Umar as someone who was questioning the meaning of some unclear words in the Qur'ān and was, therefore, severely beaten by 'Umar and banished from

theological debates,[6] which they always considered non-Islamic and of Jewish or Christian origin.[7]

Early in its history in the first decades of the second/eighth century the overwhelming trend in Imāmite Shī'ism was against *kalām* theology. The idea was that because the Imām was the supreme religious authority, all questions must be submitted to him, and his instructions, which were considered by his followers to represent the pure truth, must be followed. There was no room, therefore, for rational argument or personal opinion in religion.[8] Moreover, any debate on the nature of God and questions such as predestination and man's free will, about which the human mind could not reach proper, final conclusions, was regarded as inappropriate.[9] The Imāms refrained from involving themselves in that genre of debates[10] but

---

Medina to Baṣra with a public governmental announcement that nobody should ever contact him) in Dārimī, *Sunan*, 1:67; Ājurrī, *Sharī'a*: 73–4; Ibn Qudāma, *Dhamm al-ta'wīl*: 5; Ibn al-Jawzī, *manāqib 'Umar*: 108–10; Suyūṭī, *Ṣawn al-manṭiq*: 17–18. For other examples see Suyūṭī, *al-Durr al-manthūr*, 6:317, 321.

6. See the opinion of the eminent early Sunnite scholars, especially those of the founders of the four Sunnite legal schools, in Ibn Qutayba, *'Uyūn al-akhbār*, 2: 157; 'Uthmān b. Sa'īd al-Dārimī, *al-Radd 'ala 'l-jahmiyya*: 101–102; Abu 'l-Ḥasan al-Ash'arī, *Risāla fī istiḥsān al-khawḍ fi 'l-kalām*: 3; Khaṭīb, *Sharaf aṣḥab al-ḥadīth*: 78; Sahmī, *Ta'rīkh jurjān*: 98; Ibn 'Abd al-Barr, *Jāmi' bayān al-'ilm*: 364–6; Dhahabī, *al-'Uluww li 'l-'alī al-ghaffār*: 101–9; idem, *Siyar a'lām al-nubalā'*, 8:89, 90, 95; Ibn Qudāma, *Dhamm al-ta'wīl*: 5–6; Ibn 'Asākir, *Tabyīn kidhb al-muftarī*: 333–45; Tāj al-Dīn al-Subkī, *Ṭabaqāt al-shāfi'iyya*, 1:241; Zarkashī, 2:78; Suyūṭī, *Ṣawn al-manṭiq*: 31 ff.
7. See, for instance, Khaṭīb, *Ta'rīkh baghdād*, 7:61; Shahrastānī, 1:121; Ibn Ḥajar, *Tahdhīb*, 10:226; idem, *Lisān*, 2:29–30; Ibn Taymiyya, *al-'Aqīda al-ḥamawiyya*, 435.
8. See, for instance, Kulaynī, 1:179.
9. Ibid., 1: 92–4, 102, 103.
10. See Kashshī, 147–8. See also Ibn Bābawayh, *I'tiqādāt*: 74. Later, however, the Imāms had to take a position on some theological debates and topics, a fact especially true with 'Alī al-Riḍā because of the nature of the court of Ma'mūn. In an answer to a letter that described to the Imām the disagreements in the Imāmite community over the question of the attributes of God, Ḥasan al-'Askarī again emphasized the point that the people should not debate on divinity (Kulaynī, 1:103).

followed[11] the Qur'ān and instructed their followers to adhere[12] to it. However, the situation soon started to change, influenced by the general trend in the larger Muslim community at the time. A number of the disciples of Imām Ja'far al-Ṣādiq, including some of their elders who had been trained by his father and who were generally considered to be competent and well-informed authorities in religious matters,[13] engaged in theological debates and formulated their own opinions on various theological topics.[14] Among these men were such scholars as Zurāra b. A'yan (d. 148-150/765–767),[15] Abū Mālik al-Haḍramī,[16] Muḥammad b. 'Abd Allāh al-Ṭayyār (d. before 148/765),[17] Abū Ja'far al-Aḥwal Ṣāḥib al-Ṭāq,[18] Muḥammad

11. See Durust b. Abī Manṣūr, 162; Kulaynī, 1:150.
12. See, for instance, Kulaynī, 1:100, 102, 103.
13. See Durust b. Abī Manṣūr: 165–6.
14. See especially Madelung, "The Shī'ite and Khārijite Contribution to Pre-Ash'arite *Kalām*": 122–24.
15. On him see Kashshī: 133–60; Ibn al-Nadīm: 276; Najāshī: 175; Ṭūsī, *Fihrist*: 74–5; Nashwān: 164.
16. On him see Najāshī: 205; also Kulaynī, 1:410; Kashshī: 278; Mas'ūdī, *Murūj*, 4:28, 237. For his theological opinions see Abu 'l-Ḥasan al-Ash'arī, 1:115, 117, 124, 2:200; *Farq*: 52; Ibn Ḥazm, 4:158; Ibn Abi 'l-Ḥadīd, 3:224.
17. On him see Durust b. Abī Mansūr: 161; Barqī: 213; Kashshī: 210, 271, 275–6, 347–9; Mufīd, *Taṣḥīḥ*: 55. For his opinions see, for instance, Mufīd, *Awā'il*: 69.
18. On him see Kashshī: 185–191; Ibn al-Nadīm: 224; Najāshī: 325–6; Ṭūsī, *Fihrist*: 131–2. See also Khayyāṭ: 6; Khaṭīb, *Talkhīṣ al-mutashābih*, 1:249; Ibn Ḥajar, *Lisān*, 5:300–301. For his theological opinions see Abu 'l-Ḥasan al-Ash'arī, 1:111–12, 116, 118, 123, 291–2, 3:38, 184; *Farq*: 53; Ibn Ḥazm, 2:269, 4:158, 5:39; Isfarā'īnī: 40–41, 121; Maqdisī, 5:132; Shahrastānī, 1:218–19; Nashwān: 149. The Shī'ites call him Mu'min al-Ṭāq and the Sunnites Shayṭān al-Ṭāq. During his life, however, he was known among the Shī'ites as Ṣāḥib al-Ṭāq. See Kulaynī, 1:101, 351; Kashshī: 185, 186, 190, 282. See also Najāshī: 325. (The title of one of the works of Hishām b. al-Ḥakam is given in Najāshī: 433 as *Kitābuhu 'alā shayṭān al-ṭāq*. The reference is, however, taken from Ibn al-Nadīm: 224 as is well attested by the fact that the titles mentioned by Najāshī before and after that work follow their arrangement in Ibn al-Nadīm's list. The name that is obviously given to the book by the bibliographers, therefore, does not necessarily reflect that the Shī'ites ever called this scholar Shayṭān al-Ṭāq, especially if one keeps in mind Ibn Ḥajar's report in *Lisān*, 5:301, that Hishām was the first who called Abū Ja'far al-Aḥwal, Mu'min al-Ṭāq.)

b. Ḥakīm al-Khath'amī,[19] Hishām b. al-Ḥakam[20] (d. 179/795–796) and Hisham b. Sālim.[21]

A main difference between the Shī'ite scholars and other Muslim theologians of their time was the position that human reason had in each group's ideology. Unlike their Sunnite counterparts Shī'ite theologians regarded the Imām, and not mere human reason, as the ultimate source of knowledge, and they derived theological principles from the teachings of the Imāms.[22] Zurāra b. A'yan, whose opinions on several theological topics including the question of *istiṭā'a,* that is, whether man's capability precedes or coincides with the act, are quoted in the general works of *kalām,*[23] maintained, for instance, that he derived his own opinions on this latter topic from some remarks of Imām Ja'far al-Ṣādiq, although the Imām himself did not notice the collateral conclusion of his remarks because he was not thoroughly familiar with the nature of the theological debates that were going on at the time.[24] It is reported that once Abu 'l-Hudhayl al-'Allāf, the Mu'tazilite theologian (d. 235/849–850), and Hishām b. al-Ḥakam were engaged in a debate on a theological question in which Abu 'l-Hudhayl told Hishām that he would debate with him if the defeated party would agree to follow the doctrine of the victorious one. Hishām answered that this was not fair: "I would rather debate with you on the basis that if I defeat

19. On him see Kashshī: 448–9; Kulaynī, 1:56; Najāshī: 357; Ṭūsī, *Fihrsit*: 149. For his opinions see, for instance, Abu 'l-Ḥasan al-Ash'arī, 1:116.
20. On him see the article *Hishām b. al-Ḥakam* in *EI*², 3:496–8 (by Madelung).
21. On him see Kashshī: 269, 276–7, 279, 281–5, 478; Najāshī: 434; Ṭūsī, *Fihrist*: 174. See also Kulaynī, 1:351–2. For his opinions see Khayyāṭ: 6, 57; Kulaynī, 1:101, 105, 106; Abu 'l-Ḥasan al-Ash'arī, 1:109, 115–18, 283, 2:38, 199; 'Abd al-Qāhir al-Baghdādī, *Uṣūl al-dīn*: 337; idem, *Farq*: 65, 68–9; Murtaḍā, *Mas'ala fī nafy al-ru'ya*: 281,; Ibn Ḥazm, 4:158; Isfarā'īnī: 39–40, 120; Shahrastānī, 1:216–17; Nashwān: 149. See also Madelung, "The Shī'ite and Khārijite Contribution": 121–2, 125, 129–31, 134, 136.
22. This was specifically instructed by Imām Ja'far al-Ṣādiq. See Mufīd, *Taṣḥīḥ*: 55–6.
23. See, for instance, Abu 'l-Ḥasan al-Ash'arī, 1:110–11, 116; Mufīd, *Awā'il*: 69; *Farq*: 52; Isfarā'īnī: 40, 121; Shahrastānī, 1:218. See also Kashshī: 268; Sam'ānī, 6:278.
24. Kashshī: 147–8. Cf. Durust b. Abī Manṣūr: 162.

you, you follow my doctrine, but if you defeat me, I would go to my Imām."[25] This view of the subordination of reason to the Imām, or in other words, that reason is a means and not a source, remained the main characteristic of the Shī'ite theology for the next one hundred years[26] until the middle of the third/ninth century.[27] All prominent Imāmite Shī'ite theologians who appeared in that period belonged to the same trend,[28] including scholars such as 'Alī b. Ismā'īl al-Maythamī,[29] 'Alī b. Manṣūr,[30] Yūnus b. 'Abd al-Raḥmān al-Qummī,[31] Abū Ja'far al-Sakkāk[32] and Faḍl b. Shādhān al-Naysābūrī[33] whose views on many theological subjects are recorded in the sources.

25. Ibn Bābawayh, *I'tiqādāt*: 74. See also Kulaynī, 1:170–171 where Hishām b. al-Ḥakam is quoted as telling Ja'far al-Ṣādiq that he derived his principles from the Imām's teachings.
26. See Shahrastānī, 1:193.
27. This might have been one of the reasons that Ibn Abi 'l-Ḥadīd, 3:224, called these Shī'ite theologians *mustaḍ'afū* 'l-*mutakallimīn*.
28. See, for instance, Ibn Ḥazm, 5:39–40 (for Maythamī); Kashshī: 499 (for Yūnus).
29. On him see Khayyāṭ: 6, 99, 142; Kashshī: 262–3, Ibn al-Nadīm: 223; Najāshī: 251; Ṭūsī, *Fihrist*: 87; Ibn Ḥazm, 4:158; Khaṭīb, *Talkhīṣ al-mutashābih*, 1:218, 249. For his views and theological debates see Khayyāṭ: 6, 99, 142; Kulaynī, 1:101; Abu 'l-Ḥasan al-Ash'arī, 1:115, 126, 2:200; Mufīd, *Majālis*, 1:5–6, 9–10, 31, 39–40, 44, 52; Murtaḍā, *mas'ala fī nafy al-ru'ya*: 281; Ibn Ḥazm, 5:39–40; *Farq*: 69.
30. On him see Khayyāṭ: 6; Kashshī: 256, 278; Kulaynī, 1:72; Najāshī: 255, 433; Mas'ūdī, *Murūj*, 4:238–9. See also Abu 'l-Ḥasan al-Ash'arī, 1:134; Shahrastānī, 1:225. For his theological views see Murtaḍā, *Mas'ala fī nafy al-ru'ya*: 281; Ibn Ḥazm, 4:158, Ibn Abi 'l-Ḥadīd, 3:228, 229.
31. On him see Kashshī: 483–99; Abu 'l-Ḥasan al-Ash'arī, 1:134–5; Ibn al-Nadīm: 276; Najāshī: 446–8; Ṭūsī, *Fihrist*: 181–2; Shahrastānī, 1:225. For his opinions see Sa'd b. 'Abd Allāh: 98; Abu 'l-Ḥasan al-Ash'arī, 1:110; Murtaḍā, *Mas'ala fī nafy al-ru'ya*: 281; *Farq*: 52–3; Isfarā'īnī: 40, 120; Shahrastānī, 1:220; Ibn Abi 'l-Ḥadīd, 3:228, 229.
32. On him see Khayyāṭ: 6, 110–11, 142; Kashshī: 539; Ibn al-Nadīm: 225; Abu 'l-Ḥasan al-Ash'arī, 1:135; Najāshī: 328–9; Mas'ūdī, *Murūj*, 4:240; Ṭūsī, *Fihrist*: 132; *Ma'ālim*: 97; Shahrastānī, 1:225. For his opinions see Khayyāṭ: 6, 110–11, 142; Abu 'l-Ḥasan al-Ash'arī, 1:287, 291, 2:181; Ibn Ḥazm, 4:158, 5:40; Ibn Abi 'l-Ḥadīd, 3:228, 231.
33. See above, chapter 2. For his views on theological matters see, for instance, Ibn Abi 'l-Ḥadīd, 3:288.

This tendency, however, remained a minor one in the Shī'ite community, the overwhelming majority[34] of whose scholars refrained from any sort of rational argument and theological debate and devoted themselves to transmitting the teachings of the Imāms. There was bitter opposition, for instance, to Zurāra and his disciples among the circle of traditionists around Ja'far al-Ṣādiq to the degree that each of the two groups called the other infidel.[35] Hishām b. al-Ḥakam also faced hostile treatment from the Shī'ite community of his time.[36] His student Yūnus b. 'Abd al-Raḥmān, who had established a circle of followers in Baghdad,[37] received similar hostile treatment from the Shī'ite community of Qum[38] and of Baṣra[39] as well as from the disciples of Imām 'Alī al-Riḍā. The latter went so far as to declare Yūnus and his followers infidels.[40] A major factor in these reactions was that although the Imāmite theologians drew upon the teachings of the Imāms, their theological conclusions in some cases substantially deviated from those teachings and ran against what was commonly accepted by the Imāmite community. The widely cited opinions of Hishām b. al-Ḥakam and Hishām b. Sālim on the divine body and form,[41] whatever their real intentions may have been, were, at face value, prime examples of that sort of contradiction and were sources of more divisions within the Imāmite community for several decades.[42] The severe conflicts and disputes between these scholars themselves[43] and between their followers[44] only added to

34. See Ibn al-Rāwandī, *Faḍīḥat al-mu'tazila*: 105 (Khayyāṭ: 4), Ibn Qiba, *Naqḍ kitāb al-ishhād*: para. 34; Fakhr al-Dīn al-Rāzī, *Maḥṣūl*, 2:188.
35. Kashshī: 498.
36. Ibid., 270.
37. Ibid., 496.
38. Ibid.: 489, 495–7.
39. Ibid.: 487, 490.
40. Ibid.: 498–9.
41. See Madelung, "The Shī'ite and Khārijite Contribution": 122.
42. At least until the year 255/869. See Kulaynī, 1:102–3, 108. For similar theological disagreements among the Imāmites in the early period see ibid., 1:159–60; Abu 'l-Ḥasan al-Ash'arī, 1:106–33. Ṭūsī, *'Udda*, 1:364–5. See also Ibn Bābawayh, *'Uyūn*, 1:142; Murtaḍā, *Ibṭāl al-'amal bi-akhbār al-āḥād*: 310; Najāshī: 329, 373 (also 140); 438; Ṭūsī, *Fihrist*: 37; *Ghayba*: 138; Malaṭī: 38; Shahrastānī, 1:193, 203.
43. See, for instance, Kashshī: 268, 279, 284–5; Najāshī: 433; Pseudo Mufīd, *Ikhtiṣāṣ*: 47.
44. See examples of that in Kashshī: 279, 498; Kulaynī, 1:102–3, 108, 159–60.

the difficult environment in which that rational tendency continued its life.

An important factor helped many Shīʿite theologians to enjoy the support of the Imāms and a reasonable degree of respect within the Shīʿite community. Since the decline and subsequent fall of the Umayyads, the topic of the imāmate had attracted some of the most heated debates in the Muslim community. Although debate on this topic was not confined to the theologians, it was the theologians who debated the most and the most seriously. For the Shīʿite theologians, debating this topic in support of Shīʿite points of view was the main task. The Imāms always encouraged and praised the ability of the ingenious[45] Shīʿite theologians in dialectics, as well as their endeavors to support the Shīʿite doctrine,[46] although at times they pointed out that rational argument is good as a means in dialectic, but no belief should be constructed upon it, because religion is the realm of revelation, not reason.[47]

The traditional school of Shīʿite theology continued until the end of the period of the "presence" of the Imāms in the mid-third/ninth century as the only theological trend in Imāmite Shīʿism. From the middle of that century, however, Muʿtazilite points of view were gradually introduced into Shīʿism by a new generation of scholars who helped form a new and more reason-oriented school of Shīʿite *kalām*.[48] The followers of this new school adopted the main principles of Muʿtazilite doctrine concerning the attributes and justice of God and man's free will while retaining and strongly defending the Shīʿite doctrine of the Imāmate. Unlike what the Muʿtazilite Khayyāṭ stated[49] (with a clear sectarian bias), it seems

45. See Kashshī: 319, 349, 448–9; Mufīd, *Taṣḥīḥ al-iʿtiqād*: 55–6.
46. See Kulaynī, 1:171, 173; Kashshī: 186, 268, 278, 349, 483–90; Mufīd, *Taṣḥīḥ al-iʿtiqād*: 55–6. See also Abū Manṣūr al-Ṭabrisī, 2:259 where it is quoted that ʿAlī al-Hādī gave the highest honor to an Imāmite scholar who had debated with an anti-Shīʿite debater and defeated him.
47. Kashshī: 189. See also Kulaynī, 1:56–8; *Kamāl*: 324.
48. For the specifications and doctrines of this new Shīʿite school of *kalām*, see especially Madelung, "Imāmism and Muʿtazilite Theology." for the relation between the Shīʿites and Muʿtazilites see further ʿAbd al-Jabbār, *Ṭabaqāt*: 291; Tanūkhī, 8:70; Abu 'l-Maʿālī: 34; Ibn Taymiyya, *Minhāj al-sunna*, 1:46; Ibn Ḥajar, *Lisān*, 4:459.
49. See his *Intiṣār*: 6, 127, 144.

that this new trend did not start with some individuals who had been formerly associated with the Mu'tazilites but by some Shī'ite scholars who approached the doctrines and teachings of the theological schools of their time with considerable independence,[50] such as Abu 'l-Aḥwaṣ Dāwūd b. Asad al-Baṣrī[51] and 'Abd al-Raḥmān b. Aḥmad b. Jabrawayh al-'Askarī,[52] both from the mid-third/ninth century. The trend was then followed by such philosophy-minded scholars from the younger generation as the two Nawbakhtīs,[53] Abū Sahl Ismā'īl b. 'Alī (d. 311/924)[54] and Abū Muḥammad Ḥasan b. Mūsā (d. 300–310/912–922),[55] and further strengthened by the contributions of some scholars who had started as Mu'tazilites but later converted to Shī'ism,[56] such as Abū 'Abd Allāh Muḥammad b.

50. See Madelung, "Imāmism and Mu'tazilite Theology": 16.
51. On him see Abu 'l-Ḥasan al-Ash'arī, 1:135; Najāshī: 157; Ṭūsī, *Fihrist*: 190; Asad Allāh al-Tustarī: 204.
52. On him see Najāshī: 236. His opinions on the nature of faith is quoted in Abu 'l-Ḥasan al-Ash'arī, 1:125–6. According to this source, he agreed with the Mu'tazilites on their opinion concerning God's unconditional fulfillment of his threat of punishment of the sinners (*wa'īd*). For other supporters of this idea among the Imāmite scholars see Najāshī: 381 (on Abu 'l-Ḥusayn al-Sūsanjirdi); al-Sharīf al-Raḍī, *Ḥaqā'iq al-ta'wīl*: 16–17 (on himself); Ibn al-Muṭahhar, *Khulāṣa*: 148 (on Muḥammad b. al-Ḥasan al-Ṭūsī). See also Shahrastānī, 1:193, 203.
53. *Banū Nawbakht*, as always referred to by Mufīd (see Madelung, "Imāmism and Mu'tazilite Theology": 15–16). Murtaḍā, *Dhakhīra*: 114, however, quoted an opinion that Mufīd (*Sarawiyya*: 217) attributed to *Banū Nawbakht* as the view of *ibnā Nawbakht* (= *abnā' Nawbakht*?). The family produced many scholars and notables during the third and fourth/ninth and tenth centuries. 'Abd al-Jalīl al-Qazwīnī: 209 mentioned that it produced some forty scholars, all authors of books (see also pp. 184 and 186 where two of these scholars, Abū Sahl and Ibrāhīm [apparently author of *Kitāb al-Yāqūt* who was possibly from the fifth/eleventh century; see Madelung, "Imāmism and Mu'tazilite Theology": 15] are named.) Mufīd also refers to the followers of the Banū Nawbakht (*Awā'il*: 33).
54. On him see the article "Abū Sahl Nawbakhtī" in *Encyclopaedia Iranica*, 1:372–3 (by W. Madelung).
55. On him see 'Abbās Iqbāl: 125–140.
56. The trend of conversion from Mu'tazilism to Shī'ism had allegedly already started early in the third/ninth century (see Majlisī, 50:187), and continued well after that century. For examples from later periods see Najāshī: 269, 403.

'Abd Allāh b. Mumlak al-Iṣfahānī[57] and Abū Ja'far b. Qiba al-Rāzī.

* * * * *

Abū Ja'far Muḥammad b. 'Abd al-Raḥmān b. Qiba[58] al-Rāzī was a prominent Shī'ite theologian at the turn of the third/ninth century and is described by some of his biographers as the head of the Imāmite community in his time,[59] although very little biographical information is available about him. It is known only that he started as a Mu'tazilite and later converted to Imāmite Shī'ism; that he lived in Ray where he also died; that he lived in the second half of the third/ninth century, probably into the beginning of the next century; and, as attested by the following story about the scholarly exchange between him and Abu 'l-Qāsim al-Balkhī, he died before Sha'bān 319/August 931 when Balkhī died. His biographers[60] all praised him for his mastery in *kalām,* but, according to one of them,[61] he was a transmitter of *ḥadīth* as well, and Abū Ja'far Muḥammad b. Ja'far b. Aḥmad b. Buṭṭa al-Qummī al-Mu'addib,

57. On him see Ibn al-Nadīm: 226; Najāshī: 380; Ṭūsī, *Fihrist*: 193; *Ma'ālim*: 142. His name and opinion on the nature of accidents (*a'rāḍ*) appear in Abu 'l-Ḥasan al-Ash'arī, 2:47. He had a discussion with his contemporary Mu'tazilite theologian, Abū 'Alī al-Jubbā'ī, on the question of the imāmate that Ibn al-Nadīm: 226 has mentioned. Among the writings of Ḥasan b. Mūsā al-Nawbakhtī listed by Najāshī: 63 is a book called *Sharḥ majālisihi mak'a abī 'abd allāh b. mumlak raḥimahu 'llāh.*
58. This is the correct form of his grandfather's name according to Ibn al-Muṭahhar, *Īḍāḥ*: 286 on the authority of Ṣafī al-Dīn Muḥammad b. Ma'add al-Mūsawī, a well-informed expert on the biographical data (see also idem, *Khulāṣa*: 143). This has also been the common and traditional pronunciation of the name among the Shī'ite scholars of all generations (*Īḍāḥ*: 286. See also 'Alam al-Hudā: 297–8). The word must have been the Arabicized form of an old Persian word.
59. See Ibn al-Nadīm: 225; Najāshī: 375–6; Ṭūsī, *Fihrist*: 132; *Ma'ālim*: 95; Ibn al-Muṭahhar , *Khulāṣa*: 143. See also Shahrastānī, 1:225 where his name is mentioned among the early Shī'ite authors; also Asad Allāh al-Tustarī, *Kashf al-qinā'*: 204–5, quoting al-Sharīf al-Murtaḍā who put the name of Ibn Qiba on the beginning of a list of the authorities of the Shī'ite school whose agreement was essential if a consensus was to be formed on any religious question (see also Murtaḍā, *Shāfī*, 1: 127, 2: 323).
60. Ibn al-Muṭahhar, *Khulāṣa*: 143 (copied in Sarawī: 271–2).
61. Najāshī: 375.

a prolific Shī'ite traditionist of the early fourth/tenth century,[62] mentioned him in the index he wrote of his teachers as one of his authorities in *ḥadīth*.[63] He was actively involved in both written and oral sectarian debates in support of the Shī'ite doctrines against supporters of other schools as attested by the titles of his works as well as examples of his oral debates that are recorded in his writings.[64]

He also had correspondence and scholarly exchanges with other scholars of his time. Two works are mentioned in the list of the writings of his contemporary, Abū Muḥammad Ḥasan b. Mūsā al-Nawbakhtī as *Jawābātuhu li-abī ja'far ibn qiba* and *Jawābāt ukhar li-abī ja'far ayḍan*.[65] There was an exchange of polemics between him and his Mu'tazilite contemporary, Abu 'l-Qāsim 'Abd Allāh b. Aḥmad b. Maḥmūd al-Balkhī, also known as Ka'bī (d. 319/931).[66] It was facilitated by a contemporary theologian of Ray,[67] Abu 'l-Ḥusayn al-Sūsanjirdī,[68] a frequent traveler[69] and an acquaintance of both men, who visited Balkhī in his hometown of Balkh and gave him a copy of Ibn Qiba's main polemic on the Imāmate question, *Kitāb al-Inṣāf fi 'l-imāma*. Balkhī read the book and refuted it in a book he called *al-Mustarshid fi 'l-imāma*. Sūsanjirdī then went

62. On him see Najāshī: 373.

63. Muḥsim al-Amīn, 9:380, mentions that Abū Muḥammad Ḥasan b. Hamza al-'Alawī al-Ṭabarī, known as Mar'ash (d. 358/967–8), also related *ḥadīth* from Ibn Qiba. This must be an error caused by the fact that this scholar transmitted the works of Ibn Buṭṭa (Najāshī: 373). His narration from Ibn Qiba must, therefore, have been through Ibn Buṭṭa, not direct.

64. See Mufīd, *Majālis*, 1:4 quoting from Ibn Qiba's *Kitāb al-Inṣāf*.

65. Najāshī: 63.

66. On him see the article "Abu 'l-Qāsim al-Ka'bī" in *Encyclopaedia Iranica*, 1:359–62 (by J. Van Ess).

67. Sūsanjirdī's biographers did not mention that he lived in Ray, but this may be inferred from his own statement in the previously mentioned story in which he says that he went to Balkh and then "returned" to Ray.

68. Abu 'l-Ḥusayn Muḥammad b. Bishr al-Ḥamdūnī al-Sūsanjirdī, a pious Shī'ite theologian with strong Mu'tazilite tendencies (as can be attested by his support of the Mu'tazilite aforementioned doctrine of *wa'īd*), a pupil of Abū Sahl al-Nawbakhtī, and author of several books including two works on the question of Imāmate called *al-Muqni'* and *al-Munqidh* (or *al-Inqādh*). See Ibn al-Nadīm: 226; Najāshī: 376, 381; Ṭūsī, *Fihrist*: 132; *Ma'ālim*: 96; Ibn Ḥajar, *Lisān*, 5:93.

69. Najāshī: 376, 381 quotes that he went fifty times on the annual pilgrimage to Mecca.

back to Ray and gave Balkhī's book to Ibn Qiba who, in turn, wrote a refutation of it, *al-Mustathbit fi 'l-imāma.* Next Sūsanjirdī carried this last refutation to Balkhī who refuted it in a book called *Naqḍ al-mustathbit.* When Sūsanjirdī next brought that book to Ray to show it to Ibn Qiba, he found that the man had already died.[70] In the list of Balkhī's works in Ibn al-Nadīm's *Kitāb al-Fihrist,* a book is mentioned as *Kitāb al-Kalām fi 'l-imāma 'alā ibn qiba,*[71] which should refer to one of his two books in that chain of polemical exchange.

Ibn Abi 'l-Ḥadīd, a later Mu'tazilite, claimed that Ibn Qiba had been a student of Balkhī.[72] There is, however, no evidence to support this claim; indeed, the exchange mentioned may indicate that they regarded each other as peers. It seems, therefore, quite plausible to suggest that Ibn Abi 'l-Ḥadid's assertion is a Mu'tazilite's biased interpretation of the same story. It should also be noted that among the Mu'tazilite theologians of the third/ninth century was a certain Ṣāliḥ Qubba[73] whose name and views are quoted in many later works.[74] Some modern writers,[75] clearly confused by the fact that the two words *qubba* and *qiba* are spelled the same way in Arabic script, have identified Ṣāliḥ Qubba with Ibn Qiba. This is clearly a mistake. The two scholars even lived in different periods;

70. Najāshī: 376.
71. Ibn al-Nadīm: 219.
72. Ibn Abi 'l-Ḥadid, 1:206, transcribed by Ibn Maytham, 1:252.
73. According to Abu 'l-Ḥasan al-Ash'arī, 2:15, the man was called Qubba (dome) because this word was used by one of his opponents in a counter-argument that Ṣāliḥ had to acknowledge and submit to. Shahrastānī, 1:160, however, mentions a certain Ṣāliḥ b. Qubba b. Ṣubayḥ b. 'Amr alongside theologians such as Ghaylān, Jahm b. Ṣafwān, Burghūth and Ibn Karrām, who is apparently the same man; thus, Qubba was his father's name.
74. See, for instance, Abu 'l-Ḥasan al-Ash'arī, 2:15, 64–5, 82–3, 107, 220, 221; 'Abd al-Jabbār, *Ṭabaqāt al-mu'tazila*: 281; idem, *al-Muḥīt bi 'l-taklīf*: 380; Murtaḍā, *Mas'ala fi 'l-manāmāt*: 10; *Farq*: 18, 93, 193; Ibn Ḥazm, 3:34, 5:71, 123; Shahrastānī, 1:160, 165.
75. Nashshār: 78 and the editors of 'Abd al-Jabbār's *al-Muḥīt bi 'l-taklīf* (Cairo, 1965): 439 and Ibn Ḥazm's *Fiṣal* (Riyadh, 1982): 3:34, 5:71. The same should be said of Ibn Baṭṭa's inclusion of Ṣāliḥ Qubba among the theologians of the Shī'ites in his *Kitāb al-Sharḥ wa 'l-ibāna*: 92.

Ṣāliḥ Qubba lived at the time of the Abbasid Wāthiq (r. 227–232/842–847)[76] and so preceded Ibn Qiba by two generations.

Among the writings of Ibn Qiba the following are known:

1. *Kitāb al-Inṣāf fi 'l-imāma,*[77] or *al-Inṣāf wa 'l-intiṣāf* as mentioned by al-Sharīf al-Murtaḍā.[78] This was apparently Ibn Qiba's main contribution on the topic of the Imāmate. The work was extant until the seventh/thirteenth century.[79] Paragraphs of it are quoted in other books from the late fourth/tenth to the mid-seventh/thirteenth century,[80] but nothing is known about the book after that.[81] Balkhī's refutation of this book is also lost.

2. *Al-Mustathbit fi 'l-imāma,*[82] the polemic he wrote in defense of his *Kitāb al-Inṣāf* against Balkhī's refutation and which was, in turn, refuted by another book by Balkhī. Neither of these works seems to have survived.

76. 'Abd al-Jabbār, *Ṭabaqāt*: 281.
77. Ibn al-Nadīm: 225; Najāshī: 375; Ṭūsī, *Fihrist*: 132; *Ma'ālim*: 95.
78. Murtaḍā, *Shāfī*, 2: 323–4.
79. Ibn Abī 'l-Ḥadīd, 1:206.
80. They include (1) a long section quoted by al-Sharīf al-Murtaḍā in his *Shāfī*, 1:127 (transcribed in Ṭūsī's *Talkhīṣ al-shafī*, 2:119–23, referred to also by Fakhr al-Dīn al-Rāzī in his *Muḥaṣṣal*: 363) as well as two other passages in 2: 324–5; (2) a paragraph in Mufīd's *Majālis*, 1:4; (3) a reference in Ibn Abi 'l-Ḥadīd, 1:206 (transcribed in Ibn Maytham, 1:252), which stated that many paragraphs of one of 'Alī's sermons, the one that is known as the *Shiqshiqiyya*, are quoted in Ibn Qiba's *Kitāb al-Inṣāf*; and (4) several paragraphs in 'Abd al-Jabbār's *Mughnī*, including 20(1): 125–7, 145–6, 156, 158, all of which are quoted from an unnamed Imāmite author in his book, but as attested to by al-Sharīf al-Murtaḍā in his *Shāfī*, 2: 323, all are taken from Ibn Qiba's *Kitāb al-Inṣāf* (the paragraph on *Mughnī*, 20[1]: 158 is the same as that quoted in *Shāfī*, 1: 127). According to Murtaḍā, this section of the *Mughnī* essentially addresses Ibn Qiba's arguments in *Kitāb al-Inṣāf*.
81. Āghā Buzurg, 2:396, suggests that the early thirteenth/nineteenth century Shī'ite author, Muḥammad b. 'Abd al-Nabī al-Naysābūrī al-Akhbārī (d. 1233/1818) may have had a copy of this book because he quotes from it in his work *Maṣādir al-anwār*. What Akhbārī quotes in that work (fol. 2a) is, however, Ibn Qiba's *Naqḍ kitāb al-ishhād* (which he calls *Kitāb al-Naqḍ 'ala 'l-zaydiyya*) on the basis of the text preserved in Ibn Bābawayh's *Kamāl al-dīn* (see below).
82. Najāshī: 375; Ṭūsī, *Fihrist*: 132; *Ma'ālim*: 95. This may be identical with *Kitāb al-Imāma* that Ibn al-Nadīm: 225 mentions after *Kitāb al-Inṣāf fi 'l-imāma*.

3. *Al-Radd 'alā abī 'alī al -jubbā'ī.*[83] Abū 'Alī Muḥammad b. 'Abd al-Wahhāb al-Jubbā'ī (d. 303/916) was a prominent Mu'tazilite theologian whose opinions on many topics were disputed by other theologians of his and later times. It is not clear what topic Ibn Qiba's work was on or which opinion of Jubbā'ī he refuted. The work is otherwise unknown.

4. *Al-Ta'rīf fī madhhab al-imāmiyya wa fasād madhhab al-zaydiyya,*[84] or *Kitāb al-Ta'rīf 'ala 'l-zaydiyya* as recorded by Ṭūsī,[85] and apparently identical with *Kitāb al-Radd 'ala 'l-zaydiyya* mentioned by Najāshī.[86] Also lost.

5. *Al-Mas'ala al-mufrada fi 'l-imāma,*[87] apparently identical with the tract that Ibn Bābawayh has quoted in his *Kamāl al-dīn*[88] as Ibn Qiba's answer to an Imāmite of his time in defense of the Imāmite opinion concerning the Twelfth Imām against the Mu'tazilites' criticisms.

6. *Naqḍ kitāb al-ishhād li-abī zayd al-'alawī.*[89] This work too, a refutation of *Kitāb al-Ishhād,* an anti-Imāmite work by Abū Zayd al-'Alawī, a Zaydite scholar whose name and work are only known through Ibn Qiba's refutation, is quoted in full, with the exception of the opening formula (*khuṭba*) and introductory remarks, by Ibn Bābawayh in the book mentioned.[90] Many parts of the refuted book are preserved in this work by Ibn Qiba, because in many places he quotes it paragraph by paragraph and gives his answers to them.

7. *Al-Naqḍ 'alā abi 'l-ḥasan 'alī b. aḥmad b. bashshār,* refutation of a tract written by Abu 'l-Ḥasan 'Alī b. Aḥmad b. Bashshār on the Occultation question. Ibn Bashshār himself was, obviously, a supporter of Ja'far, the brother of the eleventh Imām. His tract,

83. Najāshī: 375.
84. *Ma'ālim*: 93–96.
85. Ṭūsī, *Fihrist*: 132.
86. Najāshī: 375.
87. Ibid.
88. *Kamāl*, 60–63.
89. *Ma'ālim*: 96. It may have been this work that Najāshī refers to as *al-Radd 'ala 'l-zaydiyya*. As noted, Muḥammad b. 'Abd al-Nabī al-Naysābūrī al-Akhbārī calls it *Kitāb al-Naqḍ 'ala 'l-zaydiyya* in his *Maṣādir al-anwār*: 2a.
90. *Kamāl*: 94–126.

together with Ibn Qiba's critique, is quoted in full, again with the omission of the opening formulas and introductory remarks, in the work mentioned of Ibn Bābawayh.[91] This work of Ibn Qiba is not specifically mentioned by his biographers.

* * * * *

Apart from his active engagement in oral and written debates in defense of the Imāmite Shī'ite doctrine, Ibn Qiba's most obvious contribution to Imāmite Shī'ite thought was his effort to formulate a refined, straightforward, and defensible Shī'ite theory of the Imāmate. The main points of this theory, as will be noted in all three works of his that follow, can be summarized as follows: The successor to the Prophet must always be a member of his family, as attested by a widely transmitted quotation from him. This person must be the most knowledgeable and pious of that family, and so quality and merit, not lineage, determines the holder of the position of Imāmate in each generation.[92] However, because the people themselves cannot determine, or at least agree on, who is the most qualified, the Prophet and then each Imām have the obligation to clearly and explicitly designate their successors.[93] This designation

91. Ibid.: 51–60.

92. On this question, however, he is inconsistent. See his *Naqḍ kitāb al-ishhād*: para. 21; *Naqḍ ibn bashshār*: para. 5.

93. This is the principle of *naṣṣ* or *waṣiyya*, which did not necessarily require that the Imāmate be hereditary. Many of the early Imāmite reports do not, in fact, mention the lineage among the conditions of the Imām but emphasize that he is the one who is the most qualified and is designated by the previous Imām (see, for instance, Ṣaffār: 489; Kulaynī, 1:277, 285; Nu'mānī: 242; Ibn Bābawayh, *Khiṣāl*: 428. See also Majlisī, 25:115–75). Muslim heresiographers note that the Imāmites in early centuries were divided among themselves on this question; some held that the Imāmate is hereditary; others rejected this opinion and maintained that it follows the designation and not lineage ('Abd al-Qāhir al-Baghdādī, *Uṣūl al-dīn*: 285–6; Nashwān: 150. Cf. Pseudo Qāsim b. Ibrāhīm: 104a, 105a; Sa'd b. 'Abd Allāh: 102, 106, 107 which attributed the view that it is hereditary to all Imāmites). They also mentioned that the first view is supported by the majority of the Imāmites, which seems to be true (see Ḥimyarī: 146; Abū Sahl al-Nawbakhtī: 92; Kulaynī, 1:284–6, 351; 'Alī b. Bābawayh: 179, 188–9, 191; Kashshī: 254, 458; Nu'mānī: 242; *Kamāl*: 323, 426).

becomes binding upon those who are living in the same age as the Prophet or the Imām and who hear the designation from him in person. It will become binding upon others who are living in different places or times through the reports of those who heard it from the Prophet or the Imām. This report must be a sound and safe one, widely known and transmitted by groups of people in different places in each generation so that no possibility exists for the transmitters to collaborate and fabricate a lie. Such a report, technically called *mutawātir,* is regarded by Muslim scholars from all schools to be indisputable proof.

It is this, in Ibn Qiba's opinion, that separates the mainstream Imāmites from splinter groups, because the mainstream has that sort of widespread report to prove that its Imām in each generation was designated by the previous Imām, whereas the splinter groups do not. This transmission was, of course, widespread among the Shī'ite transmitters themselves, but Ibn Qiba insisted that their widespread transmission in these cases is as valid as that of any other group in any other matter because their number reached the number required for the *tawātur.* If the authority of their reports on the designation by each Imām of his successor as held by the Imāmites could be contested and the acknowledgment of people other than the Imāmite Shī'ites themselves were required for the validity of such reports, no report in the world could constitute a valid proof. Therefore, the validity of all religions and miracles, except for the Qur'ān, would be doubted and questioned because all of these are proved through the same sort of reports and none has received the acknowledgment of all mankind.[94]

The Prophet's designation of 'Alī was clear and explicit. However, the majority of the early Muslims who did not follow that designation did not deviate from Islam, as some early Shī'ites thought. In the confused situation that immediately followed the death of the Prophet, an interpretation was offered of the Prophet's statement concerning the question of leadership of the Muslim community after his death, which suggested that it was up to the people to decide who their next leader should be. Most of those

94. The same analysis and argument is also offered by Abū Sahl al-Nawbakhtī: 89.

who did not follow 'Alī did so on good faith on the basis of that interpretation. It was wrong, but it was not an intentional violation of the Prophet's decree.[95]

Unlike what the extremists suggested, the Imāms were merely prominent pious scholars of the *sharī'a.* They did not possess the knowledge of the unseen, a privilege that only God enjoys. Whoever believes that anyone apart from Him knows the unseen is a polytheist. Whoever says that God changes His mind because of changing circumstance is an infidel.[96]

Ibn Qiba's influence on the later Imāmite theology in this topic was immense and longlasting. Scholars such as the Sharīf al-Murtaḍā and Ṭūsī not only followed him on all of these points, with the exception of the question of lineage, but even used his actual phrases.[97] The repetition of the remaining paragraphs from

95. See below, chapters 5–7.
96. See below, chapter 7.
97. For example, his argument with the widespread Shī'ite report of the designations by the Prophet and the Imāms of their successors is adopted in al-Sharīf al-Raḍī, *Khaṣā'iṣ al-A'imma*, p. 41; Khazzāz: 314, 326, 328; Murtaḍā, *Shāfī*, 2: 76–80, 3:145–6; idem, *Dhakhīra*: 463, 502; Ṭūsī, *Mufṣiḥ*: 118, 134; idem, *Iqtiṣād*: 203, 235; idem, *Tamhīd*: 353, 393, 399; Abu 'l-Ṣalāḥ al-Ḥalabī, *Kāfī*: 70, 100; idem, *Taqrīb*: 137; Ṭabrisī, *I'lām*: 207, 272, 296, 345; Ibn Maytham, *Qawā'īd*: 190. (Ṭabrisī, however, questions the validity of this argument in pp. 257, 357 [see also 265] on the basis that the suppression and fear that existed during the time that the Umayyads and Abbasids were in full control did not permit the Shī'a to freely talk about their Imāms, let alone to transmit the explicit designation of one for another as the next head of the religion, which would be tantamount to an open challenge to the authority of the caliphs. He, therefore, maintains that the right argument to prove the succession of 'Alī Zayn al-'Ābidīn, Muḥammad al-Bāqir, 'Alī al-Hādī, and, in fact, that of most of the Imāms [p. 257], would be a rational one based on external evidence, not a widespread *naṣṣ*.) His discussion on the meanings of the word *mawlā*, used in a Prophetic statement about 'Alī and his argument with Arabic poetry to suggest that it means head and leader (Mufīd, *Majālis*, 1:4; 'Abd al-Jabbār, *Mughnī*, 20(1):145– 6, 155) is adopted in *Shāfī*, 2: 268–73; *Dhakhīra*: 448–50; *Mufṣiḥ*: 134–8; *Iqtiṣād*: 217–22; *Tamhīd*: 395–9; *Taqrīb*: 151–5 (see also Bāqillānī: 169–72). His analysis about a different interpretation of the Prophetic statements that led the early Muslims to choose their own *imām* is adopted in *Shāfī*, 1: 127 (also see Murtaḍā, *al-Ṭarābulusiyyāt al-thāniya*: 340); *Mufṣiḥ*: 126–7; *Iqtiṣād*: 211–12; *Tamhīd*: 385–6.

his *Kitāb al-Inṣāf,* mostly in abridged forms and without reference to him, in the later works gives an impression that many of these works were modeled after that book and used its arrangement and arguments.

* * * * *

On the topic of the occultation of the Twelfth Imām, Ibn Qiba repeatedly insisted that it was the logical conclusion of the Imāmite doctrine of the Imāmate, and it should not be discussed separately. If one accepts the idea that there must always be a living Imām who is to be designated by his predecessor, the eleventh Imām must have delegated the position to someone after himself.[98] The number of people who have quoted such a designation from the eleventh Imām of his son meets the requirement of a *mutawātir* report, so if their testimony is rejected, the whole institution of report and with it the whole structure of the *sharī'a* will collapse. Because this son has not been seen in public, one concludes that he must be in occultation. An Imām is still the Imām even though he is absent from the people's vision, just as the Prophet was still a prophet when he was in similar situations although for much shorter periods.[99] When he reappears, the Imām may have to accompany his claim to the Imāmate with a miracle should God decide that it is in the best interest of mankind to manifest such a miracle by his hand. Ibn Qiba also argues with the statements that some of the early Imāmites quoted from the previous Imāms, long before the situation came up, which predicted the occurrence of such an occultation.

As in the topic of the Imāmate, Ibn Qiba was followed in the main points of his argument in this topic by scholars after him.[100]

98. The same line of argument is adopted by Iba Qiba's contemporary, Abū Sahl al-Nawbakhtī: 92.

99. The same argument and its parallel to the situation of the Prophet appear also in Abū Sahl al-Nawbakhtī: 90; Sa'd b. 'Abd Allāh: 103.

100. See especially Mufīd, *al-Risāla al-khāmisa fi 'l-ghayba*: 399; Murtaḍā, *Tanzīh al-anbiyā'*: 184; idem, *Risāla fī ghaybat al-ḥujja*: 293–5, 296; Ṭūsī, *Iqtiṣād*: 232–5; idem, *Ghayba*: 3, 13, 57, 61, 100–101; Abu 'l-Ṣalāḥ al-Ḥalabī, *Taqrīb*: 198–9, 215 (see also idem, *Burhān*: 53).

* * * * *

The absolute majority of the Imāmite scholars until the end of the third/ninth century refrained from legal reasoning and restricted themselves to transmitting and collecting the statements and opinions expressed by the Imāms on various questions. The idea was that, however learned a man may be, *sharī'a* was the realm of revelation, not reason, and because the Imām was the authoritative source of knowledge for what was revealed to the Prophet, then there was no room for speculation and rational reasoning in the field of religion.[101] The legal situation of every problem is stipulated in the Qur'ān, but the mind of the people does not comprehend the stipulated law,[102] a statement from Ja'far al-Ṣādiq declared. The common understanding among the Shī'a was that any specific case might have a different legal status and that it was only the Imām who knew what that law was. The Imāmite law was, therefore, supposed to depend exclusively on explicit designation (*naṣṣ*).[103] There was, however, another tendency among some of the most learned disciples of the Imāms that supported and practiced rational argument in law, a derivation of the specific law for each case reasoned from general norms.[104] Some of them maintained that even the Imāms themselves applied the same method for arriving at the law for each specific case, as noted above.[105]

Ibn Qiba supported the opinion that the institution of law is firmly based on explicit instruction and that the laws are to be received from the Imām. After all, according to his theory of the Imāmate, this was the main function of the Imāms[106] as pious scholars of the Qur'ān and the Prophetic tradition. However, he

101. See Durust b. Abī Manṣūr: 165–6; Barqī: 212–13, 215; Ṣaffār: 302–3; Kulaynī, 1:56.
102. Kulaynī, 1:60. See other similar statements in Barqī: 209–15; Ṣaffār: 302; Kulaynī, 1:59–62; *Jāmi' aḥadīth al-shī'a*, 1:275–6.
103. See Barqī: 214 (*naḥnu gawmun nattabi'u 'l-athar*).
104. See my *An Introduction to Shī'ī Law*: 24–31.
105. Sa'd b. 'Abd Allāh: 98; Mufīd, *Taṣḥīḥ*: 114. See also Ṣaffār: 301, 387–90; 'Ayyāshī, 1:299; Kulaynī, 1:62.
106. See also Barqī: 213–14; Ḥimyarī: 157.

explained that this did not mean that the law for each specific instance was necessarily given by a particular statement from the Imāms. It meant rather that there were enough general principles in the Qur'ān and the teachings of the Prophet and the Imāms to cover all possible cases; whatever problem came up was an instance of a general principle given in the Qur'ān or explained by the Prophet or the Imāms. There was, therefore, neither need nor room for independent mental exertion or rational speculation.[107] This idea seems to be quite in line with the legal tendency of such former Imāmite theologians as Yūnus b. 'Abd al-Raḥmān and Faḍl b. Shādhān. They apparently followed the same mode of reasoning in law although their contemporaries and successors confusedly thought theirs a kind of analogical reasoning tantamount to the Sunnite concept of *qiyās*.[108] It became, however, the standard method of legal reasoning in the Imāmite Shī'ite law for several centuries to come before other more sophisticated methods were developed by Imāmite scholars. In more recent centuries, some of the supporters of the Akhbārī school of Shī'ite law, which advocated the return to the more simple and original method of legal reasoning, have offered Ibn Qiba's description of the nature of Shī'ite law as the earliest and most authoritative picture of it. They maintain that his analysis properly explains the pattern and framework for that legal system and draws a clear line between it and other non-Shī'ite schools of Islamic law.[109]

* * * * *

Ibn Qiba's name is associated in the Shī'ite tradition with an idea about the validity of reports, as well—that it is rationally impossible for the *sharī'a* to authorize uncertain reports.

Generally speaking, the theologians accepted a report as a valid source of knowledge only if it had been so widely transmitted that,

107. Ibn Qiba, *Naqḍ kitāb al-ishhād*, para. 68.

108. See Ḥimyarī: 157; Murtaḍā, *Ibṭāl al-'amal bi-akhbār al-āḥād*: 311. See also my *An Introduction to Shī'ī Law*: 30–31.

109. See, for instance, Akhbārī, *Maṣādir al-anwār*: 2a.

as noted, there would be no doubt about its authenticity and no possibility of collusion by its transmitters to fabricate a lie.[110] In the early period of Islam this concept was clearly understood to refer to common sense of all Muslims, that which all Muslims agreed upon even though it was not explicitly mentioned in the Qur'ān, such as the number of daily prayers and the cycles of each.[111] Such things were later termed *ḍarūrāt al-shar'*, indisputable facts of religion. This sort of report is what the theologian Wāṣil b. 'Aṭā' (d. 131/748–749) called *khabar mujma' 'alayh*[112] (a report that everybody has accepted) and a later Shī'ite scholar described as *sunnat al-rasūl al-mutawātira al-muttafaq 'alayhā*[113] (the Prophetic tradition that is widely transmitted and which has received unanimous acceptance). This is also what some early Khārijites meant by their proposition that nothing is obligatory in the *sharī'a* "except what is explicitly mentioned in the Qur'ān or what all Muslims from all sects have reported."[114] It is also clearly what the two early theologians, Ḥafṣ al-Fard and Ḍirār b. 'Amr (both from the second/eighth century) meant by "consensus" when they suggested that the religious norms "can only be proved after the Prophet through consensus, so whatever is quoted from him by individuals [i.e., not by the entire community] cannot be accepted."[115] These statements are important because they shed light on the original perceptions of the three concepts of *ijmā', khabar mutawātir,* and *akhbār al-āḥād.*[116] Later, however, the terminology changed. The old concept of *mutawātir* gave way to the new concept of consensus; one of its categories to be the "con-

110. On the philosophical background of this entire discussion, see Ḥasan b. Sahl's *Risāla fī awṣāf al-akhbār allatī akhbara bi-ha 'l-kathīrūn.*

111. See Sarakhsī, *Uṣūl*, 1:282–3.

112. Abū Ḥilāl al-'Askarī, *Awā'il*, 2:134. According to this source, Wāṣil was the first to classify the valid sources of religious knowledge into four categories: the Qur'ān, unanimously accepted Tradition, consensus, and reason, a classification adopted by the sixth/twelfth century Imāmite jurist Ibn Idrīs al-Ḥillī (see his *Sarā'ir*, 1: 46) and then, with more flexibility in Tradition, by all later Uṣūlī Shī'ite jurists as the main sources of the *sharī'a*.

113. Ibn Idrīs al-Ḥillī, *Sarā'ir*, 1: 46.

114. Nāshi': 69.

115. Shahrastānī, 1:103.

116. See further Mufīd, *Majālis*, 1:60.

sensus of the entire community of the faithful." *Mutawātir* was then first reduced to a "report related by countless individuals" in each generation, a definition that the Muʿtazilite Ibrāhīm al-Naẓẓām believed fell short of eliminating the possibility of falsity,[117] whereas others maintained that such a report never existed in Islam.[118] The required number of transmitters was later greatly reduced,[119] especially by the Traditionists, some of whom tended to regard as *mutawātir* any report that was transmitted by more than two[120] or three[121] individuals. The concept of *akhbār al-āḥād* consequently changed its meaning from the original sense, that is, what is reported by individuals as against the entire community, to reports that are related by one or very few individuals.

Theologians and Traditionists disagreed sharply on the validity of *akhbār al-āḥād.* The theologians normally maintained that these reports were of no value, whatever the situation of the transmitters might be,[122] unless a report was supported by indisputable external evidence.[123] Such an indisputable report was naturally included in what some of them called *al-sunna al-maqṭūʿ bihā* (tradition that is undoubtedly genuine).[124] The Traditionists, however, held that any report related by a reliable transmitter is a proof and tried to support their opinion by evidence from the Qur'ān and common Muslim practice. The theologians rejected those arguments for the validity of *akhbār al-āḥād* with legal counterarguments; some tried to strengthen those counterarguments with a theological analysis that suggested that it is logically impossible for the *sharīʿa* to sanction this sort of report as a valid source of knowledge. Nothing that does not result in certain and indisputable knowledge can be

117. *Farq*: 128.
118. Bahārī, *Musallam al-thubūt*, 2:87.
119. See, for instance, Āmidī, 2: 25.
120. *Kamāl*: 84.
121. Bahārī, 2: 88–9.
122. See Ṭūsī, *Tibyān*, 9:344.
123. See, for instance Mufīd, *Tadhkira*: 193; Juwaynī, *Irshād*: 416; Āmidī, 2:49–50. See also Sarakhsī, *Sharḥ al-siyar*, 3:58; idem, *Uṣūl*, 1:332.
124. Murtaḍā, *al-Mawṣiliyyāt al-thālitha*: 209, 210; Ḥimmaṣī, *Munqidh*, the chapter on the Imāmate.

sanctified by the *sharīʿa*. Many of the *akhbār al-āḥād* are inevitably false; by sanctioning them, the *sharīʿa* would mislead people and expose them to all sorts of disbelief, sin, and evil that the false reports might contain. Even the claim of the prophets, which was by itself a report of God's authorizing them as prophets, was not to be accepted without the putative prophet's performing a miracle to prove the truth of his report. How then could the *sharīʿa* possibly order the people to accept the reports of some ordinary individuals without indisputable proof? This was an important argument because if it could be accepted, there would remain no room for any further argument on the topic. It was originally suggested by the Muʿtazilite Abū ʿAlī al-Jubbāʾī[125] but rejected by most other theologians who held that it was logically possible for the *sharīʿa* to pronounce *akhbār al-āḥād* as valid sources of legal knowledge, although no evidence suggests that such a validation ever took place.

Among prominent Shīʿite scholars the only one[126] who is known by name to have supported the view of rational impossibility is Ibn Qiba.[127] It is still firmly associated with his name as the view is known up to the present in Shīʿite jurisprudence as the paradox (*shubha*) of Ibn Qiba. The opinion has been quoted and discussed by most Shīʿite scholars of *uṣūl al-fiqh* since the mid-seventh/thirteenth century, and his name thus appears in most Shīʿite works on that discipline up to the present.[128]

* * * * *

In the following chapters, the texts of three works of Ibn Qiba that are preserved in Ibn Bābawayh's *Kamāl al-dīn* are reproduced

125. Āmidī, 2: 44–5; ʿAlāʾ al-Dīn al-Bukhārī, 2:370; Bahārī, 2:95. Cf. Murtaḍā, *Dharīʿa*, 2:529 where the sentence reads as if this idea were supported by Ibrāhīm al-Naẓẓām, too.
126. The Sharīf al-Murtaḍā in his *al-Mawṣiliyyāt al-thālitha*: 202 (also quoted by Ibn Idrīs, 1: 47) attributed the view to *qawmun min shuyūkhinā raḥimahumu ʾllāh*.
127. The oldest available source to have quoted this opinion from Ibn Qiba that I have so far come across is al-Muḥaqqiq al-Ḥillī, *Maʿārij al-wuṣūl*: 141.
128. See, for instance, Ḥasan b. Zayn al-Dīn al-ʿĀmilī: 215; Abu ʾl-Qāsim al-Qummī, 1: 432; Muḥammad Ḥusayn al-Iṣfahānī: 271; Anṣārī: 23; Ḥāʾirī: 349; Nāʾīnī, 3: 89; Ḍiyāʾ al-Dīn al-ʿArāqī, 3: 55; Khumaynī, 2: 130–31.

from the most recent edition of that book (Tehran, 1390/1970–1971) with numerous corrections on the basis of some of the manuscripts of this work[129] that are not used for that edition. (In a few cases, a clear error was shared by all manuscripts.) The Tehran, 1301/1883 lithograph of this work was also used in a single case. The variances given in the charts at the end of each text reflect the main differences among the manuscripts; the obvious misspellings and errors are not included. The brief descriptions in the beginnings of the texts are by Ibn Bābawayh. A translation immediately follows each text.

129. They are MS 6324 of the Central Library of the University of Tehran (described in its catalog, 16:242) and MSs 382 Ṭabāṭabā'ī, 808 Ṭabāṭabā'ī, 4185 and 4973 of Majlis Library, Tehran (the last two described in the Library's catalogue, 11:190, 14:264–5).

V

A Debate with the Mu'tazilites

THE FOLLOWING ESSAY was written, as Ibn Bābawayh pointed out, in answer to a letter that was sent to Ibn Qiba by a Shī'ite who questioned him about the validity of the Mu'tazilites' argument against the Imāmate of the vanished Imām. Two points are of concern in the argument: that the claim that the eleventh Imām designated someone as his successor is baseless and that even if one assumes that he designated someone, how does one determine whether someone who appears in the future and claims that he is the designated one is correct and truthful? The eleventh Imām never introduced his successor to society because, the Shī'a claimed, he feared for the successor's life, and that person is believed to have been in occultation since. The people, therefore, never had a chance to meet him to verify whether the future claimant was the designated successor or a different person.

In response to both points, Ibn Qiba mentions the circle of close associates of the eleventh Imām who were now running the affairs of the house of the Imāmate. The designation and existence of the vanished Imām, he states, were proved to us by their testimony, so they should be the ones to verify whether a future claimant is or is not the true Imām who had been in occultation. (This indicates that the tract presented here was written before approximately 285/898, by which time almost all close associates of the eleventh Imām had died.)[1] Moreover, if one accepts the Imāmites' viewpoints that a living Imām must exist on earth in each period until the end of time and that any Imām must explicitly designate his successor before he passes away, the necessary conclusion will be that the eleventh Imām did designate his successor before he died. Like the Prophets who had to support their claims to be messengers with miracles, whoever appears in the future and

1. Abū Sahl al-Nawbakhtī: 93.

claims to be the formerly vanished Imām may have to perform a miracle to prove his veracity, if there is no other way for the people to decide whether his claim is correct or not.

مسألة في الإمامة

[كتب بعض الإماميّة إلى أبي جعفر بن قبة كتاباً يسأله فيه عن مسائل فورد في جوابها:]

[1] أمّا قولك - أيّدك الله - حاكياً عن المعتزلة أنّها زعمت أنّ الإماميّة تزعم أنّ النصّ على الإمام واجب في العقل، فهذا يحتمل أمرين: إن كانوا يريدون أنّه واجب في العقل قبل مجيء الرسل وشرع الشرايع فهذا خطأ، وإن أرادوا أنّ العقول دلّت على أنّه لا بدّ من إمام بعد الأنبياء فقد علموا ذلك بالأدلّة القطعيّة وعلموه أيضاً بالخبر الّذي ينقلونه عمّن يقولون بإمامته.

[2] وأمّا قول المعتزلة: إنّا قد علمنا يقيناً أنّ الحسن بن علي مضى ولم ينصّ، فقد ادّعوا دعوى يخالفون فيها وهم محتاجون إلى أن يدلّوا على صحّتها، وبأيّ شيء ينفصلون ممّن زعم من مخالفيهم أنّهم قد علموا من ذلك ضدّ ما ادّعوا أنّهم علموه؟.ومن الدليل على أنّ الحسن بن علي قد نصّ إثبات إمامته، وصحّة النصِ من النبيّ - صلّى الله عليه وآله وسلّم - وفساد الاختيار، ونقل الشيعة عمّن قد أوجبوا بالأدلّة تصديقه أنّ الإمام لا يمضي أو ينصّ على إمام كما فعل رسول الله - صلّى الله عليه وآله وسلّم - إذ كان الناس محتاجين في كلِّ عصر إلى من يكون خبره لا يختلف ولا يتكاذب، كما اختلفت أخبار الأمّة عند مخالفينا هؤلاء وتكاذبت، وأن يكون إذا أمر أُئتُمر بطاعته ولا يد فوق يده ولا يسهو ولا يغلط، وأن يكون عالماً ليعلّم الناس ما جهلوا وعادلاً ليحكم بالحقّ. ومن هذا حكمه فلا بدّ من أن ينصّ عليه علّام الغيوب على لسان من يؤدّي ذلك عنه، إذ كان ليس في ظاهر خلقته ما يدلُّ على عصمته.

[3] فإن قالت المعتزلة: هذه دعاوى تحتاجون إلى أن تدلّوا على صحّتها.

قلنا: أجل! لا بدَّ من الدلائل على صحّة ما ادّعيناه من ذلك وأنتم، فإنّما سألتم عن فرع والفرع لا يُدلُّ عليه دون أن يدلَّ على صحّة أصله، ودلائلنا في كتبنا موجودة على صحّة هذه الأصول. ونظير ذلك أنَّ سائلاً لو سألنا الدليل على صحّة الشرايع لاحتجنا أن ندلَّ على صحّة الخبر وعلى صحّة نبوَّة النبيّ – صلّى الله عليه وآله وسلّم – وعلى أنّه أمر بها، وقبل ذلك أنَّ الله عزَّ وجلَّ واحدٌ حكيمٌ، وذلك بعد فراغنا من الدليل على أنَّ العالم محدث. وهذا نظير ما سألونا عنه.

[4] وقد تأمّلت في هذه المسألة فوجدت غرضها ركيكاً وهو أنّهم قالوا لو كان الحسن بن علي قد نصَّ على من تدّعون إمامته لسقطت الغيبة. والجواب في ذلك أنّ الغيبة ليست هي العدم، فقد يغيب الإنسان إلى بلد يكون معروفاً فيه مشاهداً لأهله ويكون غائباً عن بلد آخر، وكذلك قد يكون الإنسان غائباً عن قوم دون قوم وعن أعدائه لا عن أوليائه فيقال إنّه غائب وإنّه مستتر. وإنّما قيل غائب لغيبته عن أعدائه وعمّن لا يوثق بكتمانه من أوليائه، وأنّه ليس مثل آبائه – عليهم السلام – ظاهراً للخاصّة والعامّة. وأولياؤه مع هذا ينقلون وجوده وأمره ونهيه، وهم عندنا ممّن تجب بنقلهم الحجّة إذ كانوا يقطعون العذر لكثرتهم واختلافهم في هممهم ووقوع الاطمئنان مع خبرهم، ونقلوا ذلك كما نقلوا إمامة آبائه – عليهم السلام – وإن خالفهم مخالفوهم فيها. كما تجب بنقل المسلمين صحّة آيات النبيّ – صلّى الله عليه وآله وسلّم – سوى القرآن وإن خالفهم أعداؤهم من أهل الكتاب والمجوس والزنادقة والدهريّة في كونها. وليست هذه مسألة تشتبه على مثلك مع ما أعرفه من حسن تأمّلك.

[5] وأمّا قولهم: إذا ظهر فكيف يعلم أنّه محمّد بن الحسن بن علي؟ فالجواب في ذلك أنّه قد يجوز بنقل من تجب بنقله الحجّة من أوليائه كما صحّت إمامته

عندنا بنقلهم. وجواب آخر وهو أنّـه قد يجوز أن يظهر معجزاً يدلُّ على ذلك. وهذا الجواب الثاني هو الّـذي نعتمد عليه ونجيب الخصوم به، وإن كان الأوّل صحيحاً.

[6] وأمّـا قول المعتزلة: فكيف لم يحتجَّ عليهم علي بن أبي طالب بإقامة المعجز يوم الشورى؟ فإنّـا نقول: إنَّ الأنبياء والحجج إنّما يظهرون من الدلالات والبراهين حسب ما يأمرهم الله عزَّ وجلَّ به ممّـا يعلم الله أنه صالح للخلق، فإذا ثبتت الحجّـة عليهم بقول النبي - صلّى الله عليه وآله وسلّم - فيه ونصّه عليه فقد استغنى بذلك عن إقامة المعجزات. اللهمَّ إلّا أن يقول قائل إنَّ إقامة المعجزات كانت أصلح في ذلك الوقت، فنقول له: وما الدليل على صحّـة ذلك؟ وما ينكر الخصم من أن تكون إقامته لها ليست بأصلح وأن يكون الله عزَّ وجلَّ لو أظهر معجزاً على يديه في ذلك الوقت لكفروا أكثر من كفرهم ذلك الوقت ولادَّعوا عليه السحر والمخرقة؟ وإذا كان هذا جائزاً لم يعلم أنَّ إقامة المعجز كانت أصلح.

[7] فإن قالت المعتزلة: فبأيِّ شيء تعلمون أنَّ إقامة من تدَّعون إمامته المعجز على أنّـه ابن الحسن بن علي أصلح؟

قلنا لهم: لسنا نعلم أنّـه لا بدَّ من إقامة المعجز في تلك الحال وإنّما نجوّز ذلك. اللهمَّ إلّا أن يكون لا دلالة غير المعجز فيكون لا بدَّ منه لإثبات الحجّـة، وإذا كان لا بدَّ منه كان واجباً، وما كان واجباً كان صلاحاً لا فساداً. وقد علمنا أنَّ الأنبياء قد أقاموا المعجزات في وقت دون وقت ولم يقيموها في كلِّ يوم ووقت ولحظة وطرفة وعند كلِّ محتجٍّ عليهم ممّن أراد الإسلام، بل في وقت دون وقت على حسب ما يعلم الله عزَّ وجلَّ من الصلاح. وقد حكى الله عزَّ وجلَّ عن المشركين أنّـهم سألوا نبيّـه - صلّى الله عليه وآله وسلّم - أن يرقى في السماء وأن يسقط السماء عليهم كسفاً أو ينزِّل عليهم كتاباً يقرؤونه وغير ذلك

ممّا في الآية فما فعل ذلك بهم، وسألوه أن يحيي لهم قصيّ بن كلاب وأن ينقل عنهم جبال تهامة فما أجابهم إليه، وإن كان قد أقام لهم غير ذلك من المعجزات. فكذا حكم ما سألت المعتزلة عنه. ويقال لهم كما قالوا لنا: لم نترك أوضح الحجج وأبين الأدلّة من تكرُّر المعجزات والاستظهار بكثرة الدلالات؟

[8] وأمّا قول المعتزلة: إنّه احتجّ بما يحتمل التأويل، فيقال: فما احتجّ عندنا على أهل الشورى إلّا بما عرفوا من نصِّ النبيّ – صلّى الله عليه وآله وسلّم – لأنّ أولائك الرؤساء لم يكونوا جهّالاً بالأمر وليس حكمهم حكم غيرهم من الأتباع. ونقلب هذا الكلام على المعتزلة فيقال لهم: لِمَ لم يبعث الله عزّ وجلّ بأضعاف من بعث من الأنبياء؟ ولمَ لم يبعث في كلِّ قرية نبيّاً وفي كلِّ عصر ودهر نبيّاً أو أنبياء إلى أن تقوم الساعة؟ ولمَ لم يبيّن معاني القرآن حتّى لا يشكّ فيه شاكٌّ؟ ولمَ تركه محتملاً للتأويل؟ وهذه المسائل تضطرُّهم إلى جوابنا.

An Essay on the Imāmate

[One of the Imāmites wrote a letter to Abū Ja'far b. Qiba in which he asked him about several matters. The following was received in answer to those questions:]

[1] As for your words, may God support you, relating from the Mu'tazilites that they said that the Imāmites say that it is a rational necessity that the [succeeding] Imām be explicitly designated [by the previous one], this may mean one of two things: If they mean that it is a rational necessity before the advent of the prophets and the revelation of the religions, this is wrong; but if they mean that reason decides that there must be an Imām after the prophets, then this is what they [the Imāmites] came to know by indisputable proofs and also through a report that they narrate from those whose Imāmate they profess.

[2] As for the Mu'azilites saying: "We know for certain that Ḥasan b. 'Alī [al-'Askarī] passed away without designating [a successor]," they are making a claim in which they are challenged, and they need to demonstrate that it is correct. How can they distinguish themselves from those among their opponents who said that on this [matter] they came to know the opposite of what they [the Mu'tazilites] claimed to know? Among the proofs that Ḥasan b. 'Alī did designate [someone] is [the juxtaposition of the following facts]: that the truth of his Imāmate was established; that the Prophet, may God bless him and his Family and grant them peace, explicitly designated [his successor], and the idea that the people had the choice to elect [his successor] was false; and that the Shī'ites have quoted from those that they have proved their authority that an Imām does not pass away without designating an[other] Imām as did the Messenger of God, may God bless him and his Family and grant them peace. [This is] because people in every age need someone whose narration is not varied or inconsistent such as the reports that our opponents have received through the community are varied and contradictory; someone to be obeyed when he commands and there is no authority above his; who does not neglect or err and is knowledgeable (so that he may inform the people of that which they do not know) and just (so that he may judge with the truth).

The person thus qualified has to be explicitly designated by the Omniscient through the tongue of one who announces it on His behalf, because there is nothing in such a person's outward appearance that indicates his infallibility.

[3] If the Mu'tazilites say: "These are claims that you need to validate," we say: Indeed! We both have to prove the correctness of our claims. But you asked about a subsidiary matter, and a subsidiary matter cannot be demonstrated without [first] demonstrating the truth of the basis on which it depends. Our proofs for the truth of these principles are to be found in our writings. It is the same as if someone were to ask us for the proof of the validity of religious laws, in which case we would be required to prove the truth of the traditions, the truth of the prophethood of the Prophet, may God bless him and his Family and grant them peace, and that he [the Prophet] commanded those religious laws. And before this, [we would be required to prove] that God, to Whom belong might and majesty, is One and Wise, and this after we had finished proving that the universe is created [to prove that there is a creator]. This is like what they asked us about.

[4] I thought over that assertion [of the Mu'tazilites] and found that what it is trying to prove is devious; it is that they said: If Ḥasan b. 'Alī had designated the one whose Imāmate you allege, there would have been no occultation. The answer to this is that the occultation is not nonexistence, for a man can disappear to a land in which he is known [and] visible to its people and yet be absent from another land; similarly, a man can be absent from one people and not another or from his enemies and not from his friends; so he will be described as absent and hidden. He [whose Imāmate we allege] is described as absent because of his absence from his enemies and from those among his friends who cannot be trusted to conceal a secret, and he is not, like his forefathers, peace be upon them, visible to his followers and others. Despite this his close associates communicate his existence and his commands and prohibitions, and they are, in our opinion, among those whose reports constitute an indisputable proof, because they cut off any excuse [against their narration] by their great numbers, their differences in tendency, and the reassurance their reports engender. They reported this in the same way as they reported the Imāmate of his

forefathers, peace be upon them, even though their opponents disagreed. This is just like the truth of the supernatural signs of the Prophet, may God bless him and his Family and grant them peace, other than the Qur'ān, being proved by the narrations of the Muslims, even though their enemies among the People of Scripture [the Jews and the Christians], the Magians, the atheists, and the materialists disagreed on the existence of those signs. This is not a point that can be obscure to the likes of you with what I know of your good deliberation.

[5] As for their saying: When he [the vanished Imām] appears, how can it be known that he is Muḥammad b. al-Ḥasan b. 'Alī? the answer to this is that it is possible through the assertion of a number of his close associates whose reports constitute an indisputable proof, in the same way as his Imāmate was verified for us by their transmission. Another answer is that it is possible that he will perform a miracle that attests to that. It is this second answer that we rely on and with which we answer adversaries, even though the first is [also] correct.

[6] As for the Mu'tazilites saying: "So why did 'Alī b. Abī Ṭālib not perform a miracle to vindicate himself against them [his adversaries] on the Day of the Consultation?",[2] we say: The prophets and the proofs [i.e. the Imāms] only show supernatural signs and clear demonstrations as they are ordered to by God, the Mighty, the Exalted, according to God's knowledge of what is appropriate for the people. When a proof is already established for them through a saying of the Prophet, may God bless him and his Family and grant them peace, concerning him ['Alī] and after the Prophet explicitly designated him [as his own successor], no need remains to perform miracles. Someone, however, may assert that performing miracles would still have been more appropriate at that time; then we will say to him: What is the proof that this assertion is correct?

2. *Yawm al-shūrā*, the day after the death of the caliph 'Umar in 26 Dhu 'l-Ḥijja 23/3 November 644 when a committee appointed by him on his deathbed to choose his successor met and discussed the question of succession. See Ṭabarī, 4:227–240.

How can the disputant deny that performing miracles would not have been more appropriate, and that if God, the Mighty, the Exalted, had divulged a miracle at his ['Alī's] hands at that time, they [the opponents of 'Alī] would have disbelieved even more than their disbelief at that time and would have accused him of sorcery and trickery. If that could have been possible, it would not be known that performing miracles was more appropriate.

[7] If the Mu'tazilites say: So how do you know that the performance of miracles by the one whose Imāmate you claim—to prove that he is son of Ḥasan b. 'Alī—is more appropriate? We say to them: We do not know that he definitely has to perform miracles in these circumstances; we only say that it is possible. If, however, there were no other sign than miracles, he would have no other recourse to establish the proof, and if there were no other recourse for him, it would be obligatory, and whatever is obligatory is proper and not inappropriate. For we know that the prophets performed miracles at certain times, not in every period of time, or at every moment or instant, nor for every person who argued with them among those who desired to submit to the true religion, but from time to time according to what God, the Mighty, the Exalted, saw fit. God, the Mighty, the Exalted, described how the polytheists asked the Prophet, may God bless him and his Family and grant them peace, to ascend to the sky and make the sky fall down to them in pieces, or to bring down to them a letter to read, and the other things that are mentioned in the verse [of the Qur'ān],[3] but he did not do this for them. They [also] asked him to resurrect Quṣayy b. Kilāb[4] and to move the mountains of Tihāma away from them,[5] but he did not grant them this, even though he did perform other miracles for them. The same is true with what the Mu'tazilites ask. It should be said to them, just as they said to us: Why should we renounce the clearest of proofs and the most obvious of signs

3. Qur'ān, 17:90–93.

4. Quṣayy b. Kilāb b. Murra b. Ka'b b. Lu'ayy, a great grandfather of the Prophet and head of the tribe of Quraysh in his time (Ibn Sa'd, 1:36–42; Ibn Hishām, 1:123–38; Ṭabarī, 2:254–60). See also the article "Ḳuṣayy" in *EI*², 5:519–20 (by G. Levi Della Vida).

5. See Ibn Hishām, 1:316; Ṭabarī, *Jāmi' al-bayān* (Cairo, 1954), 15:165.

for the repetition of miracles and the seeking of support through multiplicity of supernatural signs?

[8] As for the Mu'tazilites assertion that "he ['Alī] put forward as an argument something that could be disputed," it should be said that, in our opinion, he argued with the People of the Consultation[6] with what they knew of the designation by the Prophet, may God bless him and his Family and grant them peace, because these leaders were not ignorant of the matter, and their situation was not the situation of the other people among the rank and file. We turn this argument around against the Mu'tazilites and ask them why God, the Mighty, the Exalted, did not send many times more prophets than He has sent? Why did He not send to every community a prophet or in every age and time a prophet or prophets until the day of resurrection? Why did He not clarify the meaning of the Qur'ān so that no one would have any doubts about it [but instead] left it open to different interpretations? These questions require them [to accept] our answer.

6. *Ahl al-shūrā*, the committee of six that was appointed by 'Umar to choose his successor.

VI

A Debate with the Followers of Ja'far b. 'Alī

THE FOLLOWING TREATISE was written by Ibn Qiba to refute a tract that Abu 'l-Ḥasan 'Alī b. Aḥmad b. Bashshār, a supporter of Ja'far, the younger son of 'Alī al-Hādī, wrote against the mainstream Imāmites who believed in the Imāmate of the vanished son of the eleventh Imām.

The main point of Ibn Bashshār's argument is that the claim of the associates of the eleventh Imām that he had a son is baseless; no one had seen or heard about such a son, nor has anyone seen him since the claim was made. The Imāmite Shī'ite doctrine requires that there always be an Imām from the house of the Imāmate to whom people can bring their religious concerns. Now that Ḥasan al-'Askarī has passed away, the only person from the House available to the people is Ja'far, and so, logically, he has to be regarded as the Imām.[1]

In response to this argument, Ibn Qiba stressed that Imāmite Shī'ism is based on the divine necessity that an Imām exist on the earth in each age, but it also requires that the next Imām always be a descendant of the previous one. The Imāmate of Ḥasan al-'Askarī was established in his time through widespread reports of his appointment by his father, 'Alī al-Hādī, whose Imāmate was a matter of consensus between the mainstream Imāmites and the followers of Ja'far. If the authority of such a widespread Imāmite report on 'Alī al-Hādī's designation of Ḥasan al-'Askarī can be contested, no report in the world can constitute a valid proof, and, the validity of all religions will be doubted and questioned. The combination of these facts necessarily leads to the conclusion that Ḥasan al-'Askarī, who was the true Imām in his time, had a son who became the Imām, even though he was not apparent in society. For the Imām to be available to the people does not require that he be

1. See also Kulaynī, 1: 331, *Kamāl*: 511; *Ghayba*: 175.

accessible to the public as long as he is available through his close associates. Even the Prophet was hidden and unavailable to the public during his flight from Mecca to Medina when he was forced to hide in a cave.

Nothing is known about the author of the tract, ʿAlī b. Aḥmad b. Bashshār, except that he, as noted, was clearly a supporter of Jaʿfar b. ʿAlī.[2] The tract was clearly written when Jaʿfar was still alive although Ibn Qiba's refutation may have been written after Jaʿfar passed away. The author may well be ʿAlī al-Ṭāḥin whom the sources described, as noted in chapter 3 above, as a powerful disputant *mutakallim,* a well-known figure in the Faṭḥite community of Kūfa, the chief supporter of Jaʿfar, and head of his followers.

2. Ibn Bābawayh transmits a report in *Kamāl*: 524 on the authority of Muḥammad b. ʿAlī b. Bashshār al-Qazwīnī, who was already dead by the time that the book was written in the mid-fourth/tenth century. It is plausible to think that this transmitter may have been a son of the author of the tract. The omission of some names in the genealogical line was a common practice in cases where the name of the ultimate ancestor was uncommon and rare like Bashshār, which was not a commonly used name.

النقض على أبي الحسن علي بن أحمد بن بشّار في الغيبة

[قد تكلّم علينا أبو الحسن علي بن أحمد بن بشّار في الغيبة، وأجابه أبو جعفر محمّد بن عبد الرحمن بن قبة الرازي. وكان من كلام علي بن أحمد بن بشّار علينا في ذلك أن قال في كتابه:]

[1] أقول: إنَّ كلَّ المبطلين أغنياء عن تثبيت إنّيّة من يدَّعون له وبه يتمسّكون وعليه يعكفون ويعطفون، لوجود أعيانهم وثبات إنّياتهم، وهؤلاء [يعني أصحابنا] فقراء إلى ما قد غني عنه كلُّ مبطل سلف من تثبيت إنّيّة من يدَّعون له وجوب الطاعة. فقد افتقروا إلى ما قد غني عنه سائر المبطلين، لأنَّ الزيادة من الباطل تحطُّ والزيادة من الخير تعلو. والحمد لله ربِّ العالمين.

[ثمَّ قال:]

[2] وأقول قولاً تعلم فيه الزيادة على الإنصاف منّا، وإن كان ذلك غير واجب علينا. أقول: إنّه معلوم أنّه ليس كلُّ مدَّع ومدَّعى له بمحقٍّ، وأنّ كلَّ سائل لمدَّع تصحيح دعواه لمنصف. وهؤلاء القوم ادَّعوا أنَّ لهم مَن قد صحَّ عندهم أمره ووجب له على الناس الانقياد والتسليم. وقد قدَّمنا أنّه ليس كلُّ مدَّع ومدَّعى له بواجب له التسليم، ونحن نسلّم لهؤلاء القوم الدعوى ونقرُّ على أنفسنا بالابطال – وإن كان ذلك في غاية المحال – بعد أن يوجدونا إنّيّة المدَّعى له ولا نسألهم تثبيت الدعوى. فإن كان معلوماً أنَّ في هذا أكثر من الإنصاف فقد وفينا بما قلناه. فإن قدروا عليه فقد أبطلوا، وإن عجزوا عنه فقد وضح ما قلناه من زيادة عجزهم عن تثبيت ما يدَّعون على عجز كلِّ مبطل عن تثبيت دعواه،

وأنّـهم مختصّون من كلِّ نوع من الباطل بخاصّة يزدادون بها انحطاطاً عن المبطلين أجمعين لقدرة كلِّ مبطلٍ سلف على تثبيت دعواه إنّيّة من يدَّعون له وعجز هؤلاء عمّا قدر عليه كلُّ مبطل. إلّا ما يرجعون إليه من قولهم إنّه لا بدَّ ممّن تجب به حجّة الله عزَّ وجلَّ، وأجل لا بدَّ من وجوده – فضلاً عن كونه – فأوجدونا الإنّيّة من دون إيجاد الدعوى.

[3] ولقد خبّرت عن أبي جعفر بن أبي غانم أنّه قال لبعض من سأله فقال: بم تحاجُّ الّذين كنت تقول ويقولون إنّه لا بدَّ من شخص قائم من أهل هذا البيت؟ قال له: أقول لهم هذا جعفر. فيا عجبا! أيختصم الناس بمن ليس هو بمخصوم. وقد كان شيخ في هذه الناحية – رحمه الله – يقول: قد وسمت هؤلاء باللابدّية، أي أنّه لا مرجع لهم ولا معتمد إلّا إلى أنّه لا بدَّ من أن يكون هذا الّذي ليس في الكاينات، فوسمهم من أجل ذلك، ونحن نسمّيهم بها. أي أنّهم دون كلِّ من له بدّ يعكف عليه، إذ كان أهل الأصنام الّتي أحدها البدُّ قد عكفوا على موجود وإن كان باطلاً، وهم قد تعلّقوا بعدم ليس وباطل محض. وهم اللابدّية حقّاً، أي لا بدَّ لهم يعكفون عليه إذ كان كلُّ مطاع معبود. وقد وضح ما قلنا من اختصاصهم من كلِّ نوع الباطل بخاصّة يزدادون بها انحطاطاً. والحمد لله.

[ثمّ قال:]

[4] نختم الآن هذا الكتاب بأن نقول: إنّما نناظر ونخاطب من قد سبق منه الإجماع على أنّه لا بدَّ من إمام قائم من أهل هذا البيت تجب به حجّة الله ويسدُّ به فقر الخلق وفاقتهم، ومن لم يجتمع معنا على ذلك فقد خرج من النظر في كتابنا فضلاً عن مطالبتنا به، ونقول لكلِّ من اجتمع معنا على هذا الأصل الّذي قدَّمنا في هذا الموضع: كنّا وإيّاكم قد أجمعنا على أنّه لا يخلو أحد من بيوت هذه الدار من سراج زاهر، فدخلنا الدار فلم نجد فيها إلّا بيتاً

واحداً، فقد وجب وصحَّ أنَّ في ذلك البيت سراجاً. والحمد لله ربِّ العالمين.

[فأجابه أبو جعفر محمّد بن عبد الرحمن بن قبة الرازي بأن قال:]

[1] إنّا نقول وبالله التوفيق: ليس الإسراف في الإدّعاء والتقوُّل على الخصوم ممّا يثبت بهما حجّة، ولو كان ذلك كذلك لارتفع الحجاج بين المختلفين واعتمد كلُّ واحد على إضافة ما يخطر بباله من سوء القول إلى مخالفه، وعلى ضدِّ هذا بني الحجاج ووضع النظر، والإنصاف أولى ما يُعامل به أهل الدين. وليس قول أبي الحسن ليس لنا ملجأ نرجع إليه ولا قيّماً نعطف عليه ولا سنداً نتمسّك بقوله حجّة لأنَّ دعواه هذا مجرَّد من البرهان، والدعوى إذا انفردت عن البرهان كانت غير مقبولة عند ذوي العقول والألباب. ولسنا نعجز عن أن نقول: بلى! لنا – والحمد لله – من نرجع إليه ونقف عند أمره ومن كان ثبتت حجّته وظهرت أدلّته.

[2] فإن قلت: فأين ذلك؟ دلّونا عليه.

قلنا: كيف تحبّون أن ندلّكم عليه؟ أتسألوننا أن نأمره أن يركب ويصير إليكم ويعرض نفسه عليكم؟ أو تسألونا أن نبني له داراً ونحوِّله إليها ونعلّم بذلك أهل الشرق والغرب؟ فإن رمتم ذلك فلسنا نقدر عليه ولا ذلك بواجب عليه.

[3] فإن قلتم: من أيِّ وجه تلزمنا حجّته وتجب علينا طاعته؟

قلنا: إنّا نقرُّ أنّه لا بدَّ من رجل من ولد أبي الحسن عليّ بن محمّد العسكريّ تجب به حجّة الله. دللناكم على ذلك حتّى نضطرّكم إليه إن أنصفتم من أنفسكم. وأوَّل ما يجب علينا وعليكم أن لا نتجاوز ما قد رضي به أهل النظر واستعملوه ورأوا أنَّ من حاد عن ذلك فقد ترك سبيل العلماء، وهو أنّا

لا نتكلّم في فرع لم يثبت أصله. وهذا الرجل الّذي تجحدون وجوده فإنّما يثبت له الحقُّ بعد أبيه، وأنتم قوم لا تخالفوننا في وجود أبيه فلا معنى لترك النظر في حقِّ أبيه والاشتغال بالنظر معكم في وجوده، فإنّه إذا ثبت الحقُّ لأبيه فهذا ثابت ضرورة عند ذلك بإقراركم وإن بطل أن يكون الحقُّ لأبيه فقد آل الأمر إلى ما تقولون وقد أبطلنا. وهيهات لن يزداد الحقُّ إلّا قوّة ولا الباطل إلّا وهناً وإن زخرفه المبطلون.

[4] والدليل على صحّة أمر أبيه أنّا وإيّاكم مجمعون على أنّه لا بدَّ من رجل من ولد أبي الحسن تثبت به حجّة الله وينقطع به عذر الخلق، وإنَّ ذلك الرجل تلزم حجّته من نأى عنه من أهل الإسلام كما تلزم من شاهده وعاينه. ونحن وأكثر الخلق ممّن قد لزمتنا الحجّة من غير مشاهدة، فننظر في الوجه الّذي لزمتنا منه الحجّة ما هي، ثمَّ ننظر من الأولى من الرجلين الّذين لا عقب لأبي الحسن غيرهما فأيّهما كان أولى فهو الحجّة والإمام ولا حاجة بنا إلى التطويل. ثمَّ نظرنا من أيِّ وجه تلزم الحجّة من نأى عن الرسل والأئمّة، فإذا ذلك بالأخبار الّتي توجب الحجّة وتزول عن ناقليها تهمة التواطؤ عليها والإجماع على تخرُّصها ووضعها. ثمَّ فحصنا عن الحال فوجدنا فريقين ناقلين، يزعم أحدهما أنَّ الماضي نصَّ على الحسن وأشار إليه ويروون – مع الوصيّة وما له من خاصّة الكبر – أدلّة يذكرونها وعلماً يثبتونه، ووجدنا الفريق الآخر يروون مثل ذلك لجعفر، لا يقول غير هذا فإنّه أولى بنا. نظرنا فإذا الناقلة لأخبار جعفر جماعة يسيرة، والجماعة اليسيرة يجوز عليها التواطؤ والتلاقي والتراسل، فوقع نقلهم موقع شبهة لا موقع حجّة، وحجج الله لا تثبت بالشبهات. ونظرنا في نقل الفريق الآخر فوجدناهم جماعة متباعدي الديار والأقطار، مختلفي الهمم والآراء متغايرين، فالكذب لا يجوز عليهم لنأي بعضهم عن بعض ولا التواطؤ ولا التراسل والاجتماع على تخرُّص خبر ووضعه، فعلمنا أنَّ النقل الصحيح هو

نقلهم وأنَّ المحقّ هؤلاء، ولأنّـه إن بطل ما قد نقله هؤلاء على ما وصفنا من شأنهم لم يصحّ خبرٌ في الأرض وبطلت الأخبار كلّـها. فتأمّل – وفّقك الله – في الفريقين فإنّك تجدهم كما وصفت، وفى بطلان الأخبار هدم الإسلام وفى تصحيحها تصحيح خبرنا، وفى ذلك دليل على صحّـة أمرنا. والحمد لله ربِّ العالمين.

[5] ثمَّ رأينا الجعفريّـة تختلف في إمامة جعفر من أي وجه تجب؟ فقال قوم: بعد أخيه محمّـد، وقال قوم: بعد أخيه الحسن، وقال قوم: بعد أبيه، ورأيناهم لا يتجاوزون ذلك. ورأينا أسلافهم وأسلافنا قد رووا قبل الحادث ما يدلُّ على إمامة الحسن، وهو ما روي عن أبي عبد الله قال: « إذا توالت ثلاثة أسماء محمّـد وعلي والحسن فالرابع القائم » وغير ذلك من الروايات. وهذه وحدها توجب الإمامة للحسن، وليس إلّا الحسن وجعفر. فإذا لم تثبت لجعفر حجّـة على من شاهده في أيّـام الحسن، والإمام ثابت الحجّـة على من رآه ومن لم يره، فهو الحسن اضطراراً. وإذا ثبت الحسن، وجعفرٌ عندكم تبرَّأ منه والإمام لا يتبرَّأ من الإمام، والحسن قد مضى ولا بدَّ عندنا وعندكم من رجل من ولد الحسن تثبت به حجّـة الله، فقد وجب بالاضطرار للحسن ولدٌ قائم.

[6] وقل يا أبا جعفر – أسعدك الله – لأبي الحسن – أعزّه الله –: يقول محمّـد بن عبد الرحمن قد أوجدناك إنّـيّـة المدَّعى له فأين المهرب؟ هل تقرُّ على نفسك بالإبطال كما ضمنت أو يمنعك الهوى من ذلك فتكون كما قال الله تعالى: وَإِنَّ كَـثِيراً لَـيُضِلُّـونَ بِأَهْـوَائِهِمْ بِغَـيْـرِ عِلْمٍ؟

[7] فأمّـا ما وسم به أهل الحقِّ من اللابدّية لقولهم: « لا بدَّ ممّن تجب به حجّـة الله » فيا عجبا! أفلا يقول أبو الحسن لا بدَّ ممّن تجب به حجّـة الله؟ وكيف لا يقول وقد قال عند حكايته عنّـا وتعييره إيّـانا: « أجل لا بدَّ من وجوده فضلاً عن كونه ». فإن كان يقول ذلك فهو وأصحابه من اللابدّية، وإنّما

وسم نفسه وعاب إخوانه، وإن كان لا يقول ذلك فقد كفينا مؤونة تنظيره ومثله بالبيت والسراج. وكذا يكون حال من عاند أولياء الله، يعيب نفسه من حيث يرى أنّه يعيب خصمه. والحمد لله المؤيّد للحقِّ بأدلّته. ونحن نسمّي هؤلاء بالبُدّيّة، إذ كان عبدة البدِّ قد عكفوا على ما لا يسمع ولا يبصر ولا يغني عنهم شيئاً، وهكذا هؤلاء.

[8] ونقول: يا أبا الحسن – هداك الله –: هذا حجّة الله على الجنِّ والإنس ومن لا تثبت حجّته على الخلق إلّا بعد الدعاء والبيان، محمّد – صلّى الله عليه وآله وسلّم –، قد أخفى شخصه في الغار حتّى لم يعلم بمكانه ممّن احتجَّ الله عليهم به إلّا خمسة نفر. فإن قلت: إنَّ تلك غيبة بعد ظهوره وبعد أن قام على فراشه من يقوم مقامه. قلت لك: لسنا نحتجُّ عليك في حال ظهوره، ولا استخلافه لمن يقوم مقامه من هذا في قبيل ولا دبير، وإنّما نقول لك: أليس ثبتت حجّته في نفسه في حال غيبته على من لم يعلم بمكانه لِعلّة من العلل؟ فلا بدَّ من أن تقول: نعم، قلنا: وتثبت حجّة الإمام وإن كان غائباً لعلّة أخرى وإلّا فما الفرق. ثمَّ نقول: وهذا أيضاً لم يَغِب حتّى ملأ آباؤه – عليهم السلام – آذان شيعتهم بأنّ غيبته تكون وعرَّفوهم كيف يعملون عند غيبته. فإن قلت في ولادته فهذا موسى – عليه السلام – مع شدَّة طلب فرعون إيّاه وما فعل بالنساء والأولاد لمكانه حتّى أذن الله في ظهوره، وقد قال الرضا – عليه السلام – في وصفه: «بأبي وأمّي شبيهي وسميَّ جدّي وشبيه موسى بن عمران».

[9] وحجّة أخرى – نقول لك: يا أبا الحسن أتقرُّ أنَّ الشيعة قد روت في الغيبة أخباراً؟ فإن قال: لا، أوجدناه الأخبار، وإن قال: نعم، قلنا له: فكيف تكون حالة الناس إذا غاب إمامهم فكيف تلزمهم الحجّة في وقت غيبته؟ فإن قال: يقيم من يقوم مقامه، فليس يقوم عندنا وعندكم مقام الإمام إلّا الإمام، وإذا

كان إماماً قائماً فلا غيبة، وإن احتجَّ بشيء آخر في تلك الغيبة فهو بعينه حجّتنا في وقتنا لا فرق فيه ولا فصل.

[10] ومن الدليل على فساد أمر جعفر موالاته وتزكيته فارس بن حاتم وقد تبرّأ منه أبوه وشاع ذلك في الأمصار حتّى وقف عليه الأعداء فضلاً عن الأولياء. ومن الدليل على فساد أمره استعانته بمن استعان في طلب الميراث من أمّ الحسن وقد أجمعت الشيعة أنَّ آباءه – عليهم السلام – أجمعوا أنَّ الأخ لا يرث مع الأمّ. ومن الدليل على فساد أمره قوله « إنّي إمام بعد أخي محمّد » فليت شعري متى تثبت إمامة أخيه – وقد مات قبل أبيه – حتّى تثبت إمامة خليفته؟ ويا عجبا إذا كان محمّد يستخلف ويقيم إماماً بعده وأبوه حيٌّ قائم وهو الحجّة والإمام فما يصنع أبوه؟ ومتى جرت هذه السنّة في الأئمّة وأولادهم حتّى نقبلها منكم؟ فدلّونا على ما يوجب إمامة محمّد حتّى إذا ثبتت قبلنا إمامة خليفته. والحمد لله الّذي جعل الحقَّ مؤيَّداً والباطل مهتوكاً ضعيفاً زاهقاً.

[11] فأما ما حكى عن ابن أبي غانم – رحمه الله – فلم يُرِد الرجل بقوله [إنّه] عندنا يثبت إمامة جعفر، وإنّما أراد أن يعلّم السائل أنَّ أهل هذا البيت لم يفنوا حتّى لا يوجد منهم أحدٌ.

[12] وأمّا قوله: « وكلٌّ مطاع معبود » فهو خطأ عظيم، لأنّا لا نعرف معبوداً إلّا الله ونحن نطيع رسول الله – صلّى الله عليه وآله وسلّم – ولا نعبده.

[13] وأمّا قوله: « نختم الآن هذا الكتاب بأن نقول: إنّما نناظر ونخاطب من قد سبق منه الإجماع بأنّه لا بدَّ من إمام قائم من أهل هذا البيت تجب به حجّة الله – إلى قوله – وصحَّ أنَّ في ذلك البيت سراجاً، ولا حاجة بنا إلى دخوله » فنحن – وفّقك الله – لا نخالفه وإنّه لا بدَّ من إمام قائم من أهل هذا البيت تجب به حجّة الله، وإنّما نخالف في كيفيّة قيامه وظهوره وغيبته. وأمّا ما مثّل به من البيت والسراج فهو مُنى وقد قيل: إنّ المنى رأس مال المفلس. ولكنّا

نضرب مثلاً على الحقيقة لا نميل فيه على خصم ولا نحيف فيه على ضدٍّ بل نقصد فيه الصواب فنقول: كنّا ومن خالفنا قد أجمعنا على أنّ فلاناً مضى وله ولدان وله دار، وأنّ الدار يستحقّها منهما من قدر على أن يحمل بإحدى يديه ألف رطل، وأنّ الدار لا تزال في يدي عقب الحامل إلى يوم القيامة، ونعلم أنّ أحدهما يحمل والآخر يعجزه، ثمّ احتجنا أن نعلم مَن الحامل منهما فقصدنا مكانهما لمعرفة ذلك فعاق عنهما عائق منع عن مشاهدتهما غير أنّا رأينا جماعات كثيرة في بلدان نائية متباعدة بعضها عن بعض يشهدون أنّهم رأوا أنّ الأكبر منهما قد حمل ذلك، ووجدنا جماعة يسيرة في موضع واحد يشهدون أنّ الأصغر منهما فعل ذلك، ولم نجد لهذه الجماعة خاصّة يأتوا بها. فلم يجز في حكم النظر وقضيّة الإنصاف وما جرت به العادة وصحّت به التجربة ردُّ شهادة تلك الجماعات وقبول شهادة هذه الجماعة، والتهمة تلحق هؤلاء وتبعد عن أولائك.

[14] فإن قال خصومنا: فما تقولون في شهادة سلمان وأبي ذرّ وعمّار والمقداد لأمير المؤمنين – عليه السلام – وشهادة تلك الجماعات وأولائك الخلق لغيره، أيّهما أصوب؟

قلنا لهم: لأمير المؤمنين – عليه السلام – وأصحابه أمور خُصَّ بها وخصّوا بها دون من بإزائهم، فإن أوجدتمونا مثل ذلك أو ما يقاربه لكم فأنتم المحقّون. أوّلها أنّ أعداءه كانوا يقرُّون بفضله وطهارته وعلمه، وقد روينا ورووا له معنا أنّه – صلّى الله عليه وآله وسلّم – أخبر أنّ الله يوالي من يواليه ويعادي من يعاديه، فوجب لهذا أن يتّبع دون غيره. والثاني أنّ أعداءه لم يقولوا نحن نشهد أنّ النبيَّ – صلّى الله عليه وآله وسلّم – أشار إلى فلان بالإمامة ونصبه حجّة للخلق، وإنّما نصبوه لهم على جهة الاختيار كما قد بلغك. والثالث أنّ أعداءه كانوا يشهدون على أحد أصحاب أمير المؤمنين – عليه السلام – أنّه لا يكذب، لقوله – صلّى الله عليه وآله وسلّم – « ما أظلّت الخضراء ولا أقلّت

الغبراء على ذي لهجة أصدق من أبي ذرّ »، فكانت شهادته وحده أفضل من شهاداتهم. والرابع أنَّ أعداءه قد نقلوا ما نقله أولياؤه ممّا تجب به الحجّة وذهبوا عنه بفساد التأويل. والخامس أنَّ أعداءه رووا في الحسن والحسين أنّهما سيّدا شباب أهل الجنّة، ورووا أيضاً أنّه – صلّى الله عليه وآله وسلّم – قال: « من كذب عليَّ متعمّداً فليتبوَّأ مقعده من النّار »، فلمّا شهدا لأبيهما بذلك وصحَّ أنّهما من أهل الجنّة بشهادة الرسول وجب تصديقهما، لأنّهما لو كذبا في هذا لم يكونا من أهل الجنّة وكانا من أهل النار وحاشا لهما الزكيّين الطيّبين الصادقين. فليوجدنا أصحاب جعفر خاصّة هي لهم دون خصومهم حتّى يقبل ذلك. وإلّا فلا معنى لترك خبر متواتر لا تهمة في نقله ولا على ناقليه وقبول خبر لا يؤمن على ناقليه تهمة التواطؤ عليه ولا خاصّة معهم يثبتون بها، ولن يفعل ذلك إلّا تائه حيران.

[15] فتأمّل – أسعدك الله – في النظر فيما كتبت به إليك ممّا ينظر به الناظر لدينه المفكّر في معاده المتأمّل بعين الخيفة والحذار إلى عواقب الكفر والجحود موفّقاً إن شاء الله تعالى. أطال الله بقاءك وأعزّك وأيّدك وثبّتك وجعلك من أهل الحقّ وهداك له وأعاذك من أن تكون من الّذين ضلَّ سعيهم في الحيوة الدنيا وهم يحسبون أنّهم يحسنون صنعاً ومن الّذين يستزلّهم الشيطان بخدعه وغروره وإملائه وتسويله، وأجرى لك أجمل ما عوَّدك.

Refutation of Abu 'l-Ḥasan 'Alī b. Aḥmad b. Bashshār on the Occultation

[Abu 'l-Ḥasan 'Alī b. Aḥmad b. Bashshār argued against us on the Occultation, and Abū Ja'far Muḥammad b. 'Abd al-Raḥmān b. Qiba al-Rāzī answered him. In his argument against us on this [question], 'Alī b. Aḥmad b. Bashshār said [the following] in his book:]

[1] I say [that] all wrong thinkers need not substantiate the existence of the ones they put forward a claim for and to whom they cling, adhere, and lean because those [subjects of devotion] exist in the external world and their being is proved. But these people [meaning our community] need to [do] what no previous wrong thinker had to do, that is, to substantiate the being of the one to whom they claim obedience must be given. Therefore, they need what other wrong thinkers do not need. That is because additional falsehood debases whereas additional good elevates. Praise belongs to God, the Lord of the Worlds.

[Then he said:]

[2] I shall now say something by which you will come to know that we are supremely fair although this is not incumbent on us. I say: It is known that not everyone who makes a claim is right and not all claims are true and that everyone who asks any claimant to confirm his claim is being fair. Now this group claims that they have someone whose authority is established and to whom the people must yield and submit. We have already said that it is not required to concede the truth of everyone who makes a claim or the truth of what he claims. We do, however, concede the truth of the claim of this group and we shall accept that we are wrong (although this is the utmost impossibility) if they convince us of the existence of the one they make their claim for; we shall not ask them to prove the claim. If it is clear that this [proposal] is more than fair, then we have fulfilled our promise. Therefore, if they can do that, they will rescind [our argument]. But if they cannot, then what we have said will become evident, that is, that their inability to prove what

they claim is greater than that of every [other] wrong thinker to do so and that they are marked by a characteristic through which they sink lower than all [other] wrong thinkers. Because every previous wrong thinker was able to establish his claim, to the existence of the one about whom he was making claims, but these people are unable to do what every [other] wrong thinker has been able to do. Their only resort is the argument that there must be someone through whom the proof of God, the Mighty, the Exalted, could be established. True! The actual existence of such a person, let alone his mere conceptual being, is necessary. Therefore, prove to us the reality [of the one whose existence you allege] with a proof, not with mere allegation.

[3] I have been informed that someone asked Abū Ja'far b. Abī Ghānim[3]: "How do you argue with the people that you and they used to say that there must always be an incumbent [Imām] from the people of this [the Prophet's] House?" He said to him: "I say to them here is Ja'far." What a surprise! Will one argue with the people using a person who is outside the controversy? A senior man in this region, may God have mercy upon him, used to say: "I call these people the *lābuddiyya* [followers of inevitability] that is, that they have no recourse or source of support except to [say] that this person, who cannot be found anywhere in the world, must

3. Abū Ja'far 'Abd Allāh b. Abī Ghānim al-Qazwīnī, clearly a prominent figure in the Imāmite community in the beginning of the period of Minor Occultation, most likely not a son of Abū Ghānim, the servant of the eleventh Imām (*Kamāl*: 408, 431, 492). After the death of Ḥasan al-'Askarī, Ibn Abī Ghānim denied that the Imām had left a son to succeed him and, thus, was engaged in a tough dispute with the community over the question of succession. The community wrote a letter to the Holy Threshold in which they reported the dispute. A rescript issued to the community in answer to that letter by the hand of the Agent expressed the Imām's sadness that some of the Shī'ites were in doubt (*Ghayba*: 172–3). Sa'd b. 'Abd Allāh al-Ash'arī transmitted *ḥadīth* from the son of this person, Muḥammad b. 'Abd Allāh b. Abī Ghānim al-Qazwīnī (*Kamāl*: 381). (In a footnote in *Kamāl*: 52 the editor misidentified Abū Ja'far b. Abī Ghānim as 'Alī b. Abī Ghānim al-Harrānī, an Imāmite scholar from the sixth/twelfth century.)

inevitably exist." So he branded them with that title because of this. We call them this too, in the sense that they are inferior to all those who have [at least] a *budd* (idol)[4] to which to give devotion because the worshippers of idols (one of which [idols] to be *Budd*) cling to an existent thing even though it is false. These people [who believe in a vanished Imām] are devoted to an absolute nonexistence and a complete falsehood. They are the true *lābuddiyya,* that is, they do not even have a *budd* to cling to for everything that is obeyed is worshipped. This explains our statement that they are especially singled out by a characteristic of false by which they are further debased. Praise be to God.

[Then he said:]

[4] We shall now bring this book to a close by saying that we are only arguing with and addressing those who already had a consensus that an incumbent Imām must always exist from among the people of this House, through whom the proof of God can be established and the needs and wants of people will be met. Those who do not agree with us on this [point] are not being addressed in this book, let alone being appealed to. We say to everyone who does agree with us on the fundamental point that we outlined above: We and you agreed that one of the rooms of this house always contains a brilliant light; then we entered the house and found that there is only one room in it; so it necessarily follows that there is a light in this room. Praise belongs to God, the Lord of the Worlds.

[Abū Ja'far Muḥammad b. 'Abd al-Raḥmān b. Qiba al-Rāzī answers him, as follows:]

[1] We say, and through God comes success: Exorbitance in accusation and allegation against opponents does not prove anything.

4. See Ibn Durayd, 1:65, who was unable to trace the origin of the word; Ibn Manẓūr, 3:82, who noted that it is the Arabicized form of the Persian word *bot*; Nashwān: 216, who identified it as an Indian word, presumably referring to the word Buddha.

If it could, the dispute between the opponents would be eliminated, and each side could depend on ascribing whatever evil he could think of to his opponent. [The concepts of] debate and dialectic are constructed in contrast to that [method]. Fairness is the most proper thing for religious people to put into practice. What Abu 'l-Ḥasan [Ibn Bashshār] said, that we have no refuge to retreat to, no support to turn to, and no authority to cling to, is not a valid argument because this claim of his is devoid of any proof. When not accompanied by a proof, a claim is unacceptable to the intelligent and the reasonable. We are not unable to say: Indeed! We have, thank God, someone to whom we can have recourse and to whose authority we submit and one whose proof has been established and whose signs have been made manifest.

[2] If you say: Where is this person? Point him out to us! we say: How do you want us to point him out to you? Are you asking us to order him to mount and set out to meet you and to show himself to you? Or are you asking us to build him a house and transfer him there and [then] broadcast this to everyone in the east and the west? If this is what you mean, we are unable to do it nor is this incumbent on him.

[3] If you say: In what way does his proof become incumbent upon us and obedience to him necessary? we say: We have established that there must be a man among the descendants of Abu 'l-Ḥasan 'Alī b. Muḥammad al-'Askarī [that is, 'Alī al-Hādī] through whom God's proof is established. We demonstrated this to you to oblige you [to accept] it, if you treat this matter fairly on your part. The first thing that is incumbent on us and you is not to stray outside the limits of that [principle] with which rational people are satisfied and which they use, believing that anyone who contravenes this [principle] has deviated from the path of the learned, that is, to speak about a subsidiary matter without first establishing the basis on which it depends. This man whose existence you deny, the right can only be established for him after his father. You are a group that does not disagree with us about the existence of his father; so it only makes sense to examine [first] the right of his father rather than to engage in the debates on his [the son's] existence. This is

because if the right of his father is established, that [existence] will be then necessarily established by your [own] acknowledgment; but if the idea that the right belonged to his father proves false, then your claim will be established and ours will prove wrong. But how absurd! Truth can only flourish and falsehood only wither even if the wrong thinkers embellish it.

[4] The proof that demonstrates the correctness of his father's Imāmate is that both we and you agree that there must be a man from among the descendants of Abu 'l-Ḥasan ['Alī al-Hādī] through whom God's proof is established and people are denied any excuse and that the proof of this man is compelling for the Muslims who are far from him in just the same way as it is compelling for those who see him. We and most people are of the group for whom the proof became compelling without seeing with our own eyes, so we must examine the way through which the proof became compelling for us. Then we should consider who is more qualified among the two men who are Abu 'l-Ḥasan ['Alī al-Hādī]'s only offspring who survived him. Naturally, whichever is the more qualified is the proof and [is] the Imām, and we need go no further. We then looked to see in which way the proof is compelling for those who are far from the prophets and Imāms, and found that it is through [a great number of] reports that result in an undeniable proof and dismiss from their transmitters any accusation of collusion concerning the reports and agreement to fabricate or invent them.

Next, we examined this specific case and found two groups of transmitters; one claims that the departing Imām designated Ḥasan and pointed him out, and—together with the testament and the seniority he has—they narrate evidence that they adduce and knowledge that they substantiate; the other group narrates similar things about Ja'far and nothing else of what we [as members of the first group] more deserve to offer. Then we investigated further and found the narrators of the reports of Ja'far to be an insignificant group. It is possible for a small group to collude and to come together and write to each other, so their narration produces suspicion and cannot stand as proof for God's proofs are not established through doubtful means.

We investigated the narration of the other group and found them to be a group that was widely separated in locality and region, with differing aims and conflicting views, so deceit was not possible because they were so far from each other nor was collaboration or collusion through correspondence or in a gathering to fabricate and invent a report. So we came to know that the correct narration is theirs and that it is they who tell the truth. If what they have narrated, with what we described of their status, were false, no report on this earth could be substantiated, and the whole [institution of] report would collapse. So consider you—may God grant you success—these two groups carefully, and you will find them as I described. The collapse of [the institution of] report means the destruction of Islam; and the recognition of its reliability equals the acceptance of the authenticity of our report. This demonstrates the truth of our doctrine. Praise be to God, the Lord of the Worlds.

[5] Then we noticed that the Ja'fariyya [that is, the supporters of Ja'far b. 'Alī al-'Askarī][5] differed among themselves about how the Imāmate of Ja'far was established. One group said: After his brother Muḥammad. Another group said: After his brother Ḥasan. And [yet] another group said: After his father. We saw that they get no further than this. We saw that their and our predecessors had already narrated before the Event [the Occultation] what demonstrates the Imāmate of Ḥasan, that is, a report quoted from Abū 'Abd Allāh [Ja'far al-Ṣādiq] who said: "When three names follow one another, Muḥammad and 'Alī and Ḥasan, the fourth will be the *qā'im*"[6] and other reports. This leads by itself to the necessary conclusion that the Imāmate belongs to Ḥasan, for there is no one apart from Ḥasan and Ja'far. Then, if there is no proof concerning Ja'far for someone who saw him in the time of Ḥasan,

5. The name is used in the above-mentioned sense also in Fakhr al-Dīn al-Rāzī, *I'tiqādāt*: 68.

6. Nu'mānī: 179–80; Khuṣaybī: 374; Ibn Bābawayh, *Nuṣūṣ* (quoted by Majlisī, 51:158); idem, *Kamāl*: 333–4; al-Ṭabarī al-Shī'ī: 236; Khazzāz: 325; Mufīd, *al-Risāla al-khāmisa fi 'l-ghayba*: 400; *Ghayba*: 139– 40.

whereas the Imām is the one whose proof is firmly established for both those who saw him and those who did not see him, then [the Imām] must necessarily be Ḥasan. Now that Ḥasan is confirmed [in the Imāmate], and, according to you, Ja'far disowned him, while the Imām never disowns another Imām, and Ḥasan passed away, and, according to both us and you, there must be a man from the offspring of Ḥasan through whom the proof of God can be established, then Ḥasan had necessarily to have a living son.

[6] Say, O Abū Ja'far [meaning himself], may God give you happiness, to Abu 'l-Ḥasan [Ibn Bashshār], may God confer dignity upon him: Muḥammad b. 'Abd al-Raḥmān [Ibn Qiba] says: We have proved to you the existence of the one whose Imāmate we claim, so how to escape? Do you acknowledge the falsity [of your argument] as you promised, or does [your] passion prevent you, so that you become as God said: "And many are lead astray by their passions without any knowledge."[7]

[7] As for [the name] *lābuddiyya* with which he branded the followers of truth because they say that there must be someone through whom the proof of God can be established, how amazing! Does Abu 'l-Ḥasan [Ibn Bashshār] not say that there must be some-one through whom the proof of God can be established? How can he not say [that] while he said when quoting and reproaching us: "Indeed! The actual existence of such a person, let alone his mere conceptual being, is necessary." If he believes this, then he and his companions are from *lābuddiyya,* so he is only branding himself and reproaching his brothers. If he does not believe this, it saves us the trouble of [answering] his [later] comparison and reference to the room and the light. This is the fate of him who opposes the friends of God; he actually finds fault in himself when he thinks he is finding fault in his opponent. Praise be to God Who confirms the truth with His signs. We call these people *buddiyya* because those who worship *budd* cling to what "cannot hear or see or make them needless of anything,"[8] and these people are like that.

7. Qur'ān, 6:119.
8. Ibid., 19:42.

[8] We say: O Abu 'l-Ḥasan, may God guide you on the right path, here is the Proof of God for the jinn and mankind, and the one whose authority is established only after public call and clear declaration, Muḥammad, may God bless him and his Family and grant them peace. He concealed himself in the cave so that only five people of those to whom God had sent him as a proof knew of his whereabouts. If you say: This concealment was after he had been manifest and after he had left someone in his bed in his place, I say to you: We do not argue with you about his status while he was manifest nor is his appointing the person who took his place relevant here in any way at all. We only say to you: Was not his proof established in him while he was in concealment for those who did not know his whereabouts for one reason or another? You must answer: Yes, indeed. We say: The proof of the Imām is established even though he is in concealment for another reason; otherwise, what is the difference? Then we say: He too did not go into concealment until his forefathers, peace be upon them, had thoroughly informed their followers that his concealment would take place and let them know how they should act during the concealment. Should you say anything about his birth, here is Moses, peace be upon him, despite Pharaoh's desperate search for him and what he did to the women and the children to find his whereabouts, [no one knew about his birth] until God permitted him to reveal himself. [Imām 'Alī] al-Riḍā, peace be upon him, said describing him [the vanished Imām]: "By my father and my mother, the one who is like me and is my grandfather's namesake, and is like Moses, the son of Amran."[9]

[9] Another proof: We say to you: O Abu 'l-Ḥasan, do you admit that the Shī'a have narrated Traditions concerning the Occultation? If he says no, we will show him the Traditions, and if he says yes, we would say to him: What is the position of the people when their Imām goes into occultation, how are they bound by the Proof in the time of his concealment? If he says: He appoints one who takes his place, then, according to both us and you, no one can take the place of the Imām except an Imām, and if there is an

9. See *Kamāl*: 371 where the latter part of the statement reads "who is my grandfather's namesake and is like me and like Moses, the son of Amran."

incumbent Imām, then there is no occultation. If he offers another argument for that occultation, that will precisely be our argument for our time. There is no difference nor any distinction between the two cases.

[10] Among the proofs that demonstrate that Ja'far's status was corrupt is his amity to, and attestation of, Fāris b. Ḥātim while his father disclaimed him. This [action by Ja'far's father] became well known everywhere so that even the enemies [of the Shī'ite community]—not to mention the friends—came to know it. Another proof of the falsity of his claim is his recourse to those he resorted to in his claiming the legacy from Ḥasan's mother, whereas the Shī'a agreed that his forefathers, peace be upon them, were in accord that the brother cannot inherit together with the mother.[10] Another proof of the falsity of his claim is his statement: "I am the Imām after my brother Muḥammad"; if only I could understand when the Imāmate of his brother could have been established—while he died before his father—so that the Imāmate could be established for his successor. How amazing it would be if Muḥammad appointed a successor and designated an Imām after him while his father was still alive and holding that position and was the Proof and the Imām; what was his father up to then? When was this practice the norm among the Imāms and their sons so that we could accept it from you? Show us what makes the Imāmate of Muḥammad incumbent so that, when it is proven, we may accept the Imāmate of his successor. Praise be to God who has confirmed the truth and discredited, weakened, and enfeebled falsehood.

[11] As for what he related from Ibn Abī Ghānim, may God have mercy on him, the man did not intend by what he said to affirm that we recognize the Imāmate of Ja'far. He only wanted to inform the questioner that the people of this House had not perished in such a way that none of them really exited.

[12] As for his saying: «Everything that is obeyed is worshipped», this is a grave error, for we know no object of worship apart

10. See Shalmaghānī: 288; 'Ayyāshī, 2:72; Kulaynī, 7:82, 91; Kashshī: 134; Ibn Bābawayh, *Faqīh*, 4:269; Ṭūsī, *Tahdhīb*, 9:251, 270, 283, 292, 310, 317.

from God; and we obey the Messenger of God, may God bless him and his Family and grant them peace, and do not worship him.

[13] As for his saying: «We shall now bring this book to a close by saying: We are only arguing with and addressing those who already had a consensus that an Imām must always rise up from among the people of this House, through whom the proof of God can be established—up to his words—it necessarily follows that there is a light in this room», and we do not need to enter the room [to make that judgment]. We, may God grant you success, do not disagree with this; there must be an Imām from among the people of this House through whom the proof of God can be established. We differ [with you] only about how he rises up and about his manifestation and occultation. As for the comparison he made with the room and the light, it is a wish, and it is said that "wish is the capital of the bankrupt." However, we cite a correct example, one by which we do not intend to attack an opponent or act prejudiced against an adversary but [to find] the truth. We say: [Suppose that] we and our opponent had agreed that someone passed away, leaving two sons and a house, and that the house should belong to the one who was able to hold one thousand pounds in one of his hands, and that the house would remain in the hands of the offspring of the holder till the Day of Judgment. We knew that one of the two sons could hold [this amount] but the other could not. We needed to know which of them could hold it. So we went to where they were in order to find out, but some obstacle in our way prevented us from seeing them. However, we found large groups of people in many countries, separated by great distances from each other, who testified that they had seen the elder of the two carry that weight. We also found a small group in one place who testified that the younger of the two did that. We did not find any special characteristic that this [latter] group could advance. Neither the judgment of reason or the requirements of justice nor anything in customary practice or valid experience permits us to reject the testimony of the former group and accept that of the latter, for suspicion attaches to them but not to the former.

[14] If our opponents say: What do you say about the testimony of Salmān [al-Fārsī], Abū Dharr, 'Ammār, and Miqdād in favor of

the Commander of the Faithful ['Alī],[11] peace be upon him, and the testimony of all those groups of people in favor of another? Which of them was the more correct?

We say to them: There were matters that were particular to the Commander of the Faithful, peace be upon him, and his companions that did not apply to anyone else. If you prove to us that you have the same or similar qualifications, then you would be right. The first of these [matters] is that his enemies acknowledged his superiority, his saintliness, and his knowledge. Both we and they narrated concerning him that [the Prophet], may God bless him and his Family and grant them peace, announced that God befriends anyone who is his ['Alī's] friend and is an enemy of anyone who is his enemy.[12] Because of this it was obligatory to obey him and no one else. The second [matter] is that his enemies did not say: We testify that the Prophet, may God bless him and his Family and grant them peace, identified that other person for the imāmate and set him up as a proof for mankind. They appointed him over themselves through election, as you are informed. The third [matter] is that his enemies testified for one of the companions of the Commander of the Faithful, peace be upon him, that he would never tell a lie, because he [the Prophet], may God bless him and his Family and grant them peace, said: "The sky has never stood over, nor has the earth ever supported, anyone with a tongue more truthful than Abū Dharr";[13] then his testimony was by itself worth more than their [combined] testimonies. The fourth [matter] is that his ['Alī's] enemies transmitted the same [statements] that established the proof [for him] as did his friends but disregarded it through wrong interpretation. The fifth [matter] is that his enemies narrated that Ḥasan and Ḥusayn were the two chiefs of youth of Paradise.[14] They also narrated that [the Prophet], may God bless him and his Family and grant them peace, said: "Whoever intentionally attri-

11. Abū Manṣūr al-Ṭabrisī, 1: 99–101. See also Jāḥiẓ, *'Uthmāniyya*: 172, 180–81; Nāshi': 10; Balādhurī, 1:591.

12. See 'Abd al-Ḥusayn al-Amīnī, 1:9–158 and the many sources cited therein.

13. Aḥmad, 2:175, 223, 5:197, 6:442; Ibn Māja, 1:55; Tirmidhī, 13:210.

14. See Nūr Allāh al-Tustarī, 10: 544–95, 19:232–51 where the statement is quoted from many sources.

butes to me what I have not said will occupy his place in the fire."[15] So when they [Ḥasan and Ḥusayn] witnessed for their father [that he was the Imām] and we already came to know that they were among the people of Paradise through the testimony of the Prophet, it became obligatory to accept [what they witnessed]. If they had lied in their witness they would not have been among the people of Paradise but among the people of the fire; far be it from them! the two guiltless, the two pure, and the two truthful.

Let the companions of Ja'far find for us a special characteristic that they have whereas their opponents do not so that [their testimony] may be accepted. Otherwise, there is no sense in abandoning a widely transmitted report whose narrators cannot be accused, and accepting a report that has no safeguard against the suspicion that the narrators colluded over it nor any special characteristic that validates [their narration]. Only a perplexed, confused person would ever do that [that is, abandon the former kind of report for the latter].

[15] So think over, may God grant you happiness, about what I have written to you concerning matters that are of concern to one who reflects about his religion, who thinks about his afterlife, and who contemplates with the eye of fear and caution the consequences of unbelief and rejection of the truth, [may you] be successful, God willing. May God prolong your life, give you strength, support you, make you steadfast, place you among the people of truth, guide you to the right path, and protect you from becoming one of "those whose efforts have been wasted in worldly life, while they reckon that they are doing good,"[16] or one of "those whom Satan causes to slip"[17] by his guile and deceit, his insinuations and temptations. And may He bring about for you the most favorable of what he always gives you.

15. Aḥmad, 2:159, 171 (and many other cases mentioned in Wensinck, 5:549); Bukhārī, 1:39–40; 2: 372–4; Muslim, 1:10; Ibn Māja, 1:13–14; Abū Dāwūd, 3:32; Tirmidhī, 10:126, 128, 137; Ibn Bābawayh, *Faqīh*, 4:364.

16. Qur'ān, 18:104.

17. Ibid., 3:155.

VII

A Debate with the Zaydites

THE FOLLOWING WORK is a refutation of *Kitāb al-Ishhād,* an anti-Imāmite work by a certain Abū Zayd al-ʻAlawī, obviously a Zaydite scholar of the late third/ninth century. The original work, *Kitāb al-Ishhād,* was written around that time as attested by a reference to the passing away of Jaʻfar b. ʻAlī and that his followers were rotating the Imāmate among his descendants through inheritance and will (para. 24). The author attacks the Imāmite doctrine on three main points: that they have restricted the Imāmate without reason to a certain clan of the descendants of Ḥusayn, that they hold the Imāmate to be established through designation from one Imām to the next while they always disagree on who has actually been designated, and that they recognize as Imāms some members of the House of the Prophet who never rose against injustice and never tried to establish the rule of truth, whereas the Zaydites accept as *imām* only those who call for the establishment of a just government and rebel against injustice. He also criticizes the Imāmites for their belief in a hidden Imām and their claim of knowledge of the unseen for their Imāms.

Ibn Qiba tried to respond to all of these criticisms while simultaneously demonstrating that those criticisms apply in much the same way to the Zaydites' own theories and practices. He tried to construct a consistent Imāmite theory of the Imāmate that could be protected from all of those criticisms. As in his other works, he offered the concept of the indisputable validity of the Imāmites' widespread reports to prove the authority of the chain of Imāms that the Imāmites believe in (paras. 18, 22, 28, 29, 35, 44). He rejects the idea that the Imāmate is based on lineage, supporting the idea that it is only based on merit and quality so that the Imām has always to be the most qualified among the descendants of the Prophet (paras. 9, 10, 44, 48, 50). He also forcefully denies that the Imāmites ever attributed knowledge of the unseen to the Imāms, an idea that only the "infidel polytheist" extremists held. He emphasizes that the Imām is only a pious scholar with thorough knowledge of the Qur'ān and the Prophetic tradition (paras. 25, 34, 55).

The text is also of considerable value for the students of the early history of Zaydism. The reference to the division of the Zaydite community into two camps of Mu'tazilites and *Muthbita* (para. 67) is a valuable attestation to the fact that Mu'tazilite doctrines had already gained a solid ground in Zaydism by the late third/ninth century.[1] The reference to Zaydite inactivity in that period (para. 71) goes well with Madelung's analysis of the politics of the Zaydite *imām* Qāsim b. Ibrāhīm al-Rassī (d. 246/860).[2]

1. Cf. Madelung, *Der Imām al-Qāsim b. Ibrāhīm*: 91–4, 140–45.
2. Ibid.: 163–7.

نقض كتاب الإشهاد لأبي زيد العلوي

[قال أبو جعفر محمّد بن عبد الرحمن بن قبة الرازي في نقض كتاب الإشهاد لأبي زيد العلوي:]

[1] قال صاحب الكتاب بعد أشياء كثيرة ذكرها لامنازعة فيها: « وقالت الزيديّة والمؤتمّة: الحُجّة من ولد فاطمة لقول الرسول المجمع عليه في حجّة الوداع، ويوم خرج إلى الصلاة في مرضه الّذي توفّي فيه: أيّها الناس قد خلّفت فيكم كتاب الله وعترتي، ألا وإنّهما لن يفترقا حتّى يردا عليَّ الحوضَ، ألا وإنّكم لن تضلّوا ما إن تمسّكتم بهما ». ثمَّ أكّد صاحب الكتاب هذا الخبر وقال فيه قولاً لا مخالفة فيه. ثمَّ قال بعد ذلك: « إنَّ المؤتمّة خالفت الإجماع وادَّعت الإمامة في بطن من العترة ولم توجبها لسائر العترة، ثمَّ لرجل من ذلك البطن في كلِّ عصر ».

[2] فأقول وبالله الثقة: إنَّ في قول النبيّ – صلّى الله عليه وآله وسلّم – على ما يقول الإماميّة دلالة واضحة. وذلك أنَّ النبيَّ – صلّى الله عليه وآله وسلّم – قال: « إنّي تارك فيكم ما إن تمسّكتم به لن تضلّوا، كتاب الله وعترتي أهل بيتي ». دلَّ على أنَّ الحجّة من بعده ليس من العجم ولا من سائر قبائل العرب بل من عترته أهل بيته. ثمَّ قرن قوله بما دلَّ على مراده فقال: « ألا وإنّهما لن يفترقا حتّى يردا عليَّ الحوض ». فأعلمنا أنَّ الحجّة من عترته لا يفارق الكتاب، وأنّا متى تمسّكنا بمن لا يفارق الكتاب لن نضلَّ، و[أنّ] من لا يفارق الكتاب [فهو] ممّن فرض على الأمّة أن يتمسّكوا به. ويجب في العقول

أن يكون عالماً بالكتاب مأموناً عليه، يعلم ناسخه من منسوخه وخاصّه من عامّه وحتمه من ندبه ومحكمه من متشابهه ليضع كلَّ شيء من ذلك موضعه الّذي وضعه الله عزَّ وجلَّ، لا يقدِّم مؤخّراً ولا يؤخّر مقدَّماً. ويجب أن يكون جامعاً لعلم الدين كلّه ليمكن التمسّك به والأخذ بقوله فيما اختلفت فيه الأمّة وتنازعته من تأويل الكتاب والسنّة، لأنّه إن بقي منه شيء لا يعلمه لم يمكن التمسّك به. ثمَّ متى كان بهذا المحلِّ أيضاً ولم يكن مأموناً على الكتاب لم يؤمن أن يغلط فيضع الناسخ منه مكان المنسوخ والمحكم مكان المتشابه والندب مكان الحتم إلى غير ذلك ممّا يكثر تعداده، وإذا كان هكذا صار الحجّة والمحجوج سواء. وإذا فسد هذا القول صحَّ ما قالت الإماميّة من أنَّ الحجّة من العترة لا يكون إلّا جامعاً لعلم الدين معصوماً مؤتمناً على الكتاب. فإن وجدت الزيديّة في أئمّتها مَن هذه صفته فنحن أوَّل من ينقاد له، وإن تكن الأخرى فالحقُّ أولى ما اتُّبع.

[3] وأمّا قوله: «إنَّ المؤتمّة خالفت الإجماع وادَّعت الإمامة في بطن من العترة»، فيقال له: ما هذا الإجماع السابق الّذي خالفناه؟ فإنّا لا نعرفه. اللهمَّ إلّا أن تجعل مخالفة الإماميّة للزيديّة خروجاً من الإجماع، فإن كنت إلى هذا تومي فليس يتعذَّر على الإماميّة أن تنسبك إلى مثل ما نسبتها إليه وتدَّعي عليك من الإجماع مثل الّذي ادَّعيته عليها. وبعد فأنت تقول إنَّ الإمامة لا تجوز إلّا لولد الحسن والحسين، فبيّن لنا لم خصّصت ولدهما دون سائر العترة لنبيّن لك بأحسن من حجّتك ما قلناه. وسيأتي البرهان في موضعه إن شاء الله.

[4] ثم قال صاحب الكتاب: وقالت الزيديّة: الإمامة جائزة للعترة كلّهم لدلالة رسول الله – صلّى الله عليه وآله وسلّم – عليهم عامّاً لم يخصّص بها بعضاً دون بعض، ولقول الله عزَّ وجلَّ لهم دون غيرهم بإجماعهم: «ثُمَّ أَوْرَثْنَا الْكِتَابَ الَّذِينَ اصْطَفَيْنَا مِنْ عِبَادِنَا – الآية».

[5] فأقول، وبالله التوفيق: قد غلط صاحب الكتاب فيما حكى، لأنَّ الزيديّة

إنّما تجيز الإمامة لولد الحسن والحسين خاصّة. والعترة في اللغة العمُّ وبنو العمّ، الأقرب فالأقرب، وما عرف أهل اللغة قطُّ ولا حكى عنهم أحدٌ أنَّـهم قالوا العترة لا تكون إلّا ولد الإبنة من ابن العمّ. هذا شيء تمنّته الزيديّـة وخدعت به أنفسها وتفرَّدت بادّعائه بلا بيان ولا برهان، لأنَّ الّـذي تدَّعيه ليس في العقل ولا في الكتاب ولا في الخبر ولا في شيء من اللغات، وهذه اللغة وهؤلاء أهلها فاسألوهم تبيّن لكم أنَّ العترة في اللغة الأقرب فالأقرب من العمّ وبني العمّ.

[6] فإن قال صاحب الكتاب: فلِمَ زعمت أنَّ الإمامة لا تكون لفلان وولده، وهم من العترة عندك؟

قلنا له: نحن لم نقل هذا قياساً وإنّما قلناه اتّـباعاً لما فعله – صلّى الله عليه وآله وسلّم – بهؤلاء الثلاثة دون غيرهم من العترة، ولو فعل بفلان ما فعله بهم لم يكن عندنا إلّا السمع والطاعة.

[7] وأمّـا قوله: « إنَّ الله تبارك وتعالى قال: ثُمَّ أَوْرَثْـنَـا الْكِتَـابَ الَّـذِينَ اصْطَـفَـيْـنَـا مِنْ عِبَـادِنَـا – الآية »، فيقال له: قد خالفك خصومك من المعتزلة وغيرهم في تأويل هذه الآية وخالفتك الإماميّـة، وأنت تعلم مَن السابق بالخيرات عند الإماميّـة. وأقلُّ ما كان يجب عليك – وقد ألّـفت كتابك هذا لتبيّن الحقَّ وتدعو إليه – أن تؤيّـد الدعوى بحجّـة، فإن لم تكن فاقناع، فإن لم يكن فترك الاحتجاج بما لم يمكنك أن تبيّن أنّـه حجّـة لك دون خصومك، فإنَّ تلاوة القرآن وادّعاء تأويله بلا برهان أمرٌ لا يعجز عنه أحدٌ. وقد ادَّعى خصومنا وخصومك أنَّ قول الله عزَّ وجلَّ: كُـنْـتُمْ خَـيْـرَ أُمَّـةٍ أُخْـرِجَـتْ لِلنَّـاسِ – الآية، هم جميع علماء الأمّـة، وأنَّ سبيل علماء العترة وسبيل علماء المرجئة سبيل واحد، وأنَّ الإجماع لا يتمُّ والحجّـة لا تثبت بعلم العترة، فهل بينك وبينها فصل؟ وهل تقنع منها بما ادَّعت أو تسألها البرهان؟ فإن قال: بل أسـألها

البرهان، قيل له: فهات برهانك أوّلاً على أنَّ المعنيّ بهذه الآية الّتي تلوتها هم العترة، وأنَّ العترة هم الذرّيّة، وأنَّ الذرّيّة هم ولد الحسن والحسين دون غيرهم من ولد جعفر وغيره ممّن أمّهاتهم فاطميّات.

[8] ثمّ قال: « ويقال للمؤتمّة: ما دليلكم على إيجاب الإمامة لواحد دون الجميع وحظرها على الجميع؟ فإن اعتلّوا بالوراثة والوصيّة قيل لهم: هذه المغيريّة تدّعي الإمامة لولد الحسن ثمّ في بطن من ولد الحسن بن الحسن في كلّ عصر وزمان بالوراثة والوصيّة من أبيه وخالفوكم بعد فيما تدّعون كما خالفتم غيركم في ما يدّعي ».

[9] فأقول وبالله الثقة: الدليل على أنَّ الإمامة لا تكون إلّا لواحد أنَّ الإمام لا يكون إلّا الأفضل، والأفضل يكون على وجهين: إمّا أن يكون أفضل من الجميع أو أفضل من كلّ واحد من الجميع، فكيف كانت القصّة فليس يكون الأفضل إلّا واحداً، لأنّه من المحال أن يكون أفضل من جميع الأمّة أو من كلّ واحد من الأمّة وفى الأمّة من هو أفضل منه. فلمّا لم يجز هذا، وصحّ بدليل تعترف الزيديّة بصحّته أنَّ الإمام لا يكون إلّا الأفضل، صحّ أنّها لا تكون إلّا لواحد في كلّ عصر. والفصل في ما بيننا وبين المغيريّة سهلٌ واضحٌ قريب، والمنّة لله، وهو أنَّ النبيَّ – صلّى الله عليه وآله وسلّم – دلَّ على الحسن والحسين دلالة بيّنة وبانهما من سائر العترة بما خصّهما به ممّا ذكرناه ووصفناه، فلمّا مضى الحسن كان الحسين أحقُّ وأولى بدلالة الحسن لدلالة الرسول – صلّى الله عليه وآله وسلّم – عليه واختصاصه إيّاه وإشارته إليه. فلو كان الحسن أوصى بالإمامة إلى ابنه لكان مخالفاً للرسول – صلّى الله عليه وآله وسلّم – وحاشا له من ذلك. وبعد فلسنا نشكُّ ولا نرتاب في أنّ الحسين أفضل من الحسن بن الحسن بن علي، والأفضل هو الإمام على الحقيقة عندنا وعند الزيديّة. فقد تبيّن لنا بما وصفنا كذب المغيريّة وانتقض الأصل الّذي بنوا عليه مقالتهم.

[10] ونحن لم نخصّ عليَّ بن الحسين بن عليّ بما خصّصناه به محاباة ولا قلّدنا في ذلك أحداً، ولكنَّ الأخبار قرعت سمعنا فيه بما لم تقرع في الحسن بن الحسن. ودلّنا على أنّه أعلم منه ما نقل من علم الحلال والحرام عنه وعن الخلف من بعده وعن أبي عبد الله، ولم نسمع للحسن بن الحسن بشيء يمكننا أن نقابل بينه وبين ما سمعناه من علم علي بن الحسين. والعالم بالدين أحقُّ بالإمامة ممّن لا علم له. فإن كنتم يا معشر الزيديّة عرفتم للحسن بن الحسن علماً بالحلال والحرام فأظهروه، وإن لم تعرفوا له ذلك فتفكّروا في قول الله عزَّ وجلَّ: أَفَمَنْ يَهْدِي إِلَى الْحَقِّ أَحَقُّ أَنْ يُتَّبَعَ أَمَّنْ لاٰ يَهِدّي إِلاٰ أَنْ يُهْدىٰ فَمَا لَكُمْ كَيْفَ تَحْكُمُونَ. فلسنا ندفع الحسن بن الحسن عن فضل وتقدُّم وطهارة وزكاة وعدالة، والإمامة لا يتمُّ أمرها إلّا بالعلم بالدين والمعرفة بأحكام ربِّ العالمين وبتأويل كتابه. وما رأينا إلى يومنا هذا ولا سمعنا بأحد قالت الزيديّة بإمامته إلّا وهو يقول في التأويل – أعني تأويل القرآن – على الاستخراج وفى الأحكام على الإجتهاد والقياس. وليس يمكن معرفة تأويل القرآن بالاستخراج، لأنَّ ذلك كان ممكناً لو كان القرآن إنّما أنزل بلغة واحدة وكان علماء أهل تلك اللغة يعرفون المراد، فأمّا القرآن فقد نزل بلغات كثيرة وفيه أشياء لا يعرف المراد منها إلّا بتوقيف مثل الصلاة والزكاة والحجّ وما في هذا الباب منه، ممّا نعلم وتعلمون أنّ المراد منه إنّما عرف بالتوقيف دون غيره، فليس يجوز حمله على اللغة لأنّك تحتاج أوّلا أن تعلم أنَّ الكلام الّذي تريد أن تتأوّله ليس فيه توقيف أصلاً لا في جمله ولا في تفصيله.

[11] فإن قال منهم قائلٌ: لِمَ ينكر أن يكون ما كان سبيله أن يعرف بالتوقيف فقد وقف الله رسوله – صلّى الله عليه وآله وسلّم – عليه، وما كان سبيله أن يستخرج فقد وكّل إلى العلماء وجعل بعض القرآن دليلاً على بعض، فاستغنينا بذلك عمّا تدّعون من التوقيف والموقّف.

قيل له: لا يجوز أن يكون ذلك على ما وصفتم، لأنّا نجد للآية الواحدة تأويلين متضادَّين كلّ واحد منهما يجوز في اللغة ويحسن أن يتعبّد الله به. وليس يجوز أن يكون للمتكلّم الحكيم كلامٌ يحتمل مرادين متضادَّين.

[12] فإن قال: ما ينكر أن يكون في القرآن دلالة على أحد المرادين وأن يكون العلماء بالقرآن متى تدبّروه علموا المراد بعينه دون غيره.

فيقال للمعترض بذلك: أنكرنا هذا الّذي وصفته لأمر نخبرك به: ليس تخلو تلك الدلالة الّتي في القرآن على أحد المرادين من أن تكون محتملة للتأويل أو غير محتملة. فإن كانت محتملة للتأويل فالقول فيها كالقول في هذه الآية، وإن كانت لا تحتمل التأويل فهي إذاً توقيف ونصٌّ على المراد بعينه ويجب أن لا يشكل على أحد عَلِمَ اللغة معرفة المراد. وهذا ما لا تنكره العقول وهو من فعل الحكيم جائز حسن. ولكنّا إذا تدبّرنا آي القرآن لم نجدها هكذا، ووجدنا الاختلاف في تأويلها قائماً بين أهل العلم بالدين واللغة. ولو كان هناك آياتٌ تفسّر آياتٍ تفسيراً لا يحتمل التأويل لكان فريق من المختلفين في تأويله من العلماء باللغة معاندين، ولأمكن كشف أمرهم بأهون السعي، ولكان من تأوّل الآية خارجاً من اللغة ومن لسان أهلها لأنَّ الكلام إذا لم يحتمل التأويل فحملته على ما لا يحتمله خرجت عن اللغة الّتي وقع الخطاب بها. فدلّونا يا معشر الزيديّة على آية واحدة اختلف أهل العلم في تأويلها وفي القرآن ما يدلُّ نصّاً وتوقيفاً على تأويلها. وهذا أمر متعذِّر، وفي تعذُّره دليلٌ على أنّه لا بدَّ للقرآن من مترجم يعلم مراد الله تعالى فيخبر به. وهذا عندي واضحٌ.

[13] ثم قال صاحب الكتاب: « وهذه الخطّابيّة تدَّعي الإمامة لجعفر بن محمّد من أبيه بالوراثة والوصيّة ويقفون على رجعته ويخالفون كلَّ من قال بالإمامة ويزعمون أنّكم وافقتموهم في إمامة جعفر وخالفوكم في من سواه ».

[14] فأقول وبالله الثقة: ليس تصحُّ الإمامة بموافقة موافق ولا مخالفة مخالف وإنّما

تصحُّ بأدلّـة الحقِّ وبراهينه. وأحسب أنَّ صاحب الكتاب غلط فالخطابيّـة قوم غلاة وليس بين الغلوِّ والإمامة نسبة. فإن قال: فإنّي أردت الفرقة الّتي وقفت عليه، قيل له: فيقال لتلك الفرقة نعلم أنَّ الإمام بعد جعفر موسى بمثل ما علمتم أنتم به أنّ الإمام بعد محمّـد بن علي جعفر، ونعلم أنّ جعفراً مات كما نعلم أنَّ أباه مات، والفصل بيننا وبينكم هو الفصل بينكم وبين السبائيّـة والواقفة على أمير المؤمنين – صلوات الله عليه – فقولوا كيف شئتم. ويقال لصاحب الكتاب: وأنت فما الفصل بينك وبين من اختار الإمامة لولد العبّـاس وجعفر وعقيل – أعني لأهل العلم والفضل منهم – واحتجَّ باللغة في أنّـهم من عترة الرسول وقال إنَّ الرسول – صلّى الله عليه وآله وسلّم – عمَّ جميع العترة ولم يخصَّ ثلاثة هم أمير المؤمنين والحسن والحسين – صلوات الله عليهم –؟ عرّفناه وبيّن لنا.

[15] ثمَّ قال صاحب الكتاب: « وهذه الشمطيّـة تدَّعي إمامة محمّـد بن جعفر بن محمّـد من أبيه بالوراثة والوصيّـة. وهذه الفطحيّـة تدَّعي إمامة إسماعيل بن جعفر عن أبيه بالوراثة والوصيّـة، وقبل ذلك قالوا بإمامة عبد الله بن جعفر ويسمّـون اليوم إسماعيليّـة لأنّـه لم يبق للقائلين بإمامة عبد الله بن جعفر خلف ولا بقيّـة. وفرقة من الفطحية يقال لهم القرامطة قالوا بإمامة محمّـد بن إسماعيل بن جعفر بالوراثة والوصيّـة. وهذه الواقفة على موسى بن جعفر تدَّعي الإمامة لموسى وترتقب لرجعته ».

[16] أقول: الفرق بيننا وبين هؤلاء سهل واضح قريب:

أما الفطحيّـة فالحجّـة عليها أوضح من أن تخفى لأنَّ إسماعيل مات قبل أبي عبد الله، والميّت لا يكون خليفة الحيّ، وإنّما يكون الحيُّ خليفة الميّت، ولكنَّ القوم عملوا على تقليد الرؤسـاء وأعرضوا عن الحجّـة وما في بابها. وهذا أمر لا يحتاج فيه على إكثار لأنّـه ظاهر الفساد بيّن الانتقاد.

[17] وأما القرامطة فقد نقضت الإسلام حرفاً حرفاً، لأنّـها أبطلت أعمال

الشريعة وجاءت بكلِّ سوفسطائيّة. وإنَّ الإمام إنّما يحتاج إليه للدين وإقامة حكم الشريعة، فإذا جاءت القرامطة تدَّعي أنَّ جعفر بن محمّد أو وصيّه استخلف رجلاً دعا إلى نقض الإسلام والشريعة والخروج عمّا عليه طبايع الأمّة لم نحتج في معرفة كذبهم إلى أكثر من دعواهم المتناقض الفاسد.

[18] وأمّا الفصل بيننا وبين سائر الفرق فهو أنَّ لنا نقلة أخبار وحملة آثار قد طبّقوا البلدان كثرة، ونقلوا عن جعفر بن محمّد من علم الحلال والحرام ما يُعلم بالعادة الجارية والتجربة الصحيحة أنَّ ذلك كلّه لا يجوز أن يكون كذباً مولّداً، وحكوا مع نقل ذلك عن أسلافهم أنَّ أبا عبد الله أوصى بالإمامة إلى موسى، ثمَّ نقل إلينا من فضل موسى وعلمه ما هو معروف عند نقلة الأخبار، ولم نسمع لهؤلاء بأكثر من الدعوى. وليس سبيل التواتر وأهله سبيل الشذوذ وأهله. فتأمّلوا الأخبار الصادقة تعرفوا بها فصل ما بين موسى ومحمّد وعبد الله بني جعفر، وتعالوا نمتحن هذا الأمر بخمس مسائل من الحلال والحرام ممّا قد أجاب فيه موسى، فإن وجدنا لهذين فيه جواباً عند أحد من القائلين بإمامتهما فالقول كما يقولون. وقد روت الإماميّة أنَّ عبد الله بن جعفر سئل كم في مئتي درهم؟ قال: خمسة دراهم، قيل له: وكم في مائة درهم؟ فقال: درهمان ونصف. ولو أنَّ معترضاً اعترض على الإسلام وأهله فادَّعى أنَّ ههنا من قد عارض القرآن وسألنا أن نفصل بين تلك المعارضة والقرآن، لقلنا له: أمّا القرآن فظاهر، فأظهر تلك المعارضة حتّى نفصل بينها وبين القرآن. وهكذا نقول لهذه الفرق: أمّا أخبارنا فهي مرويّة محفوظة عند أهل الأمصار من علماء الإماميّة، فأظهروا تلك الأخبار الّتي تدَّعونها حتّى نفصل بينها وبين أخبارنا. فأمّا أن تدَّعوا خبراً لم يسمعه سامع ولا عرفه أحدٌ ثمَّ تسألونا الفصل بين أخبارنا وبين الخبر فهذا ما لا يعجز عن دعوى مثله أحدٌ. ولو أبطل مثل هذه الدعوى أخبارَ أهل الحقِّ من الإماميّة لأبطل مثلُ هذه الدعوى من البراهمة أخبارَ المسلمين. وهذا

واضح ولله المنّة. وقد ادَّعت الثنويّة أنَّ ماني أقام المعجزات وأنَّ لهم خبراً يدلُّ على صدقهم، فقال لهم الموحّدون: هذه دعوى لا يعجز عنها أحدٌ فأظهروا الخبر لندلّكم على أنّه لا يقطع عذراً ولا يوجب حجّة، وهذا شبيه بجوابنا لصاحب الكتاب.

[19] ويقال لصاحب الكتاب: قد ادَّعت البكريّة والإباضيّة أنَّ النبيَّ – صلّى الله عليه وآله وسلّم – نصَّ على أبي بكر، وأنكرت أنت ذلك، كما أنكرنا نحن أنَّ أبا عبد الله أوصى إلى هذين. فبيّن لنا حجّتك ودلّنا على الفصل بينك وبين البكريّة والإباضيّة، لندلّك بمثله على الفصل بيننا وبين من سمّيت.

[20] ويقال لصاحب الكتاب: أنت رجلٌ تدَّعي أنَّ جعفر بن محمّد كان على مذهب الزيديّة وأنّه لم يدَّ ع الإمامة من الجهة الّتي تذكرها الإماميّة. وقد ادَّعى القائلون بإمامة محمّد بن جعفر بن محمّد خلاف ما تدَّعيه أنت وأصحابك، ويذكرون أنَّ أسلافهم رووا ذلك عنه. فعرِّفنا الفصل بينكم وبينهم لنأتيك بأحسن منه، وأنصف من نفسك فإنّه أولى بك.

[21] وفرق آخر: وهو أنَّ أصحاب محمّد بن جعفر وعبد الله بن جعفر معترفون بأنَّ الحسين نصَّ على علي، وأنَّ عليّاً نصَّ على محمّد، وأنَّ محمّداً نصَّ على جعفر. ودليلنا أنَّ جعفراً نصَّ على موسى هو بعينه دون غيره دليل هؤلاء على أنَّ الحسين نصَّ على علي. وبعد فإنَّ الإمام إذا كان ظاهراً واختلفت إليه شيعته ظهر علمه وتبيّن معرفته بالدين، ووجدنا رواة الأخبار وحملة الآثار قد نقلوا عن موسى من علم الحلال والحرام ما هو مدوّن مشهور، وظهر من فضله في نفسه ماهو بيّن عند الخاصّة والعامّة، وهذه هي أمارات الإمامة. فلمّا وجدناها لموسى دون غيره علمنا أنّه الإمام بعد أبيه دون أخيه. وشيء آخر وهو أنَّ عبد الله بن جعفر مات ولم يعقّب ذكراً ولا نصَّ على أحد فرجع القائلون بإمامته عنها إلى القول بإمامة موسى.

[22] والفصل بعد ذلك بين أخبارنا وأخبارهم هو أنَّ الأخبار لا توجب العلم حتّى يكون في طرقه وواسطته قوم يقطعون العذر إذا أخبروا. ولسنا نشاحُّ هؤلاء في أسلافهم بل نقتصر على أن يوجدونا في دهرنا من حملة الأخبار ورواة الآثار ممّن يذهب مذهبهم عدداً يتواتر بهم الخبر كما نوجدهم نحن ذلك. فإن قدروا على هذا فليظهروه، وإن عجزوا فقد وضح الفرق بيننا وبينهم في الطرف الّذي يلينا ويليهم، وما بعد ذلك موهوب لهم. وهذا واضح والحمد لله.

[23] وأمّا الواقفة على موسى فسبيلهم سبيل الواقفة على أبي عبد الله، ونحن فلم نشاهد موت أحد من السلف وإنّما صحَّ موتهم عندنا بالخبر، فإن وقف واقف على بعضهم سألناه الفصل بينه وبين من وقف على سائرهم. وهذا ما لا حيلة لهم فيه.

[24] ثمَّ قال صاحب الكتاب: « ومنهم فرقة قطعت على موسى وائتمّوا بعده بابنه علي بن موسى دون سائر ولد موسى، وزعموا أنّه استحقّها بالوراثة والوصيّة. ثمَّ في ولده، حتّى انتهوا إلى الحسن بن علي فادّعوا له ولداً وسمّوه الخلف الصالح وقد كانوا في حياة علي بن محمّد وسموا للإمامة ابنه محمداً فمات قبل أبيه، ثمَّ إنّهم رجعوا إلى أخيه الحسن وبطل في محمّد ما كانوا توهّموا وقالوا: بدا لله من محمّد إلى الحسن كما بدا له من إسماعيل بن جعفر إلى موسى، وقد مات إسماعيل في حياة جعفر. إلى أن مات الحسن بن علي في سنة ثلاث وستّين ومأتين فرجع بعض أصحابه إلى إمامة جعفر بن علي، كما رجع أصحاب محمّد بن علي بعد وفاة محمّد إلى الحسن. وزعم بعضهم أنَّ جعفر بن علي استحقَّ الإمامة من أبيه علي بن محمّد بالوراثة والوصيّة دون أخيه الحسن، ثمَّ نقلوها في ولد جعفر بالوراثة والوصيّة. وكلُّ هذه الفرق يتشاحّون على الإمامة ويكفّر بعضهم بعضاً ويكذِّب بعضهم بعضاً ويتبرّأ بعضهم من إمامة بعض وتدَّعي كلُّ فرقة الإمامة لصاحبها بالوراثة والوصيّة وأشياء من علوم

الغيب الخرافات أحسن منها. ولا دليل لكلّ فرقة فيما تدّعي وتخالف الباقين غير الوراثة والوصيّة. دليلهم شهادتهم لأنفسهم دون غيرهم قولاً بلا حقيقة ودعوى بلا دليل. فإن كان ههنا دليل فيما يدّعي كلُّ طائفة غير الوراثة والوصيّة وجب إقامته، وإن لم يكن غير الدعوى للإمامة بالوراثة والوصيّة فقد بطلت الإمامة لكثرة من يدّعيها بالوراثة والوصيّة، ولا سبيل إلى قبول دعوى طائفة دون الأخرى إن كانت الدعوى واحدة فلا سيّما وهم في إكذاب بعضهم بعضاً مجتمعون وفيما يدّعي كلُّ فرقة منهم منفردون ».

[25] فأقول والله الموفّق للصواب: لو كانت الإمامة تبطل لكثرة من يدّعيها لكان سبيل النبوّة سبيلها لأنّا نعلم أنّ خلقاً قد ادّعاها. وقد حكى صاحب الكتاب عن الإماميّة حكايات مضطربة وأوهم أنّ تلك مقالة الكلِّ، وأنّه ليس فيهم إلّا من يقول بالبداء. ومن قال إنّ الله يبدو له من إحداث رأي وعلم مستفاد فهو كافر بالله. وما كان هذا قول غير المغيريّة ومن ينحل للأئمّة علم الغيب، فهذا كفرٌ بالله وخروج عن الإسلام عندنا. وأقلُّ ما كان يجب عليه أن يذكر مقالة أهل الحقِّ، وأن لا يقتصر على أنّ القوم اختلفوا حتّى يدلّ على أنّ القول بالإمامة فاسدٌ. وبعد فإنّ الإمام عندنا يعرف من وجوه سنذكرها ثمّ نعتبر ما يقول هؤلاء، فإن لم نجد بيننا وبينهم فصلاً حكمنا بفساد المذهب ثمّ عدنا نسأل صاحب الكتاب عن أنّ أيّ قول هو الحق من بين الأقاويل.

[26] أمّا قوله إنّ « منهم فرقة قطعت على موسى وائتمّوا بعده بابنه علي بن موسى » فهو قول رجل لا يعرف أخبار الإماميّة، لأنّ كلّ الإماميّة – إلّا شرذمة وقفت وشذوذ قالوا بإمامة إسماعيل وعبد الله بن جعفر – قالوا بإمامة علي بن موسى ورووا فيه ما هو مدوّن في الكتب. وما يذكر من حملة الأخبار ونقلة الآثار خمسة مالوا إلى هذه المذاهب في أوّل حدوث الحادث، وإنّما أكثر من كثر منهم بعد. فكيف استحسن صاحب الكتاب أن يقول: « ومنهم فرقة قطعت على موسى »؟

[27] وأعجب من هذا قوله: « حتّى انتهوا إلى الحسن فادّعوا له ابناً وقد كانوا في حياة علي بن محمّد وسموا للإمامة ابنه محمّداً » [ولم يقل بإمامة محمّد] إلّا طائفة من أصحاب فارس بن حاتم. وليس يحسن بالعاقل أن يشنع على خصمه بالباطل الّذي لا أصل له. والّذي يدلُّ على فساد قول القائلين بإمامة محمّد هو بعينه ما وصفناه في باب إسماعيل بن جعفر لأنَّ القصّة واحدة وكلٌّ واحد منهما مات قبل أبيه، ومن المحال أن يستخلف الحيُّ الميّت ويوصى إليه بالإمامة، وهذا أبين فساداً من أن يحتاج في كسره إلى كثرة القول.

[28] والفصل بيننا وبين القائلين بإمامة جعفر أنَّ حكاية القائلين بإمامته عنه اختلفت وتضادَّت، لأنَّ منهم ومنّا من حكى عنه أنّه قال: إنّي إمامٌ بعد أخي محمّد، ومنهم من حكى عنه أنّه قال: إنّي إمام بعد أخي الحسن، ومنهم من قال إنّه قال: إنّي إمام بعد أبي علي بن محمّد. وهذه أخبار كما ترى يكذِّب بعضها بعضاً، وخبرنا في أبي محمّد الحسن بن علي خبر متواتر لا يتناقض، وهذا فصل بيّن. ثمَّ ظهر لنا من جعفر ما دلّنا على أنّه جاهل بأحكام الله عزَّ وجلَّ وهو أنّه جاء يطالب أمَّ أبي محمّد بالميراث، وفى حكم آبائه أنَّ الأخ لا يرث مع الأمّ، فإذا كان جعفر لا يحسن هذا المقدار من الفقه حتّى تبيّن فيه نقصه وجهله كيف يكون إماماً؟ وإنّما تعبّدنا الله بالظاهر من هذه الأمور ولو شئنا أن نقول لقلنا وفيما ذكرناه كفاية ودلالة على أنَّ جعفراً ليس بإمام.

[29] وأما قوله إنّهم « ادَّعوا للحسن ولداً » فالقوم لم يدَّعوا ذلك إلّا بعد أن نقل إليهم أسلافهم حاله وغيبته وصورة أمره واختلاف الناس فيه عند حدوث ما يحدث، وهذه كتبهم فمن شاء أن ينظر فيها فلينظر.

[30] وأما قوله: « إنَّ كلَّ هذه الفرق يتشاحّون ويكفّر بعضهم بعضاً » فقد صدق في حكايته وحال المسلمين في تكفير بعضهم بعضاً هذا الحال. فليقل كيف أحبَّ وليطعن كيف شاء فإنَّ البراهمة تتعلّق به فتطعن بمثله في الإسلام.

ومن سأل خصمه عن مسألة يريد بها نقض مذهبه إذا ردّت عليه كان فيها من نقض مذهبه مثل الّذي قدر أن يلزمه خصمه فإنّما هو رجل يسأل نفسه وينقض قوله، وهذه قصّة صاحب الكتاب. والنبوّة أصلٌ والإمامة فرع، فإذا أقرّ صاحب الكتاب بالأصل لم يحسن به أن يطعن في الفرع بما رجع على الأصل. والله المستعان.

[31] ثمّ قال: « ولو جازت الإمامة بالوراثة والوصيّة لمن يدّعى له بلا دليل متّفق عليه لكانت المغيريّة أحقُّ بها، لإجماع الكلّ معها على إمامة الحسن – الذي هو أصلها المستحقّ للإمامة من أبيه بالوراثة والوصيّة – وامتناعها بعد إجماع الكلّ معها على إمامة الحسن من إجازتها لغيره. هذا مع اختلاف المؤتمّة في دينهم، منهم من يقول بالجسم ومنهم من يقول بالتناسخ ومنهم من تجرّد التوحيد، ومنهم من يقول بالعدل ويثبت الوعيد ومنهم من يقول بالقدر ويبطل الوعيد، ومنهم من يقول بالرؤية ومنهم من ينفيها، مع القول بالبداء وأشياء يطول الكتاب بشرحها، يكفّر بها بعضها بعضاً ويتبرّأ بعضهم من دين بعض. ولكلِّ فرقة من هذه الفرق بزعمها رجال ثقات عند أنفسهم أدّوا إليهم عن أئمّتهم ما هم متمسّكون به ».

ثمّ قال صاحب الكتاب: وإذا جاز كذا جاز كذا (شيء لا يجوز عندنا ولم يأت بأكثر من الحكاية، فلا معنى لتطويل الكتاب بذكر ما ليس فيه حجّة ولا فائدة).

[32] فأقول وبالله التوفيق: لو كان الحقُّ لا يثبت إلّا بدليل متّفق عليه ما صحّ حقٌّ أبداً، ولكان أوّل مذهب يبطل مذهب الزيديّة لأنّ دليلها ليس بمتّفق عليه. وأمّا ما حكاه عن المغيريّة فهو شيء أخذته عن اليهود لأنّها تحتجُّ أبداً بإجماعنا وإيّاهم على نبوّة موسى – عليه السلام – ومخالفتهم إيّانا في نبوّة محمّد – صلّى الله عليه وآله وسلّم –. وأما تعييره إيّانا بالاختلاف في المذاهب وبأنّ

كلّ فرقة منّا تروي ما تدين به عن إمامها، فهو مأخوذٌ من البراهمة لأنّها تطعن به، بعينه دون غيره، على الإسلام. ولولا الإشفاق من أن يتعلّق بعض هؤلاء المجان بما أحكيه عنهم لقلت كما يقولون. والإمامة، أسعدكم الله، إنّما تصحُّ عندنا بالنصِّ وظهور الفضل والعلم بالدين مع الإعراض عن القياس والاجتهاد في الفرائض السمعيّة وفى فروعها، ومن هذا الوجه عرفنا إمامة الإمام. وسنقول في اختلاف الشيعة قولاً مقنعاً.

[33] قال صاحب الكتاب: « ثمَّ لم يخل اختلافهم من أن يكون مولّداً من أنفسهم أومن عند الناقلين إليهم أو من عند أئمّتهم. فإن كان اختلافهم من قبل أئمّتهم فالإمام مَنْ جَمَعَ الكلمة لا من كان سبباً للاختلاف بين الأمّة، لا سيّما وهم أولياؤه دون أعدائه ومن لا تقيّة بينهم وبينه، وما الفرق بين المؤتمّة والأمّة إذ كانوا مع أئمّتهم وحجج الله عليهم [داخلين] في أكثر ما عابوا على الأمّة الّتي لا إمام لها من المخالفة في الدين وإكفار بعضهم بعضاً. وإن يكن اختلافهم من قبل الناقلين إليهم دينهم فما يؤمنهم من أن يكون هذا سبيلهم معهم فيما ألقوا إليهم من الإمامة لا سيّما إذا كان المدّعى له الإمامة معدوم العين غير مرئيِّ الشخص، وهو حجّة عليهم فيما يدّعون لإمامهم من علم الغيب إذ كان خيرته والتراجمة بينه وبين شيعته كذّابين يكذبون عليه ولا علم له بهم. وإن يكن اختلاف المؤتمّة في دينها من قبل أنفسها دون أئمّتها فما حاجة المؤتمّة إلى الأئمّة إذ كانوا بأنفسهم مستغنين وهو بين أظهرهم لا ينهاهم وهو الترجمان لهم من الله والحجّة عليهم؟ هذا أيضاً من أدلِّ الدليل على عدمه وما يدّعى من علم الغيب له، لأنّه لو كان موجوداً لم يسعه ترك البيان لشيعته كما قال الله عزّ وجلّ: وَما أَنْزَلْنا عَلَيْكَ ٱلْكِتابَ إِلَّا لِتُبَيِّنَ لَهُمُ ٱلَّذِي اخْتَلَفُوا فِيهِ، فكما بيّن الرسول – صلّى الله عليه وآله وسلّم – لأمّته وجب على الإمام مثله لشيعته ».

[34] فأقول وبالله الثقة: إنَّ اختلاف الإماميّة إنّما هو من قبل كذّابين دلّسوا أنفسهم فيهم في الوقت بعد الوقت والزمان بعد الزمان حتّى عظم البلاء. وكان أسلافهم قوم يرجعون إلى ورع واجتهاد وسلامة ناحية، ولم يكونوا أصحاب نظر وتميز، فكانوا إذا رأوا رجلاً مستوراً يروي خبراً أحسنوا به الظنَّ وقبلوه. فلمّا كثر هذا وظهر شكوا إلى أئمّتهم فأمرهم الأئمّة – عليهم السلام – بأن يأخذوا بما يُجمع عليه فلم يفعلوا وجروا على عادتهم. فكانت الخيانة من قبلهم لا من قبل أئمّتهم. والإمام أيضاً لم يقف على كلِّ هذه التخاليط الّتي رويت لأنّه لا يعلم الغيب وإنّما هو عبد صالح يعلم الكتاب والسنّة ويعلم من أخبار شيعته ما يُنهى إليه.

[35] وأمّا قوله: « فما يؤمنهم من أن يكون هذا سبيلهم فيما ألقوا إليهم من أمر الإمامة » فإن الفصل بين ذلك أنَّ الإمامة تنقل إليهم بالتواتر، والتواتر لا ينكشف عن كذب، وهذه الأخبار فكلُّ واحد منها إنّما خبر واحد لا يوجب خبره العلمَ، وخبر الواحد قد يصدق ويكذب وليس هذا سبيل التواتر. هذا جوابنا وكلُّ ما أتى به سوى هذا فهو ساقط.

[36] ثم يقال له: أخبرنا عن اختلاف الأمّة هل تخلو من الأقسام الّتي قسمتها؟ فإذا قال: لا، قيل له: أفليس الرسول إنّما بعث لجمع الكلمة؟ فلا بدَّ من نعم، فيقال له: أوليس قد قال الله عزَّ وجلَّ: وَمَا أَنْزَلْنَا عَلَيْكَ ٱلْكِتَابَ إِلَّا لِتُبَيِّنَ لَهُمُ ٱلَّذِي اخْتَلَفُوا فِيهِ؟ فلا بدَّ من نعم، فيقال له: فهل بيّن؟ فلا بدَّ من نعم، فيقال له: فما سبب الاختلاف؟ عرّفناه واقنع منّا بمثله.

[37] وأمّا قوله: « فما حاجة المؤتمّة إلى الأئمّة إذ كانوا بأنفسهم مستغنين وهو بين أظهرهم لا ينهاهم » إلى آخر الفصل، فيقال له: أولى الأشياء بأهل الدين الإنصاف، أيّ قول قلناه وأومأنا به إلى أنّا بأنفسنا مستغنين حتّى يقرعنا به صاحب الكتاب ويحتجُّ علينا؟ أو أيُّ حجّة توجّهت له علينا توجب

ما أوجبه؟ ومن لم يبال بأيِّ شيء قابل خصومه كثرت مسائله وجواباته.

[38] وأما قوله: « وهذا من أدلِّ دليل على عدمه لأنّه لو كان موجوداً لم يسعه ترك البيان لشيعته كما قال الله عزَّ وجلَّ: وَمَا أَنْزَلْنَا عَلَيْكَ ٱلْكِتَابَ إِلَّا لِتُبَيِّنَ لَهُمُ ٱلَّذِي اخْتَلَفُوا فِيهِ » فيقال لصاحب الكتاب: أخبرنا عن العترة الهادية يسعهم أن لا يبيّنوا للأمّة الحقَّ كلّه؟ فإن قال: نعم، حجَّ نفسه وعاد كلامه وبالاً عليه لأنَّ الأمّة قد اختلفت وتباينت وكفّر بعضها بعضاً، وإن قال: لا، قيل: هذا من أدلِّ دليل على عدم العترة وفساد ما تدَّعيه الزيديّة لأنَّ العترة لو كانوا كما تصف الزيديّة لبيّنوا للأمّة ولم يسعهم السكوت والإمساك كما قال الله عزَّ وجلَّ: وَمَا أَنْزَلْنَا عَلَيْكَ ٱلْكِتَابَ إِلَّا لِتُبَيِّنَ لَهُمُ ٱلَّذِي اخْتَلَفُوا فِيه. فإن ادَّعى أنَّ العترة قد بيّنوا الحقَّ للأمّة غير أن الأمّة لم تقبل ومالت إلى الهوى، قيل له: هذا بعينه قول الإماميّة في الإمام وشيعته. ونسأل الله التوفيق.

[39] ثم قال صاحب الكتاب: « ويقال لهم [لِمَ] استتر إمامكم عن مسترشده؟ فإن قالوا: تقيّة على نفسه، قيل لهم: فالمسترشد أيضاً يجوز له أن يكون في تقيّة من طلبه، لا سيّما إذا كان المسترشد يخاف ويرجو ولا يعلم مايكون من قبل كونه هو في تقيّة. وإذا جازت التقيّة للإمام فهي للمأموم أجوز. وما بال الإمام في تقيّة من إرشادهم وليس هو في تقيّة من تناول أموالهم؟ والله يقول: اِتَّبِعُوا مَنْ لَا يَسْئَلُكُمْ أَجْراً، وقال: إِنَّ كَثِيراً مِنَ ٱلْأَحْبَارِ وَٱلرُّهْبَانِ لَيَأْكُلُونَ أَمْوَالَ ٱلنَّاسِ بِٱلْبَاطِلِ وَيَصُدُّونَ عَنْ سَبِيلِ اللهِ، فهذا ممّا يدلُّ على أنَّ أهل الباطل عرض الدُنيا يطلبون، والّذين يتمسّكون بالكتاب لا يسألون الناس أجراً وهم مهتدون ».

ثمَّ قال: وإن قالوا كذا قيل كذا (شيء لا يقوله إلّا جاهل منقوص).

[40] والجواب عمّا سأل: أنَّ الإمام لم يستتر عن مسترشده، إنّما استتر خوفاً

على نفسه من الظالمين. فأمّا قوله: « فإذا جازت التقيّة للإمام فهي للمأموم أجوز » فيقال له: إن كنت تريد أنَّ المأموم يجوز له أن يتّقي من الظالم ويهرب عنه متى خاف على نفسه كما جاز للإمام فهذا لعمري جائز، وإن كنت تريد أنَّ المأموم يجوز له أن لا يعتقد إمامة الإمام للتقيّة فذلك لا يجوز إذا قرعت الأخبار سمعه وقطعت عذره، لأنَّ الخبر الصحيح يقوم مقام العيان وليس على القلوب تقيّة ولا يعلم ما فيها إلّا الله.

[41] وأما قوله: « وما بال الإمام في تقيّة من إرشادهم وليس في تقيّة من تناول أموالهم والله يقول: اتَّبِعُوا مَنْ لَا يَسْئَلُكُمْ أَجْرًا » فالجواب عن ذلك إلى آخر الفصل يقال له: إنَّ الإمام ليس في تقيّة من إرشاد من يريد الإرشاد، وكيف يكون في تقيّة وقد بيّن لهم الحقَّ وحثّهم عليه ودعاهم إليه وعلّمهم الحلال والحرام حتّى شهروا بذلك وعرفوا به. وليس يتناول اموالهم وإنّما يسألهم الخمس الذي فرضه الله عزّ وجلّ ليضعه حيث أمر أن يضعه. والذي جاء بالخمس هو الرسول وقد نطق القرآن بذلك. قال الله عزَّ وجلَّ: وَاعْلَمُوا أَنَّمَا غَنِمْتُمْ مِنْ شَيْءٍ فَأَنَّ لِلهِ خُمُسَهُ – الآية، وقال: خُذْ مِنْ أَمْوَالِهِمْ صَدَقَةً – الآية. فإن كان في أخذ المال عيب أو طعن فهو على من ابتدأ به. والله المستعان.

[42] ويقال لصاحب الكتاب: أخبرنا عن الإمام منكم إذا خرج وغلب هل يأخذ الخمس وهل يجبي الخراج وهل يأخذ الحقَّ من الفيء والمغنم والمعادن وما أشبه ذلك؟ فإن قال: لا، فقد خالف حكم الإسلام، وإن قال: نعم، قيل له: فإن احتجَّ عليه رجل مثلك بقول الله عزَّ وجلَّ: اتَّبِعُوا مَنْ لَا يَسْئَلُكُمْ أَجْرًا وبقوله: إِنَّ كَثِيرًا مِنَ ٱلْأَحْبَارِ وَٱلرُّهْبَانِ – الآية بأيِّ شيء تجيبه حتّى تجيبك الإماميّة بمثله؟ وهذا – وفّقكم الله – شيء كان الملحدون يطعنون به على المسلمين، وما أدري من دلّسه لهؤلاء. واعلم – علّمك الله الخير وجعلك

من أهله – أنّه يعمل بالكتاب والسنّة ولا يخالفها فإن أمكن خصومنا أن يدلّونا على أنّه خالف في أخذ ما أخذ الكتاب والسنّة فلعمري إنّ الحجّة واضحة لهم، وإن لم يمكنهم ذلك فليعلموا أنّه ليس في العمل بما يوافق الكتاب والسنّة عيب. وهذا بيّن.

[43] ثم قال صاحب الكتاب: «ويقال لهم: نحن لا نجيز الإمامة لمن لا يُعرف فهل توجدونا سبيلاً إلى معرفة صاحبكم الّذي تدّعون حتّى نجيز له الإمامة كما نجوّز للموجودين من سائر العترة؟ وإلّا فلا سبيل إلى تجويز الإمامة للمعدومين، وكلٌّ من لم يكن موجوداً فهو معدوم، وقد بطل تجويز الإمامة لمن تدّعون».

[44] فأقول وبالله أستعين: يقال لصاحب الكتاب: هل تشكُّ في وجود علي بن الحسين وولده الّذين نأتمُّ بهم؟ فإذا قال: لا، قيل له: فهل يجوز أن يكونوا أئمّة؟ فإن قال: نعم، قيل له: فأنت لا تدري لعلّنا على صواب في اعتقاد إمامتهم وأنت على خطأ وكفى بهذا حجّة عليك، وإن قال: لا، قيل له: فما ينفع من إقامة الدليل على وجود إمامنا؟ وأنت لا تعترف بإمامة مثل علي بن الحسين مع محلّه من العلم والفضل عند المخالف والموافق. ثمَّ يقال له: إنّا إنّما علمنا أنَّ في العترة من يعلم التأويل ويعرف الأحكام بخبر النبيِّ – صلّى الله عليه وآله وسلّم – الّذي قدّمناه، وبحاجتنا إلى من يعرّفنا المراد من القرآن ومن يفصل بين أحكام الله وأحكام الشيطان، ثمَّ علمنا أنَّ الحقَّ في هذه الطائفة من ولد الحسين لما رأينا كلَّ من خالفهم من العترة يعتمد في الحكم والتأويل على ما يعتمد عليه علماء العامّة من الرأي والاجتهاد والقياس في الفرائض السمعيّة الّتي لا علّة في التعبّد بها إلّا المصلحة، فعلمنا بذلك أنَّ المخالفين لهم مبطلون. ثمَّ ظهر لنا من علم هذه الطائفة بالحلال والحرام والأحكام ما لم يظهر من غيرهم. ثمَّ ما زالت الأخبار ترد بنصٍّ واحد على آخر حتّى بلغ الحسن بن علي. فلمّا مات ولم يظهر النصُّ والخلف بعده رجعنا إلى الكتب الّتي كان أسلافنا رووها

قبل الغيبة فوجدنا فيها ما يدلُّ على أمر الخلف من بعد الحسن وأنّه يغيب عن الناس ويخفى شخصه وأنَّ الشيعة تختلف وأنَّ الناس يقعون في حيرة من أمره فعلمنا أنَّ أسلافنا لم يعلموا الغيب وأنَّ الأئمّة أعلموهم ذلك بخبر الرسول. فصحَّ عندنا من هذا الوجه بهذه الدلالة كونه ووجوده وغيبته. فإن كان ههنا حجّة تدفع ما قلناه فلتظهرها الزيديّة فما بيننا وبين الحقِّ معاندة. والشكر لله.

[45] ثمَّ رجع صاحب الكتاب إلى أن يعارضنا بما تدَّعيه الواقفة على موسى بن جعفر، ونحن فلم نقف على أحد فنسأل الفصل بين الواقفين. وقد بيّنّا أنّا علمنا أن موسى قد مات بمثل ما علمنا أنَّ جعفراً مات، وأنَّ الشكَّ في موت أحدهما يدعو إلى الشكِّ في موت الآخر، وأنّه قد وقف على جعفر قوم أنكرت الواقفة على موسى عليهم وكذلك أنكرت قول الواقفة على أمير المؤمنين – عليه السلام – فقلنا لهم: يا هؤلاء! حجّتكم على أولائك هي حجّتنا عليكم، فقولوا كيف شئتم تحجّوا أنفسكم.

[46] ثمَّ حكى عنّا أنّا كنّا نقول للواقفة: « إنَّ الإمام لا يكون إلّا ظاهراً موجوداً ». وهذه حكاية من لا يعرف أقاويل خصمه. وما زالت الإماميّة تعتقد أنَّ الإمام لا يكون إلّا ظاهراً مكشوفاً أو باطناً مغموراً، وأخبارهم في ذلك أشهر من أن تخفى. ووضع الأصول الفاسدة للخصوم أمر لا يعجز عنه أحدٌ ولكنّه قبيح بذوي الدين والفضل والعلم. ولو لم يكن في هذا المعنى إلّا خبر كميل بن زياد لكفى.

ثمَّ قال: فإن قالوا كذا قيل لهم كذا (شيء لا نقوله وحجّتنا ما سمعتم وفيها كفاية. والحمد لله).

[47] ثمَّ قال: « ليس الأمر كما تتوهّمون في بني هاشم، لأنَّ النبيَّ – صلّى الله عليه وآله وسلّم – دلَّ أمّته على عترته (بإجماعنا وإجماعكم) الّتي هي خاصّته الّتي لا يقرب أحدٌ منه كقربهم، فهي لهم دون الطلقاء وأبناء الطلقاء،

ويستحقّها واحدٌ منهم في كلِّ زمان (إذ كان الإمام لا يكون إلّا واحداً) بلزوم الكتاب والدعاء إلى إقامته، بدلالة الرسول – صلّى الله عليه وآله وسلّم – عليهم أنّهم لا يفارقون الكتاب حتّى يردوا عليّ الحوض، وهذا إجماع. والّذي اعتللتم به من بني هاشم ليس هم من ذرّيّة الرسول – صلّى الله عليه وآله وسلّم – وإن كانت لهم ولادة، لأنَّ كلَّ بني ابنة ينتمون إلى عَصَبتهم ما خلا ولد فاطمة فإنَّ رسول الله – صلّى الله عليه وآله وسلّم – عصبتهم وأبوهم، والذُرّيّة هم الولد لقول الله عزَّ وجلَّ: إِنِّي أُعِيذُهَا بِكَ وَذُرِّيَّتَهَا مِنَ ٱلشَّيْطَانِ ٱلرَّجِيمِ ».

[48] فأقول وبالله أعتصم: إنَّ هذا الأمر لا يصحُّ بإجماعنا وإيّاكم عليه وإنّما يصحُّ بالدليل والبرهان، فما دليلك على ما ادَّعيت؟ على أنَّ الإجماع بيننا إنّما هو في ثلاثة، أمير المؤمنين والحسن والحسين، ولم يذكر الرسول – صلّى الله عليه وآله وسلّم – ذُرّيّته وإنّما ذكر عترته فلم أنتم إلى بعض العترة دون البعض بلا حجّة وبيان أكثر من الدعوى، واحتججنا نحن بما رواه أسلافنا عن جماعة حتّى انتهى خبرهم إلى نصِّ الحسين بن علي على علي ابنه، ونصِّ علي على محمّد، ونصِّ محمّد على جعفر. ثمَّ استدللنا على صحّة إمامة هؤلاء دون غيرهم ممّن كان في عصرهم من العترة بما ظهر من علمهم بالدين وفضلهم في أنفسهم، وقد حمل العلم عنهم الأولياء والأعداء وذلك مبثوث في الأمصار معروف عند نقلة الأخبار. وبالعلم تتبيّن الحجّة من المحجوج والإمام من المأموم والتابع من المتبوع. وأين دليلكم يا معشر الزيديّة على ما تدَّعون؟

[49] ثم قال صاحب الكتاب: « ولو جازت الإمامة لسائر بني هاشم مع الحسن والحسين لجازت لبني عبد مناف مع بني هاشم، ولو جازت لبني عبد مناف مع بني هاشم لجازت لسائر ولد قصيّ ». ثمَّ مدَّ في هذا القول.

[50] فيقال له: أيّها المحتجّ عن الزيديّة! إنَّ هذا لَشيء لا يُسْتَحقُّ بالقرابة

وإنّما يُسْتَحقُّ بالفضل والعلم ويصحُّ بالنصِّ والتوقيف. فلو جازت الإمامة لأقرب رجلٍ من العترة لقرابته لجازت لأبعدهم . فافصل بينك وبين من ادَّعى ذلك وأظهر حجّتك. وافصل الآن بينك وبين من قال: ولو جازت لولد الحسن لجازت لولد جعفر، ولو جازت لهم لجازت لولد العبّاس، وهذا فصل لا تأتي به الزيديّـة أبداً إلّا أن تفزع إلى فصلنا وحجّتنا وهو النصُّ من واحد على واحد وظهور العلم بالحلال والحرام.

[51] ثم قال صاحب الكتاب: وإن اعتلّوا بعلي – عليه السلام – فقالوا: ما تقولون فيه أهو من العترة أم لا؟ قيل لهم: ليس هو من العترة ولكنّـه بان من العترة ومن سائر القرابة بالنصوص عليه يوم الغدير بالإجماع ».

[52] فأقول وبالله أستعين: يقال لصاحب الكتاب: أمّـا النصوص يوم الغدير فصحيح وأمّـا إنكارك أن يكون أمير المؤمنين من العترة فعظيم، فدَلِّنا على أيِّ شيء تعوّل فيما تدَّعي؟ فإنَّ أهل اللغة يشهدون أنَّ العمَّ وابن العمِّ من العترة ثمَّ أقول: إنَّ صاحب الكتاب نقض بكلامه هذا مذهبه لأنّـه يعتقد أنَّ أمير المؤمنين ممّن خلّـفه الرسول في أمّـته، ويقول في ذلك إنَّ النبيَّ – صلّى الله عليه وآله وسلّم – خلّف في أمّـته الكتاب والعترة، وإنَّ أمير المؤمنين – صلوات الله عليه – ليس من العترة، وإذا لم يكن من العترة فليس ممّن خلّـفه الرسول – صلّى الله عليه وآله وسلّم – وهذا متناقض كما ترى. اللهمَّ إلّا أن يقول: إنّـه – صلّى الله عليه وآله وسلّم – خلّف العترة فينا بعد أن قتل أمير المؤمنين – صلوات الله عليه – فنسأله أن يفصل بينه وبين من قال خلّف الكتاب فينا منذ ذلك الوقت لأنَّ الكتاب والعترة خُـلّـفا معاً، والخبر ناطقٌ بذلك شاهد به. ولله المنّـة.

[53] ثم أقبل صاحب الكتاب بما هو حجّـة عليه فقال: « ونسأل من ادَّعى الإمامة لبعض دون بعض إقامة الحجّـة » ونسي نفسه وتفرّده بادِّعائها لولد الحسن والحسين دون غيرهم.

[54] ثمَّ قال: « فإن أحالوا على الأباطيل من علم الغيب وأشباه ذلك من الخرافات وما لا دليل لهم عليه دون الدعوى عورضوا بمثل ذلك لبعض، فجاز أنَّ العترة من الظالمين لأنفسهم إن كان الدعوى هو الدليل ».

[55] فيقال لصاحب الكتاب: قد أكثرت في ذكر علم الغيب، والغيب لا يعلمه إلّا الله وما ادَّعاه لبشر إلّا مشركٌ كافر، وقد قلنا لك ولأصحابك: دليلنا على ما ندَّعي الفهم والعلم فإن كان لكم مثله فأظهروه، وإن لم يكن إلّا التشنيع والتقوُّل وتقريع الجميع بقول قوم غلاة فالأمر سهل. وحسبنا الله ونعم الوكيل.

[56] ثم قال صاحب الكتاب: « ثمَّ رجعنا إلى إيضاح حجّة الزيديّة بقول الله تبارك وتعالى: ثُمَّ أَوْرَثْنَا ٱلْكِتَابَ ٱلَّذِينَ اصْطَفَيْنَا مِنْ عِبَادِنَا – الآية ».

[57] فيقال له: نحن نسلّم لك أنَّ هذه الآية نزلت في العترة، فما برهانك على أنَّ السابق بالخيرات هم ولد الحسن والحسين دون غيرهم من سائر العترة؟ فإنّك لست تريد إلّا التشنيع على خصومك وتدَّعي لنفسك.

[58] ثمَّ قال: « قال الله عزَّ وجلَّ – وذكر الخاصّة والعامّة من أمّة نبيّه –: وَاعْتَصِمُوا بِحَبْلِ اللهِ جَمِيعاً – الآية ». ثمَّ قال: « انقضت مخاطبة العامّة ثمَّ استأنف مخاطبة الخاصّة فقال: وَلْتَكُنْ مِنْكُمْ أُمَّةٌ يَدْعونَ إِلَى ٱلْخَيْرِ – إلى قوله للخاصّة – كُنْتُمْ خَيْرَ أُمَّةٍ أُخْرِجَتْ لِلنَّاسِ». ثمَّ قال: « هم ذرّيّة إبراهيم – عليه السلام – دون سائر الناس، ثمَّ المسلمون دون من أشرك من ذرّيّة إبراهيم – عليه السلام – قبل إسلامه، وجعلهم شهداء على الناس فقال: يَا أَيُّهَا ٱلَّذِينَ آمَنُوا ٱرْكَعُوا وَٱسْجُدُوا وَٱعْبُدوا – إلى قوله – وَتَكونوا شُهَدَاءَ عَلَى ٱلنَّاسِ. وهذا سبيل الخاصّة من ذُرِّيّة إبراهيم – عليه السلام – » ثمَّ اعتلَّ بآيات كثيرة تشبه هذه الآيات من القرآن.

[59] فيقال له: أيّها المحتجّ! أنت تعلم أنَّ المعتزلة وسائر فرق الأمّة تنازعك في تأويل هذه الآيات أشدَّ منازعة وأنت فليس تأتي بأكثر من الدعوى، ونحن نسلّم

لك ما ادَّعيت ونسألك الحجّة فيما تفرَّدت به من أنَّ هؤلاء هم ولد الحسن والحسين دون غيرهم. فإلى متى تأتي بالدعوى وتعرض عن الحجّة وتهوِّل علينا بقراءة القرآن وتوهم أنَّ لك في قراءته حجّة ليست لخصومك؟ والله المستعان.

[60] ثم قال صاحب الكتاب: « فليس من دعا إلى الخير من العترة كمن أمر بالمعروف ونهي عن المنكر وجاهد في الله حقَّ جهاده سواء وسائر العترة ممّن لم يدع إلى الخير ولم يجاهد في الله حقَّ جهاده، كما لم يجعل الله مَن هذا سبيله من أهل الكتاب سواء وسائر أهل الكتاب، وإن كان تارك ذلك فاضلاً عابداً لأنَّ العبادة نافلة والجهاد فريضة لازمة كسائر الفرائض، صاحبها يمشي بالسيف إلى السيف ويؤثر على الدعة الخوف ». ثمَّ قرأ سورة الواقعة وذكر الآيات الّتي ذكر الله عزَّ وجلَّ فيها الجهاد وأتبع الآيات بالدعاوي ولم يحتجَّ لشيء من ذلك بحجّة، فنطالبه بصحّتها ونقابله بما نسأله فيه الفصل.

[61] فأقول وبالله أستعين: إن كان كثرة الجهاد هو الدليل على الفضل والعلم والإمامة فالحسين أحقُّ بالإمامة من الحسن لأنَّ الحسن وادع معاوية والحسين جاهد حتّى قُتل. وكيف يقول صاحب الكتاب وبأيِّ شيء يدفع هذا؟ وبعد فلسنا ننكر فرض الجهاد ولا فضله ولكنّا رأينا الرسول – صلّى الله عليه وآله وسلّم – لم يحارب أحداً حتّى وجد أعواناً وأنصاراً وإخواناً فحينئذ حارب، ورأينا أمير المؤمنين – عليه السلام – فعل مثل ذلك بعينه، ورأينا الحسن قد همَّ بالجهاد فلمّا خذله أصحابه وادع ولزم منزله، فعلمنا أنَّ الجهاد فرض في حال وجود الأعوان والأنصار. والعالم بإجماع العقول أفضل من المجاهد الّذي ليس بعالم. وليس كلُّ من دعا إلى الجهاد يعلم كيف حكم الجهاد ومتى يجب القتال ومتى تحسن الموادعة وبماذا يستقبل أمر هذه الرعيّة وكيف يصنع في الدماء والأموال والفروج. وبعد فإنّا نرضى من إخواننا بشيء واحد وهو أن يدلّونا على رجل من العترة ينفي التشبيه والجبر عن الله ولا يستعمل الاجتهاد

والقياس في الأحكام السمعيّة ويكون مستقلّاً كافياً حتّى نخرج معه، فإنَّ الأمر بالمعروف والنهي عن المنكر فريضة على قدر الطاقة وحسب الإمكان، والعقول تشهد أنَّ تكليف ما لا يطاق فاسدٌ والتغرير بالنفس قبيحٌ، ومن التغرير أن تخرج جماعة قليلة لم تشاهد حرباً ولا تدرَّبت بدُربة أهله إلى قوم متدرِّبين بالحروب تمكّنوا في البلاد وقتلوا العباد وتدرَّبوا بالحروب ولهم العدد والسلاح والكراع ومن نصرهم من العامّة (ويعتقدوا أنَّ الخارج عليهم مباح الدم) مثل جيشهم أضعافاً مضاعفة فكيف يسومنا صاحب الكتاب أن نلقى بالأغمار المتدرِّبين بالحروب؟ وكم عسى أن يحصل في يد داع إن دعا من هذا العدد؟ هيهات هيهات! هذا أمر لا يزيله إلّا نصر الله العزيز العليم الحكيم.

[62] قال صاحب الكتاب بعد آيات من القرآن تلاها ينازع في تأويلها أشدَّ منازعة ولم يؤيّد تأويله بحجّة عقل ولا سمع: « فافهم، رحمك الله، من أحقُّ أن يكون لله شهيداً، مَن دعا إلى الخير كما أُمر ونهى عن المنكر وأمر بالمعروف وجاهد فى الله حقَّ جهاده حتّى استشهد أم مَن لم يُر وجهه ولا عرف شخصه؟ أم كيف يتّخذه الله شهيداً على من لم يرَهم ولا نهاهم ولا أمرهم فإن أطاعوه ادَّوا ما عليهم وإن قتلوه مضى إلى الله عزَّ وجلَّ شهيداً؟ ولو أنَّ رجلاً استشهد قوماً على حقٍّ يطالِب به لم يروه ولا شهدوه هل كان شهيداً وهل يستحقُّ بهم حقّاً إلّا أن يشهدوا على ما لم يروه فيكونوا كذّابين وعند الله مبطلين؟ وإذا لم يجز ذلك من العباد فهو غير جائز عند الحكم العدل الّذي لا يجور. ولو أنّه استشهد قوماً قد عاينوا وسمعوا فشهدوا له – والمسألة على حالها – أليس كان يكون محقّاً وهم صادقون وخصمه مبطل وتمضي الشهادة ويقع الحكم؟ وكذلك قال الله تعالى: إِلَّا مَنْ شَهِدَ بِٱلْحَقِّ وَهُمْ يَعْلَمُونَ. أولا ترى أنَّ الشهادة لا تقع بالغيب دون العيان؟ وكذلك قول عيسىٰ: وَكُنْتُ عَلَيْهِمْ شَهِيداً مَا دُمْتُ فِيهِمْ – الآية ».

[63] فأقول وبالله أعتصم: يقال لصاحب الكتاب: ليس هذا الكلام لك بل

هو للمعتزلة وغيرهم علينا وعليك بأن تقول إنَّ العترة غير ظاهرة وإنَّ من شاهدنا منها لا يصلح أن يكون إماماً، وليس يجوز أن يأمرنا الله عزَّ وجلَّ بالتمسّك بمن لا نعرف منهم ولا نشاهده ولا شاهده أسلافنا، وليس في عصرنا ممّن شاهدناه ممّن يصلح أن يكون إماماً للمسلمين والّذين غابوا لا حجّة لهم علينا، وفي هذا أدلّ دليل على أنّ معنى قول النبيّ – صلّى الله عليه وآله وسلّم – « إنّي تارك فيكم ما إن تمسّكتم به لن تضلّوا كتاب الله وعترتي » ليس ما يسبق إلى قلوب الإماميّة والزيديّة. وللنظّام وأصحابه أن يقولوا: وجدنا الّذي لا يفارق الكتاب هو الخبر القاطع للعذر فإنّه ظاهر كظهور الكتاب يُنتفع به ويمكن اتّباعه والتمسّك به، فأمّا العترة فلسنا نشاهد منهم عالماً يمكن أن نقتدي به وإن بلغنا عن واحد منهم مذهب بلغنا عن آخر أنّه يخالفه والاقتداء بالمختلفين فاسد، فكيف يقول صاحب الكتاب؟

[64] ثمَّ اعلم أنَّ النبي – صلّى الله عليه وآله وسلّم – لمّا أمرنا بالتمسّك بالعترة كان بالعقل والتعارف والسيرة ما يدلُّ على أنّه أراد علماءهم دون جهّالهم والبررة الأتقياء دون غيرهم، فالّذي يجب علينا ويلزمنا أن ننظر إلى من اجتمع له العلم بالدين مع العقل والفضل والحلم والزهد في الدنيا والاستقلال بالأمر فنقتدي به ونتمسّك بالكتاب وبه. فإن قال: فإن اجتمع ذلك في رجلين وكان أحدهما ممّن يذهب إلى مذهب الزيديّة والآخر إلى مذهب الإماميّة بمن يقتدي منهما ومن يتّبع؟ قلنا له: هذا لا يتّفق، فإن اتّفق فرق بينهما دلالة واضحة إمّا نصٌّ من إمام تقدَّمه وإمّا شيء يظهر في علمه كما ظهر في أمير المؤمنين – عليه السلام – يوم النهر حين قال: « والله ما عبر النهر ولا يعبروا، والله ما يقتل منكم عشرة ولا ينجو منهم عشرة »، وإمّا أن يظهر من أحدهما مذهب يدلُّ على أنَّ الاقتداء به لا يجوز كما ظهر من علم الزيديّة القول بالاجتهاد والقياس في الفرائض السمعيّة والأحكام فيعلم بهذا أنّهم غير أئمّة. ولست

أريد بهذا القول زيد بن علي وأشباهه لأنَّ أولئك لم يظهروا ما ينكر ولا ادَّعوا أنّهم أئمّة وإنّما دعوا إلى الكتاب والرضا من آل محمّد وهذه دعوة حقّ.

[65] وأمّا قوله: « كيف يتخذه الله شهيداً على من لم يرهم ولا أمرهم ولا نهاهم » فيقال له: ليس معنى الشهيد عند خصومك ما تذهب إليه، ولكن إن عِبتَ الإماميّة بأنَّ من لم يُر وجهه ولا عُرف شخصه لا يكون بالمحلِّ الّذي يدَّعونه له فأخبرنا عنك مَن الإمام الشهيد من العترة في هذا الوقت؟ فإن ذكر أنّه لا يعرفه دخل في ما عاب ولزمه ما قدّر أنّه يلزم خصومه. فإن قال: هو فلان، قلنا له: فنحن لم نرَ وجهه ولا عرفنا شخصه فكيف يكون إماماً لنا وشهيداً علينا؟ فإن قال: إنّكم وإن لم تعرفوه فهو موجود الشخص معروفٌ عَلمه من علمه وجهله مَن جهله، قلنا: سألناك بالله هل تظنُّ أنَّ المعتزلة والخوارج والمرجئة والإماميّة تعرف هذا الرجل أو سمعت به أو خطر ذكره ببالها؟ فإن قال: هذا ما لا يضرُّه ولا يضرّنا لأنَّ السبب في ذلك إنّما هو غلبة الظالمين على الدار وقلّة الأعوان والأنصار، قلت له: لقد دخلت فيما عِبتَ وحججت نفسك من حيث قدَّرت أنّك تحاجُّ خصومك، وما أقرب هذه الغيبة من غيبة الإماميّة غير أنّكم لا تنصفون.

[66] ثمَّ يقال له: قد أكثرت في ذكر الجهاد ووصف الأمر بالمعروف والنهي عن المنكر حتّى أوهمت أنَّ من لم يخرج فليس بمحقٍّ، فما بال أئمّتك والعلماء من أهل مذهبك لا يخرجون؟ وما لهم قد لزموا منازلهم واقتصروا على اعتقاد المذهب فقط؟ فإن نطق بحرف فتقابله الإماميّة بمثله. ثمّ قيل له برفق ولين: هذا الذي عبته على الإماميّة وهتفت بهم من أجله وشنّعت به على أئمّتهم بسببه وتوصّلت بذكره إلى ما ضمّنته كتابك قد دخلت فيه وملت إلى صحّته وعوَّلت عند الاحتجاج عليه. والحمد لله الّذي هدانا لدينه.

[67] ثمَّ يقال له: أخبرنا هل في العترة اليوم من يصلح للإمامة؟ فلا بدَّ من أن

يقول: نعم، فيقال له: أفليس إمامته لا تصحُّ بالنصِّ على ما تقوله الإماميّة ولا معه دليل معجز يعلم به أنّه إمام وليس سبيله عندكم سبيل من يجتمع أهل الحلِّ والعقد من الأمّة فيتشاورون في أمره ثمَّ يختارونه ويبايعونه؟ فإذا قال: نعم، قيل له: فكيف السبيل إلى معرفته؟ فإن قالوا: يعرف بإجماع العترة عليه، قلنا لهم: كيف تجتمع عليه فإن كان إماميّاً لم ترض به الزيديّة وإن كان زيديّاً لم ترض به الإماميّة؟ فإن قال: لا يعتبر بالإماميّة في مثل هذا، قيل له: فالزيديّة على قسمين قسم معتزلة وقسم مثبتة. فإن قال: لا يعتبر بالمثبتة في مثل هذا ، قيل له: فالمعتزلة قسمان قسم يجتهد في الأحكام بآرائها وقسمٌ يعتقد أنَّ الاجتهاد ضلالٌ. فإن قال: لا يعتبر بمن نفى الاجتهاد، قيل له: فإن بقي ممّن يرى الاجتهاد منهم أفضلهم وبقي ممّن يبطل الاجتهاد منهم أفضلهم ويتبرّأ بعضهم من بعض، بمن نتمسّك وكيف نعلم المحقَّ منهما هو مَن تؤمي أنت وأصحابك إليه دون غيره؟ فإن قال: بالنظر في الأصول، قلنا فإن طال الاختلاف واشتبه الأمر كيف نصنع وبما نتفصّى من قول النبيِّ – صلّى الله عليه وآله وسلّم – « إنّي تارك فيكم ما إن تمسّكتم به لن تضلّوا، كتاب الله وعترتي أهل بيتي »؟ والحجّة من عترته لا يمكن أحداً أن يعرفه إلّا بعد النظر في الأصول والوقوف على أنَّ مذاهبه كلّها صواب وعلى أنَّ من خالفه فقد أخطأ، وإذا كان هكذا فسبيله وسبيل كلِّ قائل من أهل العلم سبيل واحد فما تلك الخاصّة الّتي هي للعترة؟ دلّنا عليها وبيّن لنا جميعها لنعلم أنَّ بين العالم من العترة وبين العالم من غير العترة فرقاً وفصلاً.

[68] وأخرى يقال لهم: أخبرونا عن إمامكم اليوم، أعنده الحلال والحرام؟ فإذا قالوا: نعم، قلنا لهم: وأخبرونا عمّا عنده ممّا ليس في الخبر المتواتر هل هو مثل ما عند الشافعي وأبي حنيفة ومن جنسه أو هو خلاف ذلك؟ فإن قالوا: بل عنده الّذي عندهما ومن جنسه، قيل لهم: وما حاجة الناس إلى علم إمامكم

الّذي لم يسمع به، وكتب الشافعي وأبي حنيفة ظاهرة مبثوثة موجودة؟ وإن قالوا: بل عنده خلاف ما عندهما، قلنا: فخلاف ما عندهما هو النصُّ المستخرج الّذي تدّعيه جماعة من مشايخ المعتزلة وأنَّ الأشياء كلّها على إطلاق العقول إلّا ما كان في الخبر القاطع للعذر على مذهب النظّام وأتباعه، أو مذهب الإماميّة أنَّ الأحكام منصوصة – واعلموا أنّا لا نقول منصوصة على الوجه الّذي يسبق إلى القلوب ولكنَّ المنصوص عليه بالجمل الّتي مَن فهمها فهم الأحكام من غير قياس ولا اجتهاد –. فإن قالوا: عنده ما يخالف هذا كلّه خرجوا من التعارف، وإن تعلّقوا بمذهب من المذاهب قيل لهم: فأين ذلك العلم؟ هل نقله عن إمامكم أحدٌ يوثق بدينه وأمانته؟ فإن قالوا: نعم، قيل لهم: قد عاشرناكم الدهر الأطول فما سمعنا بحرف واحد من هذا العلم وأنتم قوم لا ترون التقيّة ولا يراها إمامكم كما تدّعون أنَّ الإماميّة كذبت على جعفر بن محمّد، وهذا ما لا فصل فيه.

[69] مسئلة أخرى – ويقال لهم: أليس جعفر بن محمّد عندكم كان لا يذهب إلى ما تدّعيه الإماميّة، وكان على مذهبكم ودينكم؟ فلا بدَّ من نعم (اللهمَّ إلّا أن يتبرّؤوا منه) فيقال لهم: وقد كذبت الإماميّة فيما نقلته عنه وهذه الكتب المؤلّفة الّتي في أيديهم إنّما هي من تأليف الكذّابين؟ فإن قالوا: نعم، قيل لهم: فإذا جاز ذلك فلم لا يجوز أن يكون إمامكم يذهب مذهب الإماميّة ويدين بدينها وأن يكون ما يحكي سلفكم ومشايخكم عنه مولّداً موضوعاً لا أصل له؟ فإن قالوا: ليس لنا في هذا الوقت إمام نعرفه بعينه نروي عنه الحلال والحرام ولكنّا نعلم أنَّ في العترة من هو موضع هذا الأمر وأهله، قلنا لهم: دخلتم فيما عبتموه على الإماميّة بما معها من الأخبار من أئمّتها بالنصّ على صاحبهم والإشارة إليه والبشارة به، وبطل جميع ما قصصتم به من ذكر الجهاد والأمر بالمعروف والنهي عن المنكر، فصار إمامكم بحيث لا يُرى ولا يُعرف. فقولوا كيف شئتم ونعوذ بالله من الخذلان.

[70] ثمَّ قال صاحب الكتاب: « وكما أمر الله العترة بالدعاء إلى الخير وصف سبق السابقين منهم وجعلهم شهداء وأمرهم بالقسط فقال: يَا أَيُّها ٱلَّذينَ آمَنوا كونوا قَوَّامِينَ لله شُهَدآءَ بِالْقِسْطِ ». ثمَّ أتبع ذلك بضرب من التأويل وقراءة آيات من القرآن ادَّعى أنّها في العترة ولم يحتجَّ لشيء منها بحجّة أكثر من أن يكون الدعوى. ثمَّ قال: « وقد أوجب الله تعالى على نبيّه – صلّى الله عليه وآله وسلّم – ترك الأمر والنهي إلى أن هيّأ له أنصاراً فقال: وَإِذَا رَأَيْتَ ٱلَّذينَ يَخوضونَ في آياتِنا – إلى قوله – لَعَلَّهُمْ يَتَّقونَ، فمن لم يكن من السابقين بالخيرات المجاهدين في الله ولا من المقتصدين الواعظين بالأمر والنهي عند إعواز الأعوان فهو من الظالمين لأنفسهم. وهذا سبيل من كان قبلنا من ذراري الأنبياء ». ثمَّ تلا آيات من القرآن.

[71] فيقال له: ليس علينا لمَن أراد بهذا الكلام ولكن أخبرنا عن الإمام من العترة عندك من أيِّ قسم هو؟ فإن قال: من المجاهدين، قيل له: فمن هو ومن جاهد وعلى من خرج وأين خيله ورجله؟ فإن قال: هو ممّن يعظ بالأمر والنهي عند إعواز الأعوان، قيل له: فمن سمع أمره ونهيه؟ فإن قال: أولياؤه وخاصّته، قلنا: فإن اتّبع هذا وسقط فرض ما سوى ذلك عنه لإعواز الأعوان ويجاز أن لا يسمع أمره ونهيه إلّا أولياؤه فأيّ شيء عبته على الإماميّة ولمَ ألّفت كتابك هذا وبمن عرَّضت؟ وليت شعري بمن قرَّعت بآي القرآن وألزمته فرض الجهاد؟

[72] ثمَّ يقال له وللزيديّة جميعاً: أخبرونا لو خرج رسول الله – صلّى الله عليه وآله وسلّم – من الدنيا ولم ينصَّ على أمير المؤمنين – عليه السلام – ولا دلَّ عليه ولا أشار إليه أكان يكون ذلك من فعله صواباً وتدبيراً حسناً جائزاً؟ فإن قالوا: نعم، قلنا لهم: ولو لم يدلَّ على العترة أكان يكون ذلك جائزاً؟ فإن قالوا: نعم، قلنا: فأيّ شيء أنكرتم على المعتزلة والمرجئة والخوارج وقد كان يجوز أن لا يقع النصُّ فيكون الأمر شورى بين أهل الحلِّ والعقد. وهذا ما لا حيلة

فيه. فإن قالوا: لا ولا بدَّ من النصِّ على أمير المؤمنين - صلوات الله عليه - ومن الأدلّة على العترة، قيل لهم: لِمَ؟ حتّى إذا ذكروا الحجّة الصحيحة فنتقلها إلى الإمام في كلِّ زمان، لأنَّ النصَّ إن وجب في زمن وجب في كلِّ زمان لأنَّ العلل الموجبة له موجودة أبداً. ونعوذ بالله من الخذلان.

[73] مسألة أخرى - ويقال لهم: إذا كان الخبر المتواتر حجّة رواه العترة أو الأمّة، وكان الخبر الواحد من العترة يجوز على الواحد منهم من تعمّد الباطل ومن السهو والزلل ما يجوز على الواحد من الأمّة وما ليس في الخبر المتواتر ولا خبر الواحد فسبيله عندكم الاستخراج وكان يجوز على المتأوّل منهم ما يجوز على المتأوِّل من الأمّة، فمن أيِّ وجه صارت العترة حجّة؟ فإن قال صاحب الكتاب: إذا أجمعوا فإجماعهم حجّة، قيل له: فإذا أجمعت الأمّة فإجماعها حجّة، وهذا يوجب أنّه لا فرق بين العترة والأمّة، وإن كان هكذا فليس في قوله « خلّفت فيكم كتاب الله وعترتي » فائدة إلّا أن يكون فيها من هو حجّة في الدين، وهذا قول الإماميّة.

[74] واعلموا - أسعدكم الله - أنَّ صاحب الكتاب أشغل نفسه بعد ذلك بقراءة القرآن وتأويله على من أحبَّ ولم يقل في شيء من ذلك: « الدليل على صحّة تأويلي كيت وكيت ». وهذا شيء لا يعجز عنه الصبيان وإنّما أراد أن يعيب الإماميّة بأنّها لا ترى الجهاد والأمر بالمعروف والنهي عن المنكر، وقد غلط فإنّها ترى ذلك على قدر الطاقة ولا ترى أن تلقي بأيديها إلى التهلكة ولا أن يخرج مع من لا يعرف الكتاب والسنّة ولا يحسن أن يسير في الرعيّة بسيرة العدل والحقّ. وأعجب من هذا أنَّ أصحابنا من الزيديّة في منازلهم لا يأمرون بمعروف ولا ينهون عن المنكر ولا يجاهدون، وهم يعيبوننا بذلك. وهذا نهاية من نهايات التحامل ودليل من أدلّة العصبيّة. نعوذ بالله من اتّباع الهوى وهو حسبنا ونعم الوكيل.

[75] مسألة أخرى – ويقال لصاحب الكتاب: هل تعرف في أئمّة الحقِّ أفضل من أمير المؤمنين – صلوات الله عليه – ؟ فمن قوله: لا، فيقال له: فهل تعرف من المنكر بعد الشرك والكفر شيئاً أقبح وأعظم ممّا كان من أصحاب السقيفة؟ فمن قوله: لا، فيقال له: فأنت أعلم بالأمر بالمعروف والنهي عن المنكر والجهاد أو أمير المؤمنين – عليه السلام – ؟ فلا بدَّ من أن يقول: أمير المؤمنين، فيقال له: فما باله لم يجاهد القوم؟ فإن اعتذر بشيء قيل له: فاقبل مثل هذا العذر من الإمامي فإنَّ الناس جميعاً يعلمون أنَّ الباطل اليوم أقوى منه يومئذ وأعوان الشيطان أكثر، ولا تهوِّل علينا بالجهاد وذكره فإنَّ الله تعالى إنّما فرضه لشرائط لو عرفتها لقلَّ كلامك وقصر كتابك. ونسأل الله التوفيق.

[76] مسألة أخرى – ويقال لصاحب الكتاب: أتصوِّبون الحسن بن علي في موادعته معاوية أم تخطّؤونه؟ فإذا قالوا: نصوِّبه، قيل لهم: أتصوِّبونه وقد ترك الجهاد وأعرض عن الأمر بالمعروف والنهي عن المنكر على الوجه الّذي تومئون إليه؟ فإن قالوا: نصوّبه لأنَّ الناس خذلوه ولم يأمنهم على نفسه ولم يكن معه من أهل البصائر من يمكنه أن يقاوم بهم معاوية وأصحابه، فإذا عرفوا صحّة ذلك قيل لهم: فإذا كان الحسن مبسوط العذر – ومعه جيش أبيه وقد خطَب له الناس على المنابر وسلَّ سيفه وسار إلى عدوِّ الله وعدوِّه للجهاد – لما وصفتم وذكرتم فلمَ لا تُعذرون جعفر بن محمّد في تركه الجهاد وقد كان أعداؤه في عصره أضعاف من كان مع معاوية ولم يكن معه من شيعته من قد تدرَّبوا بالحروب وإنّما كان قوم من أهل السرِّ لم يشاهدوا حرباً ولا عاينوا وقعة؟ فإن بسطوا عذره فقد أنصفوا، وإن امتنع منهم ممتنع سئل الفصل. ولا فصل.

[77] وبعد فإن كان قياس الزيديّة صحيحاً فزيد بن علي أفضل من الحسن بن علي لأنَّ الحسن وادع وزيدٌ حارب حتّى قتل، وكفى بمذهب يؤدِّي إلى تفضيل زيد بن علي على الحسن بن علي قبحاً. والله المستعان وحسبنا الله ونعم الوكيل.

Refutation of *Kitāb al-Ishhād* by Abū Zayd al-ʿAlawī

[1] After mentioning many uncontroversial things, the author of the book said: «The Zaydites and the Imāmites[3] said: The Proof [of God] is one of the offspring of Fāṭima [daughter of the Prophet] because of the unanimously reported saying of the Messenger on [his] Farewell Pilgrimage, and on the day he came out for the Prayer with the illness from which he died: "O people, I left behind among you the Book of God and my *ʿitra* (Family). They will surely never separate till they are received by me at the Pool. You will never go astray so long as you hold fast to them both"».[4] Then the author emphasized the point of this report, and said something for which there is no objection. Then he went on to say: «The Imāmites opposed the consensus and claimed that the Imāmate is within a specific clan of the Prophet's family, and they do not recognize the right [to the Imāmate] of any other branch of the Prophet's family. Then [they further restricted it to] only one man from that clan in each period.»

[2] I say, and reliance is on God: There is a clear indication in the words of the Prophet, may God bless him and his Family and grant them peace, of what the Imāmites say. This is because the Prophet, may God bless him and his Family and grant them peace, said: "I leave among you something that if you hold fast to it you will never go astray: the Book of God and my *ʿitra,* my household." This indicates that the Proof [of God] after him is not a non-Arab, nor someone from other tribes of the Arabs, but from his *ʿitra,* his household. Then he added something that indicated his intention, saying: "They will surely never separate till they are received by me at the Pool." Thus he informed us that the Proof

3. The name always used by Abū Zayd al-ʿAlawī for the Imāmites is *muʾtamma*, obviously to imply that the Imāmites are not actually followers of the Imāms but pretend and claim to be so. Cf. Sulaym: 84 where a statement attributed to ʿAlī states that thirteen groups assume the love for the House of the Prophet as their main characteristic; twelve of these will be in fire and only one in Paradise, "that is the one that follows me" (*al-muʾtamma bī*).
4. Ibn Saʿd, 2:194; Aḥmad, 3:14, 17, 59, 4:371, 5:181–2; Muslim: 1873–4; Tirmidhī, 13:201; Nasāʾī: 93; Dārimī, 2:432; Bayhaqī, 2:148, 7:30, 10:113; Ḥākim, 3:109–10, 533; Khaṭīb, 3:255, 258. See further my *An Introduction to Shīʿī Law*: 2, n. 1.

[of God] from his family will not sever himself from the Book, and that when we hold fast to him who will not sever himself from the Book, we will never go astray, and that the one who will not sever himself from the Book is from those to whom the community has to hold fast. It rationally follows that he must be someone who knows the Book and is trustworthy concerning it, who knows which parts of it abrogate and which are abrogated, the parts with specific application and the parts with general application, its binding injunctions and its nonbinding recommendations, its unambiguous parts and its ambiguous parts, so that he can put each of these categories into its proper place determined by God, the Mighty, the Exalted, not putting a later part first or a preceding part later. It is necessary that such a person have comprehensive knowledge of religion so that it is possible to hold fast to him and to adhere to what he says concerning the interpretation of the Book and the Tradition which the community differs about and disputes, for if there remains any [part] of it that he does not know, one could not hold fast to him. Yet, even if he fulfills this latter condition but cannot be trusted as regards the book, he cannot be relied upon not to commit errors and to put the abrogating part in the place of what is abrogated, what is unambiguous in place of what is ambiguous, what is recommended in place of what is a binding injunction, and other things that are too numerous to enumerate. And if this were so, the Proof and those to whom he was sent would be on the same level. Now if this opinion is wrong, what the Imāmites say must be correct: that the Proof [of God] from the Prophet's family must have comprehensive knowledge of religion, must be unerring, and must be trustworthy with regard to the Book. So if the Zaydites find among their *imāms* one who has this quality, we should be the first to follow him; if it is otherwise, then truth more deserves to be obeyed.

[3] As for his saying: «The Imāmites opposed the consensus and claimed that the Imāmate is within a specific clan of the Prophet's family», it will be said to him: What is this previous consensus that we opposed? We do not know of it unless you are thinking that the disagreement of the Imāmites with the Zaydites is a departure from the consensus. If this is what you mean, it is not impossible for the Imāmites to attribute to you the likes of what you attributed

to them and to make about you the same claim regarding the consensus as you make about them. After all, you [yourself] say that the Imāmate rightfully belongs only to the descendants of Ḥasan and Ḥusayn, so show us why you specify the sons of these two and not all the Prophet's family so that we may demonstrate our opinion to you with a better proof than yours. The logical demonstration will follow in its proper place, God willing.

[4] Then the author said: «The Zaydites said: The Imāmate rightfully belongs to the entire Prophet's *'itra* because the Messenger of God, may God bless him and his Family and grant them peace, indicated them by using a general term and did not specify some of them rather than others and, also, because, according to their unanimous opinion,[5] God, the Mighty, the Exalted, spoke of them excluding others: "Then We gave the Book as inheritance unto those whom We selected of Our bondsmen..."»[6]

[5] I say, and reliance is on God: The author is mistaken in what he relates because the Zaydites allow only the descendants of Ḥasan and Ḥusayn to be *imām.* In lexicographical usage *'itra* means the father's brother and the descendants of the father's brother, the nearest living relative among them in each generation. The lexicographers never recognized, nor has anyone related from them that they ever said, that *'itra* was applied only to the sons of the daughter from the son of the father's brother. This is something that the Zaydites wish and deceive themselves with and that they alone claim with no explanation or proof; because what they claim does not arise from the intellect, nor is it in the Book or the Tradition or in any part of any language. Here is the language and these are its

5. *bi-ijmā'ihim*, referring to the concept of *ijmā' al-'itra* (the consensus of the Prophet's Family), which is regarded by the Zaydites as an indisputable valid proof. The sentence thus claims that all scholars of the descendants of the Prophet, whether those followed by the Zaydites or those followed by the Imāmites, agreed that the above-cited verse of the Qur'ān referred to the family of the Prophet and not to anybody else. The word can alternatively be read as *bi-ajma'ihim* (as a whole), meaning that the verse spoke of the family of the Prophet "altogether" and did not specify some clans or individuals rather than others.

6. Qur'ān, 35:32.

speakers; ask them to explain to you that *'itra* means the closest living relative among the father's brother and his children.

[6] If the author were to ask: Why did you say, then, that the Imāmate does not belong to so and so and his sons[7] while they are from the *'Itra* according to you?

We would say: We did not say that on the basis of [our own] analogy; we said it only in compliance with what [the Prophet], may God bless him and his Family and grant them peace, did with regard to those three ['Alī, Ḥasan, and Ḥusayn] and no others from the *'Itra.* If he had done with so and so what he did with them, we would do nothing but submit and obey.

[7] As for his saying: «God, the Mighty, the Exalted, says: "Then We gave the Book as inheritance unto those whom We selected as our bondsmen"», it should be said to him: Your adversaries among the Mu'tazilites and others differed with you over the interpretation of this verse, and the Imāmites differed with you. You know who are "the foremost in good deeds"[8] according to the Imāmites. The least that was incumbent on you—as you wrote this book of yours to make the truth clear and to propagate it—was to back up your claim with an indisputable proof, if there were none, some convincing argument, and if there were nothing persuasive, to give up arguing with what you are unable to explain is a proof for you but not for your opponents. Recitations of the Qur'ān and claims about its interpretation without a clear proof are things that anyone can do. Your adversaries and ours claim that the words of God, the Mighty, the Exalted: "You are the best community that has been raised up for mankind"[9] mean all the learned of the com-

7. This refers to 'Abbās b. 'Abd al-Muṭṭalib, uncle of the Prophet, and his grandsons, the Abbasid caliphs, who were in power when this treatise was being written.

8. This phrase is a part of the above-cited verse of the Qur'ān (35:32) where it is said that among those whom God selected as the inheritors of the Book are those who are "the foremost in good deeds," a description understood by the Imāmites as referring to their Imāms. See Ṣaffār: 44–7; 'Alī b. Ibrāhīm, 2:209; Kulaynī, 1:214–15; Ibn Bābawayh, *'Uyūn*, 1:229; idem, *Ma'ānī*: 105; Ṭabrisī, *Majma'*, 22:244; Abū Manṣūr al-Ṭabrisī, 2:139; Ibn Ṭāwūs, *Sa'd al-Su'ūd*: 107; Sharaf al-Dīn al-Najafī: 481–5.

9. Qur'ān, 3:110.

munity, that the learned of the Prophet's family are equal with those of the Murji'ite,[10] and that the consensus is not arrived at nor the proof established through the knowledge of the Prophet's Family. Is there any difference between you and them [the adversaries]? Will you be convinced by what they claim or will you ask them for a proof? If he were to say: Indeed, I shall ask them for a proof, it would be said to him: Then first give your proof that the *'itra* is what is meant by this verse that you recited, that *'itra* means the offspring, and that the offspring are the sons of Ḥasan and Ḥusayn and no one else, such as the descendants of Ja'far [b. Abī Ṭālib][11] or anyone else who descended from Fāṭima [daughter of the Prophet] on the maternal side.

[8] Then he said: «It will be said to the Imāmites: How can you demonstrate that the imāmate is required for one person and not all [of the *'Itra*] and is prohibited for all [of them]? If they argue with hereditary and testamentary right, it would be said to them: The Mughīrites[12] claim that the Imāmate belongs to the descendants of Ḥasan, then to a clan of the descendants of Ḥasan b. al-Ḥasan,[13] in every age and time, by virtue of inheritance and will from his father. Afterward they differ with you in what you claim, just as you differ with others in what they claim.»

[9] I say, and reliance is on God: The demonstration that the Imāmate always belongs to one person is that the Imām can only be the most excellent, and the most excellent can be so in one of

10. The pro-Umayyad (and basically pro-government) Sunnites. See the article "Murdji'a" in *EI*[1], 3: 734–5 (by A. J. Wensinck).

11. The cousin of the Prophet and the brother of 'Alī, who was killed in the battle of Mu'ta in the year 8/629. See the article "Dja'far b. Abi Ṭālib" in *EI*[2], 2:372 (by L. Veccia Vaglieri).

12. The followers of Mughīra b. Sa'īd al-Bajalī (d. 119/737), a former follower of Muḥammad al-Bāqir who then, after Bāqir's death, turned to the Ḥasanid branch of the House of the Prophet and advocated the cause of Muḥammad b. 'Abd Allāh b. al-Ḥasan al-Nafs al-Zakiyya as the awaited *mahdī*. See the article "al-Mughīriyya" in *EI*[2], 7:347–8 (by W. Madelung).

13. Ḥasan al-Muthannā, son of Ḥasan al-Mujtabā and father of 'Abd Allāh b. al-Ḥasan al-Maḥḍ, and a prominent member of the House of the Prophet in his time. He died during the reign of the Umayyad Walīd b. 'Abd al-Malik (86–96/705–715). See Muṣ'ab b. 'Abd Allāh: 46–9; Mufīd, *Irshād*: 196–7; 'Umarī: 36–7; Ibn 'Inaba: 98–100.

two ways: either he is more excellent than the whole or more excellent than each one of them. The only way it could be is for the most excellent to be a single person because it is impossible for him to be more excellent than all the community or than each person in the community while someone is in the community who is more excellent than he is. Now since this is not possible and because it is true according to a demonstration whose truth the Zaydites admit—that the Imām can only be the most excellent—it follows that the Imāmate belongs to a single person in every age. The difference between us and the Mughīrites is an easily understood, clear, and straightforward matter, thank God: namely, that the Prophet, may God bless him and his Family and grant them peace, clearly indicated Ḥasan and Ḥusayn, and distinguished them from the rest of the Prophet's family by distinctions which we mentioned and described. When Ḥasan died, Ḥusayn was the most entitled to and deserving of Ḥasan's designation because the Messenger, may God bless him and his Family and grant them peace, had indicated, selected, and specified him. If Ḥasan had bequeathed the Imāmate to his own son, he would have contradicted the Messenger, may God bless him and his Family and grant them peace; far be it from him. After all, we have no doubt nor any hesitation that Ḥusayn was more excellent than Ḥasan b. al-Ḥasan b. 'Alī; and the most excellent is the true Imām according to both us and the Zaydites. Through what we described, the falsehood of the Mughīrites' claim becomes clear, and the principle on which they based their allegation collapses.

[10] We did not acknowledge 'Alī b. al-Ḥusayn b. 'Alī [Zayn al-'Ābidīn] to be in the position we believe him to be in without a reason, nor did we blindly follow anyone's authority in this matter.[14] It is just that the reports that have reached our ears concerning him far outweigh anything that has reached us concerning Ḥasan b. al-Ḥasan. What is quoted from him ['Alī b. al-Ḥusayn] and from his successor [Muḥammad al-Bāqir] and Abū 'Abd Allāh [Ja'far al-Ṣādiq] concerning the knowledge of things that are licit or illicit

14. See 'Ayyāshī, 2:72; also Majlisī, 47:281 where 'Abd Allāh b. al-Ḥasan is quoted as arguing that Ḥusayn should have nominated a descendant of his brother Ḥasan as the next Imām, not his own son.

indicated to us that he was more knowledgeable than him [Ḥasan b. al-Ḥasan]. We have heard nothing pertaining to Ḥasan b. al-Ḥasan that would enable us to compare it with what we have heard about the knowledge of 'Alī b. al-Ḥusayn. The one who is knowledgeable in religion has a greater right to the Imāmite than someone who is not. If you, the Zaydites, have come across any scholarship of Ḥasan b. al-Ḥasan concerning what is licit and what is illicit, then bring it out into the open, but if you are not aware of such knowledge, then reflect upon the words of God, the Mighty, the Exalted: "Is He who leads to Truth more worthy to be followed or he who finds not the way unless he is guided? What then ails ye? How judge ye?"[15]

We are not trying to deny Ḥasan b. al-Ḥasan's good qualifications, seniority, chastity, integrity, and righteousness, but the matter of the Imāmate is concluded only by knowledge of religion and by cognizance of the precepts of the Lord of the Worlds and of the interpretation of His Book. Up to our own time, we have not seen or heard anyone whose Imāmate the Zaydites uphold who does not interpret, that is, interpret the Qur'ān, by inference or decide legal matters on the basis of his own personal opinion and analogical reasoning.[16] But knowledge about the interpretation of the Qur'ān cannot come about through inference, for that would be possible only if the Qur'ān had been revealed in one [kind of] idiom whose purport the users of that idiom could understand. However, the Qur'ān was sent down in many [kinds of idiom] and in it are things whose purport can only be understood through divine instruction, such as ritual prayer, religious alms, pilgrimage to Mecca, and other such things whose purport both we and you know can be understood only through divine instruction and in no other way. It is, then, not possible to trace the meanings of these things back to the language because in the first place you would need to know that nothing at all was in the words you were trying to interpret that depended on divine instruction in either the summary or the detailed understanding of it.

15. Qur'ān, 10:35.
16. See Majlisī, 47:275–6 for earlier instances of this argument.

[11] If one of them should say: Why should it be denied that things that could be known only through divine instruction God has already informed His Messenger, may God bless him and his Family and grant them peace, but things that could be inferred He entrusted to the religious scholars, making some parts of the Qur'ān act as pointers to others; so we are not bound by your argument about divine instruction and what can only be known through God.

It will be said to him: That which you describe is not possible, because we may find two contradictory interpretations for a single verse, each of which is permissible from a linguistic point of view and each of which can correctly lead to an act of worship of God. But it is not possible that the Wise Speaker should utter something that has two contradictory meanings.

[12] Then he may say: Why should it be denied that an indication may exist in the Qur'ān toward one of the two meanings and that those who are scholars of the Qur'ān, when they carefully consider it, can come to know that very meaning and not the other?

It will be said to the one who makes this argument: We denied what you describe because of something we shall tell you. This indication toward one of two meanings that is in the Qur'ān can either be interpreted [in different ways] or not. If it can be interpreted, then it will be subject to the same thing that was said about the verse itself. If it cannot be interpreted, it, therefore, is a divine instruction and [the sentence is] fixed for that very meaning, and so, everybody who knows the language should understand the meaning with no difficulty. This is not rationally impossible, and it is possible and good for the Wise to do it. However, when we consider the verses of the Qur'ān, we do not find them like this; we find a difference in the interpretation of them between the scholars of religion and [the scholars of] language. If there were verses that interpreted other [verses] in a way that those interpretations could not be taken to mean otherwise, then one group of those who knew the language and [nevertheless] disagreed on the interpretation of the Qur'ān were knowingly denying the truth. It would be possible to discover this fact very easily. He who interpreted the verse [against that indication] would be outside the language and the usage of the people who speak it as well because if a sentence has a fixed meaning, but you try to force it to imply [a meaning] that it cannot have, you are stepping outside the language in which the message was spoken. Show us, you Zaydites, a single verse over whose interpretation the scholars differ while something in the Qur'ān indicates its [correct] interpretation explicitly and as a divine instruction. This is impossible, and its impossibility indicates that there must be someone to expound the Qur'ān who knows and quotes what God intends. To me, this is manifestly clear.

[13] Then the author said: «These Khaṭṭābites[17] claim that the Imāmate belongs to Ja'far b. Muḥammad [al-Ṣādiq] through his father by virtue of inheritance and will, and they halt [with him] waiting for his return. They oppose everyone who lays claim to the Imāmate and contend that you agreed with them about the Imāmate of Ja'far and they differed with you over anyone apart from him.»

[14] I say, and reliance is on God: The Imāmate cannot be proved through anyone's agreement or disagreement. It can only be proved through the indications and proofs of truth. It seems to me that the author is mistaken, for the Khaṭṭābites are an extremist group and there is no connection between extremism and the Imāmate. If he says: I meant the sect that stopped with him [Ja'far al-Ṣādiq], it will be said to him: We will tell this sect that we know that the Imām after Ja'far is Mūsā in the same way as you came to know that the Imām after Muḥammad b. 'Alī [al-Bāqir] is Ja'far, and we know that Ja'far died just as we know that his father died. The difference between us and you is the same as the difference between you and the Saba'ites[18] and those who stopped with the Commander of the Faithful ['Alī], may the blessings of God be upon him. Say as you wish.

It should be said to the author: As for you, what is the difference between you and those who maintained the imāmate of the descendants of 'Abbās [uncle of the Prophet] and Ja'far and 'Aqīl [sons of

17. See above, chapter 2.

18. The followers of a possibly legendary character, 'Abd Allāh b. Saba', who allegedly maintained after the death of 'Alī that he did not actually die, but rather went into occultation and would return to the world and drive the Arabs with his stick. See above, chapter 2; also the articles "'Abd Allāh b. Sabā" and "Ghulāt" in *EI*², 1:50, 2:1093–5 (both by M.G.S. Hodgson).

Abū Ṭālib and cousins of the Prophet]—that is, the knowledgeable and outstanding among them—and argued on the basis of the lexicographical usage that they were from the *'itra* of the Messenger, saying that the Messenger, may God bless him and his Family and grant them peace, designated his entire *'itra* and not only three (viz., the Commander of the Faithful, Ḥasan, and Ḥusayn, peace be upon them)? Let us know [the difference]; explain it to us!

[15] Then the author said: «These Shamṭites[19] maintain the Imāmate of Muḥammad b. Ja'far b. Muḥammad through inheritance and will from his father. And these Faṭḥites claim the Imāmate for Ismā'īl b. Ja'far through inheritance and will from his father, and before that they maintained the Imāmate of 'Abd Allāh b. Ja'far. Today[20] they are called the Ismā'īliyya because no one is left of those who believed in the Imāmate of 'Abd Allāh b. Ja'far. A group of the Faṭḥites who are called Qarmaṭians[21] maintain the Imāmate of

19. The followers of Muḥammad al-Dībāja, a younger son of Ja'far al-Ṣādiq, who was declared *imām* by a group that rebelled against the Abbasids in Mecca in 200/815 and received the allegiance and support of the people of the Ḥijāz, but was later defeated and sent to Ma'mūn in Khurāsān where he stayed until he died in 203/818 (see Ṭabarī, 8:537–40; Abu 'l-Faraj, *Maqātil*: 537–41; Mufīd, *Irshād*: 286–7; Khaṭīb, 2:113–15; 'Umarī: 96; Ibn 'Inaba: 245). His followers are mentioned in the heresiographical works by a name that is variantly given (and can further variantly be read) as Shamṭiyya, Shumayṭiyya, Samṭiyya, Simṭiyya or Sumayṭiyya, after a head of the group named Ibn al-Ashmaṭ ('Umarī: 96) or Yaḥyā b. Abi 'l-Shumayṭ (variantly given or can further be read as Samṭ, Simṭ, Samīṭ or Sumayṭ, also with the word *abī* and the definite article or without one or the other or both). All heresiographers give the same account as in the paragraph above that after the death of Ja'far al-Ṣādiq a group of his followers maintained that Muḥammad was his successor (see Pseudo Qāsim b. Ibrāhīm: 104a; Nawbakhtī: 87; Sa'd b. 'Abd Allāh: 86–7; Nāshi': 47; Abu 'l-Ḥasan al-Ash'arī, 1:102; Abu 'l-Qāsim al-Balkhī: 180; Abū Ḥātim al-Rāzī: 286, 287, 288; Khwārazmī: 50; Mufīd, *Majālis*, 2:89; Ibn Ḥazm, 4:158; *Farq*, 23, 61–2; Shahrastānī, 1:196. See also Madelung, *Der Imām al-Qāsim b. Ibrāhīm*: 51). It seems possible, however, that the belief in his Imāmate started with the above-mentioned episode and that his followers, who were almost exclusively from the Jārūdite Zaydites (Abu 'l-Faraj: 538; Mufīd, *Irshād*: 286), followed him as someone who rose from the House of the Prophet and not as the successor to Ja'far al-Ṣādiq (see also Mufīd, *Majālis*, 92–3).

20. See above, chapter 3.

21. See the article "Ḳarmaṭī" in *EI*[2], 4:660–65 (by W. Madelung).

Muḥammad b. Ismā'īl b. Ja'far through inheritance and will. Those people who stop with Mūsā b. Ja'far claim that the Imāmate belongs to Mūsā and are awaiting his return.»

[16] I say: The difference between us and these groups is an easily understood, clear, and straightforward matter.

As for the Faṭḥites, the evidence against them is so clear that it cannot be concealed, for Ismā'īl died before Abū 'Abd Allāh [Ja'far al-Ṣādiq], and a dead person cannot succeed a living person; the only possibility is that a living person succeed a dead person. However, the group blindly followed its leaders and turned away from the proofs. This matter does not need to be dwelt on any further because it is transparently wrong and its shortcoming can clearly be noted.

[17] As for the Qarmaṭians, they contradicted Islam, letter by letter, as they abolished the acts of the *sharī'a* and brought all kinds of sophistry. The only need for an Imām is for religion and the establishment of the rule of the *sharī'a*; then, if the Qarmaṭians come and claim that Ja'far b. Muḥammad or his legatee appointed someone as his successor who called for the nullification of Islam and the *sharī'a* and to leave the normal behavior of the members of the community, there will be, in order to understand their falsehood, no need of anything more than their own selfcontradictory, vain contentions.

[18] As for the difference between us and the other groups, it is that we have narrators of Traditions and conveyors of reports who are spread throughout the countries. They reported from Ja'far b. Muḥammad so much scholarship about what is licit and what is illicit that prevalent custom and reliable experience acknowledge that it cannot be all fabricated falsehood. From such a status, they related from their predecessors that Abū 'Abd Allāh [Ja'far al-Ṣādiq] delegated the Imāmate to Mūsā. Moreover, we received on the qualities and knowledge of Mūsā all those reports that are well known to the narrators of Traditions. We have not heard from these [other sects] anything more than claims. Reports widely transmitted and accepted by great numbers of transmitters and the doctrines based on them are not comparable to those transmitted by a few people. So reflect upon the truthful reports to know the difference between Mūsā, Muḥammad, and 'Abd Allāh, the sons of Ja'far. Let

us test this with five questions about what is licit and what is illicit, concerning which Mūsā had given answers. If we find any answer by one of the other two [claimants of the Imāmate] with their supporters, we accept their claims. The Imāmites have narrated that ʿAbd Allāh b. Jaʿfar was asked how much the *zakāt* of two hundred *dirhams* would be, and he said five *dirhams*; then he was asked how much would the *zakāt* of a hundred *dirhams* be, to which he answered two and one half *dirhams*.[22]

If a disputant criticized Islam and its people and claimed that here was someone who had composed something like the Qur'ān and asked us to judge between that composition and the Qur'ān, we would say to him: As for the Qur'ān, it is accessible to everyone; so bring that composition out into the open so that we may judge between it and the Qur'ān. It is the same thing that we say to these groups. As for our reports, they are narrated and preserved among the Imāmite scholars in different cities, so show those reports to which you lay claim so that we can judge between them and our reports. That you claim a report that no one has heard and no one knows, and then ask us to decide between reports is something the like of which anyone can claim. If a claim like this could nullify the reports of the followers of truth among the Imāmites, a similar claim from the Brahmins[23] could nullify the reports of the Muslims. This is quite clear, thank God. The Dualists claimed that Manichaeus performed miracles and that they had reports that demonstrated the proof of this, but the Monotheists said to them: Anyone could make that claim. Bring the report out into the open so that we can show you that it does not bring about any conviction nor establish any proof. It is the same kind of answer that we give the author of this book.

[19] And it will be said to the author: The Bakrites and the Ibāḍites say that the Prophet, may God bless him and his Family

22. Ṣaffār: 250–51; ʿAlī b. Bābawayh: 209–10; Kulaynī, 1:351; Kashshī: 282. The problem with this answer is that in the case of cash the *zakāt* starts with two hundred *dirhams* and nothing under that limit is taxable.

23. See *Kamāl*: 83–4. On the ideas and arguments of the Brahmins as represented in *kalām*, see the article "Barāhima" in *EI*², 1:1031 (by F. Rahman) and the two recent articles by S. Stroumsa (in *Jerusalem Studies in Arabic and Islam*, 6 (1985): 229–41) and B. Abrahamov (in *Die Welt*, 18 (1987): 72–91).

and grant them peace, designated Abū Bakr,[24] whereas you deny this, just as we deny that Abū 'Abd Allāh [Ja'far al-Ṣādiq] willed [the Imāmate] to those two [sons of his, 'Abd Allāh and Muḥammad]. So explain to us your proof and demonstrate the difference between you and the Bakrites and the Ibāḍites so that we can demonstrate to you in the same way the difference between us and those [groups] you named.

[20] And it will be said to the author: You are a man who claims that Ja'far b. Muḥammad followed the doctrine of the Zaydites and that he did not lay claim to the Imāmate in the way that the Imāmites mention. Those who believe in the Imāmate of Muḥammad b. Ja'far b. Muḥammad claim the opposite of what you and your colleagues claim. They mention that their predecessors narrated this claim from him [Ja'far]. So let us know what the difference is between you and them so that we may come forward with something better than that for you. Be fair on your part for it is better for you.

[21] There is yet another difference [between us and the other groups]. The followers of Muḥammad b. Ja'far and 'Abd Allāh b. Ja'far acknowledge that Ḥusayn designated [his son] 'Alī [Zayn al-'Ābidīn] and that 'Alī designated [his son] Muḥammad [al-Bāqir] and that Muḥammad designated [his son] Ja'far [al-Ṣādiq]. Our demonstration that Ja'far designated only Mūsā is the same as their demonstration that Ḥusayn designated 'Alī. Moreover, when the Imām is present and his supporters visit him frequently, his knowledge becomes manifest and his deep familiarity with religion becomes evident. We have found that narrators of Traditions and conveyors of reports have related from Mūsā that recorded and widely known body of knowledge on what is licit and what is forbidden. What has become manifest from his surpassing merits is well known among the Shī'ites and others. These are the signs of Imāmate. Now that we have found all these signs in Mūsā and in no one else we know that he, and not his brother, is the Imām after his father. Furthermore, 'Abd Allāh b. Ja'far died leaving no male descendant

24. See Bāqillānī: 169 where the Bakrites and 'Abbāsites, who claimed that the Prophet designated either Abū Bakr or 'Abbās b. 'Abd al-Muṭṭalib as his successor, are mentioned.

and no one designated [as his successor], so those who believed in his Imāmate turned away from that [opinion] toward belief in the Imāmate of Mūsā.

[22] Having said that, the [real] difference between our reports and theirs is that the reports do not give necessary knowledge unless they are transmitted by a group whose narration leaves no room for doubt. We are not disputing with those [sects] about their predecessors; rather we would be content if they should find for us a number of narrators of Traditions and conveyors of reports who hold their doctrine at the present time through whom the report would be regarded as *mutawātir* [widely transmitted], just as we can find for them. If they can do this, then let them bring it into the open; if they cannot, then the difference between them and us will become clear in our generation, even if we take it for granted for the past [generations]. This is clear. Praise be to God.

[23] As for those who stopped with Mūsā, they have the same status as those who stopped with Abū ʻAbd Allāh [Jaʻfar al-Ṣādiq]. We did not witness the death of any of the predecessors; their death is verified for us only by reports. If someone should stop with any one of them, we will ask him what the difference is between him and those who stopped with the others.[25] This is something for which they do not have any way out.

[24] Then the author said: «Among them is a group who categorically believed in [the death of] Mūsā and followed after him his son ʻAlī b. Mūsā but no other son of his; they claimed that he [ʻAlī b. Mūsā] was entitled to the Imāmate through inheritance and will. Then [they carried on the same claim] in his offspring until they ended with Ḥasan b. ʻAlī for whom they claimed a son, whom they called the Pious Successor *{al-khalaf al-ṣāliḥ}*. During the lifetime of ʻAlī b. Muḥammad, however, they had nominated his son Muḥammad for the Imāmate, but he died before his father. Then they turned to his brother Ḥasan, and their imagination concerning Muḥammad proved false. So they claimed that a decision occurred to God to change from Muḥammad to Ḥasan, just as his mind had changed from Ismāʻīl b. Jaʻfar to Mūsā when Ismāʻīl died in the lifetime of Jaʻfar. This was until Ḥasan b. ʻAlī died in 263[26]

25. See *Ghayba*: 20 where this argument is adopted.
26. *Sic*. He actually died in 260/874 as noted before.

when some of his followers turned to belief in the Imāmate of Ja'far b. 'Alī, just as the followers of Muḥammad b. 'Alī had turned to Ḥasan after the death of Muḥammad. Some of those [who turned to Ja'far] claimed that Ja'far b. 'Alī, and not his brother Ḥasan, received the right to the Imāmate from his father, 'Alī b. Muḥammad, by inheritance and will. Then they carried it [the Imāmate] to the descendants of Ja'far through inheritance and will. All these groups contest with each other on the question of the Imāmate, accuse each other of unbelief, call each other liars, and repudiate the doctrines of the others concerning the question of the Imāmate. Each sect claims the Imāmate for its master through inheritance and will as well as through such claims as their knowledge of the unseen, [claims] that even silly nonsense is better than. None of these groups has any proof for what it claims and upon which it disagrees with the others except inheritance and will. Their proof is their witness for themselves, and not for anyone else, an utterance without reality and a claim without proof. If there is here any proof for what each group claims besides inheritance and will they must bring it forward, but if it is only the claim of the Imāmate through inheritance and will, then the Imāmate is proven void because of the large number of those who claim it through inheritance and will, and there is no way to accept the claim of one group rather than another. This would be so if the subject of claims and counter-claims were a single matter; it is much more so now that each group accuses the other of lying and each has a totally different claim.»

[25] I say, and God is the one who leads to the truth: If the Imāmate were to be proved void because of the large number of claimants, the same thing would apply to prophethood because we know that many people have laid claim to it. The author related confused narrations from the Imāmites and made it seem that this is the view of all and that there is no one among the Imāmites who does not believe in *badā'* [change in God's decision]. He who says that God changes his mind because of a new calculation or acquiring additional information is an unbeliever in God. This opinion was not held by anyone except the Mughīrites and those [extremists] who falsely attribute knowledge of the unseen to the Imāms. This, according to us [the Imāmites], is disbelief in God and deviation

from Islam. The least that he [the author] should have done was to have mentioned the opinion of the People of Truth and not confined himself to saying that the group has differed among itself to suggest that the doctrine of the Imāmate was wrong. After all, the Imām, according to us, can be recognized through various means that we shall mention; then we shall consider what these people say, and if we do not find any difference between us and them, we shall judge that the doctrine [of the Imāmate] is wrong; then we shall come back to the author to ask him which among the various opinions is right.

[26] As for his words: «Among them is a group who categorically believed in [the death of] Mūsā and followed his son 'Alī b. Mūsā after him», this is the word of a man who does not know the history of the Imāmite community because the whole Imāmite community—with the exception of a tiny group who stopped [with Mūsā] and some deviators who believed in the Imāmate of Ismā'īl and 'Abd Allāh b. Ja'far—believed in the Imāmate of 'Alī b. Mūsā and narrated concerning him what is recorded in the books. Not [even] five narrators of Traditions and conveyors of reports are mentioned to have inclined toward these opinions when these events first occurred; the increase in their numbers, wherever it happened, was a later development. So how could the author regard it appropriate to say: "Among them is *a group* who categorically believed in [the death of] Mūsā"?

[27] More strange are his words: «Until they ended with Ḥasan for whom they claimed a son. During the lifetime of 'Alī b. Muḥammad, however, they nominated his son Muḥammad for the Imāmate.» [But no one claimed that the Imāmate belonged to Muḥammad] except a group of the companions of Fāris b. Ḥātim. It is not right for a reasonable person to condemn his opponent for a falsehood that has no basis. What demonstrates the error of the opinion of the people who believed in the Imāmate of Muḥammad is the very same thing that we described concerning Ismā'īl b. Ja'far because it is the same story: each of them died before his father, and it is impossible for a living person to install a dead person as his successor and to delegate the Imāmate to him. This is so clearly wrong that there is no need to say any more to prove its falsity.

[28] The difference between us and those who believe in the Imāmate of Jaʿfar is that what they report from him is diverse and contradictory because among them and us are those who quoted him as saying: "I am the Imām after my brother Muḥammad," and among them are those who narrated that he said: "I am the Imām after my brother Ḥasan," and among them are those who narrated that he said: "I am the Imām after my father ʿAlī b. Muḥammad." These reports, as you can see, refute each other. But our report about Abū Muḥammad Ḥasan b. ʿAlī is widespread and is not self-contradictory. This is a clear difference. Moreover, we came to know from Jaʿfar what indicated to us that he was ignorant of the precepts of God, the Mighty, the Exalted, which is that he demanded the inheritance from the mother of Abū Muḥammad. It is his forefathers' ruling that the brother does not inherit while the mother is alive.[27] If Jaʿfar did not even have that much command of the religious law so that his deficiency and ignorance concerning it became clear, how could he be an Imām? God has bound us to judge these matters at their face values. If we wanted to say [more] we would, but there is enough in what we have mentioned to demonstrate that Jaʿfar was not an Imām.

[29] As for his words that «they claimed that Ḥasan had a son,» the people only claimed this after their forebearers had transmitted to them what he was like, his occultation, what would happen to him, and the disagreement among people about him when the event takes place. Here are their books. Whoever wants to look at them may do so.

[30] As for his words: «All these groups contest with each other and call each other nonbelievers», he is right in what he says. The same situation exists within the Muslim community at large where each group accuses the other of nonbelief. Let him say what he likes and discredit as he wishes, for the Brahmins will have recourse to it and discredit Islam with it. If someone, seeking to refute his opponent's beliefs, asked him a question that if turned back to him would refute his own beliefs in the same way that he wanted [to refute] his opponent, then he is [actually] posing the question to himself and refuting his own words. This is the story

27. See above, chapter 3.

of the author. Prophethood is the underlying principle, and the Imāmate is a subordinate; if the author concedes the underlying principle, he should not discredit the subordinate by using what goes back to the principle. God is the one whose help is sought.

[31] Then he said: «If the Imāmate through inheritance and will could be established for whoever claims it without an agreed proof, the Mughīrites had more right to it because everyone else agrees with them on the Imāmate of Ḥasan [al-Mujtabā]—who was the original case who was entitled to the Imāmate from his father through inheritance and will—but they [the Mughīrites] refused to recognize it for anybody else after all agreed with them on the Imāmate of Ḥasan. Add to all of this the disagreement of the Imāmites in their religion: some of them believe in [God's] corporality, some believe in the transmigration of souls, some believe in the absoluteness of divine unity, some believe in divine justice and affirm the *wa'īd* [i.e. God's unconditional fulfillment of threat of punishment of the unrepentant sinner], some believe in predestination and deny the *wa'īd,* some believe in [the possibility of] seeing [God] while others deny it; [all that] in addition to the belief in the change in the decision of God and [other] things that it would take too much space in the book to explain. They excommunicate each other for these beliefs and dissociate themselves from the others' religion. Each of these groups assumes to have its own, so they believe, trustworthy persons who transmitted to them from their Imāms what they cling to.»

Then the author said: If that is possible then this is possible [too] (referring to something that we do not allow, and he does not render anything more than quotation, so there is no sense in prolonging the book by mentioning things that have no proof nor any use).

[32] I say, and reliance is on God: If the truth were only established by a proof on which there were agreement, no truth would ever be established, and the first doctrine to prove false would be that of the Zaydites because their proof is not agreed upon. As for what he narrates from the Mughīrites, this is something that they took from the Jews because they always argue with their agreement and ours on the prophethood of Moses, peace be upon him, and their disagreement with us on the prophethood of Muḥammad,

may God bless him and his Family and grant them peace. His rebuking us with differences in belief and that every group among us reports what it professes from its Imām is taken from the Brahmins because they discredit Islam in this very way. If it were not for the concern that some of these [anti-Islam] rogues may gain the advantage of what I narrate from them [the Zaydites], I would say [about them] as they do. The Imāmate, may God grant you happiness, is only proved, according to us, through explicit designation and through the manifestation of excellence and knowledge of religion while avoiding analogies and personal reasoning concerning revealed divine prescriptions and matters subordinate to them. This is how we came to know the Imāmate of the Imām. We shall [later] give a convincing explanation about the differences among the Shīʿites.

[33] The author said: «Now either their differences are generated by themselves or by their transmitters, or by their Imāms. If their differences arise from their Imāms, the Imām is the one who brings unanimity [and is] not the one who is the cause of the difference in the community, especially when they are his supporters, not his enemies, and no precautionary secrecy [*taqiyya*] is required between him and them. What is then the difference between the Imāmites and the [rest of the Muslim] community when they, together with their Imāms and the Proofs of God to them, are subject to most of the blame that they level against the [rest of the Muslim] community, which has no Imām, concerning inconsistency in religion and accusation of each other of nonbelief.[28] If their differences arose from those who transmit their religion to them, what is their guarantee that this is not their way with them concerning what they reported to them about the Imāmate, especially when the one for whom the Imāmate is claimed is invisible and cannot be seen in person. The same is the proof against them for what they claim for their Imām concerning the knowledge of the unseen, because his select group and interpreters between him and his followers are liars who attribute to him what he has not said, but he has no knowledge of them. If the differences among the Imāmites concerning their religion arose from themselves and not their Imāms, what need do they have then of the Imāms when they manage by

28. See Saʿd b. ʿAbd Allāh: 78–9 for a similar argument by earlier Zaydites.

themselves and he does not restrain them when he is in the midst of them, even though he is the interpreter between God and them and the Proof for them? This is also a most clear proof that he does not exist nor [have] the knowledge of the unseen that is ascribed to him, for if he existed, it would not be permissible for him not to give explanations to his followers; as God, the Mighty, the Exalted, said: "We only revealed the Book to you that you might make clear to them that wherein they differed."[29] Just as the Messenger, may God bless him and his Family and grant them peace, explained to his community, so it is incumbent on the Imām to do the same for his followers.»

[34] I say, and reliance is on God: The differences between the Imāmites arose only from liars who fraudulently came among them time after time and age after age till it became an immense problem. Their predecessors were people of piety, religious practice, and purity; they were not people of rational investigation or great discernment. So whenever they saw someone decorous narrating a report they looked upon him favorably and accepted him. When those [differences] became frequent and open, they complained to their Imāms, who, peace be upon them, ordered them to accept that upon which was a consensus, but they did not follow and continued their customary practice. So the irresponsibility occurred on their side, not on that of their Imāms. Also, the Imām was not informed of all those confused accounts that were being transmitted because he does not have knowledge of the unseen but is only a godly man who knows the Book and the Tradition and knows about his followers only what is reported to him.

[35] As for his saying: «And what is their guarantee that this is not their way with them concerning what they reported to them about the Imāmate,» the difference in this is that the question of the Imāmate was reported to them through *tawātur* [i.e., and indisputable widespread transmission], and *tawātur* cannot be proved false. Those reports [that the author points to], each of them is reported by an individual whose report does not produce certain knowledge. The report of an individual may prove right or false,

29. Qur'ān, 16:64.

but this is not the case with indisputable widespread reports. This is our answer, and all that he says apart from this is void.

[36] Now it should be said to him: Tell us whether the differences of the whole Muslim community escape the same subdivisions? If he says: No, he should be told: Was not the Messenger sent only to bring unanimity? He has to agree. Then he should be told: Did not God, the Mighty, the Exalted, say: "We only revealed the Book to you that you might make clear to them that wherein they differed?" He must agree. Then he should be told: Has he made it clear? He must agree. Then it will be said to him: So what is the cause of the difference? Tell us what it is and be satisfied with the same answer from us.

[37] As for his saying: «What need do the Imāmites have then of the Imāms when they manage by themselves and he does not restrain them when he is in the midst of them...,» it will be said to him: The most proper thing for religious people is fairness. What did we say to hint that we manage by ourselves, so that the author can hit us with it and use it as an argument against us? What proof can he direct against us which requires what he said? He who does not care about what he challenges his opponents with will have many questions and answers for himself.

[38] As for his saying: «This is a most clear proof that he does not exist, for if he existed it would not be permissible for him not to give explanations to his followers, as God, the Mighty, the Exalted, said: "We only revealed the Book to you that you might make clear to them that wherein they differed,"» it should be said to the author: Tell us about the guiding *'Itra,* is it lawful for them not to explain the whole truth to the community? If he says: Indeed, then he has confuted himself and his words rebound on him as unpleasant consequences, because the community did differ and vary greatly and they did accuse each other of unbelief. If he says: No, it should be said: This is a most clear proof that the *'Itra* does not exist and that what the Zaydites claim is false because, if the *'Itra* existed, the way that the Zaydites describe, they would have explained to the community, and it would not be possible for them to keep silent and withhold [guidance] as God, the Mighty, the Exalted, said: "We only revealed the Book to you that you might make clear to them that wherein they differed." If he asserts that

the *'Itra* did explain the truth to the community but the community did not accept [but instead] inclined to their worldly desires, it should be said to him: This is the very thing that the Imāmites say about the Imām and his followers. And we seek success from God.

[39] Then the author said: «And it will be said to them: Why did your Imām conceal himself from those who seek his guidance? If they say: As a precautionary measure to protect himself, it should be said to them: So it should be lawful for the one who seeks guidance, too, not to look for the Imām as a precautionary measure, especially when [as in this case] he is uncertain about the result [of his search] and does not know what will come of that because the Imām is in precautionary secrecy. If practicing precautionary secrecy is permissible for the Imām, it should be regarded to be even more so for the follower. Why is it that the Imām practices precautionary secrecy in respect to their guidance but does not practice precautionary secrecy in devouring their money? God says: "Follow those who do not ask you for recompense,"[30] and said "Indeed, many of the rabbis and monks devour the wealth of the people wantonly and debar from the way of God."[31] This is an indication that the people of falsehood are after the wealth of this world, but those who hold to the Book do not ask the people for recompense, and they are rightly guided.»

Then he said: If they say this, it will be said to them...(something which only an ignorant and mentally deficient person would say).

[40] The answer to what he asked is that the Imām did not conceal himself from those who seek his guidance; he only concealed himself because of fear of oppressors. As for his words: «If practicing precautionary secrecy is permissible for the Imām, it should be regarded to be even more so for the follower,» it should be said to him: If you mean that the follower is allowed to practice precautionary secrecy for himself just as the Imām is allowed to, this is, when he fears for himself just as the Imām is allowed to, this is, upon my life, permitted. However, if you mean that the follower has permission not to believe in the Imāmate of the Imām on the

30. Qur'ān, 36:21.
31. Ibid., 9:34.

grounds of precautionary secrecy, this is not permitted if the reports have already reached him that allow him no excuse. Sound reports have the same status as seeing with one's own eyes. There is no precaution for [what is in] the heart—no one knows what is in it except God.

[41] As for his saying: «Why is it that the Imām practices precautionary secrecy with respect to their guidance but does not practice precautionary secrecy in devouring their wealth? God says: "Follow those who do not ask you for recompense,"» the answer to this, till the end of the section, is to be said to him: The Imām does not practice precautionary secrecy against guiding those who wish guidance. How could he be doing that while he has explained the truth to them, urged them toward it, called them to it, and taught them what is licit and what is illicit, till they became well known and gained wide recognition for it? He does not devour their money; he only asks them for the *khums* that God, the Mighty, the Exalted, has fixed, to dispose of it as God ordered him to dispose of it. The one who introduced the *khums* was the Messenger, and the Qur'ān spoke of this. God, the Mighty, the Exalted, said: "And know that whatever you acquire, a fifth thereof is for God..."—to the end of the verse,[32] and He said: "Take alms of their wealth." — to the end of the verse.[33] If there is any fault in or blame against taking wealth, it is on the one who started it. God is the One Whose help is sought.

[42] It would be said to the author: Tell us about your Imām when he emerges and gains supremacy. Will he take the *khums*? Will he collect the land tax? Will he take what is due from the fixed and movable spoils of war and from the mines and so forth? If he says: No, he is at variance with the decree of Islam. If he says: Yes, it would be said to him: If someone were to argue against him using, like you, the words of God, the Mighty, the Exalted: "Follow those who do not ask you for recompense," and "Indeed, many of the rabbis and monks . . ."—to the end of the verse, how would you answer him? [Tell us] so that the Imāmites can answer you in the same way. This—may God grant you success—is something

32. Qur'ān, 8:41.
33. Ibid., 9:103.

that the unbelievers used to scorn the Muslims with and I do not know who has put it into the mouth of these people.

Know—may God teach you benevolence and make you a person endowed with it—that he [the Imām] acts according to the Book and the Tradition (*sunna*) and is not going against them. If our opponents can demonstrate for us that he is transgressing the Book and the Tradition in taking what he takes, upon my life the word will clearly be theirs. If they cannot prove this, they should know that there is no fault in acting in accordance with the Book and the Tradition. This is clear.

[43] Then the author said: «It will be said to them: We do not allow the Imāmate to belong to someone who is not known. Can you show us a way to know the master you claim so that we may allow that the Imāmate should belong to him as we allow it to belong to all existing members of the *'Itra*? Otherwise there can be no way of allowing the Imāmate to belong to nonexistent persons. Everyone who does not exist is nonexistent. So allowing the Imāmate to belong to the one whom you claim is false.»

[44] I say, seeking help in God: It will be said to the author: Do you doubt the existence of 'Alī b. al-Ḥusayn [Zayn al-'Ābidīn] and his descendants whom we recognize as the Imāms? If he says: No, it would be said to him: So is it permitted that they be Imāms? If he says: Yes, it would be said to him: So you do not know we may be correct in believing in their Imāmate and you may be wrong. This suffices as an argument against you. But if he says: No, it would be said to him: What, then, is the point in substantiating the existence of our Imām while you do not grant recognition even to the Imāmate of someone like 'Alī b. al-Ḥusayn with his rank of knowledge and excellence according to both the opponent and the partisan?

Then it will be said to him: We came to know that among the *'Itra* is one who knows the interpretation [of the Book] and the religious precepts, through the report from the Prophet, may God bless him and his Family and grant them peace, which we mentioned above, and because of our need for someone who can teach us the meaning of the Qur'ān and can differentiate between the commands of God and the commands of Satan. Then we learned that the truth lies with this group of the descendants of Ḥusayn, because we saw that all those in the *'Itra* who oppose them rely, for religious precepts and interpretation [of the Book], on the kind of personal opinion, individual judgment, and analogical reasoning that Sunnite scholars rely on in [deducing] religious duties for which there can be no reason apart from divine interest. By this we learned that those who oppose them are wrong. Then things became apparent to us—from the knowledge of this group concerning what is licit and what is illicit and the religious precepts—which did not become apparent from anyone else. Then the reports continued to arrive about the designation of one of them by another till it reached Ḥasan b. 'Alī. When he died and no designation or successor after him appeared, we referred to the books which our forebears transmitted before the Occultation. There we found that which indicated the successor after Ḥasan and that he would disappear from among the people and conceal his person, that the Shī'a would differ, and that the people would fall into confusion about his affair. We knew that our forebears did not have knowledge of the unseen but that the Imāms had informed them of this [that they, in turn, had received it] through a Prophet's communication. So in this way and by this proof, his being, his existence, and his occultation was proved for us. If there is a proof here that refutes what we said, let the Zaydites bring it forward. We have no grudge against the truth. Thank God.

[45] Then the author returned to argue against us with what those who stopped with Mūsā b. Ja'far claimed. We did not stop with anyone, so we ask what the difference is between those who stopped [with different Imāms]. We explained that we came to know that Mūsā died in the same way that we came to know that Ja'far died and that any doubt about the death of one of them prompts doubt about the death of the other. A group of people stopped with Ja'far whose idea was rejected by those who stopped with Mūsā, just as they [the first group] rejected those who stopped with the Commander of the Faithful, peace be upon him. So we said to them: O people, your argument against your predecessors is the same as our argument against you. Say what you may; you only confute yourselves.

[46] Then he relates that we used to say to those who stopped [with Mūsā b. Ja'far]: "The Imām can only be someone who is visible and existent." This is the narration of someone who does

not know the views of his opponent. The Imāmites have always maintained that the Imām is either visible and in the open or hidden and concealed. Their reports to that effect are too well known to be kept secret. To ascribe false principles to opponents is something that anyone can do, but it is indecent for the people of religion, learning, and knowledge. If there were not, on this matter, anything other than the report of Kumayl b. Ziyād,[34] it would be enough.

Then he said: If they say this, it will be said to them . . . (something that we do not say. Our proof is what you have heard, and that is quite enough. Praise be to God.)

[47] Then he said: «The matter [the Imāmate] does not, as you have imagined, belong to the descendants of Hāshim[35] because the Prophet, may God bless him and his Family and grant them peace, directed his community to his *'itra* (according to both our and your consensus). *'Itra* means his immediate family members that no one is as close to him as they are. So it belongs to them, not to the Freedmen and sons of Freedmen.[36] One of them [the Prophet's family] is entitled to it in every age (because there can only be one Imām) through firm adherence to the Book and a call to establish its authority. [This is] because the Messenger, may God bless him and his Family and grant them peace, indicated them

34. Kumayl b. Ziyād al-Nakha'ī, a disciple of 'Alī and a *tābi'ī* who was killed by Ḥajjāj b. Yūsuf al-Thaqafī, the governor of Iraq, in 82–83/701–703 (see Ṭabarī, 6:365; Ibn Ḥazm, *Jamhara*: 390; Ibn Abi 'l-Ḥadīd, 17:149–50; Ibn Ḥajar, *Tahdhīb*, 8:447–8). The author refers to a well-transmitted statement of 'Alī quoted in the sources (e.g., *Nahj al-balāgha*: 497; Thaqafī, 1:153; Ibn Bābawayh, *Kamāl*: 289–94; idem, *Khiṣāl*: 187) on the authority of Kumayl, in which 'Alī said: "The earth is never devoid of someone who stands as the Proof of God, either manifest and well known or afraid and hidden."
35. Hāshim b. 'Abd Manāf, the great grandfather of the Prophet. See the article on him in *EI*[2], 3:260 (by W. Montgomery Watt).
36. This refers to the Umayyads whose ancestors were among the Meccans who were pardoned by the Prophet on the day of conquest of Mecca in the year 8/630 when he told them: "Go, you are freed." As the arch enemies of the Prophet who fought against him and continued their hostility toward and rejection of him until the last minute, they otherwise could have been captured by the Muslims and enslaved.

with his words that "they would not part from the Book until they are received by me at the Pool." This is a matter of consensus. Those descendants of Hāshim that you use for your argument are not from among the *dhurriyya* (offspring) of the Prophet, may God bless him and his Family and grant them peace, although they were born [to the family of the Prophet]. This is because all offspring of a daughter are accounted to their paternal kin except the offspring of Fāṭima, for whom the Messenger of God, may God bless him and his Family and grant them peace, is the paternal kin and father.[37] *Dhurriyya* means offspring, as evidenced by the words of God, the Mighty, the Exalted: "I commend her and her *dhurriyya* to thy protection from Satan, the outcast."»[38]

[48] I say, and I seek refuge in God: This matter cannot be established on the basis of your consensus and ours; it can be established only through demonstration and proof. What is your proof for what you claim? Moreover, the consensus between us was only on three persons: the Commander of the Faithful, Ḥasan, and Ḥusayn. The Messenger, may God bless him and his Family and grant them peace, did not mention his *dhurriyya,* he only mentioned his *'itra;* yet you inclined to some of the *'Itra* rather than others through no other proof or explanation greater than the mere claim. We argued with what our predecessors narrated from a group until their reports led back to Ḥusayn b. 'Alī's designation of his son, 'Alī, and 'Alī's designation of Muḥammad, and Muḥammad's designation of Ja'far. Then we demonstrated the correctness of the Imāmate of these people and no one else from the *'Itra* in their time by the manifestation of their knowledge of the religion and their preeminence in themselves. Both [their] friends and [their] enemies learned from them; this fact is widely acknowledged everywhere and is well known among the transmitters of reports. Through knowledge, the Proof is distinguished from the one to whom the Proof is sent, the leader from the led, and the one who obeys from the one who is obeyed. Where is your demonstration, O community of Zaydites, for what you claim?

37. This refers to a well-known statement of the Prophet. See Majlisī, 25:247–9, 43: 228–30 and the sources quoted therein.

38. Qur'ān, 3:36.

[49] Then the author said: «If the Imāmate were legitimate for all the descendants of Hāshim in addition to Ḥasan and Ḥusayn, then it should be legitimate for the descendants of 'Abd Manāf in addition to the descendants of Hāshim, and if it were legitimate for the descendants of 'Abd Manāf[39] as well as the descendants of Hāshim it should be legitimate for all descendants of Quṣayy.»[40] Then he carried on this statement in length.

[50] It will be said to him: O debater for the Zaydites! This is a matter that is not claimed through kinship. It can only be claimed through preeminence and knowledge, and it is authenticated through explicit designation and assignment. If the Imāmate were legitimate for the closest relative in the *'Itra* because of his kinship, it would also be legitimate for the most distant. Separate yourself from those who claimed this and bring out your proof. Distinguish right now between yourself and one who said: If [the Imāmate] were legitimate for the descendants of Ḥasan, then it should be legitimate for the descendants of Ja'far [b. Abī Ṭālib], and if it is legitimate for them then it should be legitimate for the descendants of 'Abbās. The Zaydites can never make such a differentiation unless they resort to our analysis and proof, which is the designation by one of the next and the manifestation of the knowledge of what is licit and what is illicit.

[51] Then the author said: «If they use 'Alī, peace be upon him, for their argument, saying: What do you say about him? Was he one of the *'Itra* or not?, they should be told: He was not one of the *'Itra*, but he stood ahead of the *'Itra* and all other kinsfolk through the designation of him on the Day of Ghadīr,[41] which is a matter of consensus.»

39. 'Abd Manāf b. Quṣayy b. Kilāb, father of Hāshim and the chief of the Quraysh after his father. See Ibn Sa'd, 1: 42; Ṭabarī, 2: 254.

40. Quṣayy b. Kilāb (see above, chapter 5).

41. That was 18 Dhu 'l-Ḥijja 10/16 March 632 when the Prophet on his return from the Farewell Pilgrimage stopped at Ghadīr Khumm, situated between Mecca and Medina where the pilgrims used to disperse. He asked his companions to construct a dais for him. Taking 'Alī by the hand, he asked of his faithful followers whether he, the Prophet, was not closer to the Believers than they were to themselves. The crowd cried out "It is so, O apostle of

[52] I say, seeking help from God: It will be said to the author: The designation on the Day of Ghadīr is correct. However, your denial that the Commander of the Faithful was one of the *'Itra* is very serious. Point out to us what you rely on in your claim. The linguists attest that the paternal uncle and the son of the paternal uncle are of the *'Itra.* Then I say: The author has contradicted his own doctrine by what he said, because he believes that the Commander of the Faithful was designated by the Messenger as his successor in the community. In this respect, he says that the Prophet, may God bless him and his Family and grant them peace, left as his successors among the community the Book and the *'Itra,* and that the Commander of the Faithful was not one of the *'Itra.* If he was not one of the *'Itra,* he cannot have been one designated as his successor by the Messenger, may God bless him and his Family and grant them peace. This is, thus, inconsistent as you can see, except if he claims that he [the Prophet], may God bless him and his Family and grant them peace, left the *'Itra* as his successors among us after the Commander of the Faithful, may God bless him, was killed. So we ask him to differentiate between himself and those who say that he left the Book among us from that time onward. The Book and the *'Itra* were designated successors together. The Tradition narrates this and bears witness to this. Thanks be to God.

[53] Then the author turned to what is a proof against himself, saying: «We ask those who claim the Imāmate for some and not for others to establish their proof.» He forgot himself and that he is alone in claiming it for the descendants of Ḥasan and Ḥusayn and no others.

[54] Then he said: «If they resort to argument with absurd concepts such as the knowledge of the unseen and like drivel, things that they have no proof for apart from mere claim, they will be opposed with a similar claim for some other [members of the *'Itra*]. If claim can be accepted as proof, then it would be possible to claim

---

God." He then declared: "He of whom I am the *mawlā* (the patron?) of him 'Alī is [also] the *mawlā*." (See the article *Ghadīr Khumm* in *EI*², 2:993–4 [by L. Veccia Vaglieri]. For the details and sources of this event see 'Abd al-Ḥusayn al-Amīnī, 1:9–158.)

that *'Itra* are from among those people who "do injustice to themselves."»[42]

[55] It will be said to the author: You mentioned knowledge of the unseen over and over again. Only God knows the unseen, and only unbelieving polytheists attribute it to man. We said to you and your companions: Our proof for what we say is understanding and knowledge; if you have something like this bring it forward, but if there is nothing but slander and gossip and rebuking the whole community with the views of some extremists, then the matter is simple. "God suffices for us and is a perfect trustee."

[56] Then the author said: «Now we return to the elucidation of the argument of the Zaydites with the words of God, the Blessed, the Supreme: "Then We gave the Book as inheritance unto those We selected of our bondsmen"—to the end of the verse.»

[57] It will be said to him: We grant you that this verse was sent down concerning the *'Itra,* but what is your proof that "the foremost in good deeds" are the descendants of Ḥasan and Ḥusayn and no one else from among the *'Itra*? All you meant was to slander your opponents and make a claim for yourself.

[58] Then he said: «God, the Mighty, the Exalted, said—and he is mentioning the select and the ordinary people from the community of His Prophet—: "Hold fast all of you to the rope of God . . ." to the end of the verse.»[43] Then he said: «Addressing the ordinary people is now concluded and He begins to address the select: "Let there be a nation from you who call to what is good[44]—to the point that He tells the select—You are the best community

42. This phrase is from the Qur'ān, 35:32: "Then We gave the Book as inheritance unto those whom We selected of Our bondsmen, but there are among them those who do injustice to themselves." Those who do injustice can never attain the divine position of Imāmate, according to the Qur'ān, 2:124 where God tells Abraham that He appointed him as an Imām for mankind. Abraham asked: "And from my offspring?" God answered: "My covenant does not include the unjust."

43. Qur'ān, 3:103.

44. Ibid., 3:104.

that has been raised up for mankind."»[45] Then he said: «These [the select] are the offspring of Abraham, peace be upon him, and not the rest of the people, then the Muslims, and not those among the offspring of Abraham, peace be upon him, who were polytheists before they became Muslims. He [God] made them witness against the people, saying: "O you who believe, bow down and prostrate [yourselves] and worship—to the point that He said—And that you be witnesses for mankind."[46] This is the path of the select among the offspring of Abraham, peace be upon him.» Then he brought forward many verses similar in meaning to the above verses from the Qur'ān.

[59] It would be said to him: O debater! You know that the Mu'tazilites and other groups of the community are in a serious dispute with you about the interpretation of these verses, yet you bring forward nothing more than a mere claim. We grant you what you claim but ask you for the proof for that which singles you out, that is, that those [selected] are the descendants of Ḥasan and Ḥusayn and of no one else. How long will you go on bringing your claim and avoiding the proof and trying to menace us with reciting the Qur'ān, pretending that you have a proof in it that your opponents do not? God is the one Whose help is sought.

[60] Then the author said: «The one of the *'Itra* who called to good, such as the one who enjoined good and forbade evil and engaged himself earnestly in struggle in [the path of] God, is not on a parity with the rest of the *'Itra* who did not call to good nor strive earnestly in [the path of] God;[47] just as God did not make those of the People of Scripture who followed this way equal to the rest of them.[48] [This is true] even if the one who fails to do that is

45. Ibid., 3:110.

46. Ibid., 22:77–8.

47. For earlier uses of this argument by the Zaydites against the Imāmites see Nawbakhtī: 73; Sa'd b. 'Abd Allāh: 75; Kulaynī, 1:357; Kashshī: 237–8, 416.

48. Qur'ān, 3: 113–14: "They are not all alike. Of the People of Scripture there is a group who stand, recite the revelations of God all night along, falling prostrate. They believe in God and the Last Day and enjoin good and forbid evil and compete with each other in good deeds. They are of the righteous."

eminent and pious because piety is a supererogatory matter whereas the holy struggle is a duty that is obligatory like other duties; the one who performs it goes forth with the sword to meet the sword and prefers fear to meekness.» Then he recited the *Sūrat al-Wāqiʿa* and quoted the verses where God, the Mighty, the Exalted, mentioned the holy struggle. He then followed them by claims but never advanced any argument to support any of them. So we demand from him the authentication of [those claims] and counterargue with what we ask him for differentiation.

[61] So I say, seeking help from God: If much holy struggle were the proof of preeminence and knowledge and the Imāmate, then Ḥusayn had more right to the Imāmate than Ḥasan because Ḥasan took the course of peace with Muʿāwiya,[49] whereas Ḥusayn took up the holy struggle and was killed. What does the author of the book say [in this case], and by what means can he repudiate that? After all, we do not deny the obligatory nature of holy struggle, nor its merit, but we saw that the Messenger, may God bless him and his Family and grant them peace, did not wage war with anyone until he found supporters, partisans, and brothers, and only then did he wage war. We saw that the Commander of the Faithful, peace be upon him, acted in the same way. We saw that Ḥasan intended to carry on the holy struggle but that when his companions abandoned him he took the course of peace and stayed at home. So we learned that the holy struggle is obligatory in a situation where there are supporters and partisans. All minds agree that a learned person is superior to the one who carries out the holy struggle but does not have knowledge. Not all those who call to the holy struggle know its ordinances, when it is necessary to fight, when it is good to pursue peace, how to administer the affairs of the community, and what to do in the matters that concern life, property, and the honor of the people.

Yet, we would be happy with one thing from our brothers, that they show us a single person from the *ʿItra* who denies anthropomorphism and predestination, who does not use personal opinion and analogical reasoning in [deducing] religious precepts, and who is independent and competent so that we might join his

49. See Ṭabarī, 5:162–3.

revolt. Enjoining good and forbidding evil is a duty within the measure of one's capacity and possibilities. Reason witnesses that imposing a duty on someone who is incapable is wrong and that it is evil to expose oneself to danger. One instance of exposing oneself to danger is when a small band without war experience who are not skilled soldiers, goes forth to meet a trained army that controls the land, is killing people, and is accustomed to war, is numerous, well-armed and equipped, and has a body of supporters among the ordinary people (who believe that he who attacks them can be lawfully killed) that is one hundred times larger than that small band. So how can the author force us to confront skilled soldiers with inexperienced ones? How many of this number might rally to somebody who calls for revolt? Alas, this is a situation that nothing will put an end to except the support of God, the Mighty, the All Knowing, the Wise.

[62] After quoting verses of the Qur'ān for which his interpretation can be severely challenged and for which he did not offer any rational or religious proof, the author said: «Understand, may God have mercy on you, who has the greater right to be a witness to God—someone who called [the people] to good as he was commanded and forbade evil and commanded what is proper, who struggled in the path of God as he should till he was martyred, or someone whose face has not been seen and whose person is not known? How could God take him as a witness for those whom he has not seen nor ever forbade or commanded, so that if they obey him they will fulfill their obligation, and if they kill him he will pass on to God as a martyr? If a man asks a group of people to witness for him in a case that he pursues but that they had never seen nor had any personal experience with, could they be witnesses? Can he establish any right through them? [Not] unless they testify to what they have not seen, whereupon they would be liars and perjurers before God. If this is not permissible for people, it cannot be permissible for the Fair Judge Who never is unjust. But, in the same situation, if the man called as witnesses a group of people who had seen with their own eyes and heard concerning that case, and they witnessed for him, would he not be right and they tellers of the truth and his enemies perjurers and the witnessing accomplished and the judgment given? This is as the word of God,

the Mighty, the Exalted: "Only those who bear witness to the truth and they know."[50] Do you not see that no one can legally witness what he has not seen with his own eyes? This is as the words of Jesus: "I was a witness over them as long as I dwelt amongst them"—to the end of the verse.»[51]

[63] I say, taking refuge with God: It will be said to the author: These are not your words but the words of the Mu'tazilites and others against both us and you, to say that the *'Itra* are not available, that those of them whom we have seen are not fit to be the Imām, that it is not permissible that God, the Mighty, the Exalted, should command us to cling to those of them we do not know and who neither we nor our forebears have seen, that there is no one in our time whom we have seen who is fit to be the Imām of the Muslims and those whom we have not seen have no proof over us, and that this whole situation is the clearest demonstration that the meaning of the words of the Prophet, may God bless him and his Family and grant them peace: "I leave among you what, if you cling to it, you will never go astray: the Book of God and my *'itra*" is not what springs to the minds of the Imāmites and the Zaydites. It makes it also possible for Naẓẓām[52] and his followers to say: We have found that what will never [be] separated from the Book is that [sort of] report which cuts off any excuse because it is manifest as the Book is manifest.[53] It can be put to use, followed and adhered to, but we do not see any of the *'Itra* being the sort of scholar we can follow. Whenever we came to know that one of them held an opinion, we heard that another of them opposed him. Following two persons with different opinions is wrong. So what does the author have to say?

[64] Then know that when the Prophet, may God bless him and his Family and grant them peace, commanded us to cling to the *'Itra,* there was evidence in reason, common usage, and existing

50. Qur'ān, 43:86.

51. Ibid., 5:117.

52. Abū Isḥāq Ibrāhīm b. Sayyār al-Baṣrī, known as Naẓẓām (d. 221/836), the prominent Mu'tazilite theologian. On him see the article "Abū Esḥaq al-Naẓẓām" in *Encyclopaedia Iranica*, 1:275–80 (by J. Van Ess).

53. See Khayyāṭ: 52.

practice to indicate that he meant those among them who were learned, not those who were ignorant, the pious and godfearing, not others. So what is incumbent on us is to look for the one who combines knowledge of religion with intelligence, discernment, forbearance, withdrawal from worldly matters, and autonomy in commanding so that we can follow him and cling to both the Book and him.

If [someone] says: Two men combine these qualities, but one of them follows the Zaydite doctrine, and the other the Imāmite, which of them should be followed and obeyed? We say to him: This never happens, but if it were to happen, a clear sign would distinguish between them—either a designation from the Imām who preceded him, or something becoming manifest in his knowledge, as happened in the case of the Commander of the Faithful, peace be upon him, on the Day of Nahr[54] when he said: "By God, the river has not been forded, and they will not cross. By God, not ten of you will be killed, and not ten of them will be saved."[55] It may also be that the people will come to know that one of them holds an opinion that will indicate that following him would be impermissible. This is like what has become clear in the Zaydite scholarship; they believe in personal judgment and analogical reasoning concerning transmitted religious duties and injunctions by which it is known that they [the Zaydite scholars] are not Imāms. By this statement, I do not mean Zayd b. 'Alī and his like, because these people never demonstrated anything that can be rejected nor claimed to be Imāms. They simply called [the people] to the Book and the satisfaction of the household of the Prophet. This is a right call.

[65] As for his words: «How could God take him as a witness for those whom he has not seen nor ever forbade or commanded», it will be said to him: The meaning of *witness* according to your opponents is not the same as you believe. However, if you found fault with the Imāmites on the basis that someone whose face is not seen and whose person is not known cannot be of the stature they claim for him, then tell us on your part who is the Imām of the *'Itra* who is the witness in these times? If he says that he does

54. The day that the battle between 'Alī and the Khārijites took place in Nahrawān in the year 38/658–659. See Ṭabarī, 5:72–92.

55. *Nahj al-balāgha*: 93; Mas'ūdī, *Murūj*, 3:156.

not know him, he finds the same fault in himself and faces the same [problem] that he thought that his opponents faced. If he says: He is such-and-such person, we say to him: But we never saw his face, nor did we ever know his person, so how can he be an Imām for us and a witness for us? If he says: Although you do not know him, he is an existing and known person, let him know him who knows him and not know him who does not, we say: By God, we ask you whether you suppose that the Muʿtazilites, the Khārijites, the Murji'ites, and the Imāmites know this man or have ever heard of him or [whether] even the idea [of the existence of such a person] ever occurred to them? If he says: This is something that does not harm him nor does it harm us because oppressors are in full control of the Abode [of Islam] and there are few who can help and support him, then I will say to him: You included yourself in what you blamed others for and confuted yourself with the same argument that you thought you were confuting your opponents. How close this [concept of] occultation is to the [concept of] the Occultation of the Imāmites, except that you are not behaving fairly.

[66] Then it will be said to him: You have said too much about holy struggle and the concepts of enjoining good and forbidding evil to pretend that the one who does not revolt does not have legitimacy. So why is it that your Imāms and the *ʿulamā'* from your sect do not rebel? Why have they stayed at home and confined themselves to merely believing in the doctrine? If he utters a word, the Imāmites will counter him with a similar statement. Then it would be said to him, in a friendly and pleasant way: That for which you blamed the Imāmites and railed at them and reviled their Imāms and by using which you reached the conclusions that you included in your book, you are now included in it, inclined toward it, and depended on it in your reasoning. Praise be to God Who guided us to His religion.

[67] Then it will be said to him: Tell us whether there is anyone from the *ʿItra* today who merits the Imāmate? He has to say: Yes. Then it will be said to him: Is it then not the case that his Imāmate is not validated by explicit designation as the Imāmites believe [it should be], nor does he come with a supernatural proof through which it may be known that he is an Imām, nor is he, according to you, like those who were chosen and to whom allegiance

was pledged by the People of Loosening and Binding[56] from among the community after they came together and deliberated? If he says: Yes, it will be said to him: So how can he be recognized? If they say: He is recognized by the consensus of the *'Itra* on him, then we say to them: How can they agree on him? If he were an Imāmite the Zaydites would not approve him, and if he were a Zaydite the Imāmites would not approve him. If he says: The Imāmites are not considered in this kind of thing, it will be said to him: The Zaydites are of two groups: the Mu'tazilites and the *Muthbita*.[57] If he says: The *Muthbita* are not considered in this kind of thing, it will be said to him: The Mu'tazilites are of two groups: those who follow their personal judgment in [deriving] legal rulings and those who maintain this is wrong. If he says: Those who deny [the validity of] personal judgment are not considered, it will be said to him: If there remain of those who believe in personal judgment the most eminent and of those who consider it invalid the most eminent, and each dissociates himself from the other, whom do we cling to, and how do we know that the rightful of them is the one you and your companions follow and not the other? If he says: By looking into the fundamental principles, we say: If disagreement continues for long and the matter is confused, how should we act, and how can we convince ourselves that we have obeyed the words of the Prophet, may God bless him and his Family and grant them peace: "I leave among you what, if you cling to it, you will never go astray: the Book of God and my *'itra,* my household"? No one can recognize the Proof from his *'itra* without first examining the fundamental principles, and investigating whether all of his opinions are sound and whether those who oppose him are in error. If this is how it is [that is, if the matter is as you allege], then he is the

56. *Ahl al-ḥall wa 'l-'aqd*, "those who are qualified to unbind and to bind," the representatives of the community of the Muslims, who act on their behalf in appointing and deposing a caliph and serve as his consultants in major affairs of the Muslim society (See *EI*², 1:263–4).

57. Those who supported the idea that God possessed eternal attributes such as sight, speech, and knowledge, distinct from His essence and argued that it was by means of those attributes that God was seeing, speaking, knowing, and so forth. This was against the Mu'tazilites' doctrine, which maintained that God had no attributes distinct from his essence.

same as all the other learned speakers, so what special characteristic do the *'Itra* have? Show it to us and explain all of it to us so that we may know that there is some difference and distinction between the person of knowledge from the *'Itra* and the person of knowledge from outside the *'Itra*.

[68] Furthermore, it will be said to them: Tell us about your Imām these days: does he have knowledge of what is licit and what is illicit? If they say: Yes, we will say to them: Tell us whether what he knows that is not indisputable, widely transmitted Traditions is like what Shāfi'ī, Abū Ḥanīfa, and the like know or different from that. If they say: As a matter of fact, what he knows is what they know and is from the same kind, it will be said to him: So why do the people need knowledge of your Imām, whom nobody has ever heard of, when the books of Shāfi'ī and Abū Ḥanīfa are extant and available in every place? But if they say: What he knows is different from what those two [scholars] know, we say: What is different from what they know is [either] the derived principle that a group of the leaders of the Mu'tazilites claim or [the principle] that everything is lawful as it originally was unless declared unlawful by indisputable Traditions, as maintained by Naẓẓām and his followers, or the opinion of the Imāmites that all laws are explicitly designated. (It must be noted, however, that we do not mean by explicitly designated that which may spring to someone's mind [i.e., existence of individual prescription for every case], but that there are explicitly designated general principles that whoever understands them discovers all religious norms without using analogical reasoning or personal judgment.) If they say: What he knows is at variance with all of that, they go beyond common sense. If they adhere to one of the [above-mentioned] methods, it will be said to them: Where, then, is this knowledge? Has anyone whose faith and honesty can be trusted narrated it from your Imām? If they say: Yes, it will be said to them: We have been together now for a very long time, but we have never heard a single bit of this knowledge,[58] whereas you are a group that does not believe in practicing precautionary secrecy, nor does your Imām, as you claim that the Imāmites ascribed it untruthfully to Ja'far b. Muḥammad [al-Ṣādiq]. This is an argument that cannot be escaped.

58. See Majlisī, 47:275 where a similar argument is quoted from Ja'far al-Ṣādiq.

[69] Another question: It will be said to them: Do you not maintain that Ja'far b. Muḥammad did not believe in what the Imāmites claim [he did] but held the same doctrines as you? They have to say: Yes (except if they disassociate themselves from him). Then it will be said to them: So the Imāmites have lied in what they have narrated from him, and these compiled books that they possess are merely the works of liars? If they say: Yes, it will be said to them: If this is possible, then why is it not possible that your Imām holds the doctrine of the Imāmites and follows their religion and that what your predecessors and seniors relate from him is not genuine, is fabricated, and has no basis? If they say: We have no Imām at this time whom we personally know, from whom we narrate what is licit and what is illicit, but we know that there is in the *'Itra* someone who is the right person and qualified for it, we will say: You have now brought upon yourselves the same blame that you directed toward the Imāmites who have so many Traditions from their Imāms pointing to their present Imām and indicating and predicting him. This nullifies all that you have said about holy struggle and enjoining good and forbidding evil. So you now believe in an Imām who is not seen nor known. So say as you wish. And we take refuge with God against failure.

[70] Then the author said: «Just as God commanded the *'Itra* to call [others] to what is good, He described how the foremost among them precede [the others], made them witnesses, and ordered them to act justly, saying: "O you who believe, be steadfast for God, witnesses to justice."»[59] Then he followed this with some interpretations and recitation of verses from the Qur'ān that he claimed have to do with the *'Itra.* He did not, however, try to prove any of this with any greater proof than a claim. Then he said: «God, the Exalted, required of his Prophet, may God bless him and his Family and grant them peace, to leave enjoining good and forbidding evil until He had mobilized supporters for him, saying: "And when you see those who engage in vain discourse about our signs [turn away from them]—to his words—so that they may fear [God]."[60] So the one who is not of the foremost in good actions and

59. Qur'ān, 5:8.
60. Ibid., 6:68–9.

of those who struggle in [the path of] God, nor of those who follow a middle course and fulfill the duty of enjoining good and forbidding evil through preaching when they do not have enough supporters [to establish the rule of truth], is among those who are unjust to themselves.[61] The same was the case with those before us of the descendants of the Prophets.» Then he quoted some verses of the Qur'ān.

[71] It will be said to him: It is of no concern to us [now] who He meant by these words, but tell us which group your Imām from the *'Itra* belongs to. If he says: [He is] among those who struggle [in the path of God], it will be said to him: Who is he, whom has he fought with, whom has he revolted against, and where are his cavalry and infantry? If he says: He is among the ones who fulfill the duty of enjoining good and forbidding evil through preaching when they do not have enough supporters [to establish the rule of truth], it will be said to him: Who hears his enjoining and forbidding? If he says: His close associates and selected companions, we say: If he continues this course and his obligation to do anything else were dropped because of the lack of support, and it is permissible that only his close associates should hear his enjoining and forbidding, what then is the fault you found with the Imāmites? and Why have you written this book of yours? and Whom did you scorn? I wish I knew whom you are attacking with the verses of the Qur'ān and trying to convince that the holy struggle is obligatory.

[72] Then it will be said to him and to all the Zaydites: Tell us: if the Prophet, may God bless him and his Family and grant them peace, had left this world without designating the Commander of the Faithful, peace be upon him, nor indicating him nor pointing him out, would this have been a correct action and a good and permissible measure on his part? If they say: Yes, we will say to them: If he had not indicated the *'Itra,* would this have been permissible? If they say: Yes, we will say: For what did you criticize the Mu'tazilites, the Murji'ites, and the Khārijites because it would

61. This refers to the Qur'ān, 35:32, where three groups are mentioned among the inheritors of the Book: "those who do injustice to themselves, those who follow a middle course, and those who are foremost in good deeds."

be permissible not to designate, in which case the matter would be settled by the deliberation of the council of the People of Loosening and Binding. This is an argument that they cannot escape. If they say: No, the Commander of the Faithful, may the blessings of God be upon him, had to be designated and the *'Itra* had to be indicated, it will be said to them: Why? until they mention the true argument in which time we assign this to the Imām in every age—because if the designation is necessary for one period, it is necessary in all periods because its necessitating causes always exist. And we take refuge with God from failure.

[73] Another question: it will be said to them: If indisputable widely reported Traditions are proof, whether narrated by the *'Itra* or by ordinary people, and the one transmitted by a single or a few transmitters from the *'Itra* brings the possibility of as much intention to deceive and as much negligence and commission of error on behalf of one of them as it does from one of the ordinary people and what is neither in indisputable widely reported Tradition nor in the one transmitted by a limited number must, according to you, be deduced, and whatever problem possible with the legal interpreters among the ordinary people is possible with those from among the *'Itra* too, in what way, then, did the *'Itra* became a Proof? If the author says: If they concur, their consensus is proof, it will be said to him: This is true with ordinary people too, if they concur, their consensus is proof, and this produces the conclusion that there is no difference between the *'Itra* and ordinary people. If this is the case, there can be no meaning for [the Prophet's] words: "I leave behind among you the Book of God and my *'itra*," except if among them is one who is an ultimate authority in the religion. And that is what the Imāmites maintain.

[74] Know, may God bring you happiness, that the author kept himself occupied after this point with quoting the Qur'ān and interpreting it according to his fancy, but nowhere in this did he say: The evidence for the correctness of my interpretation is such and such. This is something that even children can do. His sole purpose was to blame the Imāmites on the basis that they do not consider the holy struggle and enjoining good and forbidding evil [as obligatory]. But he is wrong because they do consider these [as obligatory] as far as one can. They do not, however, believe that

they should leap into perilous situations or rebel against those who are ignorant of the Book and the Tradition and who do not know how to rule the community properly with justice and truth. More surprising is that our colleagues among the Zaydites stay in their homes and do not enjoin any good or forbid any evil nor engage in any holy struggle and yet blame us for this. This is extremely unfair and is a sign of bigotry. We take refuge with God from worldly desire. He suffices for us and is a perfect trustee.

[75] Another matter: it will be said to the author: Do you know among the truthful Imāms anyone more excellent than the Commander of the Faithful, peace be upon him? His answer will be: No. Then it will be said to him: Do you know any reprehensible thing, after polytheism and disbelief, that is more evil and grave than what the people of the Saqīfa[62] did? His answer will be: No. Then it will be said to him: Do you know more about enjoining good and forbidding evil and holy struggle or does the Commander of the Faithful, peace be upon him? He must say: The Commander of the Faithful, so it will be said to him: So what was in his mind that he did not fight those people?[63] If he gives any kind of excuse, it will be said to him: So accept a similar excuse from the Imāmites, for everyone knows that today falsehood is stronger than it was in those days and that the supporters of Satan are more [numerous]. Do not try to frighten us with the holy struggle and mention it, for God, the Exalted, only imposed it with preconditions that, if you knew them, would cut short your speech and curtail your book. And we seek success from God.

[76] Another matter: it will be said to the author: Do you approve of Ḥasan b. ʿAlī giving up the struggle with Muʿāwiya, or do you accuse him of error? If they say: We approve, it will be said to them: Do you approve of him while he desisted from holy struggle and abandoned enjoining good and forbidding evil as you

62. The elders of Quraysh and their supporters who on the day of the death of the Prophet in the year 11/632 gathered in the Saqīfa of the Banū Sāʿida in Medina and named Abū Bakr as the successor to the Prophet. See Ibn Hishām, 4:306–12.

63. This argument was reportedly used previously by an Imāmite debater, Abū Bakr al-Haḍramī, against Zayd b. ʿAlī (Kashshī: 416; see also Kulaynī, 1:357).

indicate? If they say: We approve of him because the people forsook him and he was afraid of them for his own life—he did not have that number of perspicacious persons with him to make it possible for him to stand up to Mu'āwiya and his people, it will be said to them when they recognize the correctness of that: So if Ḥasan had an excuse—while he had the army of his father and the people delivered sermons in his name from the top of the pulpits and he pulled out his sword and set out to fight his enemy and God's for the reason you just described and gave, why do you not then excuse Ja'far b. Muḥammad for abandoning armed struggle when his enemies in his time were many times more numerous than those who had been with Mu'āwiya, and he did not have among his partisans anyone with fighting skills, but a group of peaceful people who had never witnessed a war or seen combat? If they concede that he had his excuse, they are behaving justly, but if any of them denies it, he will be asked what the difference is. There is no difference.

[77] Furthermore, if the Zaydites' analogy were correct, Zayd b. 'Alī would be more excellent than Ḥasan b. 'Alī because Ḥasan appeased but Zayd fought until he was killed. It is enough disgrace for a doctrine that it leads to a preference for Zayd b. 'Alī over Ḥasan b. 'Alī. God is the one Whose help is sought. God suffices for us and is a perfect trustee.

Bibliography

An asterisk beside the name of a book in the list below means that wherever the name of its author is given in a reference without mentioning a specific work by him, it refers to this particular work marked with the asterisk.

'ABD AL-ḤUSAYN AL-AMĪNĪ:
Al-Ghadīr fi 'l-kitāb wa 'l-sunna wa 'l-adab, Beirut, 1967

'ABD AL-JABBĀR = Qāḍī Abu 'l-Ḥusayn 'Abd al-Jabbār b. Aḥmad al-Asadābādī al-Hamadānī (d.415/1024):
– * *Al-Mughnī fī abwāb al-tawḥīd wa 'l-'adl,* vol. 20, ed. 'Abd al-Ḥalīm Maḥmūd and Sulaymān Dunyā, Cairo, 1966
– * *Al-Majmū' al-muḥīṭ bi 'l-taklīf,* compiled by Ḥasan b. Aḥmad b. Mattawayh, ed. 'Umar al-Sayyid 'Azmī, Cairo, 1965
– * *Ṭabaqāt al-mu'tazila,* ed. Fu'ād Sayyid, Tunis, 1974 (in the collection of *Faḍl al-i'tizāl wa ṭabaqāt al-mu'tazila,* 135-350)
– * *Tathbīt dalā'il al-nubuwwa,* ed. 'Abd al-Karīm 'Uthmān, Beirut, 1966

'ABD AL-JALĪL AL-QAZWĪNĪ = Naṣīr al-Dīn Abū 'l-Rashīd 'Abd al-Jalīl b. Abi 'l-Ḥusayn b. Abi 'l-Faḍl al-Qazwīnī al-Rāzī (d. after 556/1161):
Kitāb al-Naqḍ = Ba'ḍ mathālib al-nawāṣib fī naqḍ ba'ḍ faḍā'iḥ al-rawāfiḍ, ed. Jalāl al-Dīn Muḥaddith Urmawī, Tehran, 1358sh/1980

'ABD AL-QĀHIR AL-BAGHDĀDĪ = Abū Manṣūr 'Abd al-Qāhir b. Ṭāhir al-Tamīmī al-Baghdādī (d. 429/1037-8):
– * *Al-Farq bayn al-firaq,* ed. Muḥammad Muḥyi 'l-Dīn 'Abd al-Ḥamīd, Cairo [1964]
– * *Uṣūl al-dīn,* Beirut, 1981

ABRAHAMOVE, Binyamin:
"The Barahima's Enigma, a Search for a New Solution," in *Die Welt,* 18 (1987): 72-91

ABŪ 'ALĪ = Muḥammad b. Ismā'īl al-Māzandarānī al-Ḥā'irī (d. 1215/1800-1801):
Muntaha 'l-maqāl fī 'ilm al-rijāl, Tehran, 1300/1882

ABŪ 'AWĀNA = Ya'qūb b. Isḥāq b. Ibrāhīm al-Naysābūrī al-Isfarā'īnī (d. 316/928-9):
Al-Musnad = Musnad abī 'awāna, Hyderabad, 1362/1943

ABŪ DĀWŪD = Sulaymān b. Ash'ath al-Azdī al-Sijistānī (d. 275/888-9): *Kitāb al-Sunan = Sunan abī dāwūd*, ed. Muḥammad Muḥyi 'l-Dīn 'Abd al-Ḥamīd, Cairo, 1935

ABU 'L-FARAJ = 'Alī b. al-Ḥusayn b. Muḥammad al-Qurashī al-Iṣbahānī (d. 356/966-7):
– * *Al-Aghānī*, the edition of Dār al-Kutub, Cairo, 1927-74
– * *Maqātil al-ṭālibiyyīn*, ed. al-Sayyid Aḥmad Ṣaqr, Cairo, 1949

ABU 'L-FUTŪḤ AL-RĀZĪ = Jamāl al-Dīn Ḥusayn b. 'Alī b. Muḥammad al-Khuzā'ī al-Naysābūrī (early 6th/12th century): *Rawḍ al-Jinān wa rawḥ al-janān fī tafsīr al-qur'ān*, ed. 'Alī Akbar Ghaffārī, Tehran, 1382-7/1963-68

ABŪ GHĀLIB AL-ZURĀRĪ = Aḥmad b. Muḥammad b. Muḥammad b. Sulaymān al-Shaybānī al-Baghdādī (d. 368/978): *Risālat abī ghālib al-zurārī ilā ibn ibnih fī dhikr āl a'yan*, ed. Muḥammad Riḍā al-Ḥusaynī, Qum, 1411/1991

ABU 'L-ḤASAN AL-ASH'ARĪ = 'Alī b. Ismā'īl b. Abī Bishr al-Baṣrī (d. 324/936):
– * *Maqālāt al-islāmiyyīn*, ed. Muḥammad Muḥyi 'l-Dīn 'Abd al-Ḥamīd, Cairo, 1969
– *Risāla fī istiḥsān al-khawḍ fī 'l-kalām*, Hyderabad, 1344/1925-26

ABU ḤĀTIM AL-RĀZĪ = Aḥmad b. Ḥamdān b. Aḥmad al-Laythī (d. 322/934): *Kitāb al-Zīna*, ed. 'Abd Allāh al-Sallūm al-Sāmarrā'ī, Baghdad, 1392/1972 (in the editor's *al-Ghuluww wa 'l-firaq al-ghāliya fi 'l-ḥiḍāra al-islāmiyya*: 227-312)

ABŪ HILĀL AL-'ASKARĪ = Ḥasan b. 'Abd Allāh b. Sahl (d. after 395/1005): *Al-Awā'il*, ed. Walīd Qaṣṣāb and Muḥammad al-Miṣrī, Riyadh, 1981

ABU 'L-MA'ĀLĪ = Muḥammad b. 'Ubayd Allāh al-Ḥusaynī al-'Alawī (d. after 485/1092-93): *Bayān al-adyān*, ed. Hāshim Raḍī, Tehran, 1964

ABŪ MANṢŪR AL-ṬABRISĪ = Aḥmad b. 'Alī b. Abī Ṭālib (early 6th/12th century): *Al-Ihtijāj 'alā ahl al-lajāj*, ed. Muḥammad Bāqir al-Kharsān, Najaf, 1966

ABŪ MUḤAMMAD AL-'IRĀQĪ = 'Uthmān b. 'Abd Allāh al-'Irāqī al-Ḥanafī (d. after 540/1145):

Al-Firaq al-Muftariqa bayn ahl al-zaygh wa 'l-zandaqa, ed. Yasar Kutluay, Ankara, 1961

ABŪ NU'AYM = Aḥmad b. 'Abd Allāh al-Iṣbahānī (d. 430/1038-9):
Ḥilyat al-awliyā' wa ṭabaqāt al-asfiyā', Cairo, 1932-38

ABU 'L-QĀSIM AL-BALKHĪ = 'Abd Allāh b. Aḥmad b. Maḥmūd al-Ka'bī (d. 319/931):
Maqālāt al-islāmiyyīn, the chapter on the Imāmite sects quoted by 'Abd al-Jabbār in his *al-Mughnī* (Cairo, 1966), 20 (2): 176-82

ABU 'L-QĀSIM AL-QUMMĪ = Abu 'l-Qāsim b. al-Ḥasan al-Jīlānī al-Qummī (d. 1231/1816):
Qawānīn al-uṣūl, Tabrīz, 1303/1885-86

ABŪ SAHL AL-NAWBAKHTĪ = Ismā'īl b. 'Alī b. Isḥāq, Ibn Nawbakht (d. 311/924):
Al-Tanbīh fi 'l-imāma, the final section of it quoted by Ibn Bābawayh in his *Kamāl al-dīn* (Tehran, 1390/1970): 88-94

ABU 'L-ṢALĀḤ AL-ḤALABĪ = Taqī al-Dīn b. Najm al-Dīn al-Ḥalabī (d. 447/1005-6):
– *Al-Burhān 'alā thubūt al-īmān*, Qum, 1408/1987 (in Ḥasan b. Abi 'l-Ḥasan al-Daylamī's *A'lām al-dīn fī ṣifat al-mu'minīn:* 44-58)
– *Al-Kāfī fi 'l-fiqh*,[1] ed. Riḍā al-Ustādī, Qum, 1403/1983
– * *Taqrīb al-ma'ārif*, ed. Riḍā al-Ustādī, Qum, 1404/1984

ABŪ ṬĀLIB = Yaḥyā b. al-Ḥusayn b. Hārūn al-Ḥasanī al-Āmulī, al-Nāṭiq bi 'l-Ḥaqq (d.424/1-33):
Al-Di'āma fī tathbīt 'l-imāma, ed. Nājī Ḥasan, Beirut, 1981 (under the title of *Nuṣrat madhāhib al-zaydiyya* and misattributed to Ṣāḥib b. 'Abbād)

ABŪ ZAYD AL-'ALAWĪ (late 3d/9th century):
Kitāb al-Ishhād, the fragments of it quoted by Ibn Qiba in his *Naqḍ kitāb al-ishhād* (see above, chapter 7)

AFANDĪ = 'Abd Allāh b. Īsā al-Iṣfahānī (d. ca. 1130/1718):
Riyāḍ al-'ulamā' wa ḥiyāḍ al-fuḍalā', ed. Aḥmad al-Ḥusaynī, Qum, 1401-2/1980-82

1. The more accurate name of this work in *al-Kāfī fi 'l-taklīf*. See the author's *al-Burhān 'alā thubūt al-īmān*: 54.

ĀGHĀ BUZURG = Muḥammad Muḥsin b. ʿAlī al-Ṭihrānī (d. 1389/1970):
– * *Al-Dharīʿa ilā taṣānīf al-shīʿa*, Tehran and Najaf, 1353-98/1934-78
– *Ṭabaqāt aʿlām al-shīʿa*, the volume on the 7th/13th century (=*al-Anwār al-sāṭiʿa fi ʾl-miʾa al-sābiʿa*), ed. ʿAlī Naqī Munzawī, Beirut, 1972

AḤMAD = Abū ʿAbd Allāh Aḥmad b. Muḥammad b. Ḥanbal al-Shaybānī al-Marwazī (d. 241/855):
– * *Al-Musnad*, Cairo, 1313/1895
– *Al-Radd ʿala ʾl-jahmiyya wa ʾl-zanādiqa*, ed. ʿAbd al-Raḥmān ʿUmayra, Riyadh, 1977

ĀJURRĪ = Abū Bakr Muḥammad b. al-Ḥusayn b. ʿAbd Allāh al-Baghdādī (d. 360/970):
Kitāb al-Sharīʿa, ed. Muḥammad Ḥāmid al-Fiqī, Cairo, 1950

AKHBĀRĪ = Muḥammad b. ʿAbd al-Nabī al-Naysābūrī al-Akhbārī (d. 1233/1818)
– *Maṣādir al-anwār fī taḥqīq al-ijtihād wa ʾl-akhbār*, MS 3682/1, Marʿashī Library, Qum
– *Risāla dar shadādat bar wilāyat dar adhān*, MS 2797/6, Majlis Library, Tehran (described in its catalogue, 10:72-3)

ʿALĀʾ AL-DĪN AL-BUKHĀRĪ = ʿAbd al-ʿAzīz b. Aḥmad b. Muḥammad (d. 730/1329-30):
Kashf al-asrār ʿan uṣūl fakhr al-islām al-bazdawī, Istanbul, 1308/1890-91

ʿALAM AL-HUDĀ = Muḥammad b. Muḥammad Muḥsin al-Kāshānī (d. after 1112/1700):
Naḍd al-īḍāḥ, ed. A. Sprenger, Calcutta, 1853 (together with Ṭūsī's *Kitāb al-Fihrist*)

ʿALĪ B. BĀBAWAYH = Abu ʾl-Ḥasan ʿAlī b. al-Ḥusayn b. Mūsā b. Bābawayh al-Qummī (d. 329/940- 41):
Al-Imāma wa ʾl-tabṣira min al-ḥayra, ed. Muḥammad Riḍā al-Ḥusaynī, Beirut, 1987

ʿALĪ B. IBRĀHĪM = Abu ʾl-Ḥasan ʿAlī b. Ibrāhīm b. Hāshim al-Qummī (d. after 307/919):
Kitāb al-Tafsīr = *Tafsīr al-qummī*, ed. Ṭayyib al-Mūsawī al-Jazāʾirī, Najaf, 1387/1967

ʿALĪ B. YŪSUF B. AL-MUṬAHHAR AL-ḤILLĪ (late 7th/13th century):

Al-'Udad al-qawiyya li-daf' al-makhāwif al-yawmiyya, ed. Madhī al-Rajā'ī, Qum, 1408/1987

ALQĀB AL-RASŪL WA 'ITRATIH, anonymous, Qum, 1406/1985-6 (in the collection of *Majmū'a nafīsa fī ta'rīkh al-a'imma*: 203-290)

ĀMIDĪ = Sayf al-Dīn Abu 'l-Ḥasan 'Alī b. Muḥammad al-Taghlibī (d. 631/1233):
Al-Iḥkām fī uṣūl al-aḥkām, Cairo, 1967

ANṢĀRĪ = Murtaḍā b. Muḥammad Amīn al-Tustarī (d. 1281/1864):
Farā'id al-uṣūl = al-Rasā'il, Tehran, 1315/1897

'ARASHĪ = Ḥusayn b. Aḥmad b. Ṣāliḥ al-Khawlānī (d. 1329/1911):
Bulūgh al-marām fī sharḥ misk al-khitām fī man tawallā mulk al-yaman min malik wa imām, ed. Anastase-Marie de St. Elie, Beirut, 1939

ARDABĪLĪ = Aḥmad b. Muḥammad al-Ardabīlī al-Muqaddas (d. 993/1585):
Majma' al-fā'ida wa 'l-burhān fī sharḥ irshād al-adhhān, ed. 'Alī Panāh al-Ishtihārdī et al., Qum, 1402/1981-

ASAD ALLĀH AL-TUSTARĪ = Asad Allāh b. Ismā'īl al-Tustarī al-Kāẓimī (d. 1234/1818-19):
Kashf al-qinā' 'an wujūh ḥujjiyyat al-ijmā', Tehran, 1317/1899-1900

'AYYĀSHĪ = Abu 'l-Naḍr Muḥammad b. Mas'ūd al-Sulamī al-Samarqandī (late 3d/9th century):
Kitāb al-Tafsīr = Tafsīr al-'ayyāshī, ed. Hāshim al-Rasūlī, Qum, 1380-81/1960-62

BAGHAWĪ = Abū Muḥammad Ḥusayn b. Mas'ūd b. Muḥammad al-Farrā' (d. 516/1122-23):
Maṣābīḥ al-sunna, ed. Yūsuf 'Abd al-Raḥmān al-Mar'ashlī et al., Beirut, 1987

BAHĀRĪ = Muḥibb Allāh b. 'Abd al-Shakūr al-Hindī (d. 1119/1707):
Mūsāllam al-thubūt, Cairo, 1326/1908

BAḤR AL-'ULŪM = Muḥammad Mahdī b. Murtaḍā al-Ṭabāṭabā'ī al-Burūjirdī (d. 1212/1797):
Al-Fawā'id al-rijāliyya = Rijāl al-sayyid baḥr al-'ulūm, ed. Muḥammad Ṣādiq Baḥr al-'Ulūm and Ḥusayn Baḥr al-'Ulūm, Najaf, 1965-7

BALĀDHURĪ = Aḥmad b. Yaḥyā b. Jābir (d. 279/892-3):
Ansāb al-ashrāf, vol. 1, ed. Muḥammad Ḥamīdullāh, Cairo, 1959

BĀQILLĀNĪ = Qāḍī Abū Bakr Muḥammad b. al-Ṭayyib al-Baṣrī (d. 403/1013):
Al-Tamhīd, ed. Maḥmūd Muḥammad al-Khuḍayrī and Muḥammad ʿAbd al-Hādī Abū Rīda, Cairo, 1947

BARQĪ = Abū Jaʿfar Aḥmad b. Muḥammad b. Khālid al-Qummī (d. 274-80/887-94):
Al-Maḥāsin, ed. Jalāl al-Dīn Muḥaddith Urmawī, Tehran, 1370/1950-51

BUKHĀRĪ = Abū ʿAbd Allāh Muḥammad b. Ismāʿīl al-Juʿfī (d. 256/870):
Al-Jāmiʿ al-ṣaḥīḥ = *Ṣaḥīḥ al-bukhārī*, ed. M. Ludolf Krehl and Th. W. Juynboll, Leiden, 1862-1907

BURSĪ = Raḍī al-Dīn Rajab b. Muḥammad b. Rajab al-Ḥillī (d. after 813/1410):
Mashāriq anwār al-yaqīn fī asrār amīr al-muʾminīn, Beirut, 1379/1959-60

DĀRIMĪ = Abū Muḥammad ʿAbd Allāh b. ʿAbd al-Raḥmān al-Tamīmī al-Samarqrandī (d. 255/869):
Sunan al-dārimī = *Al-Musnad,* ed. Muḥammad Aḥmad Dahmān, Beirut, n.d.

DHAHABĪ = Shams al-Dīn Abū ʿAbd Allāh Muḥammad b. Aḥmad b. ʿUthmān al-Dimashqī (d. 748/1348):
- *Al-ʿIbar fī khabar man ghabar*, ed. Ṣalāḥ al-Dīn al-Munajjid, Kuwait, 1960-66
- *Siyar aʿlām al-nubalāʾ*, ed. Shuʿayb al-Arnaʾut et al., Beirut, 1981-88
- *Taʾrīkh al-islām*, Cairo, 1367-9/1947-50
- *Al-ʿUluww li ʾl-ʿalī al-ghaffār*, Medina, 1968

ḌIYĀʾ AL-DĪN AL-ʿARĀQĪ (d. 1361/1942):
Nihāyat al-afkār, his lectures collected by Muḥammad Taqī al-Burūjirdī, Najaf, 1371-7/1951-58

DURUST B. ABĪ MANṢŪR al-Wāsiṭī (2d/8th century):
Kitāb durust b. abī manṣūr, Tehran, 1371/1951-52 (in the collection of *al-Uṣul al-sittatʿashar*: 158-69)

DUSTŪR AL-MUNAJJIMĪN, anonymous (mid 5th/11th century), MS Arabe 5968, Bibliothèque Nationale, Paris[2]

2. References to this work are all to the folios 344–5 of the manuscript. The

EI[1] = *Encyclopaedia of Islam*, lst edition, ed. M. Th. Houtsma et al, Leiden, 1913-36

EI[2] = *Encyclopaedia of Islam*, 2d edition, ed. H.A.R. Gibb et al, Leiden, 1960-

ENCYCLOPAEDIA IRANICA, ed. Ehsan Yarshater, London etc. 1982-

ENAYAT, Hamid:
Modern Islamic Political Thought, London, 1982

FAḌL B. SHĀDHĀN = Abū Muḥammad Faḍl b. Shādhān b. Khalīl al-Azdī al-Naysābūrī (d. 260/873):
Al-Īḍāḥ, ed. Jalāl al-Dīn Muḥaddith Urmawī, Tehran, 1972

FAKHR AL-DĪN AL-RĀZĪ = Abū 'Abd Allāh Muḥammad b. 'Umar al-Tamīmī al-Bakrī (d. 606/1210):
- *I'tiqādāt firaq al-muslimīn wa 'l-mushrikīn*, ed. Muḥammad al-Mu'taṣim bi 'llah al-Baghdādī, Beirut, 1986
- *Al-Maḥṣūl fī 'ilm al-uṣūl*, Beirut, 1988
- *Muḥaṣṣal afkār al-mutaqaddimīn wa 'l-muta'akhkhirīn*, ed. Ṭāhā 'Abd al-Ra'ūf Sa'd, Beirut, 1984
- *Al-Shajara al-mubāraka fī ansāb al-ṭālibiyya*, ed. Mahdī al-Rajā'ī, Qum, 1409/1989

FARQ = 'Abd al-Qāhir al-Baghdādī, *al-Farq bayn al-firaq*

FRIEDLAENDER, Israel:
"The Heterodoxies of the Shī'ites in the Presentation of Ibn Ḥazm," in *Journal of the American Oriental Society*, 29 (1908): 1-183

GHAYBA = Ṭūsī, *Kitāb al-Ghayba*

GHAZĀWĪ, Yaḥya Mukhtār:
Faṣl al-kalām fī dhamm 'ilm al-kalām, Beirut, 1983 (together with Ibn Rajab's *Faḍl 'ilm al-salaf 'alā 'ilm al-khalaf*, pp. 85-102)

GOLDZIHER, Ignaz:
Introduction to Islamic Theology and Law, trans. Andras and Ruth Hamori, Princeton, 1981

ḤĀ'IRĪ = 'Abd al-Karīm b. Muḥammad Ja'far al-Yazdī (d. 1355/1937):
Durar al-fawā'id, Qum, 1408/1988

---

relevant section of the work is edited by Muḥammad Taqī Dānish-Pazhūh in *Nashriyya-yi dānishkada-yi adabiyyāt-i tabrīz*, 18 (1345sh/1966): 217–20.

HALM, Heinz:
- "Das Buch der Schatten," in *Der Islam*, 55 (1978): 219-60
- *Die Islamische Gnosis*, Zürich and München, 1982
- *Die Schia*, Darmstadt, 1988

ḤĀKIM = Abū 'Abd Allāh Muḥammad b. 'Abd Allāh al-Naysābūrī (d. 405/1014-15):
Al-Mustadrak 'ala 'l-ṣaḥīḥayn, Hyderabad, 1340/1921-22

ḤASAN B. MUḤAMMAD B. AL-ḤANAFIYYA (d. ca. 100/719):
Kitāb al-Irjā', ed. Joseph Van Ess, in *Arabica*, 21 (1974): 20-25

ḤASAN AL-QUMMĪ = Ḥasan b. Muḥammad b. al-Ḥasan al-Ash'arī al-Qummī (d. after 379/989-90):
Kitāb qum = *Ta'rīkh qum*, translated into Persian by Ḥasan b. 'Alī b. 'Abd al-Malik al-Qummī in 805-6/1402-4, ed. Jalāl al-Dīn Tihrānī, Tehran, 1313sh/1934-35

ḤASAN B. SAHL = Abū 'Alī Ḥasan b. Sahl b. al-Samḥ b. Ghālib (d. 418/1027):
Risāla fī awṣāf al-akhbār allatī yukhbiru bi-hā kathīrūn, ed. Marie Bernard-Baladi, in *Royale Asiatique* (Paris), 257 (1969): 95-138, and ed. Muḥammad Taqī Dānish-Pazhūh, in *Maqālāt wa barrasīhā* (Tehran), 3-4 (1349 sh/1970-71): 239-57

ḤASAN B. SULAYMĀN = 'Izz al-Dīn Abū Muḥammad Ḥasan b. Sulaymān b. Muḥammad al-Ḥillī (early 9th/15th century):
Mukhtaṣar baṣā'ir al-darajāt, Najaf, 1950

ḤASAN B. ZAYN AL-DĪN AL-'ĀMILĪ (d. 1011/1602):
Ma'ālim al-dīn, ed. Mahdī Muḥaqqiq, Tehran, 1983

HĀSHIM AL-BAḤRĀNĪ = Hāshim b. Sulaymān al-Ḥusaynī al-Katakānī (d. 1107/1695-6):
Al-Inṣāf fi 'l-naṣṣ 'ala 'l-a'imma al-ithnā'ashar min āl muḥammad al-ashrāf, ed. Hāshim al-Rasūlī, Qum, 1386/1966-7

HAYTAMĪ = Aḥmad b. Muḥammad b. 'Alī al-Tamīmī al-Makkī (d. 974/1566-7):
Al-Qawl al-mukhtaṣar fī 'alāmāt al-mahdī al-muntaẓar, ed. Muḥammad 'Azab, Cairo, 1986

ḤIBSHĪ, 'Abd Allāh Muḥammad:
Mu'allafāt ḥukkām al-yaman, ed. Elke Niewohner-Eberkard, Wiesbaden, 1979

ḤIMMAṢĪ = Sadīd al-Dīn Maḥmūd b. ʿAlī al-Ḥimmaṣī al-Rāzī (d. after 583/1187):
Al-Munqidh min al-taqlīd wa 'l-murshid ila 'l-tawḥīd, MS 6744, Central Library, University of Tehran[3]

ḤIMYARĪ - Abu 'l-ʿAbbās ʿAbd Allāh b. Jaʿfar al-Ḥimyarī al-Qummī (d. after 297/910):
Qurb al-isnād, Tehran, n.d.

ḤURR AL-ʿĀMILĪ = Muḥammad b. al-Ḥasan al-Mashgharī (d. 1104/1693):
– *Amal al-āmil*, ed. Aḥmad al-Ḥusaynī, Najaf, 1965
– * *Wasāʾil al-shīʿa*, ed. ʿAbd al-Raḥīm al-Rabbānī al-Shīrāzī and Muḥammad al-Rāzī, Tehran, 1376-89/1956-69

HUSAMEDDIN, Aḥmad b. Saʿīd al-Rukālī (d. 1343/1925):
Kur'anin 20. asra göre anlami., vol. 1: *Fatiha ve Amme cüzü okunuşu tercümesi ve açiklamasi*, ed. M. Kāẓim Ozturk, Izmir, 1974 (*Seyyid Ahmed Husameddin Kulliyatindan*: 4)

ḤUSAYN B. ʿABD AL-WAHHĀB (d. after 448/1056):
ʿUyūn al-muʿjizāt, Najaf, 1369/1949-50

IBN ʿABD AL-BARR = Abū ʿUmar Yūsuf b. ʿAbd Allāh al-Namrī al-Qurṭubī (d. 463/1070-71):
Jāmiʿ bayān al-ʿilm wa faḍlih, Cairo, 1975

IBN ʿABD RABBIH = Aḥmad b. Muḥammad b. ʿAbd Rabbih al-Qurṭubī (d. 328/939-40):
Al-ʿIqd al-farīd, ed. Aḥmad Amīn et al., Cairo, 1940-

IBN ABI 'L-ḤADID = ʿIzz al-Dīn ʿAbd al-Ḥamid b. Hibat Allāh al-Madāʾinī (d. 655/1257):
Sharḥ nahj al-balāgha, ed. Muḥammad Abu 'l-Faḍl Ibrāhīm, Cairo, 1959-64

IBN ABĪ SHAYBA = Abū Bakr ʿAbd Allāh b. Muḥammad b. Ibrāhīm al-Kūfī (d. 235/849):
Al-Muṣannaf, ed. Saʿīd al-Laḥḥām, Beirut, 1989

IBN ABI 'L-THALJ = Abū Bakr Muḥammad b. Aḥmad b. Muḥammad b. ʿAbd Allāh b. Ismāʿīl al-Kātib al-Baghdādī (d. 325/936-7):
Taʾrīkh al-aʾimma, ed. Muḥammad Riḍā al-Ḥusaynī, Qum, 1410/1989 (as *Taʾrīkh ahl al-bayt naqlan ʿan al-aʾimma*)

3. The first half of this work has just been published in a volume (Qum, 1991).

IBN 'ASĀKIR = Abu 'l-Qāsim 'Alī b. al-Ḥasan b. Hibat Allāh al-Dimashqī (d. 573/1177-8):
- *Tabyīn kidhb al-muftarī fī maa nasab ila 'l-imām abi 'l-ḥasan al-ash'arī*, Damascus, 1347/1928-29
- *Ta'rīkh madīnat dimashq*, the section on the biography of 'Uthmān, ed. Sukayna al-Shihābī, Damascus, 1984

IBN AL-ATHĪR = 'Izz al-Dīn 'Alī b. Muḥammad b. 'Abd al-Karīm al-Jazarī al-Shaybānī (d. 630/1232-33):
Al-Kāmil fi 'l-t'arīkh, Beirut, 1965-67

IBN 'AYYĀSH = Abū 'Abd Allāh Aḥmad b. Muḥammad b. 'Ubayd Allāh al-Jawharī al-Baghdādī (d. 401/1010-11):
Muqtaḍab al-athar fi 'l-naṣṣ 'ala 'l-a'imma al-ithnā'ashar, ed. Hāshim al-Rasūlī, Qum, 1379/1960

IBN BĀBAWAYH = Abū Ja'far Muḥammad b. 'Alī b. al-Ḥusayn al-Qummī, al-Ṣadūq (d. 381/991-2):
- *Faqīh = Man lā yaḥḍuruh al-faqīh*, ed. 'Alī Akbar al-Ghaffārī, Tehran, 1392-4/1972-75
- *I'tiqādāt = Risāla fi 'l-i'tiqādāt*, Tehran, 1370/1951 (together with Miqdād al-Suyūrī's *al-Nāfi' yawm al-ḥashr fī sharḥ al-bāb al-ḥādī'ashr*, pp. 66-115)
- *Kamāl*[4] *al-dīn wa tamām al-ni'ma fī ithbāt al-ghayba wa kashf al-ḥayra*, ed. 'Alī Akbar al-Ghaffārī, Tehran, 1390/1970-71
- *Al-Khiṣāl*, ed. 'Alī Akbar al-Ghaffārī, Tehran, 1389/1969-70
- *Ma'ānī al-akhbār*, ed. 'Alī Akbar al-Ghaffārī, Tehran, 1379/1959
- *Al-Tawḥīd*, ed. Hāshim al-Ḥusaynī al-Tihrānī, Tehran, 1387/1967
- *'Uyūn akhbār al-riḍā*, ed. Mahdī al-Ḥusaynī al-Lājawardī, Qum, 1377-9/1958-59

IBN BAṬṬA = Abū 'Abd Allāh 'Ubayd Allāh b. Muḥammad b. Muḥammad b. Ḥamdān b. Baṭṭa al- 'Ukbarī (d. 387/997):
Al-Sharḥ wa 'l-ibāna 'alā uṣūl al-sunna wa 'l-diyāna, ed. Henri Laoust, Damascus, 1958 (as *La Profession de foi d'Ibn Battah*)

IBN DURAYD = Abū Bakr Muḥammad b. al-Ḥasan al-Azdī al-Baṣrī (d. 321/933):
Jamharat al-lugha, ed. Ramzī Munīr al-Ba'lbakī, Beirut, 1987

4. This is the correct form of the title of this work, not *Ikmāl* as appears in some manuscripts. See the author's *Khiṣāl:* 187 and *'Uyūn akhbār al-riḍā,* 1:54, 69.

IBN AL-GHAḌĀ'IRĪ = Abu 'l-Ḥusayn Aḥmad b. 'Ubayd Allāh al-Ghaḍā'irī (early 5th/11th century):
Kitāb al-Ḍu'afā', included in 'Ināyat Allāh b. 'Alī al-Quhpā'ī's *Majma' al-rijāl*, ed. Ḍiyā' al-Dīn al-'Allāma, Iṣfahān, 1384-7/1964-68

IBN ḤAJAR = Shihāb al-Dīn Abu 'l-Faḍl Aḥmad b. 'Alī al-'Asqalānī (d. 852/1449):
Lisān al-mīzān, Hyderabad, 1330-31/1912-13
Tahdhīb al-tahdhīb, Hyderabad, 1325-7/1907-9

IBN ḤAZM = Abū Muḥammad 'Alī b. Ahmad b. Sa'īd al-Qurṭubī al-Ẓāhirī (d. 456/1064):
– * *Al-Fiṣal fi 'l-milal wa 'l-ahwā' wa 'l-niḥal*, ed. Muḥammad Ibrāhīm Naṣr and 'Abd al-Raḥmān 'Umayra, Riyadh, 1982
– *Jamharat ansāb al-'arab*, ed. E. Lévi-Provençal, Cairo, 1948

IBN HISHĀM = Abū Muḥammad 'Abd al-Malik b. Hishām b. Ayyūb al-Ḥimyarī al-Miṣrī (d. 218/833):
Al-Sīra al-nabawiyya, ed. Muṣṭafā al-Saqqā' et al., Cairo, 1936

IBN IDRĪS = Abū 'Abd Allāh Muḥammad b. Manṣūr b. Aḥmad b. Idrīs al-'Ijlī al-Ḥillī (d. 598/1202):
Al-Sarā'ir al-ḥāwī li-taḥrīr al-fatāwī, Qum, 1410-12/1990-91

IBN 'INABA = Jamāl al-Dīn Aḥmad b. 'Alī b. al-Ḥusayn al-Ḥasanī al-Dāwūdī (d. 828/1425):
– *Al-Fuṣūl al-fakhriyya*, ed. Jalāl al-Dīn Muḥaddith Urmawī, Tehran, 1387/1968
– * *'Umdat al-ṭālib fī ansāb āl abī ṭālib*, ed. Muḥammad Ḥasan Āl al-Ṭāliqānī, Najaf, 1961

IBN AL-ISKĀFĪ = Abu 'l-Qāsim Ja'far b. Muḥammad b. 'Abd Allāh (mid 3d/9th century):
Al-Mi'yār wa 'l-muwāzana fi 'l-imāma, ed. Muḥammad Bāqir al-Maḥmūdī, Beirut, 1981 (misattributed to the author's father, Abū Ja'far Muḥammad b. 'Abd Allāh al-Iskāfī [d. 220/835]).

IBN AL-JAWZĪ = Abu 'l-Faraj 'Abd al-Raḥmān b. 'Alī al-Qurashī al-Baghdādī (d. 597/1201):
– *Manāqib 'Umar b. al-khaṭṭāb*, ed. Zaynab Ibrāhīm al-Qārūt, Beirut, 1980
– *Al-Muntaẓam fī ta'rīkh al-mulūk wa 'l-umam*, ed. Muḥammad 'Abd al-Qādir 'Aṭā et al., Beirut, 1992
– *Talbīs iblīs*, Cairo, 1368/1948-49

IBN KHALLIKĀN = Abu 'l-'Abbās Aḥmad b. Muḥammad b. Ibrāhīm al-Barmakī al-Irbilī (d. 681/1282):
Wafayāt al-a'yān, ed. Iḥsān 'Abbās, Beirut, 1968-77

IBN AL-KHASHSHĀB = Abū Muḥammad 'Abd Allāh b. Aḥmad al-Baghdādī (d. 567-8/1171-73):
Ta'rīkh mawālīd al-a'imma wa wafayātihim, Qum, 1406/1985-86 (in the collection of *Majmū'a nafīsa fī ta'rikh al-a'imma*: 158-202)

IBN MANẒŪR = Abu 'l-Faḍl Muḥammad b. Mukarram al-Anṣārī al-Miṣrī (d. 711/1311-12):
Lisān al-'arab, Beirut, 1376/1956-57

IBN MAYTHAM = Kamāl al-Dīn Maytham b. 'Alī b. Maytham al-Baḥrānī (d. 699/1299-1300):
– *Qawā'id al-marām*, ed. Aḥmad al-Ḥusaynī, Qum, 1398/1978
– * *Sharḥ nahj al-balāgha*, Tehran, 1378-84/1958-65

IBN AL-MUṬAHHAR = Jamāl al-Dīn Ḥasan b. Yūsuf b. al-Muṭahhar al-Ḥillī, al-'Allāma (d. 726/1325):
– *Īḍāḥ al-ishtibāh*, ed. Muḥammad al-Ḥassūn, Qum, 1411/1991
– *Khulāṣat al-aqwāl = Rijāl al-'allāma al-ḥillī*, Najaf, 1961
– *Al-Mustajād min kitāb al-irshād*, Qum, 1406/1985-86 (in the collection of *Majmū'a nafīsa fī ta'rīkh al-a'imma*: 292-558)
– *Tadhkirat al-fuqahā'*, Tehran, 1272/1856

IBN AL-NADĪM = Abu 'l-Faraj Muḥammad b. Isḥāq al-Warrāq al-Baghdādī (late 4th/10th century):
Kitāb al-Fihrist, ed. Riḍā Tajaddud, Tehran [1971]

IBN QIBA = Abū Ja'far Muḥammad b. 'Abd al-Raḥmān b. Qiba al-Rāzī (d. before 319/931):
– *Mas'ala fi 'l-imāma*, chapter 5 of the present work
– *Al-Naqḍ 'alā abi 'l-ḥasan 'alī b. aḥmad b. bashshār fi 'l-ghayba*, chapter 6 of the present work
– *Naqḍ kitāb al-ishhād*, chapter 7 of the present work

IBN QUDĀMA = Muwaffaq al-Dīn 'Abd Allāh b. Aḥmad al-Maqdisī (d. 620/1223-4):
Dhamm al-ta'wīl, Cairo, 1351/1932-33

IBN QŪLAWAYH = Abu 'l-Qāsim Ja'far b. Muḥammad b. Qūlawayh al-Qummī (d. 369/979-80):
Kāmil al-ziyārāt, ed. 'Abd al-Ḥusayn al-Amīnī, Najaf, 1356/1937-38

IBN QUTAYBA = Abū Muḥammad 'Abd Allāh b. Muslim al-Dīnawarī al-Marwazī (d. 276/889):
- *Al-Ma'ārif*, ed. Tharwat 'Ukāsha, Cairo, 1960
- *'Uyūn al-akhbār*, ed. Yūsuf 'Alī Ṭawīl, Beirut, 1986

IBN AL-RĀWANDĪ = Abu 'l-Ḥusayn Aḥmad b. Yaḥyā b. Isḥaq (3d/9th century):
Faḍīḥat al-mu'tazila, ed. 'Abd al-Amīr al-A'sam, Beirut, 1975-77

IBN SA'D = Abū 'Abd Allāh Muḥammad b. Sa'd Kātib al-Wāqidī: (d. 230/844-5):
Kitāb al-Ṭabaqāt al-kabīr, ed. E. Sachau et al, Leiden, 1904-15

IBN SHADQAM = 'Alī b. al-Ḥasan al-Ḥusaynī al-Madanī (d. 1033/1623-4):
Ẓahrat al-maqūl fī nasab thānī far'ay al-rasūl, Najaf, 1961

IBN SHAHRĀSHŪB = Rashīd al-Dīn Muḥammad b. 'Alī al-Sarawī (d. 588/1192):
- *Ma'ālim al-'ulamā'*, ed. Muḥammad Ṣādiq Āl Baḥr al-'Ulūm, Najaf, 1961
- *Manāqib āl abī ṭālib*, Qum, 1378/1958-59
- *Mutashābih al-qur'ān wa mukhtalifuh*, ed. Ḥasan al-Muṣṭafawī, Tehran, 1369/1949-50

IBN SHU'BA = Abū Muḥammad Ḥasan b. 'Alī al-Ḥarrānī (4th/10th century)
Tuḥaf al-'uquḷ 'an āl al-rasūl, Beirut, 1974

IBN TAGHRĪBIRDĪ = Jamāl al-Dīn Abu 'l-Maḥāsin Yūsuf b. Taghrībirdī b. 'Abd Allāh al-Atābakī (d. 874/1470):
Al-Nujūm al-Ẓāhira, the edition of Dār al-Kutub, Cairo, 1963-72

IBN ṬALḤA = Kamāl al-Dīn Muḥammad b. Ṭalḥa al-'Adwī al-Qurashī al-Naṣībī (d. 652/1254-45):
Maṭālib al-su'ūl fī manāqib āl al-rasūl, Tehran, 1285-7/1868-70

IBN ṬĀWŪS = Raḍī al-Dīn Abu 'l-Qāsim 'Alī b. Mūsā al-Ḥasanī al-Ḥusaynī al-Ḥillī (d. 664/1265-66):
- *Falāḥ al-sā'il*, Najaf, 1965
- *Muhaj al-da'awāt*, Tabrīz, 1323/1905
- *Sa'd al-su'ūd*, Najaf, 1369/1949-50

IBN TAYMIYYA = Taqī al-Dīn Abu 'l-'Abbās Aḥmad b. 'Abd al-Ḥalīm al-Ḥarrānī (d. 728/1327-28):
- *Al-'Aqīda al-ḥamawiyya al-kubrā*, Cairo, 1966 (in a collection of his treatises called *Majmū'at al-rasā'il al-kubrā*, 1:423-78)
- *Al-Istiqāma*, ed. Muḥammad Rashād Sālim, Riyadh, 1983
- *Minhāj al-sunna*, ed. Muḥammad Rashād Sālim, Cairo, 1962

IBN ZUHRA = Tāj al-Dīn b. Muḥammad b. Ḥamza b. Zuhra al-Ḥusaynī al-Ḥalabī (8th/14th century):
Ghāyat al-ikhtiṣār fī 'l-buyūtāt al-'alawiyya al-maḥfūẓa min al-ghibār, ed. Muḥammad Ṣādiq Baḥr al-'Ulūm, Najaf, 1963

'IMĀD AL-DĪN AL-ṬŪSĪ = Abū Ja'far Muḥammad b. 'Alī b. Ḥamza al-Ṭūsī (d. after 566/1171):
Al-Thāqib fī 'l-manāqib, ed. Nabīl Riḍā 'Alwān, Beirut, 1991

IQBĀL, 'Abbās:
Khāndān-i nawbakhtī, Tehran, 1311sh/1932-33

IRBILĪ = Bahā' al-Dīn 'Alī b. 'Īsā b. Abi 'l-Fatḥ (d. 692/1293):
Kashf al-ghumma fī ma'rifat al-a'imma, Qum, 1381/1961-62

ISFARĀ'ĪNĪ = 'Imād al-Dīn Abu 'l-Muẓaffar Shāhfūr b. Ṭāhir b. Muḥammad (d. 471/1078-79):
Al-Tabṣīr fī 'l-dīn, ed. Kamāl Yūsuf al-Ḥūt, Beirut, 1983

JĀḤIẒ = Abū 'Uthmān 'Amr b. Baḥr b. Maḥbūb al-Kinānī al-Baṣrī (d. 255/869):
- *Al-Bayān wa 'l-tabyīn*, ed. 'Abd al-Salām Muḥammad Hārūn, Cairo, 1968
- *Al-'Uthmāniyya*, ed. 'Abd al-Salām Muḥammad Hārūn, Cairo, 1955

JĀMI' AḤĀDĪTH AL-SHĪ'A, ed. Ismā'īl al-Mu'izzī al-Malāyirī, vol. 1, 2d edition, Qum, 1399/1979

JISHUMĪ = Abū Sa'd Muḥassan b. Muḥammad b. Kirāma al-Bayhaqī, al-Ḥākim (d. 494/1101):
- *Jalā' al-abṣār* = a section quoted by Aḥmad b. Sa'd al-Dīn al-Miswarī in his *Tuḥfat al-abrār*, ed. Wilferd Madelung, Beirut, 1987 (in *akhbār a'immat al-zaydiyya fī ṭabaristān wa daylamān wa jīlān*, pp. 119-33)
- *Risālat iblīs ilā ikhwānih al-manāḥīs*, ed. Hossein Modarressi, Qum, 1986

JUWAYNĪ = Abu 'l-Ma'ālī 'Abd al-Malik b. 'Abd Allāh b. Yūsuf, Imām al-Ḥaramayn (d. 478/1085):
Al-Irshād, ed. Muḥammad Yūsuf Mūsā and 'Alī 'Abd al-Mun'im 'Abd al-Ḥamīd, Cairo, 1950

KAMĀL = Ibn Bābawayh, *Kamāl al-dīn*

KAMMŪNA = 'Abd al-Razzāq Kammūna al-Ḥusaynī:
Mawārid al-itḥāf fī nuqabā' al-ashrāf, Najaf, 1968

KĀSHIF AL-GHIṬĀ' = Ja'far b. Khiḍr al-Janājī al-Najafī (d. 1228/1813):
'Kāshf al-ghiṭā' 'an mubhamāt al-sharī'a al-gharrā', Tehran, 1271/1854-55

KASHSHĪ = Abū 'Amr Muḥammad b. 'Umar b. 'Abd al-'Azīz (early 4th/10th century):
Kitāb ma'rifat al-nāqilīn = *Rijāl al-kashshī*, abridged by Muḥammad b. al-Ḥasan al-Ṭūsī as *Ikhtiyār ma'rifat al-rijāl*, ed. Ḥasan al-Muṣṭafawī, Mashhad, 1348sh/1970

KHALĪFA B. KHAYYĀṬ al-'Uṣfurī al-Baṣrī (d. 240/854-5):
Ta'rīkh khalīfa b. khayyāṭ, ed. Suhayl Zakkār, Damascus, 1968

KHAṬĪB = Abū Bakr Aḥmad b. 'Alī b. Thābit al-Baghdādī (d. 463/1072):
– *Sharaf aṣḥāb al-ḥadīth*, ed. Mehmed Said Hatiboqlu, Ankara, 1972
Talkhīṣ al-mutashābih fi 'l-rasm, ed. Sukayna al-Shīhābī, Beirut, 1985
**Ta'rīkh baghdād*, Cairo, 1931

KHAYYĀṬ = Abu 'l-Ḥusayn 'Abd al-Raḥīm b. Muḥammad b. 'Uthmān al-Baghdādī (late 3d/9th century):
Al-Intiṣār, ed. H.S. Nyberg, Cairo, 1925

KHAZZĀZ = Abu 'l-Qāsim 'Alī b. Muḥammad b. 'Alī al-Qummī al-Rāzī (early 5th/11th century):
Kifāyat al-athar fi 'l-naṣṣ 'ala 'l-a'imma al-ithnā'ashar, Tehran, 1305/1888 (together with Majlisī's *Kitāb al-Arba'īn*: 288-328)

KHU'Ī = Abu 'l-Qāsim b. 'Alī Akbar al-Mūsawī (d. 1413/1992):
Mu'jam rijāl al-ḥadīth, Beirut, 1983

KHUMAYNĪ = Rūḥ Allāh b. Muṣṭafā al-Mūsawī (d. 1410/1989):
Tahdhīb al-uṣūl, his lectures collected by Ja'far al-Subḥānī, Qum, 1375-82/1955-63

KHUṢAYBĪ = Abū ʿAbd Allāh Ḥusayn b. Ḥamdān al-Junbulāʾī (d. 346/958 or 358/969):
Al-Hidāya al-Kubrā, Beirut, 1986

KHWĀNSĀRĪ = Muḥammad Bāqir b. Zayn al-ʿĀbidīn al-Mūsawī al-Iṣfahānī (d. 1313/1895):
Rawḍāt al-jannāt fī aḥwāl al-ʿulamāʾ wa ʾl-sādāt, ed. Muḥammad Taqī al-Kashfī and Asad Allāh Ismāʿīliyān, Tehran and Qum, 1390-92/1970-72

KOHLBERG, Etan:
– "From Imāmiyya to Ithnāʿashariyya," in *Bulletin of the School of Orinetal and African Studies*, 39(1976): 521-34
– "Imām and Community in the Pre-Ghayba Period," in Said Amir Arjomand (ed.), *Authority and Political Culture in Shīʿism*, Albany, NY, 1988: 25-53
– "The Term Rāfiḍa in Imāmī Shīʿī Usage," in *Journal of the American Oriental Society*, 99 (1979): 39-47

KULAYNĪ = Abū Jaʿfar Muḥammad b. Yaʿqūb b. Isḥāq al-Rāzī (d. 329/941):
Al-Kāfī, ed. ʿAlī Akbar al-Ghaffārī, Tehran, 1377-9/1957-60

MAʿĀLIM = Ibn Shahrāshūb, *Maʿālim al-ʿulamāʾ*

MADELUNG, Wilferd:
– "Bemerkungen zur imāmitschen Firaq Literatur," in *Der Islam*, 43 (1967): 37-52
– *Der Imām al-Qāsim b. Ibrāhīm und die Glaubenslehre der Zaiditen*, Berlin, 1965
– "Imāmism and Muʿtazilite Theology," in Tawfiq Fahd (ed.), *Le Shīʿisme imāmate*, Paris, 1979: 13-29
– "Some Notes on Non-Ismāʿīlī Shīʿism in the Maghrib," in *Studia Islamica*, 44 (1977): 87-97
– "The Shīʿite and Khārijite Contribution to Pre-Ashʿarite Kalām," in Parviz Morewedge (ed.), *Islamic Philosophical Theology*, Albany, NY, 1979: 120-39

MAḤFŪẒ, Ḥusayn ʿAlī:
The biography of Kulaynī, published in the beginning of the first volume of the most recent edition of his *Kitāb al-Kāfī* (ed. ʿAlī Akbar al-Ghaffārī, Tehran, 1377/1957)

MAJD AL-DĪN B. AL-ATHĪR = Abu 'l-Sa'ādāt Mubārak b. Muḥammad b. 'Abd al-Karīm al-Jazarī al-Shaybānī (d. 606/1209-10):
al-Nihāya fī gharīb al-ḥadīth, Cairo, 1311/1893-94

MAJLIS LIBRARY, Tehran:
Catalogue: *Fihrist-i kitābkhāna-yi majlis-i shūrāy-i millī*, by 'Abd al-Ḥusayn Ḥā'irī et al., Tehran, 1305/1887

MAJLISĪ I = Muḥammad Taqī b. Maqṣūd 'Alī al-Iṣfahānī (d. 1070/1659-60):
Lawāmi'-i ṣāḥibqarānī, Tehran, 1331/1912-13

MAJLISĪ = Muḥammad Bāqir b. Muḥammad Taqī al-Iṣfahānī (d. 1110/1699):
Biḥār al-anwār, Tehran, 1376-90/1956-70

MALAṬĪ = Abu 'l-Ḥusayn Muḥammad b. Aḥmad b. 'Abd al-Raḥmān al-Ṭarā'ifī al-'Asqalānī (d. 377/987-8):
Al-Tanbīh wa 'l-radd 'alā ahl al-ahwā' wa 'l-bida', ed. Muḥammad Zāhid al-Kawtharī, Damascus, 1949

MANĀQIB = Ibn Shahrāshūb, *Manāqib āl abī ṭālib*

MAQDISĪ = Muṭahhar b. Ṭāhir (d. after 355/966):
al-Bad' wa 'l-ta'rīkh, ed. Clement Huart, Paris, 1899-1919

MAQRĪZĪ = Taqī al-Dīn Aḥmad b. 'Alī (d. 845/1441-2):
Al-Khiṭaṭ = al-Mawā'iẓ wa 'l-i'tibār bi-dhikr al-khiṭaṭ wa 'l-āthār, Cairo, 1853-54

MARWAZĪ = 'Izz al-Dīn Ismā'īl b. al-Ḥusayn b. Muḥammad al-Ḥusaynī (d. after 614/1217):
Al-Fakhrī fī ansāb al-ṭālibiyyīn, ed. Mahdī al-Rajā'ī, Qum, 1409/1988-89

MAS'ŪDĪ = Abu 'l-Ḥasan 'Alī b. al-Ḥusayn al-Hudhalī al-Baghdādī (d. 346/957-8):
– *Murūj al-dhahab wa ma'ādin al-jawhar*, ed. Charles Pellat, Beirut, 1965-74
– *Al-Tanbīh wa 'l-ishrāf*, ed. Michael Jan de Goeje, Leiden, 1894

MODARRESSI, Hossein:
An Introduction to Shī'ī Law, London, 1984

MUBARRAD = Abu 'l-'Abbās Muḥammad b. Yazīd al-Thumālī al-Azdī al-Baṣrī (d. 286/899):
- *Al-Kāmil*, ed. Muḥammad Abu 'l-Faḍl Ibrāhīm and al-Sayyid Shahāta, Cairo, 1956
- *Kitāb al-Ta'āzī wa l-marāthī*, ed. Muḥammad al-Dībāji, Damascus, 1976

MUDARRIS TABRĪZĪ = Muḥammad 'Alī b. Muḥammad Ṭāhir Khiyābānī (d. 1373/1954):
Rayḥānat al-adab, Tehran, 1328-33sh/1949-54

MUFĪD = Abū 'Abd Allāh Muḥammad b. Muḥammad b. al-Nu'mān al-'Ukbarī al-Baghdādī, Ibn al-Mu'allim (d. 413/1022):
- *Awā'il al-maqālāt fi 'l-madhāhib al-mukhtārāt*, ed. 'Abbās Qulī Wā'iẓ Charandābī, Tabrīz, 1371/1951-52
- *Al-Fuṣūl al-'ashara fi 'l-ghayba*, Qum, n.d. (in the collection of *'iddat rasā'il li 'l-shaykh al-mufīd*: 345-82)
- *Al-Irshād*, Najaf, 1382/1962-63
- *Al-Majālis = Al-Fuṣūl al-mukhtāra min al-'uyūn wa 'l-maḥāsin*, Najaf, n.d.
- *Al-Masā'il al-sarawiyya*, Qum, n.d. (in the above mentioned collection: 207-32)
- *Masārr al-shī'a*, Qum, 1406/1985-6 (in the collection of *Majmū'a nafīsa fī ta'rīkh al-a'imma:* 38-76)
- *Al-Risāla al-khāmisa fi 'l-ghayba*, Qum, n.d. (in the collection of *'iddat rasā'il li 'l-shaykh al-mufīd:* 399-402)
- *Risāla fi bayān al-sabab al-mūjib li-istitār imām al-zamān wa ghaybatih*, Qum, n.d. (in the above-mentioned collection: 395-8 as *al-Risāla al-rābi'a fi 'l-ghayba*)
- *Risāla fī annahu law ijtama'a 'ala 'l-imām 'iddat ahl badr thalāthami'a wa biḍ'at'ashar rajulan lawajab 'alayh al-khurūj*, Qum, n.d. (in the above-mentioned collection: 390-4 as *al-Risāla al-thālitha fi 'l-ghayba*)
- *Al-Tadhkira bi-uṣūl al-fiqh*, Tabrīz, 1322/1904-5 (in Muḥammad b. 'Uthmān al-Karājikī's *Kanz al-fawā'id:* 186-94)
- *Taṣḥīḥ al-i'tiqād = Sharḥ 'aqā'id al-ṣadūq*, ed. 'Abbās Qulī Wā'iẓ Charandābī, Tabrīz, 1371/1951-52 (together with *Awā'il al-maqālāt*)

MUḤAMMAD ḤASAN AL-NAJAFĪ (d. 1266/1850):
Jawāhir al-kalām fī sharḥ sharā'i' al-islām, ed. 'Abbās al-Qūchānī et al., Najaf, Qum, Tehran, 1377/1957-

MUḤAMMAD ḤUSAYN AL-IṢFAHĀNĪ = Muḥammad Ḥusayn b. Muḥammad Raḥīm al-Gharawī (d. 1250-54/1834-39):
Al-Fuṣūl fi 'l-uṣūl, Tehran, 1266/1849-50

MUḤAMMAD MU'MIN (B. MUḤAMMAD HĀSHIM) AL-ḤUSAYNĪ (mid 12th/18th century):
Risāla fī istiḥbāb al-shahāda bi-wilāyat 'alī b. abī ṭālib fi 'l-adhān wa 'l-iqāma, MS 2603/3, Central Library, University of Tehran (described in its catalogue, 9:1457)

MUḤAMMAD B. AL-MUTHANNĀ AL-HAḌRAMĪ (late 2d/8th century):
Kitāb muḥammad b. al-muthannā b. al-qāsim al-haḍramī, Tehran, 1371/1951-2 (in the collection of *al-Uṣūl al-sittat'ashar*: 83-93)

MUḤAMMAD NAṢIR B. MUḤAMMAD MA'ṢŪM:
Kanz al-shī'a, MS 2517, Mar'ashī Library, Qum (described in its catalogue, 7:102-103)

MUḤAMMAD B. AL-QĀSIM AL-ASTARĀBĀDĪ, al-Mufassir (early 4th/10th century)
Kitāb al-Tafsīr = al-Tafsīr al-mansūb ila 'l-imām al-ḥasan al-'askarī, Qum, 1409/1988-89

MUḤAMMAD TAQĪ AL-TUSTARĪ:
– *Al-Akhbār al-dakhīla, 1390/1970-71*
– * *Qāmūs al-rijāl*, 2d edition, Qum, 1410/1989–
– *Risāla fī tawārīkh al-nabī wa 'l-āl*, Tehran, 1391/1971 (with the author's *Qāmūs al-rijāl*, vol. 11)

AL-MUḤAQQIQ AL-ḤILLĪ = Najm al-Dīn Abu 'l-Qāsim Ja'far b. al-Ḥasan b. Sa'īd al-Ḥillī (d. 676/1277):
– *Ma'ārij al-wuṣūl ilā 'ilm al-uṣūl*, ed. Muḥammad Ḥusayn al-Raḍawī, Qum, 1403/1983
– *Al-Mu'tabar fī sharḥ al-mukhtaṣar*, Qum, 1364sh/1985

MUḤSIN AL-AMĪN al-'Āmilī (d. 1373/1952):
A'yān al-shī'a, ed. Ḥasan al-Amin, Beirut, 1986

MUḤSIN AL-ḤAKIM = Muḥsin b. Mahdī al-Ṭabāṭabā'ī (d. 1391/1971):
Mustamasak al-'urwa al-wuthqā, Najaf, 1391/1971-

MUNTAJAB AL-DĪN = 'Alī b. 'Ubayd Allāh b. Bābawayh al-Rāzī (d. after 600/1203):
Fihrist asmā' 'ulamā' al-shī'a wa muṣannifīhim, ed. 'Abd al-'Azīz al-Ṭabāṭabā'ī, Qum, 1404/1984

MURTAḌĀ = Abu 'l-Qāsim 'Alī b. al-Ḥusayn al-Mūsawī, 'Alam al-Hudā, al-Sharīf al-Murtaḍā (d. 436/1044):
- *Al-Dhakhīra fī 'ilm al-kalām*, ed. Aḥmad al-Ḥusaynī, Qum, 1411/1991
- *Al-Dharī'a ilā uṣūl al-sharī'a*, ed. Abu 'l-Qāsim Gurjī, Tehran, 1346-8sh/1967-69
- *Al-Intiṣār*, Najaf, 1971
- *Jawābāt al-masā'il al-mawṣiliyyāt al-thālitha*, Qum, 1405/1984-85 (in the collection of *Rasā'il al-sharīf al-murtaḍā*, 1:199-267
- *Jawābāt al-masā'il al-ṭarābulusiyyāt al-thāniya*, Qum, 1405/1984-85 (in the above-mentioned collection, 1:307-56, erroneously entitled as *Jawābāt al-masā'il al-ṭarābulusiyyāt al-thālitha*)
- *Mas'ala fi 'l-manāmāt*, Qum, 1405/1984-85 (in the above-mentioned collection, 2:5-14)
- *Mas'ala fī nafy al-ru'ya*, Qum, 1405/1984-85 (in the above-mentioned collection, 3:279-84)
- *Risāla fī ghaybat al-ḥujja*, Qum, 1405/1984-85 (in the above-mentioned collection, 2:291-8)
- *Risāla fī ibṭāl al-'amal bi-akhbār al-āḥād*, Qum, 1405/1984-85 (in the above-mentioned collection, 3:307-13)
- *Al-Shafī fi 'l-imāma*, ed. 'Abd al-Zahrā' al-Ḥusaynī al-Khaṭīb, Beirut, 1986
- *Tanzīh al-anbiyā'*, Najaf, 1352/1933-34

MURTAḌĀ AL-RĀZĪ = Jamāl al-Dīn Abū 'Abd Allāh Muḥammad b. al-Ḥusayn b. al-Ḥasan (6th/12th century)
Tabṣirat al-'awāmm, ed. 'Abbās Iqbāl, Tehran, 1313sh/1934

MUṢ'AB B. 'ABD ALLĀH AL-ZUBAYRĪ (d. 236/841):
Kitāb Nasab quraysh, ed. E. Lévi-Provençal, Cairo, 1953

MUSLIM = Abu 'l-Ḥusayn Muslim b. al-Ḥajjāj al-Qushayrī al-Naysābūrī (d. 261/875):
Al-Ṣaḥīḥ = *Ṣaḥīḥ muslim*, ed. Muḥammad Fu'ād 'Abd al-Bāqī, Cairo, 1955

NAHJ AL-BALĀGHA = al-Sharīf al-Raḍī, *Nahj al-balāgha*

NĀ'ĪNĪ = Muḥammad Ḥusayn b. 'Abd al-Raḥīm (d. 1355/1936):
Fawā'id al-uṣūl, his lectures collected by Muḥammad 'Alī al-Kāẓimī al-Khurāsānī, Qum, 1404-9/1984-88

NAJAFĀBĀDĪ, Ni'mat Allāh Ṣāliḥī:
Shahīd-i jāwīd, 12th edition, Tehran, 1361sh/1982

NAJĀSHĪ = Abu 'l-'Abbās Aḥmad b. 'Alī al-Asadī al-Kūfī (d. 450/1058-59):
Fihrist asmā' muṣannifī al-shī'a = Rijāl al-najāshī, ed. Mūsā al-Shubayrī al-Zanjānī, Qum, 1407/1986

NAMĀZĪ = 'Alī b. Muḥammad b. Ismā'īl al-Shāhrūdī (d. 1405/1985):
Mustadrak safīnat al-biḥār, Mashhad and Tehran [1972-]

NARĀQĪ = Aḥmad b. Muḥammad Mahdī b. Abī Dharr al-Kāshānī (d. 1245/1829):
Manāhij al-aḥkām, Tehran, n.d.

NĀSHI' = Abu 'l-'Abbās 'Abd Allāh b. Muḥammad al-Anbārī, al-Nāshi' al-Akbar (d. 293/905-6):
Masā'il al-imāma, ed. Joseph Van Ess, Beirut, 1971 (as *Frühe mu'tazilitsche Häresiographic*)

NASHSHĀR, 'Alī Sāmī and 'Iṣām al-Dīn Muḥammad 'Alī:
Firaq wa ṭabaqāt al-mu'tazila, Cairo, 1972

NASHWĀN = Nashwān b. Sa'īd al-Ḥimyarī (d. 573/1177-88):
Sharḥ risālat al-ḥūr al-'īn, ed. Kamāl Muṣṭafā, Cairo, 1948

NĀSIR KHUSRUW = Abū Mu'īn Nāṣir b. Khusruw b. Hārith al-'Alawī al-Qubādiyānī (d. 481/1088-89):
Dīwān-i ash'ār, ed. Naṣr Allāh Taqawī, Tehran, 1304-7sh/1925-89

AL-NĀṢIRĪ, Riyāḍ Muḥammad Ḥabīb:
Al-Wāqifiyya, dirāsa taḥlīliyya, Mashhad, 1409/1989

NAWBAKHTĪ = Abū Muḥammad Ḥasan b. Mūsā (late 3d/9th century):
Firaq al-shī'a, ed. Muḥammad Ṣādiq Baḥr al-'Ulūm, Najaf, 1969

NU'AYM B. ḤAMMĀD al-Marwazī (d. 228/842-3):
Kitāb al-Fitan, MS Or. 9449, British Library

NU'MĀNĪ = Abū 'Abd Allāh Muḥammad b. Ibrāhīm b. Ja'far al-Kātib, Ibn Abī Zaynab (mid 4th/10th century):
Kitāb al-Ghayba, ed. 'Alī Akbar al-Ghaffārī, Tehran, 1397/1977

NŪR ALLĀH AL-TUSTARĪ = Qāḍī Nūr Allāh b. 'Abd Allāh al-Ḥusaynī (d. 1019/1610-11):
- *Al-As'ila al-yūsufiyya*, MS 4513, Central Library, University of Tehran (described in its catalogue, 12:3463)
- *Iḥqāq al-ḥaqq wa izhāq al-bāṭil*, ed. Shihāb al-Dīn al-Ḥusaynī al-Mar'ashī al-Najafī, Tehran, 1376/1957-

PSEUDO MAS'ŪDĪ:
Ithbāt al-waṣiyya, Najaf, 1955

PSEUDO MUFAḌḌAL:
Kitāb al-Haft al-sharīf, ed. Muṣṭafā Ghālib, Beirut, 1964

PSEUDO MUFĪD:
Al-Ikhtiṣāṣ, with an introduction by Muḥammad Mahdī al-Kharsān, Najaf, 1971

PSEUDO QĀSIM B. IBRĀHĪM = Abū Muḥammad Qāsim b. Ibrāhīm b. Ismā'īl al-Ḥasanī al-Rassī (d. 246/860)]:
Al-Radd 'ala 'l-rawāfiḍ min aṣḥāb al-ghuluww,[5] MS 101 Glaser, Staatbibliothek, Berlin, folios 104a-110b

QĀḌĪ, Wadād:
– "The Development of the Term Ghulāt in Muslim Literature," in Albert Dietrich (ed.), *Akten des VII Kongresses für Arabistik und Islamwissenschaft*, Gottingen, 1976
– *Al-Kaysāniyya fi 'l-ta'rīkh wa 'l-adab*, Beirut, 1974

QĀḌĪ NU'MĀN = Abū Ḥanīfa Nu'mān b. Muḥammad al-Tamīmī al-Maghribī (d. 363/974):
Da'ā'im al-Islām, ed. Āṣif b. 'Alī Aṣghar Fayḍī, Cairo, 1951

QALAMDĀRĀN, Ḥaydar 'Alī:
Rāh-i nijāt az sharr-i ghulāt, Qum, [1974]

RĀGHIB = Abu 'l-Qāsim Ḥusayn b. Muḥammad al-Iṣfahānī (d. 402/1011-12):
Muqaddama fi 'l-tafsīr, ed. Ṣalāḥ al-Dīn al-Nāhī, Amman, 1986 (in a book entitled *al-Khawālid min ārā' al-rāghib al-Isfahānī*, pp. 79-131)

AL-RAWĀJINĪ = 'Abbād b. Ya'qūb al-Asadī al-Kūfī (d. 250/864):
Aṣl abī sa'īd 'abbād al-'uṣfurī, Tehran, 1371/1951-52 (in the collection of *al-Uṣūl al-sittat'ashar:* 14-19)

RĀWANDĪ = Quṭb al-Dīn Sa'īd b. Hibat Allāh (d. 573/1178):
Al-Kharā'ij wa 'l-jarā'iḥ, Qum, 1409/1989

RŪMLŪ, Ḥasan (d. ca. 985/1577-78):
Aḥsan al-tawārīkh, vol. 12, ed. C.N. Seddon, Calcutta, 1931

SABZAWĀRĪ = Muḥammad Bāqir b. Muḥammad Mu'min (d. 1090/1679):
Dhakhīrat al-ma'ād fī sharḥ al-irshād, Tehran, 1274/1857-58

5. For the identification of the real author of this work see Madelung, *Der Imām al-Qāsim b. Ibrāhīm*: 98–9.

SA'D B. 'ABD ALLĀH = Abu 'l-Qāsim Sa'd b. 'Abd Allāh b. Abī Khalaf al-Ash'arī al-Qummī (d. 299-301/911-14):
Kitāb al-Maqālāt wa 'l-firaq, ed. Muḥammad Jawād Mashkūr, Tehran, 1963

ṢAFFĀR = Abū Ja'far Muḥammad b. al-Ḥasan b. Farrukh al-Qummī (d. 290/902-3):
Baṣā'ir al-darajāt, ed. Muḥsin Kūchabāghī, Tabrīz, 1381/1961

ṢĀFĪ, Luṭf Allāh:
Muntakhab al-athar fi 'l-imām al-thānī'ashar, Tehran, 1373/1953

ṢĀḤIB B. 'ABBĀD = Abu 'l-Qāsim Ismā'īl b. 'Abbād al-Ṭāliqānī (d. 385/995):
Al-Kashf 'an manāhij aṣnāf al-khawārij, ed. Muḥammad Taqī Dānish-Pazhūh, Tabrīz, (in *Nashriyya-yi Dānishkada-yi Adabiyyāt-i Tabrīz*, 20: 145-50)

SAHMĪ = Abu 'l-Qāsim Ḥamza b. Yūsuf (d. 427/1036):
Ta'rīkh jurjān, Hyderabad, 1950

SAM'ĀNĪ = Abū Sa'd 'Abd al-Karīm b. Muḥammad b. Manṣūr al-Tamīmī al-Marwazī (d. 562/1166-67):
Al-Ansāb, ed. 'Abd al-Raḥmān b. Yaḥyā al-Mu'allamī al-Yamānī, Hyderabad, 1962-

SARAKHSĪ = Abū Bakr Muḥammad b. Aḥmad b. Sahl al-Ḥanafī (d. 483/1090-91):
– *Sharḥ al-siyar al-kabīr*, Hyderabad, 1335/1916-17
– *Al-Uṣūl = Uṣūl al-sarakhsī*, ed. Abu 'l-wafā al-Afghānī, Cairo, 1953-54

SĀRAWĪ = Muḥammad 'Alī b. Muḥammad Riḍā (d. after 1193/1779):
Tawḍīḥ al-ishtibāh wa 'l-ishkāl, ed. Jalāl al-Dīn Muḥaddith Urmawī, Tehran, 1345sh/1966 (in the collection of *sih risāla dar 'ilm-i rijāl*)

ṢARĪFĪNĪ = Abū Isḥāq Ibrāhīm b. Muḥammad b. al-Azhar (d. 641/1243):
Ta'rīkh naysābūr al-muntakhab min al-siyāq, ed. Muḥammad Kāẓim al-Maḥmūdī, Qum, 1403/1983

AL-SAYYID AL-ḤIMYARĪ = Ismā'īl b. Muḥammad b. Yazīd (d. ca. 173/789-90):
Dīwān, ed. Shākir Hādī Shākir, Beirut, [1966]

SEZGIN, Fuat:
Geschichte des Arabischen schrifttums, Leiden, 1967

AL-SHAHĪD AL-AWWAL = Shams al-Dīn Muḥammad b. Makkī al-'Āmilī (d. 786/1384):
- *Dhikrā al-shī'a*, Tehran, 1271/1854-55
- *Al-Lum'a al-dimashqiyya*, Tehran, 1406/1985-86

AL-SHAHĪD AL-THĀNĪ = Zayn al-Dīn b. 'Alī b. Aḥmad al-Jubā'ī al-'Āmilī (d. 966/1559):
- *Ḥaqā'iq al-īmān*, ed. Mahdī al-Rajā'ī, Qum, 1409/1989
- *Rawḍ al-jinān fī sharḥ irshād al-adhhān*, Tehran, 1303/1885
- *Al-Rawḍa al-bahiyya fī sharḥ al-lum'a al-dimashqiyya*, ed. Muḥammad Kalāntar, Najaf, 1386/1966-

SHAHRASTĀNĪ = Abu 'l-Fatḥ Muḥammad b. 'Abd al-Karīm (d. 548/1153):
Al-Milal wa 'l-niḥal, ed. 'Abd al-Amīr 'Alī Muhannā and 'Alī Ḥasan Fā'ūr, Beirut, 1990

SHALMAGHĀNĪ = Abū Ja'far Muḥammad b. 'Alī, Ibn Abi 'l-'Adhāqir (d. 322/934):
Kitāb al-Taklīf, Mashhad, 1406/1986 (as *al-Fiqh al-mansūb ila 'l-imām al-riḍā*)

SHARAF AL-DĪN AL-NAJAFĪ = Sharaf al-Dīn 'Alī al-Ḥusaynī al-Astarābādī (mid 10th/16th century):
Ta'wīl al-āyāt al-ẓāhira, Qum, 1407/1987

SHA'RĀNĪ = 'Abd al-Wahhāb b. Aḥmad b. 'Alī al-Anṣārī (d. 973/1565):
Lawāqiḥ al-anwār fī ṭabaqāt al-akhyār, Cairo, 1954

AL-SHARĪF AL-RAḌĪ = Abu 'l-Ḥasan Muḥammad b. al-Ḥusayn al-Mūsawī (d. 406/1015):
- *Ḥaqā'iq al-ta'wīl*, ed. Muḥammad Riḍā āl Kāshif al-Ghiṭā', Najaf, 1355/1936-37
- *Khaṣā'iṣ al-A'imma*, Mashhad, 1406/1985
- *Nahj al-balāgha*, an anthology of the sermons, letters, and other sayings of 'Alī, ed. Ṣubḥī al-Ṣāliḥ, Beirut, 1387/1967

SIBṬ IBN AL-JAWZĪ = Abu 'l-Muẓaffar Yūsuf b. Qizughlī al-Dimashqī (d. 654/1256):
Tadhkirat khawāṣṣ al-umma li-dhikr khaṣā'iṣ al-a'imma, Tehran, 1285/1868-69

STROUMSA, Sarah:
"The Barāhima in Early Kalām," in *Jerusalem Studies in Arabic and Islam*, 6 (1985): 229-41

SUBKĪ = Taqī al-Dīn 'Alī b. 'Abd al-Kāfī (d. 756/1355):
Fatāwā al-subkī, Cairo, 1355-6/1936-38

SULAMĪ = Yūsuf b. Yaḥyā b. 'Alī b. 'Abd al-'Azīz al-Sulamī al- Maqdisī al-Dimashqī (d. after 658/1260):
'Iqd al-durar fī akhbār al-muntaẓar, ed. 'Abd al-Fattāḥ Muḥammad al-Ḥulw, Cairo, 1979

SULAYM B. QAYS al-Hilalī al-'Āmirī al-Kūfī (early 2d/8th century ?):
Kitāb sulaym b. qays al-hilālī, Najaf, n.d. (2d edition)

ṢŪLĪ = Abū Bakr Muḥammad b. Yaḥyā al-Shaṭranjī (d. 335/946-7):
Kitāb al-Awrāq, *Akhbār al-rāḍī bi 'llāh wa 'l-muttaqī bi 'llāh*, ed. J. Heyworth Dunne, London, 1935

SUYŪṬĪ = Jalāl al-Dīn 'Abd al-Raḥmān b. Abī Bakr (d. 911/1505):
- *Al-Durr al-manthūr fī tafsīr al-qur'ān bi 'l-ma'thūr*, Cario, 1314/1897
- *Al-Itqān fī 'ulūm al-qur'ān*, ed. Muḥammad Abu 'l-Faḍl Ibrāhīm, Cairo, 1967
- *Ṣawn al-manṭiq wa 'l-kalām 'an fann al-manṭiq wa 'l-kalām*, ed. 'Alī Sāmi al-Nashshār, Cairo, 1947

ṬABARĀNĪ = Abu 'l-Qāsim Sulaymān b. Aḥmad b. Ayyūb (d. 360/970-71):
- *Al-Mu'jam al-kabīr*, ed. Ḥamdī 'Abd al-Majīd al-Salafī, Baghdad, 1978
- *Al-Mu'jam al-ṣaghīr*, ed. 'Abd al-Raḥmān Muḥammad 'Uthmān, Medina, 1968

ṬABARĪ = Abū Ja'far Muḥammad b. Jarīr (d. 310/923):
Ta'rīkh al-rusul wa 'l-mulūk = *Ta'rīkh al-ṭabarī*, ed. Muḥammad Abu 'l-Faḍl Ibrāhīm, Cairo, 1960-

AL-ṬABARĪ AL-SHĪ'Ī = Abū Ja'far Muḥammad b. Jarīr b. Rustam (early 4th/10th century):
Dalā'il al-imāma, Najaf, 1963

ṬABĀṬABĀ'Ī = Muḥammad Ḥusayn b. Muḥammad al-Tabrīzī (d. 1403/1982):
- His notes on Majlisī's *Biḥār al-anwār*, in the footnotes of the Tehran, 1376-90/1957-70 edition of that work
- *Al-Mizān fī tafsīr al-qur'ān*, Tehran, 1375/1955-

ṬABRISĪ = 'Abū 'Alī Faḍl b. al-Ḥasan, Amīn al-Islām (d. 548/1154):
- *I'lām al-warā bi-a'lām al-hudā*, Najaf, 1970
- *Majma' al-bayān fī tafsīr al-qur'ān*, Beirut, 1961
- *Tāj al-mawālīd*, Qum, 1406/1985-86 (in the collection of *Majmū'a nafīsa fī ta'rīkh al-a'imma*: 78-155)

TAHDHĪB = Ṭūsī, *Tahdhīb al-aḥkām*

TĀJ AL-DĪN AL-SUBKĪ = 'Abd al-Wahhāb b. 'Alī b. 'Abd al-Kāfī (d. 771/1370):
Ṭabaqāt al-shāfi'iyya al-kubrā, Cairo 1324/1906

TANŪKHĪ = Abū 'Alī Muḥassan b. 'Alī (d. 384/994-5):
Nishwār al-muḥāḍara wa akhbār al-mudhākara, ed. 'Abbūd al-Shāljī, Beirut, 1971

ṬAYĀLISĪ = Abū Dāwūd Sulaymān b. Dāwūd (d. 204/819-20):
Al-Musnad = *Musnad Abī dāwūd al-ṭayālisī*, Hyderabad, 1321/1904

THAQAFĪ = Abū Isḥāq Ibrāhīm b. Muḥammad al-Kūfī (d. 283/896-7):
Kitāb al-Ghārāt, ed. Jalāl al-Dīn Muḥaddith Urmawī, Tehran, 1395/1975

TIRMIDHĪ = Abū 'Īsā Muḥammad b. 'Īsā al-Sulamī (d. 279/892-3):
Al-Sunan = *Sunan al-tirmidhī*, ed. 'Abd al-Wāḥid Muḥammad al-Tāzī, Cairo, 1931-34

TUCKER, William F.:
"Bayān b. Sam'ān and the Bayāniyya," in the *Muslim World*, 65, (1975): 241-53

ṬŪSĪ = Abū Ja'far Muḥammad b. al-Ḥasan (d. 460/1067):
- *Al-Amālī*, Baghdad, 1964
- *Kitāb al-Fihrist*, ed. Muḥammad Ṣādiq Āl Baḥr al-'Ulūm, Najaf, 1356/1937-38
- *Kitāb al-Ghayba*, Najaf, 1385/1965-66
- *Al-Iqtiṣād al-hādī ilā sabīl al-rashād*, Tehran, 1400/1980
- *Al-Istibṣār*, ed. Ḥasan al-Mūsawī al-Kharsān, Najaf, 1375-6/1955-57
- *Miṣbāh al-mutahajjid*, Tehran, 1285/1868-69
- *Al-Mufṣiḥ fī 'l-imāma*, ed. Riḍā al-Ustādī, Qum, 1403/1983 (in the collection of *al-Rasā'il al-'ashr li 'l-shaykh al-ṭūsī: 115-138)*
- *Al-Nihāya fī mujarrad al-fiqh wa 'l-fatāwā*, Beirut, 1970

– *Kitāb al-Rijāl = Rijāl al-ṭūsī*, ed. Muḥammad Ṣādiq Āl Baḥr al-'Ulūm, Najaf, 1961
– *Talkhīṣ al-shāfī*, ed. Ḥusayn Āl Baḥr al-'Ulūm, Najaf, 1963
– *Tahdhīb al-aḥkām*, ed. Ḥasan al-Mūsawī al-Kharsān, Najaf, 1958-62
– *Tamhīd al-uṣūl*, ed. 'Abd al-Muḥsin Mishkwāt al-Dīnī, Tehran, 1362sh/1983
– *Al-Tibyān fī tafsīr al-qur'ān*, ed. Aḥmad Shawqī al-Amīn and Aḥmad Ḥabib Qaṣīr al-'Āmilī, Najaf, 1957-63
– *'Uddat al-uṣūl*, ed. Muḥammad Mahdī Najaf, Qum, 1983

'UMARĪ = Abu 'l-Ḥasan 'Alī b. Abi 'l-Ghanā'im Muḥammad b. 'Alī al-'Alawī al-Shajarī, Ibn al-Ṣūfī (mid 5th/11th century):
Al-Majdī fī ansāb al-ṭālibiyyīn, ed. Aḥmad al-Mahdawī al-Dāmghānī, Qum, 1409/1989

UNIVERSITY OF TEHRAN, Central Library:
Catalogue: *Fihrist-i nuskhahāy-i khaṭṭī-yi kitābakhāna-yi markazī-yi dānishgāh-i tehrān*, by Muḥammad Taqī Dānish-Pazhūh, Tehran, 1961-

'UTHMĀN B. SA'ĪD AL-DĀRIMĪ (d. 280-2/894-7):
Al-Radd 'ala 'l-jahmiyya, ed. Gosta Vitestam, Leiden, 1960

YAḤYĀ B. ḤAMZA al-'Alawī, al-Mu'ayyad bi 'llāh (d. 745-9/1344-49):
Tasfiyat al-qulūb, ed. Ismā'īl b. Aḥmad al-Jarāfī, Cairo, 1985

YA'QŪBĪ = Aḥmad b. Isḥāq b. Ja'far al-Baghdādī, Ibn Wāḍiḥ (d. after 292/905):
Kitāb al-Ta'rīkh = Ta'rīkh al-ya'qūbī, Beirut, 1960

YĀQŪT = Abū 'Abd Allāh Yāqūt b. 'Abd Allāh al-Ḥamawī (d. 626/1229):
Mu'jam al-buldān, Beirut, 1957-68

YŪSUF AL-BAḤRĀNĪ = Yūsuf b. Aḥmad b. Ibrāhīm al-'Uṣfūrī al-Darāzī (d. 1186/1772)
Lu'lu'at al-baḥrayn, ed. Muḥammad Ṣādiq Baḥr al-'Ulūm, Najaf, 1966

ZARKASHĪ = Badr al-Dīn Muḥammad b. Bahādur b. 'Abd Allāh (d. 794/1392):
Al-Burhān fī 'ulūm al-qur'ān, ed. Muḥammad Abu 'l-Faḍl Ibrāhīm, Cairo, 1957

Index